In Solidarity

In Solidarity

*Essays on Working–Class
Organization in
the United States*

Kim Moody

Haymarket Books
Chicago, Illinois

Published in 2014 by
Haymarket Books
P.O. Box 180165
Chicago, IL 60618
773-583-7884
info@haymarketbooks.org
www.haymarketbooks.org

ISBN: 978-1-60846-326-8

Trade distribution:
In the US, Consortium Book Sales and Distribution, www.cbsd.com
In the UK, Turnaround Publisher Services, www.turnaround-uk.com
In Canada, Publishers Group Canada, www.pgcbooks.ca
In Australia, Palgrave Macmillan, www.palgravemacmillan.com.au
All other countries, Publishers Group Worldwide, www.pgw.com

Special discounts are available for bulk purchases by organizations
and institutions. Please contact Haymarket Books for more information
at 773-583-7884 or info@haymarketbooks.org.

Cover design by Josh On. Cover image of protesters in the rotunda of the state
Capitol in Madison, Wisconsin, against the state budget and anti-union legislation
proposed by Republican Governor Scott Walker. Photo by Brian Kersey, UPI.

This book was published with the generous support of Lannan Foundation.

Printed in Canada by union labor.

Library of Congress CIP data is available.

10 9 8 7 6 5 4 3 2 1

MIX
Paper from
responsible sources
FSC
www.fsc.org   FSC® C103567

Contents

List of Tables

Introduction

This collection focuses above all on the organized working class in the United States. While I have written much about global capitalism and labor internationalism in the past, these essays attempt to analyze the problems and responses in the labor movement with which I am most familiar. Some of these were written for political publications or organizations. Several of the more recent essays are in academic form, for which I apologize to the reader. Whatever the format of the original publication of the essays in this collection, my objective has always been the same: to explore how the existing organs of class struggle can be improved, and in that process how can socialists connect their ideas and strategies to the living working class.

The great problem facing socialists for many decades in the United States, and perhaps to a lesser degree elsewhere, has been the separation of socialist ideas and organization from the day-to-day life of those who, at least in the Marxist view, are the necessary carriers of socialist revolution and human liberation. Outsider propaganda has been a manifest failure. Like all social movements, a socialist movement based in the working class will require human agency and direct day-to-day contact.

There are, of course, more socialists of various kinds active in US unions today than one might imagine from the behavior of most union leaders, and this book, it is hoped, will help them by providing analysis and ideas about perspectives and strategies. But since the number of socialists in unions is limited and organizationally fragmented, this collection is also meant to encourage activists from the newer movements confronting capitalism in one way or another—occupying, fighting home foreclosures, or breaking down barriers to society's excluded and oppressed—to take a critical look at the labor movement for the potential allies within.

To some, the emphasis on unions and unionized workers will seem strange or even pointless. Aren't America's labor unions continuing their long journey to oblivion? Haven't they lost millions of members to capital's relentless attacks on working-class people of all races and ethnicities, as several of the essays in this collection show? Of course they have. Yet, with nearly fifteen million members, unions remain the largest and most diverse working-class organizations in the United States. As the workforce has changed in the last several decades, so has organized labor. Women now compose 46 percent of all union members, while African Americans, Latinos, and Asians account for 30 percent, percentages that closely reflect the US population.[1] Union organization remains arguably the potentially most powerful way in which working-class resistance expresses itself within the problematic political culture of America.

Whether in growth or crisis, capital—and the "one percent" who most embody it—has undermined and destroyed the lives of millions the world around. Resistance is now evident across the globe and there is no reason to doubt that sooner or later, in one form or another, it will sweep the shores of the United States. We can see this resistance in recent uprisings from Egypt to Europe. It is in such resistance that people are transformed, their minds opened, and new possibilities created. It is there, I believe, that socialists need to be.

"The Union" Isn't Always What It Seems

Commentators, journalists, academics, socialists, and even this writer frequently refer to "the union" as though it were one thing. But what is this "thing" we call "the union"? As Sheila Cohen has argued, the union is, in fact, at least two contradictory things: the union as institution and the union as movement or membership.[2] The leadership is bound to protect the institution, a role that breeds caution. Furthermore, the leadership, in its role as negotiator, is placed in a position somewhere between the employers and the union's members, far removed from the workplace and the daily experience of the members. At the same time, "the union" is a social movement meant to reflect the needs and aspirations of the membership. The need to fight for these and, indeed, the existence of unions in the first place are rooted in the contradictions of the capital-labor relationship, that is, in the reality of exploitation that originates in the workplace and in capital's constant push for increased relative surplus value. Thus, in good times and bad, there is a tension between the union as institution and as movement. This is not to say that all union officials are the same or even that all members are always ahead of their leaders. Sometimes the leaders are to the "left" of their members on many issues. Nor do the officials always get their way, since the active members are also actors in this social dialectic. Nevertheless, at crucial times the leaders are pulled toward defending the institution, which can mean avoiding strikes, staying within the law, and abiding by the contract even as management bends or breaks it. It's not simply a question of betrayals or sellouts, but of the contradictory role of the high-level union official as both a leader of workers and a mediator between labor and capital.

As David McNally reminds us, following Marx, much in the way capitalism works is invisible yet real. We do not see markets or the circuits of capital—only the results. Yet they are all too real.[3] For example, let's look at Marx's concept of the commodity. "The commodity is, first of all, an external object, a thing."[4] As he investigates the commodity, Marx finds that its value consists not in its use or even its exchange, per se, but in the socially necessary labor it embodies. After a long examination, we discover that "it is nothing but the definite social relation between men themselves which assumes here, for them, the fantastic form of a relation between things."[5] Actual social relations are concealed, rendered invisible, in both the commodity's physical and exchange forms.

The union, of course, is not a commodity and the social relations within it are not those of exploitation, so this analogy has its limits. Nevertheless, if we look beneath the surface of the union as institution we find a somewhat complex social organism. Officials who deal regularly with management will tend to insulate themselves from the daily influence of members, or various groups of members, in order to stabilize the bargaining relationship. This leads to forms of bureaucratic rule. In the case of US unions, the administration of vast benefits programs, their "private welfare state," and elaborate, legalistic contracts adds further layers of institutional insulation. The members, however, have needs, desires, and expectations that may well go beyond what the leadership sees as realistic from its vantage point. Thus, the layers of bureaucracy and insulation become a barrier to achieving those needs and expectations.

Some socialists emphasize the relative privileges of top union leaders—their high salaries and expense accounts, their social mingling with managers and politicians, vastly improved working conditions, and so on. These are the symptoms of the problem, not the causes. No doubt most union leaders work hard and are dedicated to the cause of labor as they see it. At the same time, they are the guardians of the institution and of the "bargaining relationship." Most high-level US union officials still think, whether consciously or not, in terms of "business unionism"—in which, among other things, the bargaining relationship (more than the outcome) is the priority, the contract it produces sacrosanct, and labor politics incarcerated in the prison of the Democratic Party. Ages ago, most union leaders, often with membership support, to be sure, granted capital management's-rights and no-strike clauses in these sacrosanct contracts. In doing so, they have limited their own options as well as those of the rank and file.

As a result, it is precisely in the battle between labor and capital that the fight against bureaucracy and the norms of business unionism becomes a necessity. As contradictory organizations of class struggle, unions embody a dialectic between bureaucratization and rebellion from below. As I write in the essay on the "rank-and-file strategy," it is all too frequently, when capital and its management are the target of increased conflict, that the leadership in its role as guardian of the institution steps into the crosshairs. It is for this reason that the history of American labor is punctuated by rank-and-file rebellions at one level or another. The object of such rebellion ought not to be simply replacing one leadership group with another. It must involve the transformation of the union from the ground up. Here is one opportunity for socialists to play a leadership role from a grassroots position. It is a leadership that cannot be proclaimed by some vanguard identity or won simply by election. It must be earned in the course of struggle.

In this fight, union democracy is essential. As one *Labor Notes* book puts it in a title, *Democracy Is Power*.[6] This is about more than honest elections or better democratic forms. It should begin in the workplace with strong organization and accountable shop stewards, for here is the ultimate source of working-class power. Here direct democracy can be a reality, and it is on this basis that further democratization is possible. Union democracy should involve members in union administration and mobilization far beyond today's norms. It must also speak to the potential divisions within the unions and the working class as a whole.

Unions include groups of workers with real or potential conflicts of interest: skilled and unskilled, Black and white, men and women. To unite these sections of the membership often requires special attention to those most disadvantaged or underrepresented. It is a task that too many union leaders have avoided. Solidarity is not always a simple matter, but as countless struggles have demonstrated, it is not impossible. It is something to be built in the struggle with capital by and among the ranks themselves. Socialists have a key role to play in this.

Some Assumptions and Omissions

This is a collection of essays, most of which have been published previously elsewhere—all too often in places where too few activists would find them. As such it does not present a coherent narrative. There is some repetition and overlap, perhaps even some contradiction where my thoughts have developed over time. Nevertheless, I believe it presents a set of ideas and analyses of value to union and movement activists, based primarily in Marx's view of class struggle, spelled out in the first essay. As is always the case, the influences on my thinking have come from many sources, past and present. They, in turn, have shaped my views within the context of a particular socialist current. The shorthand self-identifier for this tendency is "socialism from below," a phase associated with the Marxist theorist Hal Draper.[7] His works have been one of the major frameworks in which the many other influences and experiences have been sorted out. This does not mean total agreement with all the many works and talks produced by Draper or his political offspring, but it does mean a general adherence to the idea of socialism from below, in which the emancipation of the working class (and humanity) is the task of the working class itself.

Coming from the same political current, the working-class socialist who first introduced me and many others to the reality, if not the idea, of rank-and-file movements was Stan Weir. His 1966 pamphlet *A New Era of Labor Revolt: On the Job vs. Official Unions* was an eye-opener for a young socialist activist not long removed from campus and only recently involved in organizing a union.[8] In it Weir revealed an aspect of the social rebellions of the 1960s that has often been overlooked. This early political and theoretical underpinning was much enriched by my involvement in the International Socialists and Solidarity and, above all, my twenty-two years with *Labor Notes* and the many staff members there, and the contact with countless rank-and-file union activists that provided. In addition I want to thank my colleagues at the Work and Employment Research Unit of the University of Hertfordshire for making it possible to produce some of the articles that appear in this collection. Many thanks, as well, to the folks at Haymarket Books for encouraging me to publish this collection and for their help in producing it, especially Anthony Arnove, Julie Fain, Sarah Grey, Rachel Cohen, and Caroline Luft. Finally, I want to acknowledge the constant contributions to my thinking and morale from my partner of many years, Sheila Cohen.

Ultimately, it has to be conceded that there is much more to building a socialist movement than union work. Unions, after all, are not revolutionary organizations. As many have pointed out they arise in the context of capitalism and exist to adjust the conditions of workers within that system. Much more in the way of organization, education, and action is needed than even militant union activism can provide. Yet unions, as movements, are also oppositional by nature. As Engels wrote to Bebel in 1875, they are "the real class organization of the proletariat, in which it carries on its daily struggles with capital, in which it trains itself."[9] No matter how imperfectly they do this or how much they retreat, they are on the front lines of class conflict more consistently than any other mass organizations in the United States. So, while there is more to socialist strategy than working in the unions, unions remain the obvious place in which to reconnect the theory and practice of socialist politics to the only force that can fulfill the vision of those politics.

Part I

Class Struggle—Theory and Strategy

1 Marx's Theory of Class and the World Today

Kim Moody

In 1978, the late E. P. Thompson wrote of class, "No historical category has been more misunderstood, tormented, transfixed, and de-historicized than the category of social class."[1] This critique referred mainly to Althusser, but also to "bourgeois sociology," both of which have reduced "class, ideology, social formations, and almost everything else, to categorical status."[2] Thompson's concern was with the absence of human self-activity and historical process in these theories. Since most of the essays in this collection deal with the labor movement and, hence, class, it seems appropriate to lay out the theory of social classes that underlies the thinking and analysis in this book, with the understanding, of course, that my thinking and understanding have evolved over time. First I will look at Marx's theory of class and class formation, then, later, at what it means today.

Marx's view of the development of the major classes of capitalist society was not a theory of stratification or a head count of the new classes. The two major classes that arise with capitalism do so in *relation* to one another, and that relation is characterized by conflict from the start. As Marx and Engels wrote in *The German Ideology*:

> The separate individuals form a class only in so far as they have to carry on a common battle against another class; otherwise they are on hostile terms with each other as competitors. On the other hand, the class in its turn achieves an independent existence over and against the individuals.[3]

In *The Poverty of Philosophy* Marx puts the question of the mutual development of the two classes and their conflict even more sharply. He wrote:

> In proportion as the bourgeoisie develops, it develops in its bosom a new proletariat, a modern proletariat: it develops a struggle between the proletarian class and the bourgeois class, a struggle which, before it is felt, perceived, appreciated, comprehended, avowed and loudly proclaimed by the two sides, only manifests itself previously by partial and momentary conflicts, by subversive acts.[4]

In this work, for the first time, Marx talks about the actual struggles of the working class, its trade union or "combinations," and Chartism.

Some of these formulations have led a number of Marxists to believe that the working class only has an existence if it is conscious and organized. Ralph Miliband, for example, wrote that "for Marx, the working class is not truly a class unless it acquires the capacity to organize itself politically" and "when it acquires consciousness."[5] Clearly, there must be a material social formation *before* acquiring and, indeed, *in order to* acquire these capacities. And that is what Marx believed when he wrote in *The Poverty of Philosophy*, "The domination of capital has created for this mass of people a common situation with common interests. This mass is already a class, as opposed to capital, but not yet for itself."[6]

To some readers this formulation will bring to mind the well-known duality of a class "in itself" versus one "for itself."[7] Although familiar, the "in itself" phrase is not Marx's.[8] His formulation, "a class, as opposed to capital" is far more dynamic and typical of the relational concept of class Marx developed. Any simple duality of this sort violates Marx's view of capitalism and the social formation that characterizes it as a historical process that arises, as Thompson put it, "at the intersection of determination and self-activity."[9] That is, class formation is determined both by the development of capital itself and by the self-activity of the working class in creating its organizations and consciousness through struggle. That Marx saw no such simple duality is clear from the fact that he eventually dropped the term "for itself," with its Hegelian overtones, as Hal Draper pointed out.[10]

The Communist Manifesto, penned by Marx and Engels in 1848, presented the most familiar picture of the development of the working class: "With the development of industry the proletariat not only increases in number; it becomes concentrated in greater masses, its strength grows, and it feels that strength more." At the same time, the conditions of the working class pushed down wages, obliterated differences within the class, and drove the workers to "form combinations against the bourgeoisie." In the end, the bourgeoisie had produced "its own gravediggers."[11] The story was as compressed as it was inspiring.

When, two years later, the dust had settled on revolutionary Europe, the specter of communism had not yet taken on flesh and blood. Reaction ruled; Marx was forced to admit that "the proletariat passes into the background of the revolutionary stage"[12] and to take a more long-range view. To those among his comrades who wanted to provoke revolution by an act of will, Marx had to caution, "We tell the workers: If you want to change the conditions and make yourselves capable of government, you will have to undergo fifteen, twenty or fifty years of civil war."[13] The idea that the working class had to prepare itself for power through prolonged struggle is key to understanding the uneven formation of class consciousness. It is a process that has had to be repeated over and over, under changing historical circumstances, as wars, moments of relative prosperity, and whole or partial defeats that characterize the class struggle undo the progress of years.

In the long period of relatively low levels of class conflict that followed the revolutions of 1848 to 1850, Marx's conception of class was deepened (though never codified in a single presentation) and made more complex. While the defining point of origin of capital and labor as social classes remained their relations at the point of production, the parameters of working-class life were spelled out in greater detail and depth in *Capital,* Volume I. Essentially, there are three major conditions here that define the social position of the working class. Providing the context, Marx wrote: "The capitalist process of production, therefore, seen as a total, connected process; i.e., a process of reproduction not only of commodities, not only surplus value, but it also produces and reproduces the capital-relation itself, on the one hand the capitalist, on the other the wage-laborer."[14]

The first of the three conditions, historically as well as logically, is the need to sell one's labor power in order to live. Here Marx somewhat ironically notes that the workers are "free" "in the double sense that they neither form part of the means of production themselves, as would be the case with slaves, serfs, etc., nor do they own the means of production, as would be the case with self-employed peasants."[15] The sale is for "a definite period of time" at the value of the worker's labor power, which is composed of "the value of the means of subsistence necessary for the maintenance of its owner," which in turn is determined by "the level of civilization attained in a country" and contains "a historical and moral element."[16] In other words, "subsistence" is not mere existence or absolute poverty. It is in the labor market that the worker faces competition from other workers. At the same time, here "the silent compulsion of economic relations sets the seal on the domination of the capitalist over the workers."[17]

The second condition, in many ways the very heart of Marx's analysis of class, is exploitation. He spells this out briefly in *Capital*:

> The owner of the money has paid the value of a day's labor-power; he therefore has the use of it for a day, a day's labor-power belongs to him. On the one hand the daily subsistence of labor-power costs only half a day's labor, while on the other hand the very same labor-power can remain effective, can work, during a whole day, and consequently the value which its use during one day creates is double what the capitalist pays for that use.[18]

Put simply, the worker produces more value than he or she requires to reproduce his or her labor-power by working longer than it takes to create that value. Facing competition and the need to expand his business, the capitalist, as we shall see, naturally does everything possible to reduce the labor time necessary for the worker's subsistence and increase the rate of exploitation.

To enforce and aggrandize exploitation, the capitalist must discipline the workers. Thus the process of valorization, of creating an expanding surplus value, "in form . . . is purely despotic." To administer this despotism as the scale of production grows, Marx writes,

> He [the capitalist] hands over the work of direct and constant supervision of the individual workers and groups of workers to a special kind of wage-labor. An industrial army of workers under the command of a capitalist requires, like a real army, officers (managers) and NCOs (foremen, overseers, etc.), who command during the labor process.[19]

Thus the working class is defined not by income layers or education or status but by its conflict-ridden relation to capital and the three major conditions it faces. These conditions of working-class life are important not only as a way to define who is and isn't working class, but also in terms of the more complex and ongoing process of proletarianization that affects people once thought of as "middle" class.

Three additional points are needed to fill out our understanding of the working class. The first is that "it is the collective worker, formed from the combination of the many specialized workers," or "labor-power socially combined," that produces surplus value. [20] Second is that the working class obviously also includes the family and other dependents. Marx writes, "The value of labor-power was determined, not only by the labor-time necessary to maintain the individual adult worker, but also by that necessary to maintain his family."[21] This is, of course, a nineteenth-century formulation of the patriarchal "family wage" idea that scarcely prevails anymore, but the point is that the class is more than its employed members.

The third condition is that "it is capital accumulation itself that constantly produces indeed in direct relation with its own energy and extent, a relatively redundant working population; i.e., a population which is superfluous to capital's average requirements for its own valorization, and is therefore a surplus population."[22] This is not only the "reserve army" of the unemployed but also the human basis for an expanding service sector, some of which will produce yet more surplus value. Those who are unemployed, part of the reserve army, are also part of the working class, since directly or indirectly (unemployment insurance, welfare, etc.) they are "paid" out of the value created by labor power.

Marx made a distinction between productive labor and unproductive (of surplus value) labor. On this I agree with Anwar Shaikh and Ahmet Tonac, who argue that the definition of exploitation lies in "the ratio of surplus labor time to necessary labor time. This concept applies to all capitalistically employed wage labor, whether it is productive or not."[23] As the production of goods and services becomes more extended and complex, more workers whose labor is necessary to the process but who do not directly produce surplus value are required. Hence workers who don't produce surplus value directly, but who conform to the conditions spelled out above, are part of the working class.

Class Formation: A Never-Ending Process

The working class, however, is not a fixed "thing." Like capital itself, the working class necessarily changes as capital expands, enters new lines of production, and changes the methods of production. As Marx wrote in *The Results of the Immediate Process of Production*:

> But capital is in itself indifferent to the *particular* nature of every sphere of production. Where it is invested, how it is invested and to what extent it is transferred from one sphere of production to another or redistributed among various spheres of production—all this is determined only by the greater ease or difficulty of selling the commodities manufactured.[24]

This, in turn, "constantly calls new branches of industry into being," thus "capitalist production has a tendency to take over all branches of industry not yet acquired."[25] In *Labor and Monopoly Capital* Harry Braverman argued that "the capitalist mode of production takes over the totality of individual, family, and social needs and, in subordinating them to the market, also reshapes them to serve the needs of capital."[26] Capital's thirst for new ways to make a profit is unquenchable.

Naturally, the work in these new branches of industry will be different, and the workers employed appear to be different as well. In the United States and most other industrial nations, one symbol of this change has been the longstanding shift from the production of goods to that of services, which have become commodities themselves. Today, of course, this process is global. So, on the one hand, we see a shift of manufacturing from the United States and other Western nations to the industrializing BRICS (Brazil, Russia, India, China, South Africa) nations, especially China. On the other hand, we have seen the rise of an intermodal "logistics" industry across the world that moves not only final commodities but production inputs as well. In other words, it is made necessary by the globalization of markets *and* production. Thus, while manufacturing jobs in the United States have contracted, employment in transportation and warehousing, the heart of "logistics," has risen from 3.5 million in 1990 to 4.2 million in 2010 despite many advances in technology. The number of warehouse workers alone has increased from 407,000 to 628,000 over those years, a growth of more than 50 percent.[27] These workers are now part of what amounts to a global assembly line in which transport and storage are essential parts of the chain of value creation.

Manufacturing jobs in the United States have been disappearing for a long time. From 1990 to 2010 the number of these core jobs fell from 17.7 million to 11.5 million, a loss of more than 6 million goods-producing jobs.[28] As mentioned above, many of these are accounted for by the shift of manufacturing to China, India, and elsewhere. But there is another reason for this decline that is built into capitalism. It is found in the concept of relative surplus value, the reduction of the time it takes to create the subsistence of the worker. In the *Grundrisse*, Marx's notebooks for the writing of *Capital*, he said:

> In the second form of surplus value, however, as relative surplus value, which appears as the development of the workers' productive power, *as the reduction of the necessary labor time relative to the working day,* and *as the reduction of the working population* relative to the population, in this form there directly appears the industrial and distinguishing historic character of the mode of production founded on capital.[29]

This is a remarkable piece of analysis, one which virtually undoes the optimistic view of an ever-growing industrial proletariat we saw in the *Manifesto*. Yet it is a central piece of Marx's analysis of the dynamics of capitalism, indeed, the "distinguishing historic character" of capitalism. The class sees its composition inevitably change precisely to the degree to which capitalism increases the productivity of labor, which under competition it must do.

The class has changed in other ways as well. Thompson's famous statement that "the working class made itself as much as it was made" had a certain validity when this class was being born in England during the late eighteenth and early nineteenth centuries, with its self-organized "trade unions, friendly societies, educational and religious movements, political organizations, periodicals."[30] The same was true of the American working class later in the nineteenth century with similar institutions, including the network of independent local and national labor newspapers that so impressed Eleanor Marx when she toured the United States in 1886.[31]

The expansion of capital into the life of society Braverman described above, however, has meant that many of the functions of the voluntary organizations of the early working class have been commodified (insurance, credit cards, etc.) or taken on by the state (welfare, Social Security). Ironically, the very successes of labor in the class struggle have undermined some of its older forms of organization. There are still various kinds of working-class community organizations—for example, immigrant-based workers' centers—but today unions are virtually the only organizations that cut across the class. Hence their centrality to socialist strategy, even though they compose only a minority of the class almost everywhere.

Proletarianization and Further Class Change

American labor leaders never tire of referring to their members as "middle class," part of the great washed masses between the "dirt poor" and the "filthy rich." This is, of course, nonsense that separates better-off workers from their poorer brothers and sisters—and to some extent white from Black and brown. There is, however, an actual middle class, not between the rich and poor but between capital and labor. There can be no clear definition of this middle class or even of where it begins and ends in relation to the working class. As Marx noted in his very brief and unfinished section in *Capital*, Volume III, entitled simply "Classes," "It is undeniably in England that this modern society and its economic articulation is most widely and classically developed. Even here, though, this class articulation does not emerge in pure form. Here, too, middle and transitional levels always conceal the boundaries."[32] In a society constantly changing under the pressures of capital accumulation, it can hardly be otherwise.

The word "transitional" is particularly interesting, as it would appear to refer to groups moving from one class to another, most commonly a process of proletarianization. While Marx's prediction that the petit-bourgeoisie and other middle layers would disappear has proven to be wrong, there has been an undeniable tendency for formerly middle-class occupations to take on more and more of the characteristics of working-class labor and life. The "autonomy" of many professions has been eroded as capital pushes them for greater output and longer hours and directs their work more closely: that is, becomes "purely despotic." Not surprisingly, more professionals have been joining unions. An outstanding example of this, covered elsewhere in this collection, is nurses, who have been joining unions and striking at higher rates than any other group.[33]

Race, Ethnicity, and Gender

The ever-expanding nature of capitalism leads it to draw in more and more human material from the rural periphery of the world. The US working class has seen a dramatic shift in its racial and ethnic composition, due heavily to increased immigration. The number of Latino/as in the civilian workforce, for example, has jumped from a little over six million in 1980 to almost twenty-three million by 2010. This inevitably rubs up against the pre-existing forms of racial and ethnic prejudice and hierarchy bred by slavery, nationalism, and imperialism. Viewing the working class in Britain in his day, Marx wrote to friends, "Every industrial and commercial center in England now possesses a working class *divided* into two *hostile* camps, English proletarians and Irish proletarians. The ordinary English worker hates the Irish worker as a competitor who lowers his standard of life."[34]

In the United States, of course, racial and ethnic divisions are far more prevalent, as the workforce has long been more diverse than that of nineteenth-century Britain and racism more deeply embedded in the institutional structure of American society. We know now that more than economic competition is involved in the constant reproduction not only of racial attitudes but of the evolving forms of institutional racism. Racial hierarchy and competition exist not only in the labor market but in every aspect of life in the United States, notably housing, education, public resources, credit. Massive immigration in recent years has collided with this pre-existing racial hierarchy to the detriment of immigrants, who are perceived as a threat by many working-class whites not only in terms of jobs but in all the areas just listed.

Women have always been more or less half of the working class, but their place in that class and in society has changed dramatically since Marx could talk about the value of the worker's labor power supporting "his family." While there have always been women in employment, from the 1950s they have entered the US labor force in growing numbers. Since 1970, the number of women in the workforce has increased from about thirty-two million to seventy-two million in 2010 to become 47 percent of the workforce. By 2010 the workforce participation rate of married women almost equaled that of unmarried women.[35] On the other hand, full-time women workers still earned only 80 percent of their male counterparts' earnings, and that due largely to the fall in male earnings. In addition, far more women than men worked in lower-paying part-time employment and held multiple jobs.[36] Nevertheless, the value of the labor power of women, whether married or not, was now a major source of the "subsistence" of the working class as a whole. While this has not brought an end to sexism or patriarchy, it has given women a more prominent place in daily affairs and in the labor movement, where women went from 25 percent of all members in the 1970s to 45 percent in 2012.

While organized labor in the United States is far from free of racism or sexism, it is nonetheless the most integrated institution in American society. Below is a table with the racial and gender composition of US unions in 2012.

Table 1.1. Race and Gender Composition of US Unions in 2012 by Number and Percentage[37]

Gender/Race	Number	Percentage
Total	14,366,000	100
Male	7,895,000	55
Female	6,470,000	45
White	11,306,000	79
Male	6,359,000	44
Female	4,947,000	34
Black	2,009,000	14
Latino	1,982,000	14
Asian	668,000	5

Race and gender groups overlap, so percentages don't add up to 100 percent.

The "Real Class Organization"

It was Engels who, in his 1844 *Conditions of the Working-Class in England,* first pointed to unions, or "combinations" as they were then called, as the major means of resisting the aggression of capital. Strikes were, he wrote, "the military school of the workingmen in which they prepare themselves for the great struggle which cannot be avoided," adding that "as schools of war, the Unions are unexcelled."[38] Later, in his 1875 critique of the Gotha program of the German Social Democratic Party (SPD by its German initials), Engels denounced the absence of trade unions in the program, calling them "the real class organization of the proletariat."[39] Similarly, in *The Poverty of Phi-*

losophy Marx wrote that it was through strikes and unions that "the proletarians effect their organization as a class."Their battles he termed "a veritable civil war."[40] In fact, Marx and Engels were the first socialists to see unions as central to the class struggle and hence to the fight for socialism.

As Draper pointed out, Marx and Engels would become critical of the conservatism of British trade unions. Nevertheless, unions remained central to their view of building class organization and consciousness. Unions were, of course, key to the founding of the International Workingmen's Association.[41] It is not just that class conflict of this sort is an unexcelled school of war; unions are the basis for the political movement of the class. Writing to a friend in 1871, Marx said: "The political movement of the working class has as its ultimate object, of course, the conquest of political power for this class, and this naturally requires a previous organization of the working class developed up to a certain point and arising precisely from its economic struggles."[42] This did not mean that every trade union struggle or every strike wave becomes political in the sense in which Marx uses the term here. But it does give a certain priority to economics—in the form of union organization—and to the possibility that economic struggle leads to political struggle—here he gives the example of the fight for an eight-hour working-day law.

That this process is not inevitable has been all too well demonstrated by the history of the US labor movement. This is precisely why trade union work by socialists is so essential to drawing out the meaning of the daily conditions and conflict as well as that of the high points of struggle. Elsewhere in this collection, various essays address this topic from different angles, particularly "The Rank-and-File Strategy" and its "Update," so I won't attempt to develop this perspective here.

Class and the World Today

In its 2008/09 *Global Wage Report*, the International Labour Office (ILO) of the United Nations revealed that nearly half the world's "employed" workforce worked for wages or salaries, rising from 43 percent in 1996 to 47 percent in 2006. This meant a shift of millions from either self-employment (peasants, independent artisans, peddlers, and others) or toward exclusion from the workforce. While not all waged workers are working class in the sense discussed above, most are. If we include dependents and the "reserve army" of labor (which would include many working as "self-employed") this might well amount to a majority for the first time in history. This shift is uneven. As the ILO described it, "Paid employment appears to be growing everywhere (with the exception of Latin America) and has been expanding particularly rapidly in East Asia."[43]

Thus, capital's drive to expand and take in more and more types of labor and commodities continues to draw in more of the world's rural population to the creation of surplus value and the conditions described above. What is more, this shift conforms to Marx's argument in *Capital* that even as the mass of labor's subsistence grows, "in relative terms, i.e., in comparison with surplus value, the value of labor-power would keep falling, and thus the abyss between the life situation of the worker and that of the capitalist would keep widening."[44] Thus the relative shift of value, and hence income and wealth, from the working class to capital prior to the Great Recession that began in 2008 is a reality. The ILO states:

> We show that over the period 1995–2007 average wages lagged behind the growth in GDP per capita, which we interpret as an indication that increases in productivity have failed to translate fully into higher wages. We also show that the recent period, characterized by growing economic integration, has seen a decline in the share of GDP distributed to wages.[45]

The rate of exploitation, therefore, has increased on a global scale.

This shift is apparent not only worldwide but also in the heartland of capitalism. In the seventeen leading countries of the OECD, capital's share in GDP rose from 25 percent in 1975 to 33 percent in 2005.[46] Looking somewhat more narrowly at the US corporate sector, capital's share of US national income rose from 18.8 percent in 1979 to 26.2 percent in 2010.[47] This has not been simply a matter of some economic trend, but the result of a class struggle in which capital has had the upper hand for some time—and all too often labor has fought with one hand tied behind its back. In the case of the United States, this is addressed in some detail in subsequent chapters in this collection. Here it is worth mentioning that this overall trend in capitalist development has produced increased worker resistance, perhaps most notably in China.[48]

It is always tempting at this point in such an essay to predict the next working-class upsurge. One thing Marxism is not so good at, however, is predicting the future. One reason is that socialist predictions are often in practice just economic predictions, and those not always on the mark—like the comrade who has predicted six of the last three recessions. Marxism, however, analyzes history as a process that is in large part guided by class conflict in its various forms; the outcome of such struggles is almost always indeterminate. We can, to a certain extent, analyze and predict trends to provide guidance for action, but outcomes are another matter. This is because class struggle itself depends in large part on the state of organization, consciousness, leadership, and analysis of the contending forces on the part of both sides. Marxism provides many tools to approach these problems, but all require organized human intervention. In the final analysis, therefore, the task is not to predict the future but to prepare for it.

2 Unions, Strikes, and Class Consciousness Today

Sheila Cohen and Kim Moody

One hundred and fifty years after the publication of the *Communist Manifesto,* the "specter" of communism can no longer be said to be haunting Europe—whether in the form of mass parties devoted to revolution or the states that inaccurately claimed that title. But class struggle, the inextinguishable source of everything the authors of the *Manifesto* meant by communism, is, it seems, as irrepressible as ever. Despite ever-stronger siren calls by social-democratic and union leaderships for "partnership" and "cooperation" with capital, old-fashioned mass strikes have recently stalked not only Europe but almost every other continent.

By the mid-1990s, this could be seen in the dramatic confrontations between major labor federations and the neoliberal, populist, and even social-democratic governments of such

This essay was originally published in Socialist Register 1998 *(New York: Monthly Review Press, 1998).*

seemingly dissimilar capitalisms as France, South Korea, South Africa, Canada, Peru, Brazil, Argentina, Belgium, Italy, and a dozen others. Alongside, sometimes preceding, and often following these political outbursts was a return to militant confrontation with capitalist employers far larger and more powerful than any Marx and Engels could have envisioned in 1848. If no manifestos appeared, no barricades were thrown up, and the red banners typically bore the initials of a trade union federation rather than a revolutionary party, the dynamics dramatically evoked throughout the original *Manifesto* were nonetheless clearly at work and a renewed class consciousness was evident across much of the industrial and semi-industrial world.

Despite all the real and apparent differences between Europe 150 years ago and today's capitalist world, two fundamental issues remain equally unresolved: the lack of fully fledged and widespread socialist consciousness and the absence of large-scale organization directed at fostering such consciousness. If Marx and Engels saw in the rise of class conflict the birth of such organization, the moves cited above toward some resurgence of class struggle may offer the opportunity for its rebirth—providing, of course, the socialist left can overcome its own isolation from the reality of this struggle. In many ways, we are faced with the same problems and limitations within the socialist movement itself as were the authors of the *Manifesto*.

Socialism and the Working Class

In 1848 as now, the socialist movement consisted of a variety of "socialisms" ranging from the idealist/populist/utopian to the avowedly revolutionary, or at least insurrectionary. The *Manifesto*'s survey of "Socialist, and Communist Literature" identified the three categories of Reactionary Socialism, Conservative or Bourgeois Socialism, and Critical-Utopian Socialism or Communism, and the forceful rejection by Marx and Engels of all these forms of "socialism" had one common theme: their mistaken abnegation of class. "German or 'True' Socialism," for example, prides itself in representing "not the interests of the proletariat, but the interests of human nature, of man in general, who belongs to no class, has no reality, who exists only in the misty realm of philosophical fantasy."[1] While more aware of "the working class, as being the most suffering class," utopian socialists like Fourier and Owen are equally castigated for considering themselves "far superior to all class antagonisms.... Hence, they habitually appeal to society at large, without distinction of class."[2] The sectarians of the era receive no gentler treatment: "They hold fast by the views of their masters [i.e., Fourier, Owen, et al.], in opposition to the progressive historical development of the proletariat."[3]

Even in the apparently revolutionary era when the *Manifesto* was written, the class-oriented politics of Marx and Engels placed them at a peculiar distance from many of the other socialists of their time. One of the most central features of this difference revolved around their consistent adherence to what they referred to as "the real working class movement"; this was shown most clearly in what was then an almost unique focus on, and endorsement of, trade union organization.

The general absence of this orientation within the intellectual and political milieu of Marx and Engels—mirrored in an equivalent distaste for "economistic" struggles in our own era—is recognized by Hal Draper: "Marx was the first leading figure in the history of socialism to adopt a position of support to trade unions and trade unionism, on principle."[4] Most other socialists, as Draper points out, were often not only indifferent but positively hostile to trade unionism; he shows this was even true of Owen as well as Proudhon, who "not only condemned trade unions and strikes on principle but vigorously approved gendarmes' shooting down strikers as enemies of society, that is, enemies of small property."[5] Even the leading Chartist, Ernest Jones, rejected trade unionism as a "fallacy," despite the fact that his views were published only a few years after the mass Chartist struggles, which centered at their height on a general strike and the attempt to found the Grand National Consolidated Trade Union.[6] Marx and Engels were in effect unique, then, among their socialist contemporaries, in consistently following an orientation toward basic trade union organization and struggle as expressions of what they referred to as the "real class movement."

But were they correct? Richard Hyman, in his 1971 pamphlet "Marxism and the Sociology of Trade Unionism," comments that despite their lifelong involvement with both theoretical and practical aspects of trade unionism, the attention of Marx and Engels to this question is "remarkably slight." Although he acknowledges that they provided a sufficient base in their writings "to be considered as a coherent theory of trade unionism," Hyman evidently regards this theory as essentially naive. "One need scarcely document the failure of subsequent experience to validate [the *Communist Manifesto*'s] optimistic prognosis; yet Marx and Engels never produced a comprehensive revision of their earlier analysis."[7] This view is echoed in John Kelly's comment, in *Trade Unions and Socialist Politics,* that "despite their contact with, and interest in, trade unionism they left behind no systematic or coherent analysis of the limits and possibilities of trade union action." The "array of seemingly contradictory insights and arguments" said to be presented by Marx and Engels on the question is contrasted critically to the sustained and internally consistent logic of Marx's economic analysis and his "constant endeavour to penetrate between the 'surface appearances' of capitalism and its *underlying essence.*"[8]

There is, however, no unified "underlying essence" to the character of trade unionism; it is an essentially *contradictory* phenomenon, and this is what accounts for Marx's and Engels's apparently "contradictory" responses to the class struggle (or lack of it) taking place around them. The contradictory character of trade unionism, and the dialectical nature of the necessary political response, are not sufficiently or explicitly theorized in the writings of Marx and Engels on trade unionism. Yet the distinction between the consistently subversive potential of basic industrial organization, the grass roots of trade unionism, and "trade unions" *as organizations* and, incipiently, bureaucracies, was the underlying reason for their apparent vacillations between feverish excitement about union struggles during working-class upsurges and strong disapproval of the general orientation of the trade unions during periods of acquiescence.

This instinctive "nose" for the class struggle potential of grassroots trade unionism is evident in Engels's delighted response to the eruption of basic class conflict into the New Unionism of the late 1880s, a development that, though sadly too late for Marx, Engels greeted like a drink of water in the desert of nineteenth-century craft trade unionism. As he wrote excitedly to Lafargue in 1889: "These new trades unions of un-skilled men and women are totally different from the old organisations of the working class aristocracy and cannot fall into the same conservative ways.... In them I see the *real* beginning of the movement here."[9] His estimation that these new unions could not "fall into the same conservative ways" was before long revised by Engels himself, with a disillusioned reassessment of leaders like John Burns and Tom Mann as symbolizing "the bourgeois 'respectability' which has grown deep into the bones of the workers."[10] But his instinctual awareness of the always-subversive undercurrents of exploitation-based grassroots class conflict had ensured that the *potential* for undermining the labor "aristocracy" was, in Engels's mind, always a possibility. This class-centered "optimism" is more than a simple naivety; it challenges the essentially *static* conception of class consciousness frequently embodied in assessments of "the unions" as implicitly monolithic organizations.

Twentieth-century analysis of trade unions is, of course, more sophisticated in its understanding of the internally stratified nature of unions as social phenomena. Yet, in most of the renditions of economists and sociologists, "modern" analysis is far more one-sided than Marx's and Engels's instinctive understanding. The internal dynamics and contradictions of trade union life have been buried in a series of static theories, from Beatrice and Sidney Webb's glorification of union bureaucracy and Robert Michels's declaration of its inevitability in his "Iron Law of Oligarchy," through the "institutional" analyses of the American Wisconsin School and the 1950s "maturity" theorists. All shared a belief in the inevitability and desirability of bureaucracy and stable labor relations. All imagined the direction of development to be a one-way street toward order and the professionalization of labor relations.[11] Marx and Engels, in contrast, saw something deeper beneath the organizational surface, in the living force of the workers themselves. The focus on the working class as the fundamental force in the struggle against capital; the recognition of the common *interests* of that class that lend it the potential, through struggle, to grow from "class in itself" to "class for itself"; the orientation, through this focus, toward the potential of basic trade union struggles as an aspect of class activity—all these aspects of Marx's and Engels's analysis both flowed from and led to their consistent awareness of where the class was rather than where they, and certainly their contemporary fellow socialists, might have liked it to be.

This crucial orientation toward *existing* class realities is expressed in the *Manifesto* in its presentation of the "theoretical conclusions of the Communists . . . [which] merely express, in general terms, actual relations springing from an existing class struggle, from a historical movement going on under our very eyes."[12] As Engels wrote later, discussing the impact of the concept of historical materialism, "Communism now no longer meant the concoction, by means of the imagination, of an ideal society as perfect as possible, but insight into the nature, the conditions and the consequent general aims of the struggle waged by the proletariat."[13]

This orientation on the part of Marx and Engels toward the "actually existing" consciousness and organization of the working class, rather than toward some separate, idealist construction of socialism, has been widely dismissed as implying a simplistic conflation of class activity with revolutionary consciousness. Certainly, the blithely determinist logic of the *Manifesto*'s statement that "what the bourgeoisie ... produces, above all, are its own grave-diggers. Its fall and the fall of the proletariat are equally inevitable" appears to sum up the crude historicism for which Marxism has been most frequently lampooned.[14] But what intervenes between such "inevitability" and the reality of reformism is, of course, the issue of class consciousness, the *subjective* arena of which objective social and material realities can at best be regarded as an erratic and unpredictable undercurrent—a "determinant in the last instance." The consistent orientation of Marx and Engels toward such objective material conditions as *generators* of working-class struggle and organization has been well noted; their awareness of the complex balance between such factors and the nature and progress of working-class consciousness and realpolitik has perhaps received less attention.

While, as we have pointed out, Marx and Engels failed to develop any explicit theory of the mutually influential relationships between concrete working-class conditions and class interests, activity, and consciousness, they were clearly aware of the importance of more than simply the "economic base" in conditioning such relationships. The essentially *dialectical* nature of the Marxist view of class consciousness, though never fully explicated, was rooted firmly in an awareness of the interrelation between material realities and the uneven, erratic, but always materially based development of such consciousness. In *The Poverty of Philosophy*, written a few years before the *Manifesto*, Marx developed the famous distinction between class "in itself" and "class for itself," which bases the development of class consciousness not in theoretical abstractions but in the concrete requirements of capitalism and the organizational forms thus generated:

> Economic conditions had first transformed the mass of the people of the country into workers. The combination of capital had created for this mass a common situation, common interests. This mass is thus already a class as against capital, but not yet for itself. In the struggle, *of which we have noted only a few phases,* this mass becomes united, and constitutes itself as a class for itself. The interests it defends become class interests.[15]

The crucial reference here is to some earlier paragraphs in which Marx enunciates a description of the significance of working-class "combinations" very similar to that put forward in the *Manifesto:* "In England they have not stopped at partial combinations which have no other objective than a passing strike, and which disappear with it. Permanent combinations have been formed, *trade unions,* which serve as ramparts for the workers in their struggles with the employers."[16]

The significance of this argument is that "economistic" struggles are not dismissed, as by so many socialists in Marx's time and since, as removed from any connection with political consciousness and socialism; rather, they are identified as the *central elements* in the development of more explicit class consciousness and thus, potentially, a wider politicization. In this sense the conception of "class for itself" does not have to be confined to those historical moments when the working class consciously recognizes its historic mission at the wholly political level of state power; it refers to a *transitional* dynamic, a *pull* through the materially based necessity of basic struggles for what are *objectively* class interests toward the beginnings of a conscious, *subjective* awareness of class identity.

Of course, this "pull" does not automatically take the form of an uninterrupted progress toward class unity, as implied by the enthusiastic young authors of the *Manifesto.* Bur the crucial insight around which Marx and Engels built their political lives was that the roots of *any* meaningful movement toward socialism by the class defined in terms of its potential for social transformation lie in the objective realities of class conflict that push workers, whatever their subjective consciousness, into resistance against capital.

Whatever the optimism of the clarion call rolled out in the *Manifesto*, it is these crucial insights we invoke in calling for a return by the left to "class consciousness"—for a shift of emphasis away from programmatic rectitude on the one hand and theoretical fixation on text or "discourse" on the other to the perhaps difficult recognition that the key to socialist advance lies in that most despised and least acknowledged expression of "socialism from below," basic material class struggles.

Contradictory Consciousness

The zeitgeist of the 1840s, when meetings of thousands of workers inspired by the "People's Charter" took place on the Yorkshire moors, and even of the second decade of the twentieth century, when American workers traveled miles across the Great Plains to attend socialist tent meetings in equal numbers, seem to belong to another world from that of late-twentieth-century consumerism and individualism. In this "postmodern" age, consciousness of so "fundamentalist" a category as class appears to have shrunk to a scarcely discernible pulse, a sluggish bleep on the blank screen of a commodity-based culture pushed relentlessly to the wildest shores of the "global village." And yet there remains a countervailing force, all the more significant for swimming *against* this overwhelming ideological stream. The persistence of highly conflictual economic struggles entered into by workers whose subjective consciousness may be profoundly reformist, not to say conservative, continues to confound prophets of "postindustrial" stability and to demonstrate, as we argue below, a transformative potential in terms of both consciousness and praxis.

Recent events in the United States, such as the change in leadership of the AFL-CIO, the waging of a number of climactic strike struggles and, at the time of writing, a key national victory—in a strike for jobs and greater pay equality—have opened up a new receptiveness to class thinking in that most individualistic of cultures. During roughly the same period, the simmering anger provoked by years of neoliberalism has been reflected in open political protest on the streets of France, South Africa, South Korea, and many other countries. Such developments can be taken to illustrate the potential for renewed class-based revolt even after years of apparent quiescence.

How and why do apparently "hegemonized" workers achieve such qualitative leaps into outright conflict with employers and the state? Marxist theoretical development in the wake of the distortions of Stalinism has concentrated almost entirely on the domination of such "superstructural" factors as ideology, culture, and political process and on their role in structuring consciousness and blanking out dissent. In urging a more thorough exploration of the complexities of working-class consciousness and "common sense," our own argument sets out to challenge this widespread assumption of the uncontested hegemony of ruling ideas.

We begin by reversing the critique. Just as a crude determinism of economic structures and interests cannot be assumed in the trajectory of class consciousness, nor can an uncontested "overdetermination" of ruling-class or even reformist ideology be assumed to be a stable property of the capitalist system. Rather than positive endorsement of the ruling ideas of the epoch, a "dull compulsion" to accept the apparently inevitable may be a more accurate description of at least some strands of working-class response to the prevailing system. And if we substitute fatalistic acceptance for coherent and positive consent, it becomes possible to sight gaps—potential breaks in the apparently seamless canvas of late-twentieth-century "common sense."

We start by citing an absence: the *absence* of ideology. What is being proposed here is not that workers do not subscribe to ruling-class ideas, wholly or in part, or that they do not accept, in one or another sense, the parameters of reformist ideology; the boundaries of that acceptance and the pervasiveness of reformist ideology are realities that if anything deserve much greater recognition in many segments of the left. Yet the impermanence, the instability, in many ways the fragility of this acceptance is also indicated when we probe more deeply into the precise nature of "actually existing" working-class consciousness. Here we discover, rather than coherent and explicit assent to a consistent set of ideas and "values," a more complex mix: one characterized less by undifferentiated ideological domination than by inconsistency, contradiction, and lack of information.

The essentially incoherent nature of working-class social and political attitudes was noted in a cluster of studies produced in the 1970s that united in indicating that workers' views on general social issues tend to exhibit a mixture of indifference and inconsistency rather than active "legitimization" of the status quo.[17] The term "pragmatic acceptance" was used by Michael Mann to express the essentially fatalistic, rather than actively participatory, dimension of workers' outlooks.[18] Later, Scott Lash provided strong grounds for a dismissal of workers' perceptions of class and similar political concepts as confused and incoherent.[19] But workers' consciousness is also *contradictory*—a crucial feature allowing a corresponding potential for struggle and subversion of ideology. Edwards and Scullion's 1982 study of workplace organization shows shop stewards subjectively endorsing the profit-related ethos of their management while objectively undermining it with their own actions: "There was, as it were, an unconscious form of resistance whereby stewards' everyday actions challenged managerial rights in many ways even though their articulated ideology involved commitment to the same aims."[20]

More recent research is less directly concerned with "consciousness" but touches nevertheless on workers' outlooks and attitudes. For example, David Croteau's 1995 study of the apparently unbridgeable gulf between "radical" and working-class politics shows that these (primarily white) workers' apparent dismissal of socialist ideas had little bearing on their endorsement of the prevailing ideology; in fact, as Croteau points out, the workers in his study were often considerably clearer as to the corrupt realities of present-day capitalism than were their "radical" counterparts. Rather, workers' perceptions of society revealed a profound cynicism and fatalism, a sense that there is nothing you can do about these problems and that it is best simply to concentrate on one's family and private concerns.[21]

This essentially abstentionist outlook confirms our hypothesis of an "absence" of ideology or indeed any positive, coherent conception of social structure. Nevertheless, the fragile balance between "pragmatic acceptance" and the underlying resentment indicated in the details of Croteau's study do not augur well for any prognosis of *stability* in the conduct of capitalist relations. While the issue of struggle is unexplored by Croteau, who leaves his workers as fatalistic and powerless as they began, such apparent resignation stands in sharp contrast to his interviewees' anger over issues of working time and labor intensification, issues which have propelled many similarly "nonpolitical" groups of workers into major industrial struggles in both Britain and America.[22]

The attempt to draw links between such material conditions and potentially subversive action has led in recent years to a revival of the old refrain about "economic determinism." Chantal Mouffe, for example, writes: "How can it be maintained that economic agents can have interests defined at the economic level which would be represented *a posteriori* at the political and ideological levels? . . . That amounts to stating that interests can exist prior to the discourse in which they are formulated and articulated."[23] The problem with this kind of argument is that it in itself advocates a crudely "deterministic" relationship between different levels of operation of capitalist production relations. Workers do not take part in resistance because of, or through, a "discourse" that explicitly rejects capitalism in political and ideological terms. Such resistance or disillusionment occurs as a result of the material impact—on those who, because of their class position, have no alternative—of the contradictions operating within capitalist production.

Many of these are expressed in the collapse of the mythical 1980s "prosperity" of Thatcherism, swallowed whole by British "New Times" discourse theorists but cruelly undercut for workers by factors that were starkly, non-"hegemonically" economic. A 1992 study of British workers in the same "Reagan Democrat" social stratum as those in Croteau's research (known as "C2s" from their position in British socioeconomic census categories) sheds light on the essential *instability* of skilled workers' adherence to the "hegemony" of the Thatcher years.[24] Rather than the "prosperity" and individualist "consumerism" emphasized in postmodernist analysis,[25] the overwhelming message that emerges from this research is one of widespread, and growing, economic insecurity. Respondents' "perceptions" were only too well-founded on direct experience of layoffs, short-term contracts, house repossessions, and the joblessness of their teenage children. The sense of insecurity and demoralization conveyed in the words of these erstwhile working-class Tories—"We are now going backwards . . . struggling to survive"; "There's always that fear at the back of my mind"; "It's dire—we've hit the bottom and can't go any further"—is potent testimony to the lack of permanence of apparently impregnable hegemonic structures. Disillusionment with Thatcher's "property-owning democracy," once acclaimed as the pinnacle of a new culture of "individual aspiration," is compounded by the massive intensification of labor, alongside pay freezes and other pressures on living standards, experienced by those lucky enough to retain "core" employment.[26]

But there is another side to the coin of this bewildered demoralization—the propensity of such economic factors to propel even the ideologically conservative "C2s" into action, which challenges both capitalist production relations and the state.

The relatively well-paid and secure workers who, in addition to the much-vaunted "self-employed," made up the subjects of the 1992 study were from the same stratum as those workers involved in key antiemployer struggles during the worst years of Thatcherism. The printworkers who fought the savage anti-Murdoch struggles at Wapping would fall almost entirely into the category hailed by postmodernist writers as swallowing whole the "consumerist" bait of Thatcherism, as would Ford workers at Dagenham, who staged a significant strike in the late 1980s that revealed the vulnerability of "just-in-time" work arrangements. Many of the ambulance workers who took part in the protracted national dispute of 1989 were characteristic South-Eastern "Tory waverers."[27]

While the "Reagan Democrats" and "C2s" of our analysis so far, as predominantly white and (at least traditionally) "privileged" workers, are generally presumed to be the most socially and politically conservative, the absence of coherent ideology and the presence of contradictory ideas are by no means exclusive to this stratum. In the face of very real fears of detention and/or deportation, immigrant workers such as farm laborers around the United States and Latino construction workers in Southern California have rebelled against their working conditions despite holding socially conservative ideas on reproductive rights, "family values," and other "hot-button" issues. The point, however, is the same; struggles and confrontations based in class experience are seldom preceded by ideological clarity or "political correctness." If anything, it is the struggle that opens the way to new ideas and ways of viewing the world.

The lesson to be drawn would seem to be that no amount of conservative social ideology in the heads of workers is, ultimately, proof against their intermittent propulsion in an entirely different, and contradictory, direction. Yet it is the *economic circumstances* of these workers, rather than their initial consciousness, that propel them into resistance with the potential to challenge some of their most basic assumptions about the nature of the world. In this sense the struggle is not *chosen,* but neither is it, in certain circumstances, avoidable. Ideology may have lifted these workers out of their actual position in capitalist production relations; economic contradictions put them firmly back again.

Our focus on working-class consciousness or "common sense" in terms of an *absence* of ideology, a "pragmatic acceptance" of existing structures in contrast to any more positive endorsement of ruling-class ideology, needs to be complemented by a recognition of the impressive capacity of basic economic struggles for opening up, as it were, an "epistemological break" in working-class consciousness. This has been testified to over and over, from the revolutionary upheavals of 1905, sparked by a dispute over compositors' piece rates, to late-twentieth-century class insights gained by Midwestern American workers through their involvement in struggles such as the strikes and lockouts at A. E. Staley in Decatur, Illinois, the Detroit newspapers, and elsewhere.[28]

For well over a decade, a new "common situation" (to borrow Marx's phrase in describing the formation of the early working class) has been experienced by ever-wider sections of workers in both industrial and semiindustrial nations through drastic upheavals in the organization of work, labor markets, and even capital itself. Mergers, acquisitions, and transnationalization have produced ever more universal and visible organizations of capital. On the other hand, downsizing, contracting out, work intensification, and generally "lean" norms of work organization now affect most working-class people directly or indirectly across the world.[29]

This "common situation" has had its impact in a measurable rise in class consciousness. A recent British survey showed the proportion assenting to the question "Do you think there is a class struggle?" rising from 48 percent in 1964 to 81 percent in 1995.[30] In the United States, the attitude toward strikes appears to have changed dramatically. While a 1984 poll showed that 45 percent of those questioned about strike situations supported management and 34 percent the strikers, in 1996 a nearly identical poll found a reversal of opinion as 46 percent sided with strikers and only 25 percent with management. More specifically, the recent wave of strikes at General Motors plants and, above all, the 1997 strike by 185,000 Teamsters against the United Parcel Service (UPS), gained majority "public" support as more and more working people saw themselves in the same situation; polls indicated that 55 percent were for the UPS strikers and 27 percent for management. The fight for full-time jobs had become a social issue for much of the working class.

Conflicting Ideologies

The story behind the successful fifteen-day strike at UPS in August 1997 provides an almost laboratory-style example of the impotence of explicit capitalist ideology in one of its most contemporary and "hegemonic" forms—when the company launched a concerted ideological offensive in preparation for 1997 collective bargaining—and, in contrast, of the impact of an *alternative* agenda of ideas and organization among rank-and-file activists.

The UPS workforce includes just about every level of the working class. The drivers, although not exclusively white or even male, are among the highly paid full-time workers described as "Reagan Democrats" or "C2s," while the sorters and loaders are racially diverse, mostly part-time, and fairly low-paid. The company believed that unity among these workers would collapse in the event of a strike and large numbers of part-timers would cross the picket lines. What happened was the opposite. The strike was characterized by high levels of participation and mobilization and a unity the company could not comprehend.

In the two years preceding the strike, the company mounted an ideological offensive meant to assure that disunity would be the order of the day. In 1995 they launched a new team concept program, which like all such programs was meant to win key sections of workers over to the company's ideology of "competitive" goals—or at least to promote internalization of this piece of up-to-date bourgeois ideology among enough workers to head off an effective strike. The company overestimated the degree to which UPS workers would buy into this view of the world and of the company because it underestimated a process that had gone on among these workers for years—specifically, the long-term role of the Teamsters for a Democratic Union (TDU) and the more recent dynamic of reform within the Teamsters as a whole in preparing the workforce for a fight.

When it was formed in 1976, UPS workers were already a major constituency for TDU. The number of UPS workers who became active TDUers over the years was small in relation to the rapidly growing workforce, but the group provided a core of knowledgeable rank-and-file leadership among both full-timers and part-timers.[31] UPS workers were no less likely to accept the pro-company logic of team concept than any others, but they had access to an alternative "common sense" in the form of the TDU activists, the regular publications of TDU, and the critical literature on the topic developed by *Labor Notes,* an independent trade union magazine and education center in Detroit that was widely used by TDU and later the Teamsters Union. At the same time, the broader reform process, with TDU as its backbone, brought an entirely new leadership, headed by former UPS worker Ron Carey, to power in the Teamsters and initiated a process of change across the union that affected many UPS workers.[32] The new leadership was one of the few in the United States to explicitly reject the "team concept" and the whole "partnership" notion.

Mike Parker tells how TDUers reacted to the launch of the UPS team concept program:

> In January 1995, UPS moved a trailer into its yard at the Ceres center (outside Modesto, California) to be used for Total Quality Management (TQM) and self-directed

work teams. Activists responded by getting *Labor Notes* and TDU material (which arrived promptly overnight via UPS, they point out) and prepared to deal with the programs from the beginning. Although the company controlled how the workers were divided up, the activists had sufficient numbers and training that they were able to effectively counter management in every team it set up.[33]

The union itself soon took up the TDU-initiated opposition to the team concept offensive. It directly confronted the pro-company ideological assumptions of the team concept and in effect turned the entire company initiative around—*against* the goals of management. Teamster staffer Rand Wilson described the impact on the 1997 contract fight: "The team concept campaign foreshadowed the contract campaign. UPS geared up its team concept activity as its preparation for the contract and by necessity we had to take them on as part of our preparation."[34] Capitalist ideology not only failed to carry the day, it actually allowed or forced the union to campaign for a higher class consciousness.

The strike itself was not about team concept ideology, but about decidedly material issues and demands—above all the transformation of thousands of part-time jobs into full-time jobs, the reduction of the gap between part-time and full-time wages, and continued union influence over the pension plan. While there was a pay increase for the drivers, they had much less to gain in the most immediate sense than the part-timers, who composed about 60 percent of the workforce. Yet they were as fervent as the part-timers.

Equally interesting in this respect was the more remote, yet sharply ideological, fight over control of the pension plan. UPS workers in much of the country were part of a broader, multi-employer Teamster pension plan. UPS demanded its workers be taken out of the "inefficient" union plan and put under a company-controlled plan, which, they claimed, would pay higher benefits. While the company's attempt to capture the pension plan may have been a bargaining ploy, the strikers took it seriously even though a certain leap in consciousness concerning the collectivist nature of the multiemployer plan was required. By the time the strike took place, that kind of collectivist consciousness was in place. UPS's attempt to convince them it could do a better job with the plan because it was an efficient business flopped completely. Union solidarity prevailed across company lines, a mini-triumph for working-class collectivism.

The UPS strike victory was followed by a strong ideological reaction from the big-business media and conservative politicians in the United States. In the wake of the strike, the court-appointed officer who had overseen the 1996 election that put Carey back in office by a 52 percent vote declared the election invalid due to campaign funding irregularities she had uncovered earlier. Although Carey himself was not implicated, consultants he had hired had in fact broken the rules. For the *Wall Street Journal*, the *New York Times*, and other papers, this was a heaven-sent opportunity. They published a barrage of anti-Carey editorials and articles, often recycling the same news, in an attempt to discredit Carey and pressure the court into disqualifying him, thus in effect throwing the election to Hoffa. The media barrage was joined by pro-Hoffa Republicans in Congress—a chorus of ruling-class outrage at the effectiveness of a rank-and-file leadership that had actually been able to fight effectively for its own side. Yet, while the negative publicity was bothersome, it did not reverse the sense of achievement or the deeper class understanding gained by many UPS workers over the past couple of years.

The argument here is not that workers are not susceptible to appeals for labor–management cooperation or the superiority of business efficiency. There are too many examples of company successes to deny that, and, of course, these ideas abound across society as today's common sense. The point is, workers are no more possessed of these ideas than they are of the working-class alternatives, which tend to already be present. When they are in struggle even over simply economic demands, the alternative ideas can make more sense. When, as in the unusual case of UPS, the ideas have an organized rank-and-file advocate and a leadership committed to them, it can be the working-class "common sense" that prevails. In this case, the working-class "common sense" became a counterhegemony that allowed the union to buck what many thought to be an irreversible trend toward low-wage contingent work.

A similar scenario—or what, with conscious organization, had the potential to become one—was suggested in the 1996 strike by British postal workers against the introduction of "teamworking" by their employer, Royal Mail. While these rank-and-file trade unionists fought the Royal Mail "Employee Agenda" proposals with a tenacity that might suggest (as indeed much of the media darkly hinted) an explicit political agenda, the reality is that their struggle was rooted in basic material resistance to proposals that ultimately threatened their job security, working conditions, and living standards.[35]

"Teamworking" (as team concept is usually called in Britain), along with many similar programs, has of course been accepted by countless union leaderships despite these implications.[36] In the case of the postal workers, an unusually clear-headed and determined rank-and-file leadership, particularly in the London area, made a conscious effort to alert an already combative membership to the real meaning of the proposals in terms of their concrete effects on working conditions, in contrast to the "empowerment" gloss invoked by management: "The truth is it is not a case of workers having more control, but managers being in total control and workers just having to accept 'flexible' working but never having it really defined what they are accepting, because the parameters are so enormous and totally defined by the business."[37]

The series of strikes carried out by postal workers during the summer of 1996 succeeded, through a level of unity and cohesion similar to that at UPS, in removing every line of the

"Employee Agenda" from the bargaining table. The dispute is by no means over, of course; a management philosophy that has been in clear evidence since the 1980s suggests that temporary worker victories are now met by more concerted attacks, rather than consolidation. London Underground workers' combined resistance—uniting two normally rivalrous unions—to the company's "Action Stations" plan in 1988 was followed by wave after wave of management offensive until the proposals were finally implemented, a melancholy example of the success of this retrenchment policy. To maintain the kind of conscious class approach shown by the postal workers' local leadership in the face of such management aggression and strategic clarity requires more than simple "militancy," although the mobilization of the membership and its willingness to fight are of course central elements.[38] It also requires a level of awareness of the overall meaning and direction of management strategy that in effect exposes its roots in capitalist production relations centering on exploitation. Such a perspective is, of course, the opposite of the "cooperation" and "social partnership" approaches with which British and American trade union leaderships forlornly aspire to court the employers' nonexistent benevolence. It denotes a sharp awareness of which sides you and they are on; an undeviating cleavage to *independent,* class-based forms of worker organization.

This kind of explicit class perspective cannot be left to chance. It requires a *strategy* of grassroots activist organization of the kind that informs *Labor Notes* and similar projects in other countries and, more immediately, the sort of rank-and-file organization exemplified in the example above. But it is also important to be clear that the possibilities of class "consciousness-raising" invoked in such activity are not the product of socialist wishful thinking but of the material roots of resistance arising from class relations and conditions themselves. The political implications of "everyday" working-class struggle are not imposed from without, but are inherent.

Looked at from a purely "political" perspective, the implications of the postal workers' resistance to teamworking, for example, are remarkable. Not only did they succeed in thwarting the goals of a multimillion-pound "corporation" in a struggle based on workers' rejection of supposedly all-powerful management ideology, they also resisted teamworking in direct defiance not only of their own union leadership but of the closely aligned "modernist" perspectives of the (then) prospective Labour government.[39] The tradition of rank-and-file militancy that made this struggle possible was itself rooted in a series of spontaneous walkouts by postal workers that consistently flouted the draconian anti-union laws introduced by the Conservatives but stoutly backed by "New Labour." For workers supposedly colonized by (if not ruling-class then at least reformist) capitalist ideology, this stand must carry massive *potential* political significance. It remains to develop ongoing organizational vehicles through which such potential can be realized.

We have already referred to the impact of cataclysmic, long-fought struggles like the Staley dispute in transforming the consciousness of their participants—in a small number of cases, with permanent effect. Yet less prolonged and dramatic strikes like the postal workers', and more recently, that of British Airways cabin crew and catering workers, are linked to the same dynamic of detachment from both the material and ideological constraints of capitalism. Such "breaks" in hegemony, which can be acknowledged to be an *ordinary* fact of capitalist class relations, do not stem from any preexisting opening up of consciousness among the workers concerned. Rather, in many ways they reflect the *ongoing* nature of working-class consciousness in its many-stranded character, which both resists and admits the potential of a wider conceptualization of existing socioeconomic structures.

British Airways staff, particularly the cabin crew involved in one dimension of the dispute, are hardly the standard cast of working-class rebellion. Yet, like countless other groups of workers propelled into struggle, they were forced to transcend subjective conformity and conservatism by the brutal reality of (in their case) a "Business Efficiency Program" based on a £1 billion cost-saving pay and conditions package that effectively froze pay and removed overtime enhancements. In the words of one senior cabin crew member: "We are being forced to strike for our basic rights."[40]

The point here, then, is not that workers need to be "incited" to resist capital by a corps of eager socialists. Rather, what is required of socialists is a commitment to focusing on and developing the implications of *existing*, contradictory, conflictual worker consciousness. The observation made by Lenin, among others, that the working class is ultimately far *more* revolutionary than any socialist "vanguard" when it comes to fully fledged struggle may seem absurd within today's round of undramatic, economically motivated confrontations. But the point we are making here is that it is not the *readiness* of the working class to resist which is in question, but the understanding, channeling, development, and sustaining of that readiness—and its potential for challenging labor movement reformism from within—by a socialist leadership locating itself within the class rather than reading that class politically correct programs from without.

Transitions

In making this point we are arguing for a reversal of standard left conceptions of socialist politics. Rather than proceeding from a carefully worked out, analytically correct program to the dissemination of such analysis to the masses (of one sort or another), this shift in perspective would abandon the pursuit of programmatic rectitude in favor of a focus on, and engagement with, existing levels of working-class consciousness and conflict.

The practical corollary is full adoption of a focus on working-class interests and struggle, a focus that has traditionally proved difficult for the left. The recent "resurgence" of labor has been enthusiastically greeted by many socialists, perhaps particularly in the United States, resulting in a welcome stimulation of debate between left union officials and radical intellectuals. Unfortunately, even this degree of left turn toward some aspects of working-class realpolitik may not be adequate for what we would define as the task in hand: that of building an alternative, explicitly class-based current of resistance to capital within at least the "advanced" sections of the class.

Such an approach calls for a consistent orientation toward the everyday "economistic" demands and actions of a working class that may exhibit, for principled socialists, a discomfiting conservatism on many issues, or at least the kind of gulf between its own conceptions and those of middle-class socialism shown in Croteau's study. Where this gulf relates to issues such as racism or sexism, it must of course be confronted; but confronted in context. Even given such difficulties, the kind of "sacrifice" of principles and program required of socialists in starting from where the working class is, rather than where they might like it to be, is in our view indispensable if existing patterns of working-class resistance are to realize their objective potential and meaning. Any such process requires from socialists the ability to see, and draw out, the political and class implications of what may appear on the face of it to be decidedly "nonpolitical" struggles.

Encouraging a process of *transition* from acting on basic economic demands to the explicit understanding of the class meaning of such demands may require forms of organization which are themselves "transitional." The concept of transition is central in shaping a politics that, through its necessary roots in working-class concerns and conditions, can act to build a "bridge" between the material conditions that continuously propel workers into struggle and a political perspective that can address and make sense of that process.

Historically, structures like soviets have been the most revolutionary forms of organization that encapsulate this transitional dynamic in arising from basic mass strike movements while pointing toward class power. Such structures are of significance not least in terms of their *spontaneous* eruption during major episodes of working-class struggle. As such, they have been a feature not only of the revolutionary era of the First World War period but also of more "up-to-date" upsurges. In 1972, Chilean workers set up *cordones* to fight for the Allende government; in 1979, Iranian workers created *shoras* to safeguard the overthrow of the Shah. The Portuguese revolution in 1974 almost immediately created workers' commissions that united workers across union barriers within the workplace; these developed rapidly into *inter-empresa* (inter-factory) committees that clearly mirrored the Russian soviets, from necessity rather than conscious imitation.

There has also been a history of political attempts to create cross-union transitional formations along the lines of the Minority Movement of the 1920s in Britain (with the Comintern encouraging similar efforts in the United States and Canada in the Trade Union Educational League, and, with less success, in France through the "friends of unity" in the CGT).[41] The Minority Movement explicitly saw itself as "a 'transitional' organization, a means of broadening the political consciousness of discontented trade unionists." The main idea was not immediately to push "the union leadership into militant actions from below" but rather to relate the Communists'"work in the trade unions directly to the creation of a revolutionary consciousness in *preparation* for the acute crisis which would arise with the outbreak of conflict in the mining industry."[42]

Along similar lines, the need to build a class-conscious, independent leadership rooted *within* the labor movement in *anticipation* of future upsurges, is now being explicitly taken up in a growing number of countries through cross-union formations of various kinds, usually based around a publication. One of the oldest of these is *Labor Notes* in the United States, but to the list of such publications and cross-union centers has been added *Trade Union News* in Britain, *Solidariteit* in the Netherlands, *Trade Union Forum* in Sweden, *Labour Notes* in New Zealand, and *Labour* in Taiwan, alongside the Transnationals Information Exchange (TIE) networks in Germany, Brazil, and North America, among others.[43] Such publications set out to make coherent what rank-and-file union activists do less visibly day in and day out as they operate on the terrain of their members' basic interests and need for class organization.

Projects like those listed above, by publishing reports of struggles and issues across the class, providing support contacts in other sectors for those in dispute, and bringing activists across employment together in schools and conferences, begin to demonstrate to rank-and-file trade unionists the class *meaning* of their everyday activity, without the need for principles and programs dictated from above. Such initiatives cannot be sufficient to *complete* the transition to a "class for itself" consciousness by the activists involved; but they are a necessary beginning for such a process.

The issue of membership control over even workplace union leaderships is another central focus of these cross-movement organizations, as indicated in the interactions between US *Labor Notes* and union rank-and-file caucuses like TDU.[44] The constant flux identified above between the bureaucratization of unions as organizations and the subversion of this by the concerns and demands of the membership has been *consciously* confronted by rank-and-file union activists in such formations with the deliberate adoption of strategies structured to pull in the *opposite* direction—toward the creation of organic links between the workplace-based concerns of the membership and the policies and actions of their representatives. In a few cases, like the rank-and-file based involvement of TDU in the demands and organization of the UPS strike, the threads come together with a powerful result.

We have seen that, with or without the support of socialists, workers will continue to organize on the basis of their own necessary, if sporadic, conflict with the system to create "ramparts" of resistance and, whatever their apparently conservative consciousness, intermittently enter into outright confrontation with employers and the state. Socialists have never been required to *generate* class struggle and organization; where they may be useful is in pointing out its class meaning and potential. Existing efforts to adopt this approach remain slight in comparison to the yawning gaps in consciousness and organization they confront, yet they present a crucial perspective on, and example of, *cross-movement* currents of opposition and resistance rooted in the labor movement that can begin to build toward a class response to the deepening social crisis.

3 Contextualizing Organized Labor in Expansion and Crisis: The Case of the United States

Kim Moody

The relative well-being of the working class depends to a large extent on its state of organization and combativeness. But the ability of unions to improve living and working conditions also depends strongly on the economic, political, and social context in which struggles occur. In discussing the "general law of capitalist accumulation" in *Capital,* Marx argued that "the conditions which are the most favorable to the workers" are those of "reproduction on an expanded scale, i.e., accumulation."[1] This is more or less what happened in the United States during the long expansion that followed World War II and lasted until the early 1970s. Shaikh, for example, argues that this expansion was based on growing productivity, which allowed for an increase in the rate of surplus value of 24 percent from 1948 to

Originally published as "Contextualising Organised Labour in Expansion and Crisis: The Case of the US" in Historical Materialism *20(1): 3–30, 2012.*

1976. This, in turn, allowed for a substantial increase in real wages for most of this period, despite a falling rate of profit.[2] In this period, the US working class, including both the productive workers who produced this increasing surplus value and the unproductive sections of the class, achieved a growing share of national income at the expense of capital. From 1959 to 1979 the "labor" share of US GDP rose from 68.3 percent to 73.9 percent. Eventually, by the mid-1970s, the declining rate of profit brought the great postwar expansion to an end.[3] When expansion returned it would be on the basis of a continued fall in real wages and productivity growth through the intensification of work.

Expansion Returns

A new upward trend in both profit rates and growth began in 1982. McNally argues that this was the result, among other things, of a generalized attack on organized workers that produced wage compression and a rising rate of exploitation, along with a restructuring of capital worldwide and imbalances in the global economy. In addition, there was significant destruction of capital in Europe and North America with the loss of millions of manufacturing jobs.[4] In the United States alone, some six billion dollars of real private manufacturing assets were destroyed between 1980 and 1983, while business failures soared from 7,600 in 1979 to 31,300 in 1983. Between 1979 and 1983, some two and a half million manufacturing production jobs were lost.[5] In this same period the rate of surplus value jumped by over 9 percent.[6] It was this substantial devalorization, and along with it a sharp rise in the rate of surplus value, that produced a renewed period of capitalist expansion in the 1980s.[7]

This period of expansion and accumulation, however, was very different from that of the postwar years. There was, as Shaikh shows, a continuing rise in productivity following 1982, but this time real wages lagged far behind allowing for a rapid rise in the rate of exploitation.[8] Far from rising as a proportion of US GDP, labor income, broadly defined, fell from 73.9 percent in 1979 to 70.4 percent in 2006.[9] Whereas profit rates had fallen during the postwar boom, from 1982 until about 1997, by most measures they rose.[10] While there were a number of factors that explain this return to growth, it seems clear that it was in large part due to capital's ability to accelerate the rate of exploitation quickly and continuously, as productivity outstripped wages. Shaikh and Tonak show that the rate of surplus rose by 20 percent from 1979 through 1989. Whereas the average annual rate of surplus value had increased by a modest 0.6 percent from 1948 to 1980, from 1980 to 1989 it increased by 1.8 percent a year. Mohun calculated that this ratio increased by 40 percent from 1979 through 2000 as the value of labor power in the United States plunged.[11] Far from providing "the conditions . . . most favorable to workers," the expansion that began in 1982 was built on the relative and, in the case of the United States, the absolute decline of working-class living and working standards. Capital's expansion was now predicated more than ever on the decline of labor's fortunes.

The Collapse of Union Resistance in the United States

From the mid-1960s through the 1970s, much of the industrial world experienced a major labor upheaval. America witnessed its largest labor upsurge since the 1930s, mainly in response to capital's attack on organized labor, which began in the late 1950s with what Mike Davis calls "the management offensive of 1958–63." Spurred by falling profit rates, this was specifically an attack on work standards and shop-floor organization in the major, highly unionized industries, notably automobiles, steel, and electrical goods.[12] By the mid-1960s, rank-and-file resistance to this management offensive surfaced with a wave of wildcat strikes. Strike levels often surpassed those of the huge 1945–46 strike wave, peaking at just over six thousand strikes in 1974.[13] It was an era of worker self-activity in which unofficial strikes, contract rejections, and rank-and-file rebellions within major unions all challenged both the routine of American business unionism and the bureaucratic rule that supported it. Alongside the social movements of the era, and often inspired by and overlapping them, this worker upsurge thwarted the efforts of capital to recoup its falling profits rates for several years. The labor upsurge would continue for a decade and a half.[14]

The movement's momentum, however, was broken first of all by two recessions, 1973–75 and 1980–82, in which the eight largest US unions, major sites of the rebellion, lost 2.2 million members.[15] Also key to the loss of momentum was the dialectic of constant struggle between rank-and-file activists and leaders in most of these major unions, who, in business-union fashion, resisted the assault from the ranks on bureaucratic rule and increasingly sided with management in the restoration of workplace authority and company competitive priorities. It was a conflict that eventually exhausted both sides and left the leadership unable to mobilize the ranks to resist the employers' offensive their unions now faced.[16] As the momentum of the upsurge wore down, capital moved in with what one union leader called, with unintended irony, "one-sided class war." And all too one-sided it was, for beginning in 1979, much of the US union leadership, with a sometimes resistant membership following, began a rapid retreat as it simply surrendered in the face of employer attacks, recession, and restructuring.

It was the United Auto Workers (UAW), long considered one of the country's most effective unions, that led the retreat in November 1979 when its leader, Doug Fraser, of "one-sided class war" fame, agreed to major concessions at the Chrysler Corporation, even before the US Congress passed a Chrysler "bailout" that required concessions from the unions. From that time on, one union after another agreed to wage cuts and freezes as well as changes in working conditions, almost always without a fight. This essentially political choice would lay the basis for further retreat.[17]

The surrender of 1979 led to a dramatic collapse in almost every major form of trade union activity across the US economy. This collapse began even before the 1980–82 recession took hold, and well before Ronald Reagan fired fifteen thousand air-traffic controllers when their union, PATCO, struck in August 1981. Between 1979 and 1983, union membership in the private sector fell by 26 percent. Although largely due to the recession, this loss revealed that concessions alone could not stop employment reductions.[18] New organizing, which might have helped stem the continued loss of members, declined by more than half as organizing efforts were abandoned. From 1979 to 1981, the total number of strikes dropped by almost half, while the number of strikes involving more than a thousand workers had fallen by two-thirds by 1984. Negotiated annual wage increases in major collective bargaining agreements in manufacturing dropped from 6.1 percent in 1981 to 1.5 percent in 1984, falling far behind inflation even as the annual rate of increase in the Consumer Price Index fell by more than half.[19] Concessions, however, were not only about wages. A third of all concessionary agreements reached in 1982 involved changes in work rules designed to increase productivity. By 1983 changes in work organization had been conceded in auto, steel, meatpacking, tires, petroleum refining, and air and rail transport.[20]

The virtual collapse of union activity and resistance was at least one reason the rate of surplus value rose by over 9 percent between 1979 and 1983 alone, by far the biggest increase for any five-year period in the entire postwar era. This represented a real increase in the mass of surplus value of $520 billion over a brief period. The growth in the rate and mass of surplus value would continue throughout the 1980s, bringing an increase in real surplus value of $1.2 trillion from 1982 through 1989, a 70 percent increase. Meanwhile, fixed capital assets grew by a more modest 48 percent, allowing an increased rate of profit.[21] Concessions on wages and benefits could explain some of such a significant shift in income, but major changes in both the structure of industry and the organization of work were also required to sustain the period of growth initiated in 1982.

Industry Restructures

The failure to unionize the US South after World War II opened the door to the creation of a competitive, low-wage region for American industry. Basic industry in the United States began its journey away from the highly unionized Northeast and Midwest into the largely rural South at the close of the war. Between 1947 and 1972, value added in manufacturing grew by nearly four times in the South compared to just under twice in the country as a whole. Between 1972 and 1989 this Southern growth rate slowed to 60 percent, but nevertheless remained over twice that for the nation as a whole.[22] The shift to the low-wage, nonunion South played a significant role in depressing the value of labor power in the 1980s and beyond. The regional wage differentials made further moves from highly unionized states, particularly in the Midwest, well worthwhile. In 1979, the hourly wage differential between the South as a whole and the Northeast and Midwest was about 10 percent. For those states that saw a large part of the shift before and after 1979, the wage gap in that year was 15 to 16 percent between Georgia, North Carolina, and Tennessee, major gainers, on the one hand, and Michigan and Illinois, significant losers, on the other. By 2000, the percentage of payroll employment in manufacturing in North and South Carolina, Arkansas, and Mississippi surpassed that of Michigan, Illinois, and all of the states of the upper Midwest and the Northeast. In that year, union density was 3.5 percent in South Carolina, 3.2 percent in North Carolina, 6.2 percent in Mississippi, and 7.5 percent in Arkansas, compared to 21.5 percent in Michigan and 18 percent in Illinois.[23]

Industry-wide bargaining in the form of wage and benefit patterns or master contracts had been organized labor's major means of reducing labor market competition and increasing worker incomes since the end of World War II. Tempted by wage differentials and pushed by growing competition at home and abroad, firms began to break away from existing industry agreements or wage/benefit patterns in order to strike their own deals or escape unionization altogether and improve their own position in the increasingly competitive world economy. As productivity and profitability necessarily differ between firms in the same industry at any given moment, the desire to break away from the imposed labor costs of pattern bargaining in a period where competition is increasing is almost irresistible. This is particularly true where new firms with higher productivity levels or lower labor costs enter the industry, as was the case in auto, meatpacking, and trucking, or where international competition intervenes, as in textiles, garments, and textiles, which will be examined below. Such trends contributed to the decentralization of collective bargaining in those industries that had established some form of industry-level bargaining. The number of union contracts to be negotiated and administered rose from 120,000 in the 1960s, when union density was about 30 percent, to 180,000 in 2006, with density down to 12 percent, less than 8 percent in the private sector.[24]

In the 1980s, systems of "pattern" and "master" agreement bargaining that had held wages up since the late 1940s broke down in most key industries, including automobiles, meatpacking, steel, coal mining, and road haulage. Beginning in the late 1970s and accelerating in the 1980s, the automobile industry moved south, led primarily by Japanese and European firms.[25] As the Big Three and their suppliers consolidated, outsourced, and shrank, UAW membership plunged from a high of 1.5 million in 1970, when a majority of members were auto, aerospace, or agricultural implement workers, to 355,000 in 2010, with only about half the members from its traditional core industries.[26]

Unions in meatpacking faced a similar fate as new, aggressive firms like IBP and ConAgra entered the industry in the 1970s and shifted its center from the East and Midwest to the South and the West. By the mid-1980s the meatpacking union's pattern settlement had shattered, and in real terms average union wages fell from $10.65 an hour in 1979 to $6.68 in 1990.[27] Coal miners similarly saw more and more employers abandon their national agreement with the Bituminous Coal Operators Association after 1981.[28]

In three major industries, deregulation, a neoliberal innovation of the late 1970s, aided restructuring and the fragmentation of collective bargaining. The first industry to experience deregulation was air transportation. Here the system of pattern bargaining at the major airlines was rapidly dismantled. Between 1978, when airline deregulation was passed by Congress, and 1988, only a little more than half of the new collective agreements covering the unionized workforce saw any wage increase. More than a quarter of settlements included a wage freeze or cut, while one in five introduced a two-tier wage system. As a result, average real wages of airline mechanics fell by about 40 percent from 1979 to 1989, while flight attendants lost almost half their monthly income in the same period.[29]

In road haulage, following deregulation in 1980, the Teamsters' National Master Freight Agreement, which had covered 277,000 workers in 1979, saw this drop to 160,000 by 1985 and Teamster earnings fall by 11 percent in real terms from 1979 to 1983. Deregulation had opened the industry to new competition, particularly from Southern-based giants such as Overnite and J. B. Hunt.[30] Telecommunications workers also fell victim to the new neoliberal atmosphere when their employer, the American Telephone and Telegraph, was broken up as a result of a 1984 challenge in the courts to its monopoly status, ending the national agreement and forcing the Communications Workers of America to deal with seven regional telecom companies as well as the residual AT&T itself.[31]

Three more key unionized industries saw their bases rapidly eroded by the larger global restructuring already under way.

Job losses in textiles, garments, and primary metals accounted for 80 percent of the decline in production-worker employment from 1980 to 1990, due largely to imports.[32] In textiles and garments, the unions lost almost all their traditional industrial base. In the steel industry, beset by international competition for some time, production worker employment fell from 342,000 in 1979 to 171,000 in 1984. The following year, the United Steelworkers' pattern agreement with the major steel companies was terminated by the employers.[33]

By the end of the 1980s, the structure of industry and that of organized labor and its bargaining practices had been substantially altered. Bargaining was highly decentralized and, hence, more competitive. The political and social climate in which the unions functioned had also changed dramatically. The social movements of the 1960s and 1970s had faded and the "Keynesian" era had been replaced by an increasingly aggressive neoliberalism. The ideas of Hayek and Friedman had been given a power boost by the centers of capital in the 1970s through organizations such as the Business Roundtable, a coalition of the leaders of the nation's biggest corporations in industry, commerce, and finance founded in the mid-1970s.[34] As one journalist put it, "During the 1970s, business refined its ability to act as a class."[35] These developments were followed by the election of Ronald Reagan in 1980 and the dominance of neoliberalism in US politics. But capital's power grew not only in the political arena; the 1979–82 defeat of organized labor had allowed it to increase capital's power in the workplace as well. And in the 1980s business wasted no time in reorganizing work in an effort to increase productivity and profitability even more.

"Our Most Valuable Asset"
Continuous gains in surplus value and profitability could not be sustained on the basis of ad hoc concessions from the unionized sections of the workforce alone. The productivity increases of

the 1980s were not primarily due to technology, old or new. Here periodization is important. Investment in equipment and software actually grew more slowly in the 1980s than in the 1960s, 1970s, or 1990s in real terms. In manufacturing it grew by only 18 percent in the 1980s, almost half the level for the private sector as a whole and far less than in any other decade from 1960 through the 1990s. Manufacturing productivity, on the other hand, rose by almost 5 percent a year in that decade.[36]

Thus, with unions weakened and resistance low, capital turned away from capital investment as the main source of increasing productivity and profitability to reorganize work. Ideas that had been around and largely ignored for some time were now reformulated and taken up by managers desperate to compete and continue to improve profitability. These managerial innovations came in a cluster in the mid-1980s, as rapid as the union decline of 1979–82. Virtually all were about intensifying work through various types of work reorganization schemes, motivation techniques, and/or methods of control. While "human resource management" (HRM) had a gestation period in which it overtook "personnel," it was in 1984 that the two major statements of this new approach to controlling and motivating the workforce were published. The two major schools of HRM were represented by the publication in 1984 of *Strategic Human Resource Management* by Formbrun et al., representing the University of Michigan school, and *Managing Human Assets* by Beer et al., representing the Harvard version. The two schools were allegedly differentiated, respectively, as the "hard" and "soft" versions of HRM.[37] The mantra of all was that the employee, as individual, was the company's most valuable asset.

In the same year, Atkinson published his model of the "flexible firm." This placed a new emphasis on peripheral workers, contingent work, and outsourcing, a design that seemed to contradict the notion of the employee as a firm's most valuable asset.[38] The effectiveness of these new management approaches in sustaining the expansion that began in the

1980s is debatable. What matters is that they provided management with new, or at least refined, tools with which to introduce change and cheapen and/or intensify work. Furthermore, the ideology that underlay HRM and flexibility was designed, as Keenoy argues, to "undermine, if not destroy, the institutional basis of collectivism and legitimate the transition to an individualized unitary concept of the employment relationship."[39] Their uptake was a reflection of management's hunger for new ways to motivate or simply push the workforce to perform more efficiently, as well as for an ideology appropriate to the new demands of international competition.

Even more important than these managerial prescriptions was the rapid introduction of "lean production" in the United States during the 1980s. Termed "management-by-stress" by critics Parker and Slaughter, this characterization captured the way in which these new production norms reduced inputs while increasing output. This import from Japan combined teamworking, continuous improvement, speedups, just-in-time delivery, multitasking, extensive outsourcing, "reengineering," and Total Quality Management (TQM) to produce a constant tightening of the production system. It was not a replacement for mass production or Taylorism, as many of its exponents argued at the time, but a means of removing barriers to faster production with fewer workers.[40] The introduction of lean norms in the United States was led by Japanese firms adept at it. Between 1979 and 1989 Japanese auto companies opened eleven "lean" assembly plants in the United States, only two with a union workforce, while the US Big Three closed nine unionized assembly plants. With the UAW failing to organize these new plants, by the end of the 1980s 39 percent of the industry was nonunion. In the parts sector of the industry nonunion facilities proliferated as outsourcing increased, bringing the nonunion workforce to 76 percent of that sector.[41]

The new competition from Japanese firms producing in the United States forced the US automobile companies to introduce lean methods as rapidly as possible. This typically involved the carrot of employee participation or labor-management cooperation, schemes that were rapidly embraced by most union leaders. Although originated in 1982, it was, once again, in 1984 that General Motors negotiated its fully elaborated "Jointness" program, giving the union representation on a complex of committees meant to consult, though not bargain, on production problems and plans.[42] The following year, NUMMI, the GM-Toyota joint venture, was opened in California with the entire range of lean production procedures and record-breaking speeds of production.[43] From their incubation in auto, lean norms, including TQM and other "quality" programs, "reengineering," teamworking, and the extensive outsourcing associated with lean production, spread across manufacturing in the 1980s. Estimates of the extent of lean methods vary from at least one-quarter of all US firms to 80 percent of industrial firms having some version of these by the early 1990s.[44]

Lean methods would spread beyond manufacturing in the 1990s. In 1993, for example, lean hit the telecommunications industry at US West in the form of reengineering, reorganization, and flexibility. In the same year, AT&T adopted its "Workplace of the Future" program of labor-management cooperation and lean reorganization.[45] Greenbaum's study of office work found that by the early 1990s, TQM, "broadbanding," work reorganization, "reengineering," and flexibility were invading office work.[46] In the 1990s they had spread even to the nation's healthcare industry. As Kumar wrote about US hospitals, "Over the years, they have adapted Lean Manufacturing, Six Sigma and supply chain strategies in order to become more efficient."[47]

Did lean production, enabled by HRM, TQM, and employee involvement, aid the sustainability of the 1980s expansion? I would argue that it did. Smith's review of the literature on the effectiveness of lean methods shows that most studies judge it more effective than older production methods or other strategies, such as downsizing, in terms of productivity.[48] While overall productivity growth during the 1980s was not impressive, in manufacturing, where lean production was now common, it was. There, productivity rose by 37 percent or 4.6 percent a year from 1982 to 1989, twice the average rate for the 1960s and 1970s. In the automobile industry, incubator of lean production, it rose by 47.4 percent from 1980 through 1988, an average of 5.3 percent a year.[49]

Smith's review of the literature also concludes that "*the most significant contemporary attempts to legitimate the contemporary social order all invoke the lean production model*" (emphasis in original).[50] In other words, not only is the cluster of new techniques associated with lean production more successful in terms of productivity measures, but it also plays an ideological role in legitimating the competitive arguments put forth by management. It thus seems clear that working under lean conditions, driven by new management tactics, and, given the reality of plant closures, fearful of job loss, US workers in manufacturing not only involuntarily initiated the expansion that began in 1982 after the collapse of union activity but sustained it through the 1980s under a regime of work intensification *and* a continuing fall in real wages.

There was, to be sure, some resistance to all of this. High-profile strikes in the 1980s at Hormel in Minnesota, Watsonville Canning, International Paper, and the shipyards at Jay, Maine; the successful mobilization strategy at NYNEX in the Northeast in 1989; and the massive civil disobedience in the UMWA strike against Pittston, also in 1989, all signaled that the labor movement was not quite dead yet.[51] In some unions, notably the New Directions Movement in the UAW and the Teamsters for a Democratic Union (TDU) in the International Brotherhood of Teamsters (IBT), rank-and-file reform movements fought consistently against the increasingly cooperative attitudes of the leadership toward new management methods.[52]

Nevertheless, the level of resistance and even of conventional strikes in the 1980s remained low. Aside from the exhaustion of the upsurge discussed above and the obvious fear of job loss that prevailed in many restructuring or shrinking industries after the 1980–82 recession, two other economic factors allowed for a low level of resistance from the ranks. The first was the relatively low level of inflation that followed the recession. The Consumer Price Index would fall from a high of 13.3 percent for 1979 to 3.8 percent in 1982 and then to 1.1 percent in 1986, rising again to 4.6 percent at the end of the decade.[53] While this was high enough to wipe out real gains in wages, it was far below the rising levels of the 1970s. Second, compensating for the loss of real buying power was what Shaikh calls "the extraordinary fall in the interest rate," which, among other things, allowed working-class families to continue consuming through the accumulation of household debt.[54] This relative lack of grassroots resistance also allowed most union leaders to accommodate to labor-management cooperation and subsequent implementation of lean production norms. In the face of continually falling union density in all but a few industries, the survival "strategy" of the leaders of most large unions in this period and beyond was based on three practices: bargaining concessions not only on wages but on benefits and working conditions as well; various forms of labor-management cooperation or "partnership" usually associated with lean production methods; and union mergers to bolster falling membership figures.[55] The first two represented accommodation to capital's new management strategies and practices, while the latter tended to reduce the urgency of new organizing for many unions.

Nevertheless, new organizing became a major issue in the 1990s as several unions turned seriously to new organizing techniques. As a result, significant leadership changes would take place in the AFL-CIO, as Service Employees International Union (SEIU) president John Sweeney beat old-guard standard-bearer Lane Kirkland and TDU-backed Ron Carey became president of the Teamsters, leading to one of the most important anti-lean strikes of that decade at UPS in 1997.

Grassroots militancy in the face of drastic lean methods would explode once again on the prairies of the Midwest, this time at A. E. Staley in Decatur, Illinois.[56] Yet the basic practices of labor-management cooperation adopted by most business union leaders in the 1980s would continue into the 1990s.

With resistance low, productivity gains would increase somewhat, in some recovery years very rapidly, real wages would continue to fall until a brief reprieve in the late 1990s, and increases in the exploitation of labor would remain a central factor in the expansion of the 1990s, as Mohun's figures on the rate of surplus value cited earlier indicate. In that decade and later, financial and overseas profits would play a growing role in holding up profits as the epicenter of capitalist investment moved from West to East, above all to China, until the drop in the mass of profits that began in late 2006.[57]

To summarize the analysis, the collapse of union resistance beginning in 1979, intensified by the recession that followed, sparked the recovery that began in 1982. Accelerated industrial restructuring undid "pattern" bargaining, labor's first line of defense since the end of World War II, undermining resistance and contributing to the continued fall in real wages. The introduction of "lean production" methods enabled significant productivity increases, first in manufacturing in the 1980s and then more generally in the 1990s. The combination of these trends produced a fall in the value of labor power, contributing to the sustainability of the expansion over this whole period.

US Labor in the Early Twenty-First Century

Despite the recession of 2000–01, in the early years of the new century, US capital would continue to be favored by a continued fall in the value of labor power. In the first several years of the new century, real wages remained essentially stagnant, while productivity rose by more than 20 percent from 2000 through 2008. The gap between the two grew, indicating a further fall in the value of labor power.[58] Union membership, however, after rising slightly in the late 1990s, began to slip again with the recession of 2000–01, falling from 16.3 million in 2000 to 15.4 million in 2006, with *all* of the loss in the private sector.[59] First year increases in union negotiated agreements averaged 3.5 percent from 2001 through 2007, generally staying slightly ahead of inflation and clearly somewhat better than the average worker.[60] But with union density down to about 8 percent in the private sector, these agreements had less and less influence on working-class incomes overall. While there was, as always, some resistance in the years before the Great Recession, the level of strike activity continued to plummet in the new century, falling by more than half from 392 in 2000 to 119 in 2009, a record low.[61] The most important developments in organized labor in the first few years of the twenty-first century up to the "Great Recession" of 2008, however, were the changing nature of the unions, the increasing centrality of the SEIU, the split in the AFL-CIO, and the virtual "civil war" that exploded in 2009 between several important unions.

The first thing to note is that the unions that faced capital in the twenty-first century were very different from those of the late 1970s. For one thing, the industrial distribution of union members had changed significantly. Unions in traditional strongholds such as steel, auto, transportation, and apparel all lost members as employment dropped or shifted south, or held their own through mergers or absorptions of smaller unions. Union density in manufacturing had fallen from 32.3 percent in 1980 to 14.8 percent in 2000 and would fall further to a little over 11 percent in 2007, while density in a small number of service industries grew, most notably in hospitals, where it grew from 13.8 percent in 2000 to 15.3 percent in 2007, twice the level for the private sector as a whole.[62]

The industrial shift meant that union members had changed in terms of occupations and demographics as well. In 1978, 65 percent of union members were in manual occupations in manufacturing, mining, construction, transport, and telecommunications. By 2008 fewer than half were in those industries. There were by then as many workers in health and education services as in manufacturing. Women now comprised 48 percent of union members, whereas in 1978 they were less than a quarter. In 2008, while the proportion of African American members remained the same as in 1983 at about 12 percent, the percentage of Latinos had doubled from just under 6 percent to just over 12 percent. Between 2000 and 2010 half a million Latinos had joined unions.[63] This reflected the growth and increased importance of immigrant workers in the US labor force and in the unions. If the decline of unionism in manual occupations symbolized labor's weakening position in the economy, the industrial and demographic shifts brought some new strengths.

The first of these was the rising importance of immigrant workers in the United States referred to above. In 2000, the AFL-CIO abandoned its past restrictionist policy on immigration and came out in favor of amnesty.[64] Recognizing the centrality of immigrant workers in its industries, the Hotel Employees Restaurant Employees (HERE) took the lead in organizing the Immigrant Workers' Freedom March in 2003.[65] An even more graphic reminder of the importance of immigrant labor came on May 1, 2006, when five million immigrants demonstrated across the United States for immigrant rights, many taking the day off of work. The Los Angeles waterfront was paralyzed, half the nation's meatpacking operations closed, and construction was hit hard in areas of high immigrant population such as Southern California.[66] Immigrant workers would also play an important role in the growth of the SEIU, which became the largest union in the AFL-CIO as the new century unfolded. Membership gains in the private sector came mostly in growing service-sector industries such as food services, hospitality, and health care.[67]

The scale of new organizing, however, was not sufficient to prevent overall shrinkage from 2000 to 2006. The number of NLRB representation elections involving new organizing dropped from 3,162 in 1999 to 1,503 in fiscal year 2008.[68] NLRB elections had been declining for many years as that route to representation was undermined by employer resistance. A number of unions had turned to pressuring employers for "neutrality" agreements and "card check" schemes with some success. These are procedures in which an employer agrees to a simple majority show of authorization cards for recognition. Although organizing targets tend to be larger in these campaigns and the number recruited larger, the incidence of these new types of "voluntary" organizing tactics deployed remains small, rising from 227 to a high of 420 in 2001 and then falling to 258 in 2004, never amounting to more than 15 percent of all organizing efforts. What was clear was that the general level of new union organizing had been down for some time.[69]

In terms of growth, the great success story of the period was the SEIU, which had grown from 981,331 in 1995 to 1.8 million in 2009.[70] Its most famous campaign was Justice for Janitors, drawing on the new immigrant workforce, which won a high-profile victory in 1990. By 2008 SEIU had gained representation for 225,000 building service and security employees. Some of this growth came from mergers, such as the 1998 absorption of New York's huge health care workers' Local 1199, which brought in 125,000 members. Another major source of growth was the 365,000 home and child-care workers organized between 1996 and 2007. This was largely the result of political deals struck with governors in several states, due to SEIU's generous donations to the campaigns of these governors. In 2004, it had even given half a million dollars to the Republican Governors Association. SEIU was the biggest political donor in the AFL-CIO. In the 2007–08 election cycle, SEIU raised more than sixty million dollars in political contributions.[71]

In the name of more effective organizing and political clout, however, SEIU president Andy Stern transformed this union into a highly centralized, top-down organization. Beginning with the "New Strength Unity" program in 2000, more and more authority was given to the president while local unions were merged, so that by 2009 57 percent of the union's members were in fifteen "mega-locals." Trusteeships, where local unions are placed under the direct rule of the national union, were a frequent tool in this transformation, with twenty-six locals facing control imposed by the president between 2000 and 2007.[72] Stern also adopted what many viewed as an extreme version of labor-management cooperation schemes which he called "value-added employer relationships." The theory being, he wrote, that "improved quality, increased corporate revenues, and increased workers' skills and opportunities should lead all to more equitably distributed financial rewards."[73] Linked to that is an effort to move away from workplace organization, the battleground of the last three decades, and substitute call centers for shop stewards as a means of dealing with growing on-the-job pressures, a direction that seems to be the exact opposite of what is needed. All of this was presented as *the* strategy for growth and renewed union power. This model would become increasingly controversial.[74]

Frustrated by the unwillingness of the AFL-CIO to prioritize organizing above all else, SEIU's Stern and the leaders of the Teamsters and Carpenters formed the New Unity Partnership in 2003 to pressure the federation to adopt a more aggressive organizing policy and a basic reorganization of the AFL-CIO and its unions. Unable to move the AFL-CIO, in 2005 six unions, again led by SEIU, left the AFL-CIO to form their own Change to Win (CTW) Federation.[75] At first it might have seemed as though the new federation was organizing where others had failed. In the two years prior to the recession, US unions were actually growing. In 2007, unions had a net gain of 311,000 members, 133,000 in the private sector, while in 2008 they gained 428,000, 151,000 in the private sector. The largest increase from 2006 through 2008 was in healthcare services, the major base of the SEIU, where union membership increased by 214,000.[76] Despite SEIU's gains, CTW as a whole, after slight growth from 2006 to 2007, actually lost nearly half a million members from 2007 to 2008.[77]

The aggressiveness of the SEIU leadership toward other unions went beyond the formation of CTW to spark a virtual civil war in organized labor. Much of this centered on the highly controversial efforts of the SEIU to raid a number of unions. One was the California Nurses' Association (CNA), which was successfully competing with SEIU in recruiting nurses not only in California but around the country. Another major target of SEIU aggression was UNITE-HERE, the recently merged union of garment and hotel workers. This ended in a split in UNITE-HERE, with perhaps a third of its members leaving to join SEIU.[78] The CNA, for its part, went on to lead the merger of three nurses' unions to form the National Nurses United in 2009 with 150,000 members.[79]

As Stern aggressively merged dozens of SEIU into giant "mega-locals," he ran into resistance. The strongest opposition to forced mergers *and* to Stern's increasing willingness to cut deals with healthcare systems in order to gain members came from the leadership of SEIU's militant 150,000-member United Healthcare West (UHW). When Stern moved to put this rebel local into trusteeship in 2009, the leaders and thousands of UHW members left SEIU to form the independent National Union of Healthcare Workers (NUHW). As UHW's membership was technically under agreements signed by the SEIU International, however, the members were not able to simply transfer their loyalty. NUHW suffered a serious setback in 2010 when it lost a representation election for forty-five thousand workers at Kaiser Permanente, the huge California-based healthcare system. Nevertheless, it went on to win representation for some ten thousand healthcare workers by mid-2011.[80]

Eventually, after alienating much of the leadership of both federations, the SEIU reached truces with UNITE-HERE and CNA and Stern resigned as SEIU president. The war against NUHW, however, continued.[81] If the worst of labor's "civil war" was over by 2010, it had arguably been a factor in the unions' loss of the one piece of legislation they most sought from the Obama administration, the Employee Free Choice Act, which would have made union organizing somewhat easier. Despite growth in some areas, the US labor movement as a whole had entered the recession in disarray.

Crisis and Decline, Once Again

The rate of profit began its fall in 2006. By the fourth quarter of that year the mass of profits in the nonfinancial sector fell. This was before the subprime collapse was evident and well before the big financial meltdown of 2008.[82] As employers responded to this decrease in profits, unemployment began to edge upward in the first quarter of 2007, when the unemployment rate was 4.5 percent. By March 2008 it was 5.1 percent, with 7.8 million out of work. By October 2009 official unemployment hit 10 percent with 15.6 million out of work, a third of them for twenty-seven weeks or more. If we include the 5.6 million considered "not in the labor force" but who wanted work, the total is more than twenty-one million.[83] Some six million private-sector production-worker jobs were lost between May 2007 and October 2009.[84]

The fate of the unions in this situation was predictable. In 2009 unions saw a net loss of 771,000 members, 834,000 in the private sector, more than wiping out the gains of the previous two years.[85] The outcomes of collective bargaining followed the pattern of union loss. First-year wage increases in new collective bargaining agreements rose to an average of 3.6 percent in 2007 for all new agreements and 3.2 percent for those in manufacturing, but by 2009 new wage settlements had dropped to 2.3 percent and 2.0 percent respectively, and by September 2010 they had fallen to 1.7 percent and 1.1 percent. Whereas 14 percent of workers covered by these agreements had received no first-year increase in 2007, by 2010 it was 35 percent.[86] The number of strikes, while already very low by the 2000s, fell to an all-time low in 2009 of 119 strikes.[87] Management aggression in collective disputes in 2009 and 2010 was evident in at least three lockouts; those of borate miners in California, uranium-processing workers in Illinois, and Red Cross workers across six states.[88] To be sure, there was worker resistance as well. The strike figures above included groups ranging from food-processing workers in New York State to nurses in Philadelphia and Minneapolis. Even the UAW, desperately on the defensive in the automobile industry, struck against Bell Helicopter for twenty-seven days.[89] But, as in 1979–82, the employers had the upper hand.

Productivity was once again up significantly. In 2009, productivity took several leaps, the biggest being in the second quarter when it grew by 8.4 percent for nonfarm business, as employers shed workers while production rose in the second half of that year. In manufacturing, the third quarter of 2009 brought an unprecedented 16.9 percent jump in productivity. Unit labor costs fell rapidly in manufacturing from mid-2009 through the first three quarters of 2010.[90] Looking at these productivity leaps in late 2009, *Businessweek's* economic editor explained them as follows: "So people working shorter hours had to do the same work as before, or more. People who kept their jobs had to pick up work of ex-colleagues. Many workers probably put in extra hours that weren't counted in the statistics in order to get all their work done."[91] He went on to note that this produced the "largest decrease [in labor costs] since the series began in 1948." While such huge productivity spikes cannot be sustained, it is clear that capital continues to push for the combination of wage restraint and increased relative surplus value as their means of recovery.

In 2011, the attack on working-class living standards moved on to the public sector in accelerated form as Republican governors in several states, responding to the nervousness of state bondholders and the continued desire of businesses and the wealthy for tax cuts, attempted to deprive state and local government employees of collective bargaining rights altogether. The fiscal squeeze found forty-six or fifty states in deficits by 2009, in large part because of cuts on business taxes. The proportion of state revenues drawn from corporate taxes had fallen from 9.7 percent in 1980 to 6.7 percent in 2006. Public workers had faced concessions and staff reductions for some time. By 2009 thirty-four states had begun reducing their workforces.[92]

This attack had already accelerated in 2004 in Indiana, where Governor Mitch Daniels repealed collective bargaining rights for state workers. The consequence was that union membership among state workers fell from 16,408 in 2005 to 1,490 in 2011. No doubt inspired by events in Indiana, right-wing governors in Wisconsin, Ohio, and Michigan pushed legislation that would abolish or severely limit bargaining for public workers.[93] This brought an enormous, largely unexpected reaction in these states, above all in Wisconsin. There the state Capitol Building was occupied for two weeks, with thousands in the street through the week; weekend demonstrations drew seventy thousand union members and supporters in the first week and a hundred thousand in the second. Polls showed that a majority of people across the country opposed depriving workers of bargaining rights, and most of these laws are under challenge in the courts. Nevertheless, Democratic legislators in several states soon joined those trying to repeal the bargaining rights of public workers.[94]

Underlying the attack on public workers is an effort to reduce the cost of "nonproductive," though necessary, labor—that is, labor that for the most part does not produce surplus value and, in this case, must be paid out of it in the form of taxation. It is simply another way of accomplishing what direct austerity programs are attempting to do to public workers and the poor in Southern Europe.[95] Interestingly, Marx noted that the huge increases in productivity brought about by large-scale industry in the nineteenth century allowed for "a larger and larger part of the working class to be employed unproductively," mostly as domestic servants in his day.[96] Clearly, the problems of accumulation are such that even substantial productivity growth no longer allows such a luxury from capital's point of view.

With productivity rising, corporate profits reached $1.7 trillion in the third quarter of 2010, the highest amount ever recorded by the government, and an increase of 28 percent over a year before. The biggest part of this increase came from domestic profits and the lion's share of those from nonfinancial corporations, whose profits grew by 40 percent in that period.[97] Certainly, labor, once again, will have played an involuntary role in whatever recovery should follow the Great Recession.

Conclusion

A number of conclusions flow from what has been argued above. The first is that the historic link between rising productivity and wages, so valued by Keynesian and institutional labor economists, and so central to collective bargaining theory, has been broken. The liberal economists at the union-backed Economic Policy Institute called the failure of wages to rise when productivity was growing rapidly in 2000–06 "extraordinary."[98] Actually, it had become the norm. In Marxist terms, the most favorable condition for workers, "reproduction on an expanded scale, i.e., accumulation," had been stood on its head. The conditions for accumulation have become *falling* real wages linked to increases in productivity—a downward trend in the value of labor power. It is not in the realm of theory that the productivity-wage link was broken, of course, but in that of class struggle—an altogether too "one-sided class war." The combination of capital's industrial and neoliberal strategies and practices on the favorable terrain of global restructuring and labor's weak reaction and largely misplaced strategic choices and practices have broken the link. The "secret" of the 1982 recovery and whatever subsequent expansion follows the Great Recession is found largely in this broken link.

The evidence for this lies not only in the trends in the United States discussed in this chapter, but on a world scale. Labor's share of income fell not only in the United States but also in the seventeen leading Organisation for Economic Co-operation and Development (OECD) countries, where it dropped from 75 percent in the mid-1970s to 66 percent by 2005.[99] Nor was this redistribution of surplus value limited to the developed economies. The International Labour Office (ILO), in its 2008–09 *Global Wage Report*, argues that real wages have fallen as a share of world GDP at least since 1995 in pretty much the same way as in the United States. Waged labor, they point out, now makes up half the world's economically active population. That is, this half is now employed for the most part by capital even if many of these jobs are contingent. The world economy, they calculate, grew by 3.3 percent from 1995 to 2007, while wages grew by only 1.9 percent. As a result, labor's share of income fell, "an indication that increases in productivity have failed to translate fully into higher wages."[100] Capital has succeeded in restraining wages while simultaneously extracting productivity increases on a world scale, thus lowering the value of labor power across the planet. Much of this was made possible by the opening of vast new low-wage areas of the world to investment after 1990.

With a geographic expansion on the scale of the 1990s no longer possible and the incentive for major technological breakthroughs blunted by declining relative labor costs, it is reasonable to assume that capital will continue to be wedded to this strategy for profitability at least until its limits are reached in the physical degradation or rebellion of the working class. Thus, for the foreseeable future, "the conditions which are most favorable to the workers" will not emerge on their own or as a result of the behavior of capital.

The second conclusion has to do with the organized working class itself. Obviously, the strategies of retreat that have characterized the decisions and practices of most US union leaders since the late 1970s have failed. Chief among these were labor-management cooperation or "partnership," the near-abandonment of the strike as a weapon, the mergers so common in the 1990s, and bureaucratic reorganization along the lines of the SEIU. Even the new organizing tactics based on employer "neutrality" have proved inadequate in a period when most employers who do not already have a union presence are disinclined to remain "neutral."[101] Simple changes in the leadership and even the structures of US unions, as badly needed as they are, won't be enough if working-class organization is to spread and dig roots in a changed industrial terrain. The workplace, the central battleground over productivity, will be the key to sustained resistance and mobilization. At the same time, more attention needs to be given to the sort of political and social upheaval that has recently spread around the world, from Bolivia to Mexico to America's immigrant communities, to North Africa and the Middle East, and to Wisconsin—mass, continuous street mobilizations, necessarily involving work stoppages.[102]

Here it is good to bear in mind the decisions and strategies employed by capital discussed in this chapter. Ultimately, the division of surplus value is not simply a matter of mathematics, technology, or inevitability, but of power. Capital mobilized not only itself but its states and global institutions to bring about the shift in wealth we have seen in the era of neoliberalism. The value composition of capital presents limits, but not absolute limits. Pushing back the borders of profit is, in the final analysis, a matter of organization, politics, and force. Ironically, perhaps the only way capitalism might be forced to "kick the habit" of dependency on wage compression and work intensification is to force capital to shift some of its surplus to labor, perhaps encouraging increased investment in new "labor-saving" technology. The other possibility, of course, is that increased struggle on a mass scale eventually runs up against the limits of capital, in which case far more is involved than the behavior of unions, as we can see in Greece and elsewhere.

Even the growth of unions, however, seldom comes about incrementally. Rather, as Kelly, Clawson, and others argue, union growth is a function of an upsurge in class conflict.[103] The precise mechanisms required to create the human agency that makes such an upsurge possible is a matter of considerable debate, but two things seem clear. One is that changes in the way capital organizes labor and the conditions that workers must face have a great deal to do with it, as they did in the 1930s and in the 1960s. This is why the workplace or the "job" is key. The other is that such upheavals transform the very human agents who carry it out, expanding the realm of possibility.

While there is no automatic mechanism that creates such an upturn in worker self-activity, the worker-led resistance that has commenced on a fairly large scale in Europe, Latin America, and more recently in China suggests the possibility of a new upsurge. Even such seemingly disconnected events as the plant occupation at Republic Windows and Doors in December 2008 and the spectacular mass movement in Wisconsin in early 2011 may be signs of things to come.[104] It is also worth noting that where the strike has been revived, as in hotels and hospitals, among other settings, it has often worked. The choices made by union leaders and many workplace leaders in the 1980s opened certain possibilities for capital. The question now is: can workers in and out of today's unions make different choices and bring about different outcomes? Whether America's weakened labor movement can rise to the occasion, as it did in the early 1930s, when it had hit low levels of organization comparable to those of today, is as much a matter of practice and politics as of economics.

4 The Rank-and-File Strategy

Kim Moody

Introduction: The Problem

America, it has been said, is the exception. It is the only devel oped industrial nation where no mass socialist movement took root in the working class in the twentieth century. To be sure, there have been times of mass upheaval and even the growth of sizable left organizations with a significant working-class membership. In the years before World War I and in the 1930s, socialist, communist, Trotskyist, and anarcho-syndicalist organizations had some impact on the development of organized labor and even on US politics. But then, unlike their European counterparts, they shrank to be marginalized as political relics or sects.

Some scholars saw the problem as one of "American exceptionalism." The United States, it was argued, had too much upward mobility, too much available farmland, too regular a

Originally published as a pamphlet in 2000 (Detroit: Solidarity).

turnover as old ethnic groups worked their way up into the "great American middle class." While these theories always had limited powers of explanation, much of the period of economic expansion that followed World War II lent them credibility. Not only did the so-called middle class grow and prosper, but even much of the traditional industrial working class achieved a living standard never before achieved by blue-collar or even most white-collar workers anywhere in the world. African Americans, Latinos, and other people of color were largely excluded from this upward march to prosperity, which is one reason why the enormous movements of Black and Latino people exploded in the 1950s and 1960s. For the majority of white working-class people and those people of color lucky or forceful enough to break into the unionized blue-collar workforce in those years, the "American Dream" seemed within reach.

Today, the upward mobility theories look as outmoded and irrelevant as a *Dick and Jane* first-grade reader with its tranquil, all-white world. Only the top 20 percent of US families have seen anything like upward mobility in terms of income. For the vast majority, today's forced march is downhill all the way. For African Americans, Latinos, and single women it is more like a free fall. The proportion of poor people is on the rise. The gap between the rich and the rest has grown to obscene and highly visible levels. Even the wages of unionized workers in the big corporations are lower in real terms than they were in the 1970s.

There is no more "American exception," no more "American Dream." There is no more upward mobility for the vast majority. A highly internationalized capitalism is dragging most of us down, here and abroad. The crisis of capitalist "globalization" was never more evident. And all across the world, we see growing resistance to the power of capital and its neoliberal political allies. Even in the United States, there are signs of revitalization and renewed militancy in organized labor. This is not just a matter of more strikes like those at UPS (1997), General Motors (1994–98), and US West (1998), although, as we shall see, they represent something very important. We also see more and more attempts by rank-and-file union members to make their unions more democratic and more effective in fighting today's highly aggressive employers and in organizing the unorganized. At the same time we see the beginnings of class independence in the political sphere, with the formation of the Labor Party by several national and scores of local unions in 1996.

Yet at no time since the 1950s has the isolation of socialists from the working class been greater. Socialist organizations in the United States, including Solidarity, remain small and largely populated by people with an educated middle-class background. Many socialist groups' connection with the working class is limited to support work for various strikes. The gap between the socialist organizations and the active sections of the working class who are the organizers of much of the resistance to the employers and rebellions within the unions is too great. The gap has many facets: some arise from different class origins, others from the habit of defeat on the left and the proclivity for symbolic actions and campaigns that flows from it. Most of the gap, however, is one of consciousness. The left, with its highly theorized, often moralistic politics, and the worker activists, with an untheorized, pragmatic outlook, are often like trains passing in the night. This can be true even where left groups or individuals work within the unions.

The rank-and-file strategy attempts to bridge that gap. We call this the rank-and-file strategy because it is based on the very real growth of rank-and-file activity and rebellion that occurs in periods of intensified class struggle. The theory behind the strategy tells us that the conflict inherent in capitalist social relations of production becomes more intense under conditions of increased competition and crisis. The experience of this conflict, the reality of intensified exploitation, contradicts older, embedded conservative ideas. The old ideas are not so much a clear pro-capitalist ideology as a mixture of contradictory ideas and sentiments held by most people in our society. Within the working class, rudimentary democratic and collectivist ideas co-exist with, and sometimes combat, both socially conservative ideas (from racism to cynicism and feelings of powerlessness) and a general acceptance of things as they are.

The task of socialists in this situation is not simply to offer an alternative ideology, a total explanation of the world, but to draw out the class consciousness that makes such bigger ideas realistic. The notion of a transitional set of ideas is key to this strategy. The socialist analysis of capitalism and what capitalism is doing to workers today relates directly to the daily experiences of more and more working-class people. But the fact that the vast majority of working people lack even a consistently class-conscious way of looking at the world makes it difficult for socialism to get a hearing. The gaping lack in the United States at this time is the lack of a sea of class-conscious workers for socialist ideas and organizations to swim in. How do we help create that sea (with all due respect to Mother Nature)? Socialists can build transitional organizations and struggles that help to raise the class consciousness of activist workers in order to enlarge the layer of workers in the class who are open to socialist ideas. The existence of a strong current of active, class-conscious workers is a precondition for the development of a strong current of socialist workers—and a socialist party. We need to be, at the same time, bringing our socialist ideas directly to workers who are already ready to hear them, and also helping to create the struggles that produce more such workers.

Such struggles and such organizations are expressions of worker self-activity and self-interest. But capitalism attempts to demobilize and disempower workers; our experience is that it often takes people trained in organization, with a commitment and perspective of worker organization—that is, socialists—to take the lead in pulling ongoing organization together.

Transitional organizations include rank-and-file reform movements and caucuses rooted in the workplace and the unions. The best-known example is Teamsters for a Democratic Union (TDU), but there are many others. Community-based worker organizations (sometimes called workers' centers) that organize on a class basis, usually in specific racial or ethnic communities, are also transitional worker organizations. Some examples of these are the Latino Workers' Center in New York, the Black Workers for Justice Center in North Carolina, and the Xicano Development Center in Detroit. At a slightly higher level are organizations that cut across union, industry, racial, and gender lines and give a classwide perspective to the daily workplace and union experience. This includes organizations and projects like Jobs with Justice, *Labor Notes*, local cross-union support committees, or more political organizations such as local living-wage campaigns or the new Labor Party.

This chapter will explain why such organizations and rank-and-file rebellion in general are the result of real social forces. It is this social reality that makes rank-and-file rebellion key to a successful strategy for building a revolutionary socialist workers movement in the United States.

This strategy starts with the experience, struggles, and consciousness of workers as they are today, but offers a bridge to a deeper class consciousness and socialist politics. Most of all, it is a strategy for ending the isolation of socialists and socialist organizations from the day-to-day struggles and experiences of the organized sections of the working class. It is not a panacea, a quick fix, nor guaranteed to succeed. The strategy does not assume that socialist consciousness flows automatically from "economic" struggles. If it did, no strategy would be necessary. Those looking for a way out of the dilemma of socialism's isolation from its natural base are urged to join the discussion this chapter aims to provoke.

The Setting: Why the Unions?

The rank-and-file strategy for socialism in the United States focuses on the unions and the workplace. This is not because these are the only places where consciousness is formed or struggles conducted. I am well aware of the many community-based campaigns, organizations, and struggles by working-class people. Indeed, some of these play a role in the rank-and-file strategy. I also understand that one's identity or consciousness in this society is shaped by many forces in many different settings. Class consciousness never exists alone; it is accompanied by the consciousness of other oppressions, such as those of race or gender, or their mirror images in the relative advantages of "whiteness."

Indeed, part of the transitional approach involves projecting a labor movement that is more than the unions. I see the working-class movement as composed of a variety of organizations, each with a distinct role to play in creating the sort of diverse, class-based movement that points toward a new society. Socialism, of course, will not be based primarily on union organization, but on a range of democratic organizations and structures that bring all the exploited and oppressed to power. The movement we build today will in some degree prefigure the goals of the future. The unions take a central role in our conception of a broad working-class movement by virtue of their size and their place at the heart of capitalist accumulation, a position that gives them great potential power, but our vision of a labor movement is far broader.

I want to make it clear that I do not proceed from some faceless, raceless, neutered idea of the working class. I endorse the thoughts of the Caribbean revolutionary Aimé Césaire, who rejected the crude Stalinist version of class "universality" held by the French Communist Party when he resigned in 1955. In his resignation letter he wrote, "I have a different idea of a universal. It is a universal rich with all that is particular, rich with all the particularities there are, the deepening of each particular, the coexistence of them all." Nowhere does diversity shape the particularities of the working class more than in the United States. Nowhere is this diversity more central to the divisions, diversions, and strengths experienced by working-class people in different ways. Nowhere do working-class people see themselves and one another in such different, usually distorted, ways. The prism of race, in particular, is highly distorting of class perceptions, even though in different ways for different groups— although it is also a source of class strength for many people of color. Indeed, the problems and potential of diversity is a theme our movement will return to again and again as we address questions of consciousness and organization.

One reason for focusing on the unions is that with some notable exceptions they are the most socially integrated organizations in American life. African Americans compose 15 percent of union members, compared to 11 percent of the employed workforce. Latinos make up 9 percent, slightly less than their share of the workforce. They are, however, the fastest-growing ethnic group in the unions. Women, who were only 25 percent of union members in the 1970s, now account for 40 percent of union membership, just under the 45 percent of the workforce they compose. In 1987, two-thirds of all union members were white males. Today they are just half, albeit due largely to the decline of once male dominated industries. As America and its workforce change, so do the unions.

An even more basic reason is that unions bring people together at the heart of the social relations of production. This is where both class formation and class conflict begin. Except on those rare occasions when the class struggle breaks into open political warfare, it is at the workplace that the tug of war between labor and capital is sharpest and most recurring. It is at the workplace that the conservative ideas and assumptions that blunt class consciousness are most consistently confronted.

This confrontation is typically social in nature—not only in the sense of labor versus capital, but of working people functioning together. In this context people from different races and backgrounds are most likely to join forces to combat the employer. The education received in class conflict on the job or originating in work is a social one. Some, of course, will learn faster, while some will not care or participate actively except in rare moments of struggle. But here is where the activist layer of the unions takes shape.

Finally, the unions provide a political/organizational setting in which ongoing education, organization, and struggle can be conducted. While most union work is done at the local level, the union also provides a national or international context that cuts across workplace lines and these days, with most unions recruiting in many industries, even across industry lines. Unions also provide the most concentrated working-class organization for intervention in community affairs. The living-wage campaigns of recent years are a good example of union-organized or -backed political action. The cross-union activist organization Jobs with Justice is another. Union backing has made the Labor Party, founded in 1996, a viable project with the potential of creating a genuine class politics in the United States for the first time in decades.

Unions, of course, are far from perfect political organizations. They are bureaucratic. They often embody or protect racist and/or sexist practices. Their official ideology, which we will call business unionism, is a mass of contradictions, including the idea of labor-management partnerships. Their leaders generally do their best to straddle class conflict. Yet it is precisely some of these contradictions that make the rank-and-file strategy realistic. Today those contradictions within unions are interacting with the pressures that come from employers' efforts to remake the workplace and with the intensified competition of world capitalism. It is that interaction—between employers' pressure on workers and union leaders' inaction or collaboration—that creates rank-and-file rebellion and potential for the rank-and-file strategy.

The Deep Roots of Working-Class Self-Activity

The roots of worker self-activity and self-organization in opposition to the employer lie, in the first place, in the reality of exploitation, that is, the wage relationship—the very heart of capitalist accumulation, expansion, and growth.

Put simply, this means that workers produce more value or wealth than they make in the wages and benefits that make up their standard of living. So, for example, in 1995 manufacturing companies made $5.39 of value added per hour for each $1.00 in hourly wages they paid production workers.

This ratio is not constant. While we hear much from the capitalists about their competition for market share, the fact is that growth in profitability (the rate of profit or return on investment) actually comes from increases in this ratio. So for each dollar capital paid to workers in the United States, capital skimmed $2.47 in 1947, $3.23 in 1967, $3.73 in 1977, $4.64 in 1987, and $5.39 in 1995. This rip-off ratio grows in spite of the fact that hourly wages also rise. The reason the ratio rises is that productivity increases.

While this neutral-sounding economic category seems harmless, it is not. Over time the workers' increased productivity reduces the amount of time they spend producing their own wages and benefits and expands that devoted to producing the surplus from which profits are taken. This might be the result of new technology that eliminates workers' jobs or of increased effort by the workers or, typically, a combination of both.

New technology is hardly ever introduced without attempts to increase worker effort as well. The introduction of lean production methods in the last twenty years has emphasized increased effort along with downsizing and work reorganization. To put it simply, capital does not get these increases without putting enormous pressure on the workers.

More and more workers, facing the pressure for more production and all the rhetoric about competition these days, understand that it is they who create this profit. One UAW member expressed this in an ironic way when he wrote to his union newspaper, "Believe me, we know how hard it is to make a profit—we spend 50 to 60 hours a week at the company working to make a profit for our employers."[1]

The struggle over what workers produce does not take place only at the workplace. The government backs capital with policies that redistribute the surplus between classes, limit the social safety net, impose greater market discipline on workers through deregulation and "free" trade agreements, and limit union action. Broad political struggles around these and other social issues play an important role in the development of class consciousness. At critical moments, they can make the difference between mass mobilization and fragmented struggles—even revolution and defeat.

Communities, too, are an important site of struggle. National, racial, or ethnic identities and neighborhoods often provide a starting point for mobilizing against oppression. The workers' centers mentioned above provide one form of resistance, consciousness, and organization for working-class people of color and women—particularly those not working for wages or outside the unions. Like the workplace, these are essential pieces of the class puzzle.

But it is in the workplace, in the basic social relations of production, where the fight over the extra product of productivity occurs most sharply on a regular basis and where even perceptions of bigger events can be shaped in a class perspective. The workplace is also, of course, where workers have the most power to act on their class consciousness, whatever its source may be.

Karl Marx analyzed these relationships and saw them as the basis of worker self-activity in resistance to all the employer attempts to increase the rate of exploitation. Trade unions and other working-class organizations arose in the nineteenth century around this most basic struggle between labor and capital over the surplus. Trade unions are a natural outcome of capitalism. These organizations expand beyond the workplace into labor federations and workers' political parties, but it is the experience of exploitation and its intensification that lies behind the great labor upheavals of the last century and a half.

Karl Marx and Friedrich Engels were the first leading socialists to see in the trade unions the potential for a growing class consciousness and organizational experience that would make socialist ideas common currency across the working class. They didn't think unions were revolutionary organizations themselves. They understood well, long before most economists, that their basic purpose was, as modern labor economists put it, to "take labor out of competition" in the fight to prevent falling wages. Engels noted this early on in his 1845 *Conditions of the Working Class in England*, when he wrote:

> The active resistance of the English workingmen has its effect in holding the money-greed of the bourgeoisie within certain limits, and keeping alive the opposition of the workers to the social and political omnipotence of the bourgeoisie, while it compels the admission that something more is needed than trade unions to break the power of the ruling class. But what gives these unions and the strikes arising from them their real importance is this, that they are the first attempt of the workers to abolish competition.[2]

This reminds us of just how closely linked were the origins of trade unions and the socialist movements of the time in Europe, North America, and elsewhere. The abolition of competition is certainly a classic socialist goal. The difference, of course, is that unions only reduce competition among workers, not among capitals, and leave industry in the hands of capital.

Additionally, however, Marx and Engels saw the unions that arose in the nineteenth century as "schools" in which workers learned the realities of the system firsthand and also developed the organizational, tactical, and political skills needed to take the struggle further to the political and revolutionary levels. Marx and Engels's assessment of just how well trade unions performed these tasks waxed and waned with the level of struggle, the rising conservatism of the craft unions, and, in Engels's lifetime, the explosion of the "New Unionism" that brought tens of thousands of unskilled workers into more struggle-oriented unions. But the notion that unions had a role in capitalism beyond their obvious economic collective-bargaining function, a role in raising class consciousness, remained basic to their view of society.

The notion that unions could raise consciousness and train workers in various political skills rested, of course, on the assumption that the members and not only the officials actually played an active role in the conduct of unionism—that they are democratic organizations. Most of today's unions appear to fall far short of that assumption. They are hierarchical and bureaucratic. At the national level they are typically dominated by full-time officials, appointed reps, and staffers. The members tend to be excluded from the union's administration and decision-making. So long has this been the norm that most members judge the effectiveness of their union by how well it "serves" them, rather than by how well they themselves are using it to pursue their goals.

It should be said that some national unions are more democratic than others and that the vast majority of the fifty thousand or so local unions in the United States are relatively democratic organizations—certainly in contrast to the corporations that employ their members, to the dollar-drenched national and local elections that claim the name of democracy in this country, or, indeed, to most voluntary organizations. But these local unions typically function in the context of a national or international union culture that is top-down by design, politically dead by habit, and narrowly focused on contract administration by labor "professionals."

The evolution and consequences of this sorry situation are central to the rank-and-file strategy. This bureaucratic reality gives the political conflict within unions a certain "sociological" character. Ranks versus Tops, to put it crudely. While the social aspect is real, it can also be deceptive. Just as not every leadership contest in a union has much in the way of political content, so not every shop-floor gripe or expression of distrust or hatred of the union leadership is an incipient rank-and-file rebellion. But where opposition to the old regime arises in the grassroots of the union, drawing into action at least much of the active membership and resting on the support of the majority, there is almost always an authentic political difference over the direction, culture, and politics of the union and the way it fights (or cooperates with) the employers.

It is here, whether it is a strike movement, prolonged workplace campaign, or union reform caucus, that the "school" Marx and Engels saw in the early unions in England comes back to life. It is here that the institutional attempt to suppress competition among the workers through contract administration turns into living solidarity. It is here that the opportunity for consciousness to deepen and grow presents itself again and again. It is also here that socialists have the chance to reconnect with socialism's natural base—the active working class.

The Roots of "Common Sense"

The question of bureaucracy in workers' organizations is linked to consciousness as well as to material, historical, and cultural conditions. Indeed, it is impossible to pick these elements apart completely. I will begin with the question of consciousness and then proceed to the conditions that produced the uneven consciousness of the American working class and the phenomenon of bureaucratic business unionism that is unique to the United States and, to a lesser degree, Canada.

Here I stress that while I think consciousness is crucial in building a workers' and a revolutionary movement, I am not saying that great upheaval and even revolutions require or are likely to depend on a thoroughgoing, complete revolutionary consciousness across the class. People act on their understanding of the moment, but the logic of struggle can carry them farther than that consciousness. Furthermore, consciousness is always uneven within the class, or any of its sections, even when everyone is moving in the same direction. That in fact is why understanding the relationship of action to consciousness is so important. In many situations, including revolutionary ones, action may well precede total consciousness. The proposition that social movements or revolutions are only made by people with a total understanding of social reality or some complete "political correctness" is not validated by the history of any of the great revolutionary upheavals of the last two centuries or more.

While there are many different Marxist approaches to the question of class consciousness, I will look critically at two of the more popular explanations among socialists, those of Lenin and Gramsci. Lenin's most famous statement about the limits of trade-union consciousness was in *What Is to Be Done?* where he wrote, "The history of all countries shows that the working class, exclusively by its own effort, is able to develop only trade union consciousness."[3] Trade-union consciousness was bourgeois consciousness, he argued later. Revolutionary socialist consciousness had to come from outside, from professional revolutionaries trained in socialist theory. Three years later, in 1905, a trade-union struggle grew into a mass strike movement and a revolutionary confrontation with Czarism. Lenin revised his view, allowing for the "spontaneous" development of socialist consciousness. Yet he knew that sections of the working class everywhere remained mired in reformism.

Lenin was one of the first Marxists to draw the link between reformist consciousness and the economic impact of capital's expansionary imperative explicitly. In *Imperialism*, written in 1917, he saw the problem of backward and uneven consciousness as a function of the development of a privileged layer of the class. Although he didn't use the term, it has generally become known as the "labor aristocracy" explanation. (The term was first used by Engels.) Lenin attributed the growth of imperial expansion to the economic surplus generated by monopoly profits. This same surplus, Lenin argued, allowed capital to buy off a privileged section of the working class, which became the base for reformism. The economic analysis, borrowed from a British liberal economist as well as from the Austrian Marxist Rudolph Hilferding, that imperialism is the result of a "monopoly" surplus doesn't accord with the facts of the time. A far more plausible explanation for the expansion of overseas investment and the rush for colonies, above all in Africa, that began in the late nineteenth century was the falling rate of profit that was at the roots of the worldwide crisis of the 1870s.

Lenin's view can't explain, either, the enormous employer resistance to craft unions of skilled workers in most countries throughout the entire period he writes of and after. This was the era of Taylorism (deskilling), the Homestead strike, and the "open shop" drive in the United States and of skill "dilution" everywhere. Such a vicious employer offensive directed at skilled workers is better understood in the context of the repeated crises and profitability problems of the era and contradicts the picture of the corrupting hand of capital passing out raises to craftsmen. Additionally, the "labor aristocracy" approach can't explain why these same skilled workers can become revolutionary in outlook as they did in many countries during and following the First World War. Finally, it doesn't explain why the mass of unskilled industrial workers can and did become just as conservative in outlook in the years following the Second World War.

The problems of differing skill levels and the pay differentials inevitably attached to them are inherent in a capitalist labor market. They can and typically do produce a narrow "job trust" consciousness among skilled craftsmen. At the same, however, capitalism is always attempting to dilute or eliminate these same skills and replace them with cheaper labor attached to technologies that incorporate yesterday's skills. The attempt to dilute, eliminate, and degrade skills can produce a radical consciousness, as it did even under Lenin's nose. The process of degrading skills is very much at work today.

This is not to say that Lenin wasn't right about the connection between capitalism's colonial expansion, material conditions, and conservative or reformist consciousness. Imperialism, conquest, and continental expansion are certainly major factors underlying the fact that socialist ideas have never won over the majority of American workers. Lenin's contribution remains critical because of the confusion of so many socialists over questions of national liberation then and now. The wealth extracted over the decades by these activities as well as by slavery has played a big role in the accumulation of capital in the United States. In the period following World War II, this allowed US capital to make extensive concessions to a majority of the working class. It is not monopoly but the reality of capitalist competition, however, that drives this process, as well as the fight over the ill-gotten gains of imperial expansion. We will discuss the ways in which this worked and its impact on worker organization and consciousness shortly, but first we want to look more closely at consciousness itself.

The Italian Marxist Antonio Gramsci also attempted to analyze the problems of working-class consciousness and reformism in particular. His emphasis was on the ability of the ruling capitalist class to maintain its rule through ideological means. Gramsci called this "hegemony." Many neo-Gramscians and "hegemony" theorists have turned this into an absolute, undialectical domination of working-class consciousness by bourgeois ideology. Here we want to employ a n ore contradictory concept of "hegemony" using Gramsci's idea of "common sense."

By "common sense" Gramsci meant the contradictory accumulation of ideas, beliefs, and ways of viewing the world that most people carry around. "Common sense" is not some consistent capitalist ideology. It was, as he noted, "fragmentary, incoherent."[4] It is usually a clashing collection of old ideas handed down, others learned through daily experience, and still others generated by the capitalist media, education system, religion, and so on. It is not simply the popular idea of a nation tranquilized by TV and weekends in the mall. "Common sense" is both deeper and more contradictory because it also embodies experiences that go against the grain of capitalist ideology. It is, nevertheless, capitalist "common sense" in that it tends to embody an acceptance of the capitalist system as the natural background of life. Gramsci counterposed to common sense "philosophy," meaning Marxism or socialist consciousness. While Gramsci's prison writings were necessarily highly abstract and Aesopian, his answer to the transition from "common sense" to "philosophy" or "understanding" appears to lie in the "feelings" or "passions" of the masses. Here we will interpret this to mean the drive to resistance that comes from the experience of exploitation.

Working-class life, after all, also embodies experiences that contradict many of the old ideas and assumptions. As we have argued, these contradictions tend to be sharper and more frequent at the point of production, but they can and do break out in other realms of life as well. The experience of exploitation and the intensification and reorganization of work and/or falling real incomes that inevitably accompany it push workers into collective conflict with their employers. People will put up with a lot when they feel they have to, but sooner or later some people begin to fight back; then more join in. The experience of collective struggle against the boss challenges much of the old "common sense" even more directly as people begin to think through the real power relationships they are confronting and start to feel their power as a group.

Class consciousness is a slippery item to investigate. Gains in consciousness can be gradual or rapid, partial or more or less total, depending on the magnitude of the experience that shakes up the old ideas and the alternative ideas available. But consciousness can slip back into old habits as well. While we will talk about different levels of consciousness, we do not mean to imply some stage theory of consciousness. The means by which thoughts and perceptions of the world change within an individual are clearly complex. We won't try to deal with this "psychological" side of consciousness here.

Marx made the distinction between the consciousness of being a class "in itself" and "for itself." The first is the simple recognition that the working class is a distinct class with interests opposed to those of the capitalist class. This is something like what Lenin saw as trade-union consciousness. It involves an awareness of class conflict and the need for organization, but a more-or-less unquestioned assumption that "the system" is here to stay and all that is to be done is to make it better for the workers. The consciousness of being a class "for itself" is the awareness that capitalism can be replaced and that it is the task of the working class to emancipate itself by doing just that. This is socialist consciousness.

For Marx and most twentieth-century Marxist theoreticians in Europe, class consciousness "in itself" was assumed to be a natural product of capitalism and class conflict, at least among organized workers and their communities. The great problem of the twentieth century, that which Gramsci addressed, was how to get from this given "in itself" consciousness to a revolutionary consciousness of being a class "for itself" with the historic task of abolishing capitalism and establishing socialism. Viewed in this way, as most European Marxists did, the answers tended to focus on political organization—the tasks of the revolutionary party.

In the United States and in many other countries, this consciousness of being a class "in itself," however, cannot be taken as given. Not that it is totally absent all the time. There have been times, like the 1930s, when this sort of consciousness rushes to the fore in the minds of millions. It is, not surprisingly, in such times that a small layer of the class moves beyond to socialist consciousness. In more "normal" times, however, even the "in itself" level of consciousness recedes to a small section of the class. It is this situation that underlies the isolation of socialists for the last half a century.

At least four major interrelated factors more or less unique to the United States underlie the fragility of "in itself" class consciousness within the American working class. The first is the ability of American capitalism to continue its expansion over the past century and a half regardless (or because) of depressions, wars, or the emergence of new competing powers. Second is the distorting effect of racism in US society and its deep roots in that historical accumulation process. The third is the American "business union" ideology that is largely the result of the course of capital accumulation in the United States and that attempts to deny the importance of class. The fourth, a consequence of all the preceding, is the lack of an independent mass working-class party to perpetuate rudimentary political class consciousness beyond sectional trade-union awareness and business-union ideology.

Accumulation, Class Formation, and Consciousness in the United States

The development of capitalism in what is now the United States differed from that of Western Europe and much of the Western Hemisphere as well in two major ways. First, its ruling class had to remove and/or eliminate (not, as in Europe, employ) the indigenous population in order, by the late nineteenth century, to gain uncontested, low-cost access to the land to feed and clothe the new working class as cheaply as possible, to extract the natural resources that fed and fueled industry, and to build the canals and railroads that tied it all together.[5] This is not just a matter of continental expansion per se, which might have been accomplished on a live-and-let-live basis as was somewhat more the case in Canada, but of the possession of the land and natural resources. The resistance of Native Americans to the advancing white population was as much a barrier to accumulation then as the resistance of indigenous people in Chiapas is to agribusiness and oil interests in Mexico today or as the land rights of Canada's First Nations are to extractive industries there.[6] As a result of eliminating these human barriers, burgeoning US capitalism had little need of expensive imported food or raw materials. The uncalculated wealth this contributed to accumulation in the nineteenth century was certainly enormous.

The second equally unique and involuntary contribution to US capital accumulation was African slave labor. Slavery is, of course, the opposite of capitalist wage labor. Nevertheless, the unpaid labor of millions of Africans provided the cash crops that supplied industry and a good deal of the population and also brought in foreign exchange through trade. To be sure, British and French capitalism got a big leg up from slavery, but their slave labor force was housed in the Western Hemisphere, thousands of miles from their white populations. In the United States, the fact of racial slavery within the same nation as the dominant white settlers laid the basis for a domestic racial division of labor that has never gone away completely—even though, as Jacqueline Jones has shown, that division of labor changed shapes and rationales from time to time.[7]

The ideology of modern racism took root in this historically unique social phenomenon as the slave owners and policy makers sought to justify the institution and to sell that justification (racism as a consistent ideology) to the population as a whole. It mattered little whether or not the white merchants, farmers, and artisans of the early US republic absorbed the whole pseudoscientific rationale of eighteenth- and nineteenth-century racism. It became part of the "common sense" of the white population and, hence, of the new working class as it took form. Naturally, the conquest of the Native American nations, of Mexico, and later of Puerto Rico and the Virgin Islands also fed into racism as part of the rationale for the "Manifest Destiny" of the white settler nation's ruling class.

In this unique situation, as David Roediger and others have shown, where almost all wage earners were of European descent, the social construct of "whiteness" spread first by the slave owners and their apologists became part of the very definition of "free" wage labor. For decades following the Civil War and the abolition of slavery, this attitude went largely unchallenged as the vast majority of African Americans remained tied to the land in the Old South, where large-scale cheap labor was still needed to mass-produce cash crops. While racism was common to all classes, for the working class of the nineteenth century the very idea of class identity was intertwined with that of race. Each new wave of European immigrants would learn this bit of white American "common sense." When competition between Black (or Asian or Latino) and white workers did begin to emerge, racism and the old class "common sense" provided the rationale for the exclusion of workers of color from many jobs and for the segregation of social institutions in much of the country.

The Rise of Bureaucracy and Business Unionism

There are many theories that attempt to explain the rise of trade-union bureaucracy. One-time socialist turned fascist admirer Robert Michels and elitist Fabians Sidney and Beatrice Webb saw union bureaucracy as the natural outcome of organizational growth and efficiency Michels's "Iron Law of Oligarchy" still informs much of the sociological thinking on the topic. Early in the twentieth century, the University of Wisconsin spawned two generations of institutional theorists who continued this tradition. In the 1950s and 1960s, academic "maturity" theorists reasoned that unions follow a natural pattern of development from earlier rebellious behavior to "mature" collective bargaining. This latter stage requires bureaucracy to build stable bargaining relationships.

At best, these "theories" are descriptive. They are all apologetic and meant to make the phenomenon of bureaucracy in workers' organizations of any kind seem inevitable—and a democratic socialism, thereby, impossible. The antisocialist uses of the "Wisconsin School" in the early part of the twentieth century and the Cold War convenience of the "maturity" theorists should be clear enough. These theories, however, live on past their original applications in the minds of many academics, for whom the idea of a radical, democratic working-class movement is a relic of another era. And, of course, these ideas justify the thinking of many a high-level union leader as well. Virtually all of them assume an immutable capitalism, perhaps not free of problems but inherently stable over the long run.

It is surprising that neither Marx and Engels nor the great Marxist theoreticians of the early twentieth century attempted anything like a systematic theorization of trade unions. To be sure, Lenin, Luxemburg, Trotsky, Gramsci, and others had things to say about unions and certainly observed the bureaucratic and conservative tendencies of the labor bureaucracies of their day. As people deeply involved in revolutionary struggle, it is perhaps understandable that they were so dismissive of unions. But for Marxists in countries then and now where revolution was not "around the corner," such a luxury does not exist.

Bureaucracy and conservatism in the trade-union leadership are by no means unique to the United States. To a certain extent, bureaucracy is the product of the intermediate position of full-time union leaders as negotiators and mediators between the members who work for capital and the capitalists or their representatives. In times of economic growth, the temptation to stabilize bargaining relationships by insulating this intermediate position from the rising expectations of the members is great indeed. If some sort of political "machine" already exists among the leaders, as it usually does, the leaders' ability to institutionalize their independence from constant member influence is increased. If there is no counterposed "machine" or organization in the ranks, the path to gradual bureaucratization is fairly open. If this insulated and growing machine can deliver the goods to the members, as it did for many years in the United

States, it is likely to go unchallenged by a majority of the members, although it seldom goes completely unchallenged.

What is somewhat unique to the United States is the extent and depth of bureaucracy and the explicitly pro-capitalist ideology that justifies it, among other things. While a general theory may explain the rise of permanent union bureaucracy, it cannot explain the particular development of either trade-union ideology or the dominant forms of working-class "common sense" that have been influenced by it. For this, we must turn to the history of trade unionism in the formative years of business unionism and its struggle first with the radicalism of the post–Civil War era and then with the explicitly socialist and revolutionary ideas presented by the Socialist Party and the Industrial Workers of the World after the turn of the century.

The first two decades following the Civil War were hard on the newly freed slaves of the South, the remaining Native American nations, and the emerging working class (still mostly in the North), though their experiences were still separate and distinct. African Americans lost the fight for radical Reconstruction and land and faced the onslaught of Jim Crow. The "Indian Wars" of this era saw the final military defeat of these nations. Early attempts by workers around the country to form unions generally failed. A financial crisis beginning in 1873 threw many workers onto the streets and into poverty. From the late 1870s to the mid-1880s, the growing working class turned to various forms of radicalism, including the radical and racially inclusive unionism of the Knights of Labor. This period saw the insurrectionary strikes of railroad workers in 1877, the fight for the eight-hour day that culminated in the May 1, 1886, general strike and the Haymarket incident that followed, the proliferation of labor and farmer-labor parties, and the rise of socialism within the working-class movement.

Looking at these developments, Engels was astounded at the rapidity with which this new working-class radicalism took shape in the United States in these years. He wrote that "no one could then [1885] foresee that in such a short time the movement would burst out with such irresistible force, would spread with a rapidity of a prairie-fire, would shake American society to the foundations."[8] This story has been told well by Jeremy Brecher in *Strike!* and won't be repeated here.[9]

Despite the crisis of the 1870s, this period was simultaneously very good to capital. In his 1947 work analyzing the rise of business unionism, Sidney Lens summarized the incredible growth of American capitalism from the beginning of the Civil War to the end of the century well when he wrote:

> The growth of American capitalism was phenomenal. From 1859 to 1899, the number of capitalist establishments tripled; the number of wage earners quadrupled. The value of its products went up sevenfold, and the amount of capital invested in industry increased ninefold. In the same period in England, the value of its products increased by only approximately 50 percent; in France by approximately 45 percent; in Germany, 65 percent.[10]

To this must be added the dramatic expansion of the rail system, which by 1900 totaled more miles than those of all other nations combined. To a greater extent than in Europe, which was engaged in the race for colonies abroad, this expansion took place within the nation's by-now-continental boundaries. Fueled by a combination of the exploitation of millions of new immigrant workers, the surplus of southern Black agrarian labor, and the land and natural resources taken from Mexico, Spain, and the indigenous population, American capitalism, though by no means every capitalist, flourished indeed.

Lens, in one of the few attempts to provide a material basis for the rise of business unionism, sees this expansion as a sufficient explanation. It is certainly the background that made the success of the new unions of the 1880s possible, and it allows us to understand the antisocialism that became central to business-union ideology. But it would be an enormous oversight not to integrate the impact of the preexisting racism that

informed the whole strategy of the new business unionists—
the strategy that gave them the upper hand in the fight with
the radicals in the late nineteenth century. As I argued earlier,
this racism was part and parcel of the process of accumulation
as it unfolded in what is now the United States. Business
unionism, largely a product of the rapid expansion that followed the Civil War, also incorporated the "commonsense"
racism of the prewar period.

Craft unionism was not unique to the United States. It had
existed in Britain for some time and would evolve elsewhere as
well. But almost everywhere else it would be accompanied by
some kind of class-based political party and socialist ideology
by the late nineteenth century. The major alternative in Europe
and Latin America was Christian, i.e., Catholic, unionism, not
business unionism. Indeed, even in the United States many of
the founders of the new craft unions of the 1880s regarded
themselves as socialists, and socialism would contend with business unionism and a small organized Catholic presence as the
ideology of these unions for some time. The first political contest within organized labor, however, was not primarily that between socialists and business unionists but between practically
minded craft unionists both "pure and simple" and (reform-
minded) socialist, and the labor radicalism of the 1880s.

The answer to why business unionism triumphed, however,
lies in the intersection of American capital's incredible expansion with the way the new craft unions attempted to protect
their members. The period following Haymarket in 1886 was
one of growth. Capital, however, did not see this as a reason to
be generous to the existing unions. In fact, the employers
launched a mighty antiunion offensive that destroyed the
Knights of Labor in short order. This offensive also destroyed
or drove underground those craft unions that had carved out a
place in industry. In the early 1890s, great strikes that involved
both craft and unskilled workers, like those at Homestead and
Pullman, were defeated.

The unions that survived and grew the most in this period were those based in local labor markets in the new and growing large and small industrial cities of the period. Primary among these were the building-trades unions of the new American Federation of Labor and various local transportation unions, such as the Longshoremen and Teamsters. These unions dealt with small local employers in local labor markets, not with the emerging industrial corporations. As industrial cities large and small arose across the country, these small employers had plenty of work and plenty of income building homes, new office buildings, and factories and in the growing transportation networks within and around these cities.

The craft unions regulated their wages by restricting the supply of labor to a limited union membership, rather than organizing all the workers in a given trade. Their central method was to limit and control the local labor market. The strike was used primarily to bring recalcitrant employers into line. Each craft bargained on its own, but a picket line by any union would usually be honored by all. They expressed cross-craft and industry solidarity through central labor councils (CLCs) composed of delegates of most local unions, whether AFL or not. These CLCs called strikes when necessary. In the earliest days, these new craft unions expressed some of the same egalitarian ideals embodied in the Knights of Labor. Members initiated into early AFL unions pledged, "I promise never to discriminate against a fellow worker on account of color, creed, or nationality." There were monumental struggles in which Black and white workers in AFL unions fought side by side, most notably the New Orleans general strike of 1892. Some unions, notably the United Mine Workers and Longshoremen, while by no means free of racism, recruited Black workers and had African American officers and organizers. The state AFL in Alabama fought for the inclusion of Black workers. These were, however, the exceptions.

Obviously, a restricted labor force in a growing market characterized by small, local employers feeding off the enormous expansion of capitalism in the United States gave these building trades and other local craft unions a shelter from the bigger offensive of the increasingly national corporations. It also gave them the ability to keep wages up and rising while the employer passed the cost on to cities, corporations, the wealthy, and the new middle-class consumers flush with money. None of this is to say that these craft workers were handed big wages voluntarily by their bosses. Strikes were frequently necessary. Nevertheless, the practice of collective bargaining would change significantly for these unions over the next decade or so.

First of all, the practice of limiting the labor supply of skilled workers rather than organizing all workers in a given industry rapidly took on a racial character, since most such skilled workers outside the South were white to begin with. This was soon codified in the constitutions of several craft unions. Given the unique economic context in which it arose, this exclusive craft unionism worked where the radicalism and egalitarianism of the Knights had failed. If the ideology of the Knights and of most of the embryonic labor parties of the 1880s had been classless and often rooted in monetary and land reform, the ideology that began to take shape in the craft unions was clear and well in line with much of the "common sense" of American capitalism.

Calling it "pure and simple" unionism, the bolder of the AFL leaders rejected any grand mission like socialism in favor of limited collective bargaining. The putative father of business unionism is not Samuel Gompers but his friend Adolph Strasser, a fellow cigar maker and for a while a socialist, who in the 1870s spelled out a practical and centralized version of unionism he thought compatible with the pragmatic outlook of American workers. It would be over a decade before his ideas could be put into practice. Samuel Gompers, however, did more to develop this as a self-conscious "philosophy" of labor, and by the economic crisis of 1893 it was well developed and widespread. Its main rival in the early years of the new century would not be vague radicals but socialists of various stripes, from reformists to revolutionaries.

Strasser, Gompers, and the other "pure and simple" unionists did not reject politics but had little chance to practice them at the national level until the unions began to grow after 1896, when recovery set in and the employers turned nasty. The first major entrance of the AFL into national politics was a lobbying effort in 1895 to win legislation to limit the use of injunctions against unions and for the eight-hour day.[11] After this it was a short road to the practice of hoping to win legislative influence for labor by "rewarding our friends and punishing our enemies," which meant staying well within the two-party system that had come to prevail after the Civil War. Anticipating Lenin, the "pure and simple" unionists unashamedly embraced bourgeois politics as trade-union politics in a uniquely direct way. The British Labour Party might practice bourgeois politics from an independent working-class position when it emerged at the turn of the century, but American business unionists went directly to the bourgeois parties. This fact, of course, left an indelible mark on the rudimentary class consciousness that flared up from time to time.

As the AFL grew and a new kind of liberal bourgeois politics emerged at the end of the century as "progressivism," the practical experience of the leaders of "pure and simple" unionism led them to support the "progressives" in the two major parties rather than following the minority of trade unionists into the new Socialist Party. The relative success of the building trades unions and other locally based unions in this formative period gave them and their approach credibility. They spread this ideology and, where applicable, the practices to other unions through the city central labor bodies and state federations of the AFL.

Racism and racial exclusion were built into this ideology. It is not just that the racism of the society spilled over into these unions, as it did into early industrial unions like the United Mine Workers or other unions that did not exclude Blacks; it was in the constitutions and collective bargaining agreements of a growing number of craft unions. It was in the publications of the AFL and most of these craft unions.

The triumph of business-union ideology was given an additional boost by the simultaneous development of the embryo of bureaucracy and "machine" rule in the AFL. While in most of the theories mentioned above the development of a labor bureaucracy is associated with large organizations, the development of corporations, and bargaining stability, the actual roots of American labor bureaucracy were initially the result of conflict in local labor markets.

Following the Haymarket incident, American capital went on an antiunion rampage. The new craft unions were not spared the rage of capital or even of that of the small employers for whom many of these skilled workers toiled. Union members were frequently dismissed out of hand, particularly if they raised any grievances on the job. To protect themselves, they began to select the more vocal militants as "walking delegates," the first full-time union negotiators. We know them today as business agents. This in itself was hardly bureaucracy. But as bargaining regularized itself in the years of growth before 1893, the delegates settled into routines and the citywide local unions sought to bring them under their control rather than that of the members who had originally selected them. If the members attempted to replace a complacent business agent, as they sometimes did, the business agent and local officials could turn to the employers to get rid of the troublemakers, as they increasingly did.

This period also saw the rise of the national unions, which up to now had played little role. These were the major carriers of business-union ideology. But on top of that, like the local leaders, they saw in these new full-time business agents the possibility of a political machine not unlike the urban political machines they increasingly dealt with. All of this was further intensified as the national business-union leaders of the AFL brought the formerly autonomous central labor bodies and state federations under their control. Increasingly, these practices spread to other AFL unions, taking on the characteristics of normal union practice. By today's standards this machinery was pretty minimal, but it did aid the entrenchment and insulation of business-union leaders and their ideology from a rank and file that would become increasingly restive and radical as the new century opened.

The AFL and most of its affiliated unions had survived and grown despite employer repression and the disastrous depression of 1893 to 1896, where the Knights, the labor parties, and the Populists had failed. Reflecting both this reality and the goal of stability so important to business unionism, Gompers could say with pride at the 1900 AFL convention: "It is noteworthy that while in every other previous industrial crisis the trade unions were literally mowed down and swept out of existence, the unions now in existence have manifested not only the power of resistance, but of stability and permanence."[12]

Business Unionism's Defeat of the Socialists

When the crisis of 1893 to 1896 ended, American capitalism took another leap forward. In 1898, for the first time, the United States' productivity surpassed that of its major commercial rival Britain, as well as all other industrial powers. Despite recessions, from 1870 through 1913 the growth of real per capita gross domestic product in the United States outstripped that of any industrial nation save its neighbor Canada. Unionism, too, grew rapidly, and the AFL went from 280,000 members in 1898 to 1.6 million in 1904. This time, unionism reached deep into the manufacturing industries. Along with the growth of the craft unions came the rise of new industrial unions such as the United Mine Workers, the radical Western Federation of Miners, the socialist-oriented garment workers' unions, and the revolutionary syndicalist Industrial Workers of the World. On the railroads, the craft unions turned from mutual assistance and insurance to collective bargaining.

The return of economic growth, the vast merger movement of capital, and the growth of unionism brought a quick response from the employers in the form of a national "open shop" drive led by the new National Association of Manufacturers. The years after the turn of the century through World War I saw intense class conflict, new forms of cross-craft organization in industry, and the growth of regional bargaining.

In the wake of this new class-based radicalism came the growth of the Socialist Party (SP) of Eugene V. Debs. Unlike in Europe, where both unions and parties shared a socialist outlook, however, the major trade union federation, the AFL, was ideologically hostile to the SP. Inside the unions and the AFL, Socialist Party members fought business unionists for control or at least influence. Workplace-based rank-and-file rebellions in this period typically took on a more political character as SPers challenged the "pure and simple" unionists, who were increasingly aligned with the "progressives" of the Democratic and even Republican Parties. By 1912, the Socialist leader of the typographers, Max Hayes, won a third of the votes in a contest with Gompers for leadership of the AFL.

Debs, himself a former union leader, advocate of industrial unionism, and leader of the Pullman strike, held the conservative craft-union leaders in contempt. He noted their separation from the ranks, their change in dress and habits, and their associations—notably with employers and politicians. Debs remained a supporter of the IWW. The Socialist Party, however, had no trade-union policy. It made no demands and put no pressure on members who became high-level union officials—other than that they support the SP electorally. It was a simple matter for these Socialist union leaders to separate the running of the union from their politics, to become business unionists in practice while retaining their "Socialist" membership and identity. While some Socialists held on to leadership of the AFL and of independent unions such as those in garments and textiles, the Socialist Party itself split, faced the general repression against all radicals, and then shrank after the First World War.

The triumph of the business unionists was, however, guaranteed more than anything by the impact of the First World War. As one labor historian put it, "World War I, in fact, helped make the American Federation of Labor a permanent and lasting organization by giving it the strength to survive the 1920s."[13] It did so in three ways. First was simply the growth in number of members caused by war production, to five million by 1920. Second were the wage gains that came with the swelling of war orders after 1914. These secured loyalty to incumbent leaders in many cases. Third was the government's policy of favoring AFL unions in war industries, while at the same time conducting violent repression against the IWW and SP. A corollary of this relationship with the government was the further bureaucratization as wartime decision-making moved up the hierarchy into various tripartite bodies and as attempts were made to regularize grievance handling. Business-union leaders, practices, and ideology were now deeply entrenched, while the radicals were on the defensive and their organizations severely weakened.

The First Experiment in Rank-and-File Strategy

The last years of the war and those immediately following saw sharp class conflict and industrial upheaval in the United States, as in much of the developed capitalist world. In 1918, it looked as though German workers would follow the example set in Russia a year earlier, as workers' councils spread across the country and revolution seemed an accomplished fact— though in fact the leaders of the Social Democratic Party would soon derail the revolution.

Across the industrial world, new forms of rank and file-based worker organization sprang up to deal with the massive changes in industry and work the war had brought on. The Shop Stewards and Workers' Committee Movement in Britain, the Revolutionary Shop Stewards in Germany, factory committees in Italy, and similar organizations in France exemplified the workers' effort to take on issues from which the old leaders, even so-called socialists, shrank. Indeed, by 1920 the newly formed Communist International based its strategy for revolution on these rank-and-file upsurges that swept across industry in the developed nations. As one study of this period put it, "In the Communist International's own judgment—which we share—it is primarily in the industrial struggle that the opportunities for intervention by revolutionaries are to be sought, and it is a party's performance in relation to these opportunities on which it is primarily to be judged."[14]

The United States, too, saw intense class struggle. An attempt to organize the steel industry in 1919 with a coalition of craft unions led to a strike of 365,000 workers. Soon a strike of four hundred thousand coal miners followed. A general strike in Seattle led to a near-"Soviet" situation as the unions took charge of the city. In 1920 and 1921, six hundred thousand coal miners struck, leading to a virtual civil war in West Virginia and central Illinois. In 1921 the Typographers waged a yearlong strike, while one hundred thousand textile workers in New England hit the bricks. In 1922, four hundred thousand rail shop craft workers struck.

This explosion was made possible in part by the enormous growth of the unions and the rapid economic expansion associated with the war. But it was also a response to the industrial speedup that had underlain the entire period of growth from the end of the Civil War through World War I and the carnage it produced. Industrial death rates in the United States were estimated at two to three times those in Europe. On the railroads some seventy-five thousand workers perished from the Civil War to the beginning of the First World War. In construction, the industry itself stated that each story of the new skyscrapers cost a worker's life. The Triangle Shirtwaist fire of 1911 underscored this reckless disregard of life. Alongside this and partly responsible for it were the constant and deep changes in work associated with Taylorism, skill dilution, and work intensification that drove workers to resistance.

Altogether, from 1919 through 1923 more than eight million workers struck. Almost all of the strikes, however, were defeated. In the wake of these defeats, union membership plunged from its five-million high point to 3.6 million in 1923, stabilizing at around 3.4 million later in the decade. All the issues that had led to industrial rebellion remained unresolved, the political position of labor weaker, the unions less and less able to resist while relying on the conventional methods of business unionism and of craft unionism in particular.

The political state of business unionism was aptly summarized by A. Philip Randolph and Chandler Owen in the African American socialist weekly *Messenger*, where they described the 1921 AFL convention:

> The recent convention of the American Federation of Labor held in Denver, Colorado, was colorless except for the fight for the presidency between Gompers and John L. Lewis, president of the United Mine Workers. The convention opposed trade with Russia; refused to condemn the unspeakable Ku Klux Klan; ratified Gompers' withdrawal from the Amsterdam Labor International; closed the door in the faces of Negroes and women; reelected its archaic pilots; then adjourned.[15]

While the triumph of the business unionists and their ideology had not really been in doubt, it is natural that thousands of union activists should question these leaders and their methods, including craft unionism itself. At the same time, this was the first time that capital had inflicted such a massive defeat on labor without destroying the unions. Despite the setbacks, union membership remained well above its prewar level, allowing for the growth of opposition within the unions. A symbol of this new mood was the rebellion in Gompers's home local of the Cigar Makers, which blocked his election as a delegate to the 1920 AFL convention. Opposition groups grew in several unions, notable the International Ladies' Garment Workers Union (ILGWU), the Fur Workers, the Machinists, the Carpenters, the Iron and Steel Workers, and the United Mine Workers. Though they were often led by radicals, they tended to take on a broad rather than partisan (SP, IWW) character.

In 1919 in the midst of the industrial upheaval, following a long and destructive fight in the Socialist Party, the former SP left wing formed the Communist Party (two of them, at first). After the defeat of the 1919 steel strike, its organizer William Z. Foster and other like-minded veterans of the steel strike and other struggles organized the Trade Union Educational League (TUEL) in 1920 to do revolutionary syndicalist work within the AFL. After a couple of years of infighting and underground existence, the new Communist Party (called the Workers' Party for a while) recognized the potential of the TUEL for establishing and expanding the party's roots in the organized working class.

By 1921, when Foster, like many syndicalists around the world, joined the CP and abandoned his antiparty position, the program of the TUEL took shape. It stood, above all, for industrial unionism and a labor party—two ideas that made enormous sense as the craft unions faced one defeat after another. The TUEL also stood for the end of all racial barriers to union membership, for equal status within the unions for African Americans, and for union democracy. At the same time, it supported the young Russian Soviet republic, as did many trade-union militants in its earliest years. It was endorsed by a broad cross-section of militants and officials, including Debs.

Labor historian James Barrett summarized the orientation of the TUEL aptly as follows:

> The TUEL mobilized in more than a dozen industries but built its strongest and most durable movements in the needle trades and coal mining. In each industry economic problems and competition led to dramatic confrontations

with employers, while conservative union policies precipitated rank-and-file opposition movements. League militants built united fronts with these groups by addressing genuine industrial problems and confronting unpopular leaders.[16]

There were no dues. Membership was established by subscribing to is national paper, the *Labor Herald*. The TUEL had both industrial and local geographical organizations. Its major campaign was for industrial unionism through the amalgamation of craft unions or their industry divisions, such as rail. Resolutions favoring amalgamation passed in thousands of local unions, seventeen state federations, and twenty international unions. These same militants brought their local unions into the new movement for a labor party, where TUEL also worked with progressive officials like John Fitzpatrick of the Chicago Federation of Labor.

TUEL activists, however, didn't just build the TUEL or its campaigns. They got involved in the issues confronting each industry, sometimes led strikes, and participated in or led the various rank-and-file movements of the time. Several of the TUEL industry groups were based on existing rank-and-file movements and on the new shop delegates' and shop stewards' movements. These included rank-and-file oppositions in the ILGWU, the Fur Workers, the Carpenters, the Machinists, the Amalgamated Iron and Steel Workers, and the United Mine Workers, all of which had considerable success.

The TUEL demonstrated the power of rank-and-file rebellion and the ability to organize beyond those already loyal to the left. Their day-to-day work focused on workplace issues and union democracy as well as industrial unionism, a labor party, and, less consistently, racial equality.[17] The combination of this very basic program and the activities of the TUEL moved tens of thousands of workers to action and many more to vote for resolutions and candidates backed by TUEL activists. It also linked the various rank-and-file opposition movements into a broad progressive current across the labor movement, giving these efforts a class-wide framework, a shared vision of what unionism could be, and a common basic program.

By 1924, however, the TUEL's class-wide experiment lay in shambles, with the Communists isolated from the mass of activists they had helped to motivate and organize. Probably the major reason was the vicious countermobilization of the business-union bureaucracy across the AFL. TUEL and CP activists were expelled right and left with no means of recourse. Despite big votes for opposition candidates in several unions and strong bases in many locals, the entrenched AFL leaders maintained control over the expanded machinery of their unions. For the expelled rebels there was no place to turn.

At the same time, the reaction of the bureaucracy was made all too easy by the policies of the CP and the weaknesses of the TUEL. One weakness was the resolutionary nature of its central campaign, that for amalgamation. While TUEL activists had great success in getting resolutions in favor of amalgamation passed across the labor movement, they had almost no success in actually forcing or carrying through amalgamation toward industrial unionism. Resolutions cannot be a substitute for organization and the ability to follow through on a goal. There isn't much doubt that most of the activists, including party members, who participated in the TUEL campaigns wanted such organization and influence, but the way in which the CP "ran" the TUEL made this difficult.

The greatest weakness of the TUEL was that it was controlled top-down by the CP. It never really developed a democratic structure of its own, nor an independent rank-and-file leadership to combat the growing sectarianism and erratic behavior of the CP. The TUEL's lack of independence was signaled by, among other things, its affiliation with the Moscow controlled Red International of Labor Unions. More importantly, virtually all the leaders of the various TUEL bodies were CP members. Both of these realities left

TUEL without a self-organized base and unnecessarily open to red-baiting.

The problem of party control was compounded by the sectarian direction that came from the party's central leadership in New York. Far from the daily course of class struggle and preoccupied with internal factional matters and Russian policy requirements, these leaders attempted to push their line on the CP leaders of the TUEL. This was particularly sharp in the case of Foster's work in the labor party movement. There, the CP leaders pushed for a premature launching of a farmer-labor party, which led to a break with non-Communist leaders and the collapse of the whole project. In 1924, the CP leadership guaranteed the end of the TUEL as a broad rank and file–based movement when it took the absurd step of merging the TUEL's paper, the *Labor Herald*, with two other CP-controlled papers, the *Soviet Russia Pictorial*, published by the Friends of the Soviet Union, and the *Liberator*, the CP's official paper, into the *Workers' Monthly*, which was supposed to serve as the official publication of both the TUEL and the CP.

It must also be said that Foster himself was part of the problem as well as the initiator of the solution. He had realized that the only way the new CP could overcome its isolation was to work in the AFL, building rank-and-file movements to replace business unionism with a class-struggle brand of unionism. Unlike most other top CP leaders, he understood this to be a long process. At the same time, he had a certain elitist view of this work as well as a tendency to maintain personal control of the operation. In 1922, he wrote that most rank-and-file workers were "ignorant and sluggish." In 1924, he told the socialist Scott Nearing, "Revolutions are not brought about by the sort of far-sighted revolutionaries you have in mind, but by stupid masses . . . goaded to desperate revolt by the pressure of social conditions . . . led by straight-thinking revolutionaries who are able to direct the storm intelligently against capitalism."[18] This is far from Marx's idea of trade union struggle as a school in which the masses learn political skills and come to a clearer class consciousness—though not so far from the Stalinism Foster and the CP would soon adopt. In the end, the combination of CP control and its elitist outlook killed this first experiment in conscious rank-and-file rebellion.

By the second half of the 1920s, the bureaucracies of the AFL, its affiliates, and the independent unions in garment and rail were safely entrenched. The price paid for the failure of the TUEL was high. The unions lost more members, real wages slumped, they adopted labor-management cooperation schemes, and the number of unions excluding workers of color constitutionally or by ritual actually rose from eleven in 1920 to twenty-four by the end of the decade.

The Lesson of Transitional Politics

In his assessment of the problem of CP control and the failure of the TUEL, Sidney Lens wrote:

> By permitting this state of affairs the TUEL obviated the original purpose for which it was established, to become a bridge between the Communist party and the trade unions, to offer an instrument that could neither be accused of "dual unionism" nor of being a radical force outside the unions. It was to be a class-struggle left wing, rather than a revolutionary dual union. It was to advocate militant strike tactics, democracy within the existing unions, amalgamation into industrial forms, a policy of spreading strikes to make them more effective, no faith in government arbitration machinery, and other such union strategies based on the theorem of "class against class." It was not to be the instrument of the revolution itself, as was the conception of the I.W.W. by Vincent St. John and his successors. It was to avoid the recurring difficulty of having new members endorse the idea of revolution. The TUEL in life itself, however, was so indistinguishable from the Communist Party that it isolated itself from all but party members or the closest of sympathizers.[19]

In other words, the TUEL could not serve as a bridge between the basic class consciousness of most workers and the class "for itself" politics of the revolutionaries if it was itself solely the revolutionaries' possession. That it showed so much promise in doing just this for the first three years of its brief life is testimony to the viability of this strategy. Yet the leaders of the early CP, still heady with the model of the Russian Revolution and obsessed with internal party matters, bombed their own bridge to the activist layer of the class.

The notion of a bridge between rudimentary class consciousness or trade-union militancy and socialist consciousness is the cornerstone of transitional politics and the rank-and-file strategy. The notion of a transitional program and politics was meant to replace the old idea of the minimum and maximum programs of classic social democracy, where the minimum program became the real practice and the maximum (revolutionary) program a ceremonial artifact. Sometimes employed by the early Communist International before its corruption into Stalinism, it was resurrected in the late 1930s by Leon Trotsky, who incorporated it into the founding document of the Fourth International in 1938. Formulating it primarily as a program of demands, Trotsky wrote:

> It is necessary to help the masses in the process of daily struggle to find a bridge between present demands and the socialist program of the revolution. This bridge should include a system of transitional demands, stemming from today's consciousness to wide layers of the working class and unalterably leading to one final conclusion: the conquest of power by the proletariat.[20]

For Trotsky in 1938, capitalism was in its inescapable "death agony" and the revolution blocked primarily by the degeneration of working-class leadership in the form of social democracy and Stalinism. Capitalism's obituary proved premature in the extreme and the reduction of the problems of the working-class movement to one of misleadership insufficient. We can also question whether any system of demands can by itself lead "unalterably" to revolutionary consciousness.

It is important to locate the purpose of such a transitional program. Trotsky's program was designed for a situation in which revolution seemed imminent, if only effective leadership were in place. The 1938 transitional program was meant to provide direction for a new revolutionary leadership. The far more limited program of the TUEL had a more modest purpose: to raise the general class consciousness of the activist layer of the unions and to bring the revolutionaries into a common organization and movement with these militant, but still largely trade union–minded, worker-activists.

The idea of a transitional politics and program that can serve to bridge the gap I described in the beginning of this chapter between today's "common sense" and genuine class consciousness is an important tool in overcoming both the isolation of socialists from the class and the limits of leadership within the class. Such a program for today is not so much a list of demands as a combination of demands, goals, and actions.

Before developing the idea of a transitional politics for today's labor movement, I want to look at the major competing left-wing strategy for work in the unions: permeation, or the attempt to gain influence by sidling up to the incumbent bureaucracy or its alleged progressive wing. This, above all, was the strategy of the Communist Party in the new CIO unions of the 1930s.

Permeation and the Hijacking of the CIO

The outlines of the story of the industrial upsurge that led to the formation of the CIO are well known. Most of the craft union leaders of the AFL had learned nothing from the experience of the 1920s. In the face of growing rank-and-file outbursts in the unorganized basic industries, they offered patchwork aid and solutions—when they offered anything. The first wave of strikes, from 1933 through 1935, were mostly examples of rank-and-file self-organization. Some of these workers seized on moribund local unions to create new mass organizations; some got temporary charters as AFL "federal local unions," while others simply created their own unions. The massive 1934 strikes in Toledo, Minneapolis, San Francisco, and in the textile plants, particularly in the South, were led by men and women with no more than a local title, little in the way of money, and even less in terms of staff or "labor professionals." Many of them were radicals who saw the need for industrial unionism as a priority and a training ground for a new generation of union leaders and activists—and revolutionaries.

The radicals, however, were not the only ones to read the handwriting on the wall. A handful of AFL leaders, following the lead of John L. Lewis of the Miners, began to push for industrial unionism. Lewis was no radical. In fact, he had been a lifelong Republican and as dedicated a business unionist as Gompers or anyone else. But his union was organized along industrial, not craft, lines. He had also learned a few things in his long fight against the TUEL-supported opposition movements of the 1920s. So he, Sidney Hillman of the Amalgamated Clothing Workers, and a handful of other top leaders formed the Committee for Industrial Organization to push the AFL toward organizing the mass production industries along industrial lines. They got nowhere and left to form the new Congress of Industrial Organizations (CIO) in 1936.

The men who launched the CIO as a new federation were not out to make the revolution. Rather, the new CIO leaders presented themselves as an alternative not only to the moribund AFL, but also to the rank-and-file leadership already in formation throughout industry. They did not have to do much organizing as we think of that today, for workers were already pouring into or creating unions on their own or with the help of radicals and their organizations. Indeed, as industrial struggle grew and became more confrontational, the new unions became schools of class consciousness and leadership development. The 1934 strikes in Toledo, San Francisco, and Minneapolis had all been led by socialists of one kind or another.

It would be overly simple to say that Lewis and the new CIO parachuted into this situation to save the day for capitalism. No doubt many of these leaders, like many in the ranks, saw the chance for a change in the balance of class forces within American capitalism through the organization of the mass production industries. Some, like erstwhile socialist Sidney Hillman, even brought the elements of a new labor ideology that would distinguish the CIO from the pure-and-simple business unionists of the AFL for many years—social unionism. Yet this meant that from day one, the CIO was a contradictory movement with a self-organizing rank and file in its new unions but a full-blown bureaucracy at the federation level, and within those old unions that joined, it did all in its power to keep this movement within the channels of capitalism, orderly collective bargaining, and the Democratic Party.

It would take almost two decades to turn the CIO, with its social-unionist outlook, into a modern business unionism similar enough to the AFL unions, some of which now had a more industrial character themselves, to make possible the 1955 merger that gave us the AFL-CIO. There were too many radicals and radicalized workers entrenched in the locals of the new unions, with too much support in the ranks and too good a track record in the midst of the big struggles of the second half of the 1930s, to make their taming easy. Furthermore, most of the new unions were too democratic, with plenty of open political debate and competition, to easily succumb to the bureaucratic norms of the Mine Workers or the CIO itself.

Almost all of the left organizations of the time played a significant role at one time or another: the Trotskyists in the Minneapolis Teamsters' strike, A. J. Muste's American Workers Party in the Toledo Auto-Lite strike, the Communists in San Francisco's general strike, the local Socialist Party in the Flint

Sit-Down, and so on. Had all these organizations worked together—as they often did in specific struggles like the Flint Sit-Down—in an autonomous TUEL-type rank-and-file project, the history of US labor might have been very different.

Indeed, the potential of radical-led rank-and-file mobilizations to create a class-conscious labor movement was evident not only in the new CIO unions but even in the old AFL unions, as the example of the Minneapolis Teamsters showed. Here, a small group of Trotskyists transformed a moribund craft union of truck drivers and helpers into an industrial union in the local and eventually regional freight and local cartage industries. When the process began, the entire Teamster Joint Council in Minneapolis–St. Paul had only one full-time official and fewer than a thousand members. Each step in this process of transformation involved accelerated rank-and-file mobilization not only of the members of Teamsters Local 574, but eventually of the entire labor movement in Minneapolis in the dramatic 1934 strike. The approach used by the Trotskyists is spelled out in Farrell Dobbs's book *Teamster Rebellion* and represents a classic case of the application of the rank-and-file strategy to the conditions of that time and place.

Dobbs notes that "workers were radicalizing under the goad of economic depression. To mobilize them for action it was necessary to start from their existing level of understanding. In the course of battle a majority could be convinced of the correctness of the Communist League's trade union policy." ("Communist League" was the name of the Trotskyist organization at that time, later the Socialist Workers Party.) He points to the contradictions of the union bureaucracy, but makes the important point that the direction of the struggle in these circumstances was against the employers. In all likelihood, the bureaucracy, particularly in the persons of Daniel Tobin, general president of the Teamsters, and Cliff Hall, of the Minneapolis Central Labor Council, would get in the way. As Dobbs put it, "Thus, the indicated tactic was to aim the

workers' fire straight at the employers and catch the union bureaucrats in the middle."[21]

Using this approach, Dobbs and the Minneapolis Trotskyists went on to lead a massive organizing drive followed by
three mass strikes. These strikes were models of rank-and-file
mobilization, innovative tactics such as "cruising pickets," and
alliances with other unions and farmers organizations. In the
face of massive police and vigilante violence, the strikers
mounted their own escalations with rallies reaching forty thousand people. In effect, the Trotskyist Teamsters, working with
other militants, had turned a mere organizing drive into a
major political confrontation with all the powers that be.

The 1934 strike victory did not end the problems faced by
workers in the Minneapolis trucking industry. Local 574 was
still burdened with conservative officers. The role of the Trotskyists in the strike movement, however, made them recognized leaders in practice. Dobbs and the other went about
organizing a broad rank-and-file caucus with the object of
bringing in a consistently militant leadership. But they didn't
simply run for office. Once again, Dobbs explains what is still
an important lesson for rank-and-file rebels:

> From the outset the building of a broad left wing in the
> local was rooted in the programmatic concepts essential
> to a policy of militant struggle against the employers. Al-
> though this perspective entailed an ultimate clash with
> conservative union officials, their removal from office was
> not projected at the start as an immediate aim. That could
> have given the mistaken impression that the Trotskyist
> militants were interested primarily in winning union
> posts. To avoid such a misconception a flanking tactic was
> developed. Instead of calling for a quick formal change in
> the local's leadership, the incumbent officials were pressed
> to alter their policies to meet the workers' needs.[22]

Dobbs and the other socialists allied themselves with non-
socialists who had supported their strike strategy and even-

tually changed the leadership of the local. Their rank-and-file approach didn't stop there, however. They realized that most of the trucking industry was still nonunion and that they would have a hard time holding onto wages and conditions if this remained the case. Dobbs developed a strategy for organizing the over-the-road truckers and the freight workers in other towns in the region. In effect, Dobbs did what more and more unions are finally doing today. He recognized that the best organizers are not necessarily professional staffers but committed members. So each trucker became a de facto organizer. The story of the campaign to organize the central states (Midwest) trucking industry is told in Dobbs's book *Teamster Power*. It was no easy matter. The rank-and-file Teamster organizers met with violence from the employers, police, and governments. The president of the international union, Daniel Tobin, opposed them all the way. Their fight was, of necessity, almost always a dual one against the employers and conservative union bureaucrats. The main enemy was always capital, but the business unionists were always in the way.

Although its militant leaders would eventually face enormous repression, the victory of Local 574 in Minneapolis and the organizing strategy that followed were a clear demonstration of the power of rank-and-file unionism under the leadership of revolutionaries who understood both transitional politics and the potential of a mobilized and informed rank and file. It was an alternative kind of unionism to the top-down brand favored by Lewis, Hillman, and other CIO leaders. In embryonic form it existed across the labor movement of the time. But this potential would be sidetracked by the abandonment of a rank-and-file orientation by much of the left in the second half of the 1930s.

By far the largest left organization was the Communist Party. While it is clear that the CP of the 1930s was a thoroughly Stalinized, bureaucratic party, it was also a contradictory movement. On the one hand, the CP and its thousands of worker members played a major role in building the new CIO unions from the bottom up. They and the unions they came to lead were usually well ahead of other left groups on matters of racism. And while some CP-led unions showed the same top-down tendencies as those lead by liberal social unionists, others were or would become more democratic than most.

Nevertheless, the Popular Front policy adopted around 1936, just as the big struggles were heating up, precluded any real united front with the other left parties, much less a rank-and-file strategy like the TUEL. The Popular Front meant building alliances with the leaders of the new CIO wherever possible and supporting the Roosevelt administration in the name of fighting fascism. This meant abandoning the idea of a labor party in practice and orienting more and more toward the Democrats. Such alliances inevitably led to attempts to permeate the highest levels of both government, which were not very successful, and the bureaucracy of the CIO and a number of its unions, which were more so.

The most famous case of the CP's permeationist policy was that of Lee Pressman and Len De Caux who became, as the joke went, "left-hand men" to "the Three," as the CIO's top leaders, John L. Lewis, Sidney Hillman, and Philip Murray, were known. Pressman was general counsel for the CIO, while De Caux was its publicity director. Pressman may have dropped formal membership in the party after 1935, but he continued to have those politics for a decade or so. While only a few could insinuate themselves at the top of the labor movement in this manner, many more Communists became staffers helping to build the apparatus of the CIO and some of its affiliates.

The vast majority of CP members, of course, had no hope of permeating their unions' leadership or staff. They either ran for office, often successfully, or remained rank-and-filers. But the Popular Front alliances and the permeationist orientation that flowed from it meant that the largest group on the left had checked out of any fight against the growth of bureaucracy in the new unions and in some places contributed to it. Rank-and-file CPers might still be militants in their workplace and might even resist authoritarian moves by the leadership when those leaders weren't CPers themselves, but their party had its sights set higher on the big alliance with Roosevelt, Lewis, and others.

The Second World War accelerated the process of bureaucratization and the formation of a modernized business unionism, much as the First World War had. A series of government-labor boards set the precedents and patterns of bureaucratic labor relations that shaped the whole post–World War II era. Historian Nelson Lichtenstein summed up the impact of these boards when he wrote:

> For the next four years, these boards were instrumental in setting for the first time industry-wide wage patterns, fixing a system of "industrial jurisprudence" on the shop floor, and influencing the internal structure of the new industrial unions. They were a powerful force in nationalizing a conception of routine and bureaucratic industrial relations that had been pioneered in the garment trades but that the Wagner Act and the NLRB had thus far failed to implement fully.[23]

The CP, by wartime far and away the largest left organization, saw the war not as an imperialist war but as an antifascist war for democracy. Its vigilance in supporting the war effort and war production surpassed that of ordinary antifascists or American jingoists to include opposition to any and all disruptions of production. Indeed, when Lewis broke with Murray and Hillman (and Roosevelt), first rejecting government mediation in the miners' contract in 1941 and then leading four miners' strikes in 1943, the CP sided with Hillman and Murray. They fully supported the CIO leadership's no-strike agreement. And when strikes against the inhuman pace of work or other issues began to spread in 1943, they opposed those.

The CP's elite alliance also hurt the African American liberation struggles in which they had previously played a major role in communities like Harlem. With the coming of the war, however, they played down racial struggles. They didn't support A. Philip Randolph's proposed march on Washington to demand jobs for African Americans in the burgeoning defense industries. Nor did they support the "Double-V" campaign for victory over fascism abroad and racism and segregation at home.

With the entrance of the United States into the war, the number of workers involved in strikes dropped dramatically from 2.4 million in 1941, the high point of the prewar years, to 840,000 in 1942. In 1943, however, the number shot up again to nearly two million workers and kept rising until 4.6 million workers joined the huge 1946 strike wave. Except for the coal miners' strikes, the strikes from 1943 through 1945 were almost always rank-and-file actions, frequently led by stewards willing to buck the increasingly entrenched CIO bureaucracy and the government. These were the greatest counterweight to the bureaucratic trend accelerated by the wartime institutions. Yet the largest left party opposed them—although it is likely that many rank-and-file CPers participated.

Ironically, one of the pithiest descriptions of what came next comes from Len De Caux's memoirs:

> Once the CIO won all that capitalism would allow it . . . sitdowns and mass struggle gave way to union administration, dues collection, labor board briefs, detailed negotiations. The swivel-chair tribe began its own long-lasting sitdown in union office. This tribe rode to office on the broad shoulders of Lewis and the backs of the agitators, the militants, the reds. Once they arrived they turned— dutifully, patriotically, devoutly—to kick in the face those on whom and over whom they had scrambled.[24]

The Popular Front, permeation, and wartime patriotism were repaid with Cold War purges of the Communists and then other leftists as well. When the alliances at the top shattered, the lack of an independent rank-and-file base left the radicals isolated. The Communists faced the additional problem of having lost a lot of credibility for their wartime collaboration. For the CIO as a whole, the swivel-chair crowd rapidly completed their insulation from the ranks in most unions and established the norms of modern business unionism that are still dominant. To be sure, there was plenty of rank-and-file resistance to the loss of democracy, the increased length of union contracts, the increasingly infrequent and ritualized conventions, and the cozy and stable relations with employers that more and more leaders sought. But the resisters fought alone, with few experienced political leaders among them and little or no contact with the oppositionists in other unions. The marvelous fighting democracy that had been the unions of the early thirties and then the CIO had been hijacked by leaders who soon made their peace with capital and institutionalized labor relations as the property of a layer of professional labor leaders and staffers, to a degree few had ever dreamed possible.

Modern Business Unionism and the Problem of Consciousness

The stabilization of collective bargaining and the institutionalization of modern business unionism were aided by another period of economic growth and expansion for American capital—this time as the world's leading economic and military power. This allowed a labor movement that now covered more than nine million workers, as De Caux put it, to win "all that capitalism would allow it," which in this period was more than most workers anywhere had ever seen. This, in itself, partly explains the uniquely conservative consciousness that swept most unions and their members. The Cold War repression and a political atmosphere that equated any form of leftism with the Stalinist regime of the Soviet Union was another big factor in delegitimizing any brand of socialist politics. On top of this setting, the practices of modern business unionism contributed many of the specifics to the new postwar working-class "common sense."

The knot between the new CIO and the Democratic Party had been tied by 1936. Nevertheless, labor-party sentiment reemerged during the war. In 1943, Hillman and Murray set up the CIO Political Action Committee (PAC) specifically to combat local and state labor-party initiatives and to mobilize the union ranks right down to the precinct level for Roosevelt and the Democratic Party in the 1944 elections. Thus, the new unions entered the postwar era with a political practice virtually identical to, though far more organized than, that of the AFL, with its own Labor's Non-Partisan League. This, no doubt, eased the way to the 1955 merger with the AFL. Any idea of class politics was abandoned or squelched, a fact that would shape and limit working-class consciousness enormously for decades.

By the end of the 1940s, the CIO had surrendered its political program of full employment, national health care, generous social security, civil rights for African Americans, and public housing for all who needed it when it became clear their Democratic "allies" had no interest in such reforms. This political choice meant that the liberal social-unionist ideology of the CIO turned away from the political arena and toward the narrower field of collective bargaining. The new benefits bargaining for pensions, health care, and other items previously seen as part of an expanded welfare state like those in Europe, created what some have called a "private welfare state" tied to the employers.

This had at least two long-term effects. The first was to increase the professionalization and hence the bureaucratization of collective bargaining as contracts became incredibly complex and their administration more expert-heavy. The number of full-time "International reps" grew and their power over contract administration increased. The notion and practice of the union as a service agency took root. Along with this came the erosion of basic democracy as conventions, once annual affairs, became every three or even five years in many unions.

The second was the fragmenting effect this "private welfare state" had on the consciousness of union members, along with the growing separation of their living standards from those of workers in weaker unions or in no unions. With benefits flowing from company coffers, the idea that the well-being of the company is a union goal was given a previously unknown economic underpinning. At the same time, just as any idea of a distinct class politics had been squelched, so too had the idea of the labor movement as a class movement been laid to rest. It was now a bureaucratic agency dependent on employer well-being (i.e., productivity dragged out of the workforce) to deliver services to its members and them only. Narrow "interest group" consciousness was certain at most times to beat class consciousness as a contender for this period's "common sense."

The replacement of social unionism, in all but convention-time rhetoric, by a top-down service model and fragmenting "private welfare state" was accompanied and sometimes preceded by the abandonment of the CIO's commitment to racial equality. While this commitment had always been limited and seldom carried into white bastions like the skilled trades, the alliance with the progressive organizations of the African American community had contributed to a racial egalitarianism largely absent in the older business unionism of the AFL. But when organizing, striking, and mobilizing were replaced by orderly professional bargaining in the context of economic growth, there was little need for such active alliances. When African American labor leader A. Philip Randolph proposed that the merged AFL-CIO ban racial exclusion by any union at the 1955 merger convention, not one white CIO leader voted with him. It was not that they believed in exclusion, but that they valued the alliance with their new conservative colleagues more than that with the Black community.

All of these features of modern business unionism and the economic context in which they solidified combined to bury, if not completely obliterate, the kind of basic class consciousness that had arisen in the 1930s and lasted well into the 1940s. The fragmented consciousness was reinforced by the rise in real wages and, at least for a large minority, the new benefits that brought a middle-class lifestyle to millions. Average real hourly earnings in manufacturing rose by 50 percent from 1950 through 1965. The new benefits, furthermore, meant that more of these growing wages were available for direct consumption than had ever been the case before. All this was made possible by the continued growth of the economy. From 1947 through 1967, industrial production more than doubled, while productivity grew by more than 50 percent.

While many on the left like to talk of this period as one of a "social compact" in which capital willingly handed over wage and benefit increases in exchange for increased production, the fact is that even in this period it took a high level of strike action to win this new standard of living. There were more strikes and more workers on strike in the first half of the 1950s, while the new standards of collective bargaining were being carved out, than during the years 1935 through 1939.

There was, however, a big difference. The strikes of the 1930s had been enormous battles seen by millions as part of a bigger class struggle. By the 1950s, strikes tended to be orderly affairs with token picketing. With some notable exceptions, strikes became as routine as collective bargaining itself. Furthermore, the solidaristic movement-wide pattern bargaining of 1945 and 1946 had given way to a much looser system in which each union was on its own. Most studies showed that even by the early 1950s the effect of major patterns set by the UAW or the Steelworkers was fading. The idea of solidarity was reduced to one's own union and one's own "private welfare state."

All of this produced the kind of consciousness, the "common sense," thought to be the natural state of mind of workers and union members in the United States. Neither class as an active concept nor any vision above the level of collective bargaining was a part of this consciousness for the vast majority. But the conditions that underlay the stability of this whole arrangement were beginning to change by the mid-1960s.

Fragmented Rank-and-File Rebellion

By most accounts US capitalism's rate of profit began to fall (or fall more rapidly) around the middle of the 1960s. Production actually accelerated at first, due largely to the war in Vietnam. Whereas industrial production had risen by about 50 percent from 1953 through 1963, from 1963 through 1973 it rose by 68 percent. Nevertheless, the falling rate of profit that corporations were beginning to experience more severely brought on both inflation and a push for increased productivity across much of industry. Inflation and speedups, in turn, brought forth a new period of increased resistance and rebellion within industry.

While we tend to think of the 1960s and early 1970s as the era of the mass antiwar and "new" social movements, it was also one of considerable labor unrest. Millions of public-sector workers poured into unions and for a moment, on the eve of Martin Luther King's assassination, it looked as though the labor and civil rights movements might converge. The new Black Power consciousness of the late 1960s found expression in auto assembly plants and steel foundries as well as in rebellious communities.

At the same time, the number of workers involved in strikes rose steadily from just under a million in 1965 to 2.5 million in 1971. A growing number of these strikes were wildcat strikes in violation of the contracts and against the will of the now entrenched and routinized leaderships. The strikes were typically against speedups and other management practices, but just as Dobbs had pointed out in the 1930s, the union bureaucracy—now a much bigger target—stood in the line of fire. Once again, rank-and-file rebellion was on the agenda. In the wake of these strikes came several rank and file–based organizations such as the Teamsters United Rank & File, Miners for Democracy, and the United National Caucus in the UAW. In addition, Black caucuses spread across the auto and steel industries, of which the most famous is the Dodge Revolutionary Union Movement

(DRUM). The connection of DRUM and some other Black caucuses with both Marxism and revolutionary nationalism was direct, but the exception. While leftists played a role in many of these new rank-and-file movements, there was no significant organized left in the unions in this period.

The organized left of this period was largely student-based and focused on the antiwar and social movements. While these movements also had an impact on the working class in various ways, the socialist left, except for Black radical groups like the Detroit-based League of Revolutionary Black Workers, paid little attention to this rising tide of rank-and-file rebellion. Yet the rebellion became highly visible as strikes swept the coal fields in the late 1960s, when national wildcats broke out among postal workers and Teamsters in 1970, when the Lordstown GM plant became the focus of national attention for the militancy of its young workforce, when forty thousand telephone workers in New York state struck against Nixon's wage freeze for seven months in 1971 and 1972, and when the Miners for Democracy overturned a corrupt and murderous leadership in 1972 and reshaped the United Mine Workers.[25]

The absence of a well-organized socialist left in most of these movements meant that the fragmented consciousness inherited from the modern business-union practices of the post–World War II years, though challenged by action, was not displaced with a broader class consciousness or significant movement toward independent working-class politics. Even the more visible rank-and-file organizations had little contact with one another. They fought their battles with their employers largely within the spheres of their own "private welfare states." Furthermore, they fought from a position of assumed job security, while the new militancy kept real wages ahead of inflation for most groups. As noted above, the economy was growing fast and the impact of falling profit rates on the economy as yet marginal. The "common sense" of the period had been challenged by the actions taken by millions of workers, as well as by the antiwar and social movements. But there was no socialist left within the working class, nor even a left focused on workers' struggles, that was big enough to bring these strands together.[26]

The 1974–75 recession, the deepest since the Great Depression, brought the militancy to an end and wildcat strikes virtually disappeared. Some rank-and-file movements lasted past this turning point and the Teamsters for a Democratic Union (TDU) was actually born in 1976, but the militancy and sense of confidence that made this period of rank-and-file rebellion possible and gave it its particular character was swept away as a new era of economic turbulence took shape. The fragmented consciousness encouraged by modern business unionism not only survived but was now reinforced by a sense of economic insecurity across the class that allowed the bureaucracy to reimpose its authority and to open a new period of retreat and concessions bargaining in the 1980s.

The Rank-and-File Perspective: A Contemporary Synthesis
If the fact, the reality, and the importance of rank-and-file movements and rebellions is clear, the relationship of socialists to these is still not clear. Rank-and-file movements of the twentieth century confronted three different problems. The first was a party-controlled attempt to provide a program and a class-wide framework in the early 1920s through the TUEL. This had a promising start but came to grief largely as a result of the CP's control, on the one hand, and its erratic politics, on the other. Party control meant that no independent, growing leadership developed that would give the movement the strength to replace the business-union leadership.

The second was the industrial upheaval of the 1930s. Here the major left organization, the CP, pushed an alliance with the CIO bureaucracy, or what the CP imagined to be its "progressive" wing, as well as with the Roosevelt administration. This meant permeation where possible, but also a certain passivity toward the bureaucracy by rank-and-file CPers. This crippled the possibility of independent rank-and-file organization in most CIO unions and meant the substitution of the party for an intermediate or transitional cross-union organization. Under these circumstances, the CIO bureaucracy and those of its affiliates were able to gain or maintain control, close down the rough-and-tumble democracy of the first decade or so of the CIO, and then expel their Communist allies.

The third was the rank-and-file rebellion of the late 1960s and early 1970s. The many actions and organizations of this period had very little contact with one another, let alone cross-union organization or a shared view of the changes needed to beat the speedups and inflation of the period. This rebellion, while exemplary of the self-activity and power of the working class in many ways, was hurt by the almost total absence of a political left or socialist wing within the movement. It remained the captive of the narrow consciousness of modern business unionism.

Drawing on the lessons of these major periods of class activity and rank-and-file rebellion, we need a synthesis in which socialists play a leading role in these rebellions without subjecting them to the control of any "party" or socialist organization. At its most basic, this leadership means confronting the bureaucracy within the unions and its policies by focusing on the fight with the employers over real conditions on the job and in society. This leadership role also draws on the concept of transitional politics to provide a bridge from today's consciousness to deeper and wider forms of class consciousness and organization. This requires some institutional or organizational means of bringing a class-wide perspective to the various rank-and-file groups in order to transcend the fragmented consciousness encouraged by the "private welfare states" and the intensified competition that increased international economic integration has brought. This would include cross-union formations, community-based worker organizations such as workers' centers, and steps toward active class politics.

While the pressures of capital on working-class life are always present, there are obviously times when such a perspective offers greater possibilities. The rest of the chapter will argue that today's unfolding conditions do offer such possibilities, that rank-and-file rebellions are a common contemporary response to the realities of changing conditions and bureaucratic inertia, and that there are specific things that socialists and socialist organizations can do to maximize the potential of the period and to minimize the gap between convinced socialists and the majority of worker-activists.

The Roots of a New Revolt

The closing of the twentieth century seemed to bring a resurgent hegemony to North American capital in the post–Cold War world economy. Every crisis appeared as an opportunity for the United States and its leading transnational corporations to break down barriers to its accumulation goals and impose new political/economic structures and relations that enforced its new advances. From the passage of the North American Free Trade Agreement to the new World Trade Organization, from the "drug war" on Latin America to the criminal bombing of Iraq and Yugoslavia, no force seemed able to counter US power. The recurrent economic crises of Latin America, the financial collapse in East Asia, and the overall meltdown of Russia all provided opportunities for North American capital to extend its already massive global reach. Despite the circus around Bill Clinton's scandalized presidency, big business could rest assured that the same center-right political consensus that had ruled in Washington for years was intact no matter the president's fate or which major party sat in Congress or the White House.

But the 1990s' apparent deepening of US economic and political hegemony was not a rerun of its post–World War II rise to dominance. Two major changes in the world made this renewed surge of US power far more fragile than the period of growth experienced by the United States and other major industrial nations in the quarter of a century after the end of World War II. The first was that neoliberalism, the policy of most of the world's governments, stopped working, both as a political phenomenon and as a stabilizing force for capitalism. The economic turmoil in East Asia and, above all, the prolonged and seemingly irreversible stagnation of Japan's formerly powerhouse economy were the certain signs that any hope for global stability was fading as fast as the century itself.

The symbol of neoliberalism's crisis as a political movement was the return, in the last few years, of significant opposition, primarily from the working class and proletarianized peasantry across much of the world. Mass strikes in opposition to neoliberal policies and their consequences erupted across the globe. The similarity of these mass actions in such diverse settings as Zimbabwe, Colombia, France, Greece, Russia, South Korea, Canada, and many more reminds us that while a majority of those who toil in capital's uneven global system remain outside the formal relations of wage labor, the working class has continued to grow on a world scale. Indeed, even by the narrowest measure, that of industrial workers, the industrialized OECD countries, where industrial decline and downsizing was widespread, saw a slight growth from 112 million in 1973 to 115 million in 1994. In the economic South, including the former Communist countries, the industrial workforce has risen from 285 million in 1980 to 407 million in 1994. Organized labor movements that had been repressed in the 1960s and 1970s arose again or for the first time in much of the Third World, as well as southern Europe. Fascism was overthrown in Greece, Portugal, and Spain and unions emerged and were legalized again. By the late 1990s, these movements, new and old, were expressing their opposition to the crushing impact of nearly two decades of neoliberalism.

The second difference in North American capitalism's fin-de-siècle resurgence is that, unlike the post–World War II boom where American living standards rose on average, this expansion of US corporate power has seen the living standards of the vast majority sink for twenty years. Indeed, Wall Street insider Stephen Roach calls the US economic expansion of the 1990s a "labor crunch recovery." In 1998, for example, the real wages of those who work for wages and salaries in the United States remained 12 percent below their 1979 level. This general decline has been accompanied by a sharp division between the bottom three-quarters of the population, whose incomes have fallen, and the top quarter, whose incomes have risen. The higher one goes, furthermore, the greater the increase in income and wealth. Income measures, however, only scratch the surface of what the majority of the working class has experienced in the last two decades. While there have been no mass or general strikes in the United States in recent years, the return of high-profile class struggle is now apparent and the reasons for it clear. Far from providing the material basis for the continued loyalty and ideological submission of the working-class majority, the new power of North American capital is purchased in part by the increased degradation of the working and living conditions of the vast majority within the United States.

One aspect of this change was the profound workplace and labor-market reorganization associated with "lean production." The promised brave new co-managed workplace of the future turned into a top-down, well-lit Satanic mill. Whether you worked in a hospital or an auto plant, a post office or a post-industrial techno-office, more than likely your job was worse than it was a decade ago—if you were lucky to have one that long. Whether or not it was decorated with the trimmings of employee participation, TQM, or the like, it was certainly more stressful, probably harder, and definitely more dangerous by the 1990s. US injury and illness rates in the first half of the 1990s were running anywhere from 9 percent to 100 percent higher than in the first half of the 1980s, measured by the number of cases reported. Contributing to this rise in occupational illness and injury are changing work time patterns. Full-time manufacturing workers were putting in more overtime, while millions were becoming part of the precarious workforce that fills the country's growing number of part-time, temporary, or casual jobs.

The monthly figures published by the Bureau of Labor Statistics put the number of "part-timers" (those working less than thirty-five hours a week) at twenty-one million in mid-1997, or about 18.4 percent of the workforce, up from 16.6 percent in 1975. But if those in the thirty-five- to forty-hour range are included, more than thirty-eight million people actually work less than forty hours a week, while an uncounted number of "part-timers" earning part-time pay work forty or more hours, week in and week out. More startling is the growth in temporary workers. Those who work out of "personnel supply agencies" have grown from 640,000 in 1987 to more than three million in mid-1999. An undocumented additional number of temps work directly for a growing variety of firms. A recent study by the Economic Policy Institute puts the total proportion of "nonstandard" jobs at 29.4 percent of the workforce, 34.4 percent for women workers—figures that adjust for the overlap of part-time, temporary, and contract work. With the arrival of "modular" production at the end of the 1990s, which emphasizes outsourcing and subcontracting even more than its "lean" predecessor, still more full-time and well-paid jobs will be turned in for temporary and/or lower-wage jobs.

All of this has not gone unnoticed by the majority that compose both the shrinking middle-income and the growing lower-income working class—and they are angry. Whatever glow may have accompanied the early days of labor-management partnership or workplace participation faded rapidly for many workers as their jobs were cut and/or intensified to boost profits, stock prices, and top salaries. Contesting with this anger and disillusionment, however, is fear of job loss by the same forces: downsizing, outsourcing, facility closures, or scab herding. As a *Multinational Monitor* editorial put it, "A ruthless employer class blends these multiple sources of job insecurity into a whole greater than the parts."[27]

The other side of the downsized coin, however, is work intensification. If no one with power listened to the workers who complained about this, at least a few ears perked up when Wall Street insider Stephen Roach wrote in the *Wall Street Journal* that "the so-called productivity resurgence of recent years has been on the back of slash-and-burn restructuring strategies that have put extraordinary pressures on the workforce."[28] Roach predicted a "worker backlash."

There comes a point, after all, when the pressures and inevitable indignities of intensified exploitation outweigh the fear of job loss, as it did in the Great Depression. As Marta Ojeda, director of the US-Mexico border–based Committee for Justice in the Maquiladoras put it eloquently at the 1997 Labor Notes conference in Detroit, "The hunger is stronger than the fear—hunger for justice, not only for food." First one group, then another tests the waters and open conflict returns to labor relations—despite the trimmings of company unionism or labor-management cooperation schemes. That is the meaning of the bitter strikes of the last few years in the United States. Some lose, as at Caterpillar and A. E. Staley. Some are more or less draws, like that at Wheeling-Pittsburgh. Others win something, as at UPS in 1997, at several telecommunications companies in 1998, in the seventeen local GM strikes of the last two and a half years, the brief strike at Dunlop, the sixty-nine-day Boeing strike, the weeklong general strike of Oregon state employees, the on-again-off-again strike at Yale University, and the fifty-four-day confrontational struggle at WCI Steel in Warren, Ohio.

Then there are the massive strikes of immigrant and Latino workers on the West Coast: janitors, drywallers, and carpenters in Los Angeles; waterfront truckers in LA and Seattle; and in the last days of the twentieth century, casualized waterfront workers in Southern California. To these should be added the struggle to organize twenty thousand strawberry pickers in California, the smaller number of apple pickers and processors in Washington State, and those harvesting cucumbers in North Carolina. These and similar struggles of immigrant and Latino workers around the country also point to something new—the rise of Latinos not only in the workforce but also in the unions. While union membership overall continued to decline from 1992 through 1996, the number of Latino union members grew by 12 percent.

Thus, in the long economic expansion of the 1990s, militancy returned to many sections of the US working class. What arose, however, was not the old rhythm of US collective bargaining, with a large number of relatively short, conventional strikes aimed at winning wage and benefit improvements. The strikes and struggles of the 1990s were largely defensive in nature, often very long and bitter, mostly focused on workplace and labor market changes, and increasingly "political," in the sense that they made demands that all workers could identify with (sometimes deliberately), and thus struck a sympathetic chord in the working-class public and often appealed directly for broader support. The Staley, Detroit Newspapers, and UPS strikes all did this, and the 1998 GM and telecommunications strikes also garnered majority public sympathy.

The strikes of the last few years revealed the contradictions of business unionism and its limitations in today's world economy. They also often showed the new power that many organized workers have. Strikes at Staley, Caterpillar, and the Detroit Newspapers were lost partly because local or national leaders pulled their punches or even helped derail the strike. (It is impressive that the struggle against the newspapers continued despite this, with an impressive core of activist resisters.) At General Motors in 1998, where it was clear that the union had enormous power to shut the company down, national leaders refused to use the strike to make serious gains at the national or even local levels. Instead, they settled for small, often reversible gains that didn't resolve the bigger problems of outsourcing and downsizing. Where some important things were won, as in telecommunications, it was largely because new tactics, member mobilization, and public outreach were deployed.

In 1995 a significant change occurred in the leadership of the AFL-CIO. Throughout the 1990s, rank-and-file rebellions occurred in many unions and took power for a time in the 1.4 million–member Teamsters. There would be major setbacks to these gains, but it was clear that union politics were changing as the new century approached.

Internal Union Dynamics

Most of this new consciousness and militancy comes from the activist layer of the unions. These are workers, workplace representatives, and local-level union officials who keep US unions going from day to day. They work between the upper layer of career officials and staffers, on the one hand, and the majority of members, on the other. Some are full-time, paid officials; many are not. They are forced to confront the reality of the workplace as opposed to its ideology, whether or not they accept this current partnership ideology in whole or part. A significant minority of this layer, however, rejects the labor-management ethos that comes from employers and career union officials alike. It is in this layer that the return of resistance has gathered the greatest force and, now and then, breaks through the passivity of the members and the backward-looking immobility of the top officials.

The activists and the top leaders are often at odds over how to respond to the changing workplace and labor market. Unlike in some European countries and at past times in the United States, there is only one labor federation. There is no division by political loyalty: socialist, Communist, Christian. Differences in direction or political outlook must be expressed within a union that has sole representation rights in its bargaining unit. In addition, most unions in the United States have developed bureaucratic structures beyond the reach of labor leaders in much of the world. So political conflict tends to take an almost sociological character: ranks versus bureaucrats. The forms of this clash may be many. Pressure from the activist layer to act is one, a major factor in the GM and Boeing strikes. Another is turnover at the top. The Association for Union Democracy (AUD) estimated that about a dozen union presidents were ousted in contested elections from the late 1980s through the 1991 victory of Ron Carey.

The ferment continued into the 1990s. Labor democracy attorney Paul Levy summarized it in a speech to the National Lawyers Guild in the fall of 1996 when he said:

> There is extensive intra-union activity in a large number of national unions, much more than ever before. In service unions such as the Food and Commercial Workers, the Service Employees and the Hotel Workers, construction unions such as the IBEW (Electricians) or the Bricklayers and the Carpenters and the Laborers, government unions like the Letter Carriers, the AFGE (Federal Employees) and the Treasury Employees, industrial unions like the Machinists and the Auto Workers.[29]

To this list of challenges in national unions can be added similar movements in large local unions such as the New Directions caucus in the thirty-thousand-member Transport Workers Union Local 100 in New York's transit system, the Caucus for a Democratic Union in the California State Employees/SEIU Local 1000 that has twice won control of this forty-thousand-member union, the successful rebellion in Atlanta's transit union, or the reform group in the similarly large union of New York City janitors and doormen, SEIU Local 32J/32B—John Sweeney's home local. Even the famous Justice for Janitors local union, SEIU 399 in Los Angeles, saw a massive opposition movement of Latino and African American workers, called the Multiracial Alliance, replace the old-guard executive committee—only to be placed in trusteeship by John

Sweeney, who was still SEIU president at that time. The split of the militant California Nurses Association from the more conservative American Nurses Association in 1996 represents another form of rebellion from below. Recently formed local opposition caucuses, as opposed to traditional caucuses of the "in" and the "out" opportunist union politicians, have appeared in unions as diverse as the Auto Workers, Steelworkers, Teachers, Hotel Employees, Carpenters, and the IBEW.

Nowhere was the challenge from below more successful or the process of union reform deeper than in the Teamsters. It seemed as if the reelection of Ron Carey over Jimmy Hoffa ("Junior") in 1996 not only spelled the end of the corrupt old guard but opened a new phase of transformation. As Ken Paff of the TDU explained, "We won the political battle over the value of a clean, democratic union. Hoffa had to adopt our program and promise to do even better at it. But we have not yet won the battle over the need for a new kind of union that derives its power from a mobilized and involved membership."

The dynamics of the Teamster revolution, as many TDUers call it, had brought TDU a long way from fifteen years in the wilderness as a clear-cut opposition to five years on the front lines defending the reform regime and defeating the old guard. Now the most difficult question of all was posed: how to go beyond the norms of "clean" American business unionism? For most activists, the key to anything new was an informed, activated membership. Whether speaking of winning a strike at UPS, organizing the unorganized, or building broader coalitions for bigger social goals, success would depend on mobilizing the tens of thousands of workers on whom the real power of the union rests.

This dynamic suffered a serious setback when outside consultants hired by the 1996 Carey campaign organization, along with the union's political director, were caught in an illegal scam to direct union money into the campaign coffers. Carey was disqualified from the election and eventually expelled, even though it was never proven that he was directly involved. In the wake of this turn of events, the union reform coalition around Carey fell apart. It took months for the TDU-backed union reform movement to pull itself together. The slate that it ran in the 1998 election rerun reflected the thinking of those prepared to go well beyond "clean business unionism." But its presidential candidate, Tom Leedham, was not well known and had only six months to campaign. Furthermore, the union members were made cynical by the allegations against Carey; voter turnout, at 28 percent, was no higher than in the Teamsters' first election in 1991. The old-guard candidate, Jimmy Hoffa, son of the famous Teamster leader of the 1960s, had campaigned for four years and had the best-known name in the union. He won by 54 percent.

The central role of TDU in both the reform movement and the UPS strike was no fluke. It survives the Hoffa victory. It exploded in 1999 in the strike by one thousand immigrant meatpacking workers at IBP's plant in Pasco, Washington. Here, TDU leader Maria Martinez was elected chief shop steward. Opposed by the old-guard white leadership, the TDU-led coalition fought the intolerable working conditions in the plant and eventually forced a strike. The spirit of rebellion could also be seen at Anheuser Busch, where members repeatedly rejected deals pushed on them by old-guard leaders and the Hoffa-led International.

While the TDU-backed rank-and-file movement will have to fight to regain leadership over the union, the question that faces the Teamster reformers is essentially the same question that faces the entire labor movement: What kind of unions, what kind of movement can be built that will be adequate to the challenges of corporate power, international competition, and the dominance of conservative politics?

Many of today's struggles have taken on a certain political character. As we noted, the UPS strike captured the attention and support of the working-class public. Many of the struggles mentioned above brought the state into action on the side of the employers—a fact that politicized many union activists. The struggle of members of the Transport Workers Union Local 100 in New York City's transit system illustrates another way in which "simple" union-employer conflict turns political. The fight for a new contract in late 1999 became a four-way conflict. The simple negotiating process between the union and the Transit Authority would never have taken center stage in New York as the holidays approached if it had not been for the New Directions caucus in Local 100.

New Directions began back in the 1980s as a small dissident newsletter called *Hell on Wheels*. By the late 1990s, it was a powerful movement that controlled about 40 percent of the executive board of this thirty-five-thousand-member local union and dominated the subway division. Its candidate for president of the local had come within a few hundred votes of winning in 1998. As during past contracts, it conducted its own contract campaign. The size and influence of the organization by this time, however, meant it played a significant role in the now complex negotiations. Reacting to the fear that New Directions would push the union into a crippling strike in late December, Mayor Rudolph Giuliani entered the fray by getting a court injunction not only against a strike, which was illegal in any case, but against the use of the word "strike" by any union member. The daily press in New York carried endless stories highlighting both Giuliani and New Directions leader Tim Schermerhorn.

New Directions had become more than a powerful rank-and-file movement; it was the center of city politics for a time. The main reason was that the transit contract was the first in a series of labor contracts for the city's tens of thousands of employees. For these union city workers, New Directions played the role that the UPS strike had for the country. Indeed, rank-and-file caucus activists from several of the city's public-sector unions had formed a coalition and met together for some time. Giuliani, who actually had no part in the negotiation with the Transit Authority, panicked at the idea of a series of struggles in which the outcome was an accelerating city payroll—not to mention a reenergized labor movement. A genuine class-against-class conflict was taking shape.

The Tasks of Socialists in Today's Resistance and Rebellion

Thinking about the tasks of socialists in today's United States can be overwhelming. From Reagan through Clinton, the US government has been able to launch an endless series of high-speed wars that deny us the time to organize effective opposition. The racist politics of prisons and punishment have reached such tidal proportions they, too, seem to laugh at opponents. The growth of poverty, the servitude of workfare, the threat of ecological disaster, and the seemingly unstoppable drift of mainstream politics to the right all taunt the left and tempt it to do everything at once.

To be sure, there are good signs as well. Not only rebellion in the workplace and unions, but a proliferation of community-based worker organizations, the rise of cross-union campaigns and organizations, and a new generation of student and youth activists taking on sweatshops, "free trade," and many other important issues. All of these and more came together in Seattle at the end of November 1999 to stake out their place in the global political landscape. Here and there, there are victories. But the basic problem remains one of power. The multinational corporations and the politicians they so generously fund (and, of course, the state and multilateral institutions they direct) have a lot of it and we don't.

This brings us right back to where we started, right back to Karl Marx and the working class. Marx didn't look to the working class because of some supposed moral superiority, the clarity of their ideas at any particular moment, or the infinite effectiveness of their trade unions. I have already argued that these things can be as absent among workers as individuals as among members of any other class. No, Marx looked to this class because in capitalist society they were the only other class, besides the bourgeoisie, who had the potential power to change things. Their power flowed from their position in the economy and from their numbers. "Ye are many, they are few," as the poet Shelley put it. More than that, this class has the power to create society's wealth and, acting as a class, to bring society and its production to a halt. "Without our brain and muscle not a single wheel would turn," the Wobblies sang. We might add: "Not an inch of fiber-optic cable laid, no just-in-time delivery made, not a whole ball season played." You get the picture.

The problem has always been organizing that power and giving it conscious expression for a common purpose. What is being argued here is that there is already a starting point in the form of the rank-and-file resistance and rebellions, community-based organizations, and transitional formations discussed above. While socialists can and do play an important role in building and providing direction for such movements, they don't have to invent them. The existence of the organizations, networks, projects, and activists that make up this rebellion and resistance, of course, do not solve the problems of power, or rather the left's lack of it, immediately. This is a long-range, multifaceted strategy. It is a perspective that requires a division of labor, for which reason it is most effectively conducted by organized socialists even though there is plenty for individuals to do. It is a strategy focused primarily, though not exclusively, on the unions, so it follows that most of those carrying it out will be union members, although there are roles for those not in unions.

In summary, the tasks of socialists in the labor movement include:

1. Building the rank-and-file movements and organizations that are fighting for a more effective, democratic, and inclusive union in the context of the main

fight with the bosses—the Farrell Dobbs approach of letting the bureaucratic old guard get caught in the crossfire. Realistically, however, the bureaucracy is far more omnipresent and in the way these days than in the early 1930s, so that there is no hope of avoiding internal union conflict if any progress is to be made. People are compelled into struggle by real conditions and these are mostly shaped by capital and its endless attempt to regain or improve profitability. These efforts to increase exploitation impact in all areas of working life including the different position of white and Black, men and women, in the workforce and the union. Socialists build these rank-and-file groups, acts of resistance, and movements on their own terms, but offer an analysis of the roots of the problem and a bigger vision of how to address them when appropriate. We call this social movement unionism: a unionism that is democratic, acts like a movement and not just an institution, and reaches out to other working-class and oppressed people to build a mass movement for change.

2. Building the growing number of cross-union, hence by implication class-wide, transitional organizations, publications, and projects that help provide a broader class vision for the work within the unions and direct links between activists in different unions and industries. These include both union-backed and explicitly oppositional groups. Among them are Labor Notes, the Association for Union Democracy, Jobs with Justice, strike support campaigns, and single- and social-issue campaigns, where relevant. The ongoing organizations and projects, in particular, provide opportunities to raise transitional ideas like shorter work time as well as a living demonstration of aspects of social movement unionism.

3. Building and allying with community-based working-class organizations. I have mentioned workers' centers as important, but others, like the environmental justice movement, based mainly in communities of color are also important. The significance of these organizations is that they bring to the overall movement sections of the working class, mostly people of color, who are not in unions. Like rank-and-file movements, these organizations and campaigns train the working-class leaders and activists needed to enhance the power of all working people and to deepen the reach of the broader labor movement we seek.

4. Building active international workers' solidarity. There are a growing number of opportunities to build direct links between workers in different countries as well as engage in solidarity actions at home. The Transnationals Information Exchange, the Coalition for Justice in the Maquiladoras, Labor Notes, the US/Labor Education in the Americas Project, and other groups make worker-to-worker contacts to foster internationalism.

5. Building alternative class-based politics. This would include working in and building the Labor Party, local independent campaigns with a working-class base and politics, and efforts like the living-wage campaigns that promote transitional class politics. Through these efforts transitional ideas such as national health care gain legitimacy and can be brought back into our daily work in appropriate ways.

6. Building socialist organizations that relate to all of these levels of working-class activity as well as promoting and acting on a broader socialist politics covering the entire range of social, economic, and political issues. To the degree that a significant portion of the members of the socialist organization are involved in one or more of the first four areas of activity, the organization will

have the roots in the life of the activist layer of the organized working class that lay the basis for bigger developments as events unfold. To the extent that others of its members are involved in the whole range of issues and politics, they can enrich the vision and analysis of the labor activists. Overall, socialist organization also makes possible the coordinated division of labor of its activists that is essential to the rank-and-file strategy. It is also the organization that carries the transitional ideas to their socialist conclusions: the organization that makes and trains socialists.

Each of these points begins with the word "building" because the kind of socialist politics we are talking about involves building movements, struggles, and organizations that can make a difference. Explicitly socialist education and political work must be done in connection with such work in the world of the working class. This must be done in a nonsectarian manner in which socialists from different groups work together where they agree, along with union and community activists who haven't yet drawn socialist conclusions.

Solidarity, as a revolutionary socialist organization, attempts to follow these prescriptions in its labor work as well as in other areas of political activity. We are a multitendency organization with a wide range of views on many questions, including the rank-and-file strategy. We are a "work in progress" that recognizes that the road to the type of mass democratic revolutionary socialist party (or parties) needed to end the disastrous rule of capital and usher in the rule of the working class is still a long one. While we don't claim to have the road map, we do claim to have a compass. It points to the working class and the means to expand and deepen class consciousness and organization in such a way as to make socialist ideas credible in American society. This route leads first to the active rank and file of the unions and the struggles in which they are engaged. If we carry out this rank-and-file strategy intelligently, if we can win large numbers of leftists and union activists to this strategy, and if socialism becomes the outlook of more and more of these activists, we can put socialism back on the political agenda in the United States.

5 Updating the Rank-and-File Strategy

Kim Moody

It has been well over a decade since *The Rank-and-File Strategy* was written. Since that time much has changed in the world and in the US labor movement. We have seen the Great Recession, the Eurozone crisis, resistance to the austerity these have brought on in Mediterranean Europe and elsewhere, and the Arab Spring and the disappointing retreats that often followed, to mention some of these changes. The US labor movement has continued to shrink, with most of its efforts to grow failing. Partly in response to this failure, six unions, led by the SEIU, split from the AFL-CIO in 2005, creating the Change to Win Federation. Some unions fell into a virtual civil war. Public-sector unions have seen an unprecedented attack not only on wages and conditions, but on the very right to bargain and, perhaps, exist. On the other hand, the role of immigrant workers has grown and with it new organizations and resistance. At the same time, moments of high-profile resistance like the 2011 Wisconsin upsurge or the September 2012 Chicago teachers' strike display labor's potential power. The question naturally arises: How does all of this affect the idea of a rank-and-file approach to furthering effective class action? How do they impact the hopes for building a working class–based socialist movement in the United States? The fundamental dilemma that brought forth a rank-and-file approach to the work of socialists in the unions remains the same: the disconnect between revolutionary socialism and the vast majority of organized workers—and the means to end it.

No attempt will be made here to rewrite the original article, to update every trend, or to pick out all the big and little mistakes and poor formulations. For the most part, I believe, the historical analysis stands up to scrutiny.[1] In terms of the rank-and-file perspective itself, the basic choice between permeation of the labor bureaucracy and a rank-and-file approach remains unavoidable, as all the social realities and economic pressures that conservatize the upper layers of unions remain and in many cases are even stronger under today's economic conditions. On the other hand, the pressures on the mass of workers, organized and unorganized, are if anything even greater today than a decade ago. It is precisely the clash of these contradictory pressures that from time to time gives rise to rebellion in the ranks.

There are, to be sure, some hopeful signs. Efforts at mobilization and new tactics have been adopted at least partially by a few unions. Furthermore, rank-and-file rebellions have arisen in a number of unions, mostly at the local level, as old leaders prove unable or unwilling to enlist the members in resistance or even to resist at all. More generally, there appears to be a new generation of local activists and leaders, in and out of office, who want to fight the intolerable conditions being imposed by employers both public and private. In this emerging layer there is a strong understanding of the importance of workplace organization as a power base for resistance and growth. It is in these developments, still very much minority trends to be sure, that socialists can find hope and a place to begin—again.

Old Strategies Confront Intensified Trends

It cannot be said that many of America's labor leaders haven't tried various things to halt or reverse declining union fortunes. As is their custom, however, most of these have been top-down efforts that bypass the membership or those they hope to organize. The formation of Change to Win, for example, was supposed to put new life and energy into organizing; it didn't. It was a nonstarter that led to more top-level internal conflict than new organizing.[2] Indeed, the grand troika of "new" union tactics of the 1990s and 2000s—mergers, neutrality/card check, and "leverage"—have all failed to produce the expected or intended results. Mergers, which accelerated in the 1990s and were supposed to produce the resources needed to organize, have failed to do so. Instead, they have produced a number of giant, multijurisdictional conglomerate unions that render union democracy even more difficult, without significant organizing breakthroughs or financial well-being.[3] As Steve Early reported in 2012, neutrality/card check schemes, often known as "Bargaining to Organize," have "stalled." "In the last several years," he writes, "few AFL CIO or Change to Win affiliates have made any large-scale 'Bargaining to Organize' breakthroughs."[4] Leverage, the application of outside, often indirect pressure of various kinds on the targeted company, while effective in some circumstances, has also failed to redress the deteriorating balance of class power. At best it is often an additional pressure during a hard-fought strike. At worst it becomes a substitute for member mobilization and real direct action, as it is mostly deployed and administered by union professionals.[5] Below, I will address how a rank-and-file approach relates to the question of organizing. First, I will look briefly at two major trends confronting unions and their members as well as the unorganized majority.

In the wake of the failure to organize even enough new workers to prevent continued decline, union membership has fallen further, with the Great Recession wiping out such gains as were made in 2007 and 2008. Altogether, union membership shrank from 16.3 million, or 13.5 percent of eligible workers, in 2000 to 14.8 million, or 11.8 percent, in 2011. Unlike in previous years when most losses were in the private sector, in 2011 it was the public-sector unions that lost more than sixty thousand members, reflecting the first signs of the accelerated attack on public workers and their bargaining rights.[6] The only bright spot in the 2011 figures was the unexpected gain of 110,000 union members in the private sector—almost all of them in healthcare. Along with hotels, this is one of the few areas of union growth and one in which rank and file–based mobilization tactics are frequently employed, albeit sometimes along with card check and leverage.

Employer Resistance

Two indicators of increased employer resistance to unions in the private sector were the rise in the ratio of 8a Unfair Labor Practices (ULPs) to NLRB elections filed by unions against employers and the increased use of permanent replacement workers in the face of strikes. An 8a ULP indicates that the union sees an illegal practice by management, such as firing a union activist, during a representation election.[7] The ratio of 8a ULPs to NLRB elections had been rising throughout most of the post–World War II period. But even as the number of NLRB election pursued by unions fell from 2000 to 2009, this ratio rose from 6.3 per election to 9.7.[8] The second indication of resistance to unions is the rise in the use of permanent replacement workers during strikes. Three surveys conducted from the mid-1990s to the mid-2000s show that employers not only were willing to threaten the use of scabs more in 2003 than in 1996, but increased the ratio of the actual deployment of permanent replacements during strikes from one in eight to three in four.[9] In the public sector the campaign to destroy or limit collective bargaining has mainly taken a legislative form. Yet there has been resistance in several states and it appears here, as elsewhere, that mass direction action is the key.

The point is that tactics like mergers, leverage, or Bargaining to Organize (or mere pressure politics) are not sufficient. They cannot be effective in and of themselves in the face of intensified employer efforts to extract a higher rate of surplus value in which opposition to new unionization and efforts to roll back unionism are key. It isn't simply a matter of the age-old hatred of unions American capital has harbored since the dawn of industrialization.[10] Rather, it is the realization by capital and its political representatives that profitability has come to depend on increased wage compression and workplace intensification. The increased rate of surplus value resulting from these helped create the period of growth, with its ups and downs, from 1982 through 2007. Any hopes of a general capitalist recovery since the crash of 2008 are, if anything, even more dependent on the ability to restrain wages and increase productivity through work intensification.[11] Unions, even conservative ones, in this context, represent a real or potential barrier to the achievement of an increased rate of exploitation and hence a return to profitability. This brings us to the matter of work reorganization and intensification.

Work Intensification and the Wage-Productivity Gap

The most visible statistical result of work reorganization and intensification is the wage-productivity gap that has characterized the last three decades. According to the Economic Policy Institute, while productivity rose 37.8 percent from 1995 through 2011, median real wages rose only 9.6 percent. Those for a college graduate rose 12.6 percent and those for a high-school graduate a mere 6.2 percent.[12] It is obvious from these figures that the rate of surplus value must have increased significantly as the value of labor power decreased.

Despite continued sluggish growth, profits per unit of real gross value added rose by 14 percent from the beginning of 2010 through mid-2012, while unit labor costs rose less than 1 percent.[13] In other words, wage restraint and work intensification were working for capital. Much of this is the product of lean production methods, although it appears that US capital has gone beyond the softer sides of those production methods to cruder methods of control and compulsion.

These two grim trends, union decline and work intensification, are of course linked. Bargaining power over wages, benefits, and working conditions in a majority of unionized workplaces continued to diminish. One indicator of declining union power (or possibly the willingness to use it) was that bargained wage increases have fallen from more than 3 percent a year from 2002 to 2008 to 1.7 percent in the first half of 2012, despite rising productivity and profits. Furthermore, the percentage of new contracts with no wage increase had risen to a third by 2012.[14] Things are even worse in the area of benefits and pensions. Clearly, this contributed to the continued wage-productivity gap and profitability. How does this relate to the rank-and-file strategy?

The Missing Tasks

The Rank-and-File Strategy ended with six tasks for socialist work in the unions. This list more or less stands as a general guide. However, in the light of these accelerated trends, it now seems to me there are two glaring omissions: a socialist role in organizing the unorganized and the centrality of workplace organization in a socialist approach to union work. But is there a particularly socialist approach to union or workplace organizing? I would answer yes.

We proceed from the proposition argued by Marx that consciousness grows from struggle and self-activity and that unions, despite their limitations, can be, as Engels put it, "schools of war" in which the workers prepare themselves for larger fights to come and become "fit for administrative and political work."[15] This is only true, however, if unions are in fact willing and able to struggle effectively, to mobilize the workers to engage in that struggle, and for the members to have access to the union's administration and politics (i.e., union democracy). While more unions today employ mobilization tactics, there is still often a tendency to keep things under bureaucratic control. Since most organizing as it is currently done is administered by the international unions, bureaucratic business unionism, still the norm, is a barrier to effective struggle. Of course, the socialist task is to organize against this and for basic changes in union leadership, policy, and structure. Within that longer-range task, however, are some specifics. We have long known that unions are most likely to win representation when, as Bronfenbrenner once put it, "they run aggressive and creative campaigns utilizing a rank-and-file, grassroots intensive strategy, building a union and acting like a union from the very beginning of the campaign."[16] Campaigns like UNITE-HERE's Hotel Workers Rising or those by the new National Union of Healthcare Workers and National Nurses United appear to have taken this advice more than most. Nevertheless, socialists with potential influence in organizing campaigns should fight for and help organize for this "rank-and-file, grassroots intensive" approach.

Another important path to increased organizing lies through the local union. Here, in what is likely to be a more democratic setting, stewards and members can be mobilized to organize workers in nearby and related industries or occupations and up anddown the supply chain. Some locals, like CWA Local 1037, a public-sector union in New Jersey, use members and an extensive stewards organization to recruit new members. Another example, at least when it was under TDU leadership, was Teamsters Local 174.[17]

In addition to involvement in more traditional organizing efforts, socialists can push for opening union membership beyond workplaces that win formal majority recognition, by whatever means. Prior to World War II, workers did not wait to win recognition before "acting like a union." Indeed, the CIO union would not have triumphed in the 1930s if they had. Nonmajority or "open-source" unionism could bring huge numbers into the labor movement. There are already a number of experiments with this approach.[18]

None of these approaches are panaceas, but they do point to ways to increase union power, a key goal for socialists. What is needed and what we would work for is to turn these practical approaches into is a broad working-class movement, incorporating new and old unions, immigrant organizations, workers centers, and worker resource projects, powerful enough to push the employers back and shift the center of class relations.

Power on the Job

The late historian Giovanni Arrighi observed that as industry became more capital intensive, craft workers and their unions tended to lose their "marketplace bargaining power," but as the division of labor and dependence on vast amounts of capital grew, production became more vulnerable to strikes and the workers' "workplace bargaining power" at the point of production increased.[19] Today, with endless outsourcing, subcontracting, privatizing, and so on, the picture is more complicated. Union organizing, for example, often requires both a marketplace and a workplace approach. The strategy that led to the victory of Justice for Janitors in 1990, for example, relied on a marketplace approach to organize these contract workers. That is, they had to bring all the janitors in the Los Angeles area into the union in order to reduce competition among them. In other cases, more than one layer of employers has to be fought. The Farm Labor Organizing Committee and the Coalition of Immokalee Workers had to fight and bargain with two sets of employers.

The question arises: Does this fragmentation of the workforce mean not only that marketplace approaches may be needed in some cases, but, more seriously, that the workplace power that characterized the era of industrial unionism has evaporated? On the contrary, the whole structure of the contemporary production of goods and services, frequently linked by just-in-time or "logistics" systems, is highly vulnerable to strikes and other direct actions.[20] While some workers have more workplace bargaining power than others, many possess the ability to disrupt production to the degree to which they are well organized on the job. This, in turn, opens the possibility and opportunity for solidarity actions and for the extension of unionization along the supply chain.

If Marx and Engels thought of trade unions as "schools" of war or sites where workers become "fit for administrative and political work," socialists today should understand that building workplace organization capable of disrupting the labor process is also a training ground for the wielding of greater, more extensive power down the (revolutionary) road. It is, to some degree, a transitional form of organization and power. To oversimplify, today's shop steward organization may be tomorrow's factory council—even if that is well down that road. At the moment, workplace shop stewards' organization is the key to effective resistance *and* to the greater disruptions required to shift the balance of class forces. For socialists, then, building this kind of directly elected workplace organization is both a practical and an educational task. It is the most effective base from which to hold the official accountable to the members. It is the basis of rank-and-file power on the job and in the union, as well as a base from which to extend union organizing in which the stronger help the weaker achieve organization and gain power.

Rebellion in the Unions

The Rank-and-File Strategy put considerable emphasis on rank-and-file caucuses and movement within the unions. The unfortunate heading that read "The Roots of a New Rebellion" must have given the impression that I was predicting an imminent rerun of the 1970s upsurge. And certainly the talk of "neoliberalism's crisis" was as premature then as more recent predictions of its demise have been during the current capitalist crisis, despite the bailouts and other state interventions. What that section was meant to show was simply that rank-and-file rebellions are a more-or-less constant feature of the US labor movement—a consequence of bureaucratic business unionism. Some of these movements succeed, many fail, while others eventually succumb to the pressures innate in the capital-labor relationship and its institutional superstructure. But most have the potential to help construct a new layer of experienced activists.

The 2000s, much like the 1990s, were not a decade of working-class upsurge. Yet, like the previous decade, they saw their share of rank and file–based union reform movements. Opening the decade was the reform movement in Teamsters Local 705 in Chicago, followed by Local 743 in the Windy City twelve years later. Similar movements won in Teamsters Locals 804, 805, and 814 in the New York area. The Teamsters for a Democratic Union (TDU) helped many of these Teamster reform efforts, so that today the reformers claim about thirty local unions. CWA Locals 1400 in New England and 1101 in New York saw successful rebellions. Early in the decade, rank-and-file Los Angeles teachers took over their gigantic local. A mass movement of Chicago teachers did the same in their twenty-six-thousand-member local more than a decade later. Nurses in the New York State Nurses Association brought in a new leadership, as did blue-collar workers at the University of California in AFSCME Local 3299 and longshore workers in ILA Local 1410 in Mobile, Alabama. Even in the heart of conglomerate unionism, the SEIU, several locals saw successful reform movements. Many of these local unions cover thousands of members, and there have certainly been many more such rebellions across the country in recent years. At the same time, at least two grassroots cross-union organizations have recently taken shape: Community and Postal Workers United and Railroad Workers United, both trying to build rank-and-file solidarity between workers in different locals and even different unions, offering one way to overcome the fragmentation mentioned above.

In 2012 *Labor Notes* ran an unusually frank discussion by several union reformers about the pressures and difficulties of trying to run a local union differently. Whether they were Teamsters, university workers, or longshore workers, the concerns were the same: training new grassroots leaders to broaden the base, building effective stewards organizations, creating broader forms of member mobilization and involvement, and not buying into "experts" and lawyers who are likely to push you back into "the well-worn grooves of business unionism."[21] This sort of open discussion of real problems is one way socialists, who can offer an analysis of union bureaucracy and the importance of union democracy, can contribute to the growth of rank-and-file movements.

There has been a change in the locus of rank-and-file rebellions in many unions since the 1970s. Less common these days are national rank-and-file organizations like the UAW's United National Caucus, Miners for Democracy, and Steelworkers Fight Back in the 1970s. This is partly due to the merger movement mentioned above, which has created conglomerate unions like the SEIU, Steelworkers, Teamsters, and UFCW, with their multiple, often unrelated jurisdictions. The breakup of national or master contracts and pattern bargaining, which once provided a focus for organization, has also made connections between geographically dispersed groups even in the same industry more difficult.[22]

This is not to say that it is impossible. TDU, which established a base in several Teamster jurisdictions early in its history, has been able to maintain a presence across the International Union. The Longshore Workers Committee has built a national network in the ILA. Attempting to take power at the national level, however, presents a new level of problems beyond even what the local leaders discussed in *Labor Notes*. While not all unions or union officials are the same, the higher one moves in a union, the greater the pressure to preserve the institution, reduce risky activities, and develop stable relationships with major employers mounts. Constant conflict, be it with employers or union opponents, becomes an annoyance. The pressure to professionalize and institutionalize conflict and retain office at all costs becomes hard to resist.[23] The only counter to this tendency is a powerful rank and file–based organization or movement based in strong workplace organization that can fight to keep the leadership on track. That is one reason why militant locals based on workplace power are important.

More generally, if the *Labor Notes* conferences of 2010 and 2012 are any indication, there appears to be a new generation of local leaders and activists taking shape. Attendance soared to 1,500 at the 2012 conference, an increase of 50 percent or more overmost earlier conferences. The mood and language were also more radical. This is a heartening sign. The growth of local movements also presents an opening for spreading the ideas of a rank-and-file approach to building a different unionism based on workplace power, union democracy, and a willingness to take direct action when called for.

In *The Rank-and-File Strategy* I wrote about the Trade Union Educational League (TUEL) as an early effort to build a rank-and-file movement across the entire labor movement that could fight for industrial unionism, union democracy, and independent political action. It was an organization that you joined simply by subscribing to its newspaper, the *Labor Herald*. *Labor Notes* is not a membership organization, but it has become an educational center through its publications, schools, and conferences. Its conferences provide a place to initiate or strengthen organization. The idea here is not that the *Labor Notes* staff can organize a contemporary TUEL, but that those who look to *Labor Notes* can see themselves as the core of a future working-class movement. In this context, *Labor Notes* provides a focus and a resource for a broader class consciousness in a manner similar to TUEL at its best. Changing our unions and building consciousness are not just jobs for this or that caucus, committee, or campaign in this or that union, but for a broad movement of tens of thousands pulling in the same direction.

Socialists willing to act in a nonsectarian fashion and put the broad movement before their own organizational interests have an important role to play in building this movement, providing they avoid the twin pitfalls of "party" control and permeation at the top. While new problems must be addressed and new tasks assumed, the central perspective of *The Rank-and-File Strategy* still offers a way in which to close the gap between socialist politics and working-class self-activity.

6 General Strikes, Mass Strikes: Don't Call Us, We'll Call You

Kim Moody

Inspired by the boldness of the movement, activists of Occupy Oakland "called" a general strike in that city for November 2— a sign of the movement's radicalism and its recognition of where social power lies.

One criticism of the Occupy activists was that they had not consulted the unions. Had they done so, however, it is unlikely that very many union leaders would have agreed to jointly "call" such an action. In fact, as I will argue, effective general or mass strikes are seldom simply "called" from above, if at all, or until they are well under way—and those that are "called" tend to be called off just as easily.

The result in Oakland was certainly a good demonstration, with a civil disobedience component. The city allowed its employees to participate. Members of the California Nurses'

This essay was originally published as "General Strikes, Mass Strikes" in Against the Current *160 (September/October 2012).*

Association took sick days to join in. One shift of ILWU members joined, responding to a blockade. If all this was very far from the general strike that Oakland had seen in 1946—which occurred in the context of a postwar upsurge very different from today's disastrous state of labor—it has put the issue and potential of the general strike on the agenda for discussion.

The idea of calling such a strike arises these days because some labor federations have, in fact, done so. France, Greece, Italy, Portugal, and Spain have all seen recent one- or two-day general strikes called by labor federations against the stringent austerity being imposed across much of Europe. More extended strikes played a role in the Arab Springs of Tunisia and Egypt. Closer to home, in the midst of the Wisconsin upsurge of 2011, the Madison-based South Central Federation of Labor put forth the idea of a general strike for discussion and consideration. Indeed, given the global war on the working class that has emerged out of the Great Recession and the continuing crisis of capitalism, it would be strange if this powerful idea did not arise. For this reason, it is worth taking another look at just why the idea is important and how such mass strikes actually take place.

The Power of an Idea

The idea of a massive withdrawal of labor is indeed a powerful one. The general strike goes back a long way. There was, for example, the Chartist strike for universal suffrage as well as other social demands in 1842. W. E. B. DuBois called the mass exodus of slaves from Southern plantations during the Civil War America's first general strike. This mass strike of slaves was key to Northern victory and emancipation. Neither of these, however, were "called" by some central leadership.[1] For revolutionary syndicalists and some socialists of the early twentieth century, the general strike was to be the revolutionary moment that culminated the deepening class struggle of that era. In 1906, in the Charter of Amiens, French syndicalists adopted the idea as central to the revolutionary process. They envisioned a chain of events in which strikes by individual unions led to a one-day general work stoppage, provoking a revolutionary crisis, followed by an ongoing general strike that would paralyze capitalism and the state alike. The IWW picked up this idea. Big Bill Haywood and Joseph Ettor wrote that "the general strike is the measure by which the capitalistic system will be overthrown." As a result of this "general lockout of the employing class . . . control of industry will pass from the capitalists to the masses and capitalists will vanish from the face of the earth."[2] To these revolutionaries this was not just some utopian idea. They had seen a series of mass strikes in Belgium and Geneva in 1902, in Barcelona, Bilbao, and Holland in 1903, and, of course, the mass strike that nearly tumbled the Czarist regime in Russia in 1905.[3] Though, of course, the capitalists had not vanished.

As one 1905 German syndicalist pamphlet argued, the general strike was, at that time, *the* "new weapon of the struggling proletariat" for at least two historical reasons. For one, revolution on the barricades, as in 1848, was no longer feasible in modern cities with their wide streets, not to mention the advances in military technology already apparent by then. A national or even international universal work stoppage would stretch the military too thin to break it, it was argued. For another, "modern industry, with its extremely specialized labor division and complications, is but poorly adapted to oppose a general strike," even one initiated by a minority of the working class.[4] This may be even truer today, with the just-in-time nature of production and the integrated logistics on which so much production and distribution depend. The idea was also debated in the socialist parties of the Second International, where it was more controversial. We will return later to Rosa Luxemburg's crucial contribution to that debate.

The idea of the general strike is powerful precisely because a massive and persistent withdrawal of labor can bring a capitalist city or even an entire economy to a halt. Here is a brief glimpse of the 1934 San Francisco general strike:

> The great factories were empty and deserted. No streetcars were running. Virtually all stores were closed. The giant apparatus of commerce was a lifeless, helpless hulk. Labor had withdrawn its hand. The workers drained out of the shops and plants like life-blood, leaving only a silent framework embodying millions of dollars' worth of invested capital. In the absence of labor, the giant machinery loomed like so much silent junk.[5]

The San Francisco strike was one of three major urban strikes, along with those in Minneapolis and Toledo, that took on a mass, if not always general, character in 1934 and led to both union growth and that of socialist organizations. Such a mass strike demonstrates the reality of the working class, as a whole, and the power it can wield. It also produces a sense of exhilaration and, at least where the experience has time to sink in, an expansion and deepening of class consciousness. The general strike is a powerful idea because *potentially* it is, as the syndicalists believed, a mighty weapon in the hands of the working class.

"Potentially," however, is the key word here. The strikes we have seen in Europe in the last few years seldom reach this potential because they are mostly limited to one or two days or a series of one-day strikes initiated or "staged" from the top. Writing from Montpellier in southern France about the mass strikes in 2010, Richard Greeman expressed "a disheartening feeling of déjà vu" because "the unions used the same dilatory tactics of spaced one-day public sector work stoppages in 2009, and the government simply bided its time until summer when the French go on vacation."[6] The powers that be have learned to ride out these short demonstrations of potential working-class strength. Today they certainly don't provoke the political crisis imagined by yesteryear's syndicalists. In contrast, Greeman notes, the public-sector strike of 1995 that went "wildcat" "paralyzed France for two months . . . and forced an earlier conservative government to withdraw its unpopular welfare 'reform.'" In fact, the impact was international. I visited a GM-Opel plant in eastern Germany the following summer, where I was informed the plant had closed down during the French strikes because the auto body parts, stamped in Spain, could not get through France by rail—a demonstration of the fragility of "modern industry."

If today's one-day strikes are weaker than the ongoing stoppages of 1995, they are even further removed from the impact of the French general strike of 1968. That mass strike was eventually supported, not "called," by the Communist-led CGT and the more radical CFDT only after it was well under way; union leaders reasoned that their activists would have to "swim with the tide," as Daniel Singer put it. Preceded by widespread strikes in 1967, the 1968 strikes began on May 13 at the Sud-Aviation plant near Nantes, where workers demanded a wage increase to cover income lost due to a reduction in hours. Singer writes, "The strike was not launched by the unions, but precipitated by young workers who occupied the factory and locked in the manager." On May 15 Renault workers near Rouen struck. The next day Renault workers all over France joined in, and on May 17 sit-ins spread to engineering and chemicals, and so on. The mass strike converged with the student movement and produced what Singer judged to be a revolutionary situation.[7]

In other words, we have two very different types of "general strikes": those that are "called" into being by trade-union officials, usually for a day or so, and can as easily be called off, on the one hand, and those that tend to be sparked by a particular struggle and spread due to both particular circumstances as well as those affecting broad sections of the working class.[8] We can see examples of the first type across Mediterranean Europe today, generally unable to defeat austerity even when the government changes. The more unruly extended mass strike is far rarer at the moment, but certainly cannot be ruled out given the dire circumstances faced by workers everywhere. The question is: How does such a process come about?

Luxemburg on the Mass Strike

The mass strikes that carried the 1905 Russian Revolution forward sparked a debate over the general strike in the European socialist movement. In *The Mass Strike, The Political Party and the Trade Unions,* Rosa Luxemburg condemned the anarchist and syndicalist conceptions of the general strike as both a utopian panacea and a substitute for political organization. She argued against both those who thought you could simply "put the mass strike in Germany on the calendar on an appointed day" and those trade unionists who "would eliminate the mass strike from the face of the earth" by censuring discussion of it. "Both tendencies," she argued, "proceed on the common purely Anarchist assumption that the mass strike is a purely technical means of struggle which can be 'decided' at pleasure and strictly according to conscience, or 'forbidden.'"[9]

Luxemburg drew on the recent experience of the Russian Revolution to note that those sweeping events had little to do with anarchist-style propaganda or direction from the centralized Social Democratic Party or trade union. Indeed, she appears to have chosen the term "mass strike" to distance her analysis from the equally mechanistic anarchist and Social Democratic conceptions of the "general strike." She wrote: "If, therefore, the Russian revolution teaches us anything, it teaches above all that themass strike is not artificially 'made,' not 'decided' at random, not 'propagated,' but that it is an historical phenomenon which, at any given movement, results from social conditions with historical inevitability."[10] Putting aside for the moment the notion of "inevitability" common to German Social Democratic thinking of the era, it was the conditions experienced by broad sections of the class and the specific history of the movement that propelled the strike wave of 1905. She spells out some of the history, which went back to earlier, mostly "economic" strikes in 1904, 1902, and even the textile strikes of 1896 and 1897. The great Petersburg strike that broke out in 1905, as Luxemburg tells it, was a result of the firing of two workers at the Putilov works due to their membership in the state-backed Zubatov union. Social Democratic agitators played a role in extending the strike, but "the unrest among the Putilov workers communicated itself quickly to the remainder of the proletariat, and in a few days 140,000 workers were on strike." The disciplining of two workers had been "the prologue of the most violent revolution of modern times." There was "no predetermined plan," "no organized action," but "everywhere was the revolutionary solidarity with the St. Petersburg proletariat expressly stated as the cause and aim of the strike."[11] Trotsky puts the start of the Moscow strikes in 1905 with a strike by typesetters demanding to be paid for punctuation marks—"the strike which started over punctuation marks and ended by felling absolutism."[12] Writing about '68, Singer puts it similarly: "In each factory, even in each shop, in each plant or office, it has its own roots, its own background, its own peculiarities," with "each stoppage being nourished by its predecessor and influencing the next one."[13]

A routine disciplinary case and a dispute over payment for punctuation marks led to mass solidarity strikes that, due to the inevitable clash with Czarist authority, became political, even revolutionary. War, deprivation, and repression all played a background part in making a mass strike across the Czarist empire possible (though hardly inevitable), but the timely spark of a strike by one group of twelve thousand workers in Petersburg and fewer in Moscow set things in motion. It took a few days to unfold even in Petersburg, which tells us that other groups of workers had to decide whether or not to join in the action. It took weeks for it to spread across the empire. We don't know the exact process, but Luxemburg says that "the appeals of the parties could hardly keep pace with the spontaneous rising of the masses."[14] Only later did the organized revolutionaries play a leading role. The point here, of course, is not that activists played no role in spreading the strikes. Without "human agency," the intervention of the most aware or daring workers, no mass strike is "inevitable." Rather the point is that this was not the earth-shaking event it was because some organized authority, party, or trade union, "called" the strike. For the political organization or the trade unions, the strike becomes an *opportunity*, not of their own making, to lead and grow. Unions, for example, grew substantially in 1886, 1919, 1934, and 1946 in the wake of strike waves. Radical political organizations grew in 1877 and 1934, although in 1886 and 1919 severe repression prevented the growth of socialist organization, while in 1946 the emerging Cold War already dampened radical possibilities.

Mass Strikes in America

If even the orderly one-day strikes in Europe, or for that matter the much-closer-to-home one-day strikes during the 1995–96 Ontario Days of Action, seem light-years away from what is possible in the United States today, events like 1905 in Russia or 1968 in France may appear to be from another planet. In fact, there is a history of mass or general strikes in the United States that has some lessons for us in this era of capitalist crisis. I have already mentioned the slave strike during the Civil War; here I will look briefly at mass and general strikes in 1877, 1886, 1919, and 1946.

The first truly mass strike of wage-earners exploded across the nation in July 1877. It began with a group of railroad workers in Martinsburg, West Virginia, resisting a 10-percent wage cut *and* a reorganization of work on the Baltimore & Ohio Railroad (B&O). Despite the intervention of the police and the nearby state militia, the strike just grew. This strike had been preceded by work stoppages in 1873 and 1874, but this time it spread across the nation's new transcontinental rail system—a movement aided by a new technology. The rail unions, the "Brotherhoods," had nearly collapsed and, in any case, played no role in initiating or spreading what became a near-insurrection in several cities. In fact, in the course of the strike, the workers created a new union called simply the Trainmen's Union. But even this new union was not in command. Furthermore, the strike pulled into its wake workers from many different industries.[15]

As one of the many labor newspapers of the day wrote, "There was no concert of action. It spread because the workmen of Pittsburgh felt the same oppression that was felt by the workmen of West Virginia and so with the workmen of Chicago and St. Louis."[16] Despite massive use of force by state and local authorities, the "Great Upheaval," as it came to be known, was finally broken only by the use of federal troops.

America's most famous general strike is, no doubt, the eight-hour strike of May 1, 1886. It was called as a one-day strike by the newly formed American Federation of Labor. In that sense, it might sound a little like the recent one-day strikes in Europe, but that comparison would be misleading. First, it took place in a moment of accelerating strike activity, as well as a broad movement to create local and state labor parties. The number of strikes had risen from an average of 450 a year from 1881 to 1884 to 645 in 1885 and then to 1,432 in 1886, the year of the general strike, and 1,436 in 1887. Up until 1886 almost two-thirds of strikes were over wages or wage cuts. That dropped to 63 percent in 1886. In 1886 only 53.3 percent of strikes were ordered by a union.[17] The high proportion of strikes not ordered by unions was fairly typical of the early 1880s, but may also be attributed to the way the May 1 strike took place. For one thing, it began as a strike wave in late 1885, mostly over hours, work organization, and managerial abuse.[18] For another, it was part of the broad eight-hour-day movement that began with large strikes in the 1860s and 1870s and embraced virtually the entire labor movement by the 1880s.

Although the AFL called for a general work stoppage on May 1 to impose the eight-hour day on employers, if only the new federation's 138,000 members had struck it would have been a far less memorable occasion. Almost twice that number struck on May 1 and by the end of the second week of May some 340,000 had downed tools. The reason was that thousands of members of the Knights of Labor, who had over half a million members at that time, had ignored their leadership's order not to join the strike.[19] Others not in the AFL also joined the strike.

One example was in Chicago, the epicenter of the general strike. There three union centers joined the strike: the AFL, the Knights of Labor, and the "anarchist" Central Labor Union, founded in 1884. Hostility between the three, and particularly toward the CLU, was strong enough that the AFL and Knights held a separate rally from the CLU. Nevertheless, members of all three marched and struck together on May 1.[20] Thus, the eight-hour general strike demonstrated class power in Chicago overcoming political differences through common action.

Though there would not be another nationwide mass strike in the United States, there were several local, citywide general strikes in both 1919 and 1946. The best-known general strike of 1919 was that in Seattle, which took on a revolutionary character complete with councils of soldiers, sailors, and workers. Returning veterans as well as nonunion workers were told, "Whatever you and your beliefs represent, go to your union hall and register yourself as one member of America's council of workmen." Once again, the mass strike brought together all wings of the working-class movement, as members of AFL craft unions worked with those of the IWW.[21] In that year, general strikes also broke out in Springfield, Illinois; Waco, Texas; and Billings, Montana. All these general strikes, as well as more limited ones, began in solidarity with one or another group of workers already on strike. Nineteen nineteen was, like 1877 and 1886, part of a broad strike wave that began in 1918, even before World War I had ended. The 1934 strikes mentioned above built on the acceleration of strike activity that began in 1933 and would lead to a massive strike wave in 1936 and 1937.

The next wave of general strikes came in 1946, in the midst of an enormous increase in strike activity that actually began during the war. In that year, 4.5 million union members struck, mostly for higher pay. Also that year, general strikes broke out in six US cities: Oakland, California; Houston, Texas; Stamford, Connecticut; Rochester, New York; and Pittsburgh and Lancaster, Pennsylvania. All were solidarity strikes. The Central Labor Councils usually played a role, but the strikes began before anyone "called" them.[22] The Oakland strike, for example, began in support of striking department-store clerks when police tried to move scab goods into the struck stores. Veteran socialist Stan Weir, who participated in the Oakland general strike, wrote:

> The Oakland General Strike was an extension of the national strike wave. It was not a "called" strike . . . hundreds of workers passing through downtown Oakland on their way to work became witness to police herding a fleet of scab trucks . . . The witnesses, that is, truck drivers, bus and streetcar operators and passengers, got off their vehicles and did not return. The city filled with workers, they milled about . . . and then organized themselves.[23]

Each of these strikes began in a different way, but all unfolded in solidarity with strikers under attack. In most of them the question was not whether some official body called the strike, but which group(s) of workers took the *next step* that set things in motion. Like the 1919 local general strikes, each was a demonstration of the dynamics Luxemburg had described. Each became political and clashed with local authorities, sometimes leading to political challenges in the aftermath of the strike. In some cases they ended with victory; in others they were called off by the unions or the Central Labor Council for fear of too deep a radicalization or confrontation.

Lessons for Today

All of the US mass and general strikes shared similar characteristics. First, they all occurred as part of an existing labor upsurge. The strikes of 1877, 1886, 1919, and 1946 were all preceded by a growing wave of strikes reaching levels far above those of the previous period. These periods of upsurge were the result of underlying conditions, often major changes in the organization of work and/or disruptions in living standards—not by most accounts a simple result of the "business cycle." All began as an act of solidarity, not taken all at once or "called," but unfolding as more people became aware of the struggle. Sometimes it was simply a question of which group would act next, in turn setting the precedent for the next group, as Singer described. Ironically, it is not the first group to strike—the Petersburg Putilov workers, Moscow typesetters, or Oakland store clerks, who most likely had no idea of leading a general strike—but those who take the *next steps* who are more likely to help the strike spread. The spreading of a strike, of course, also depended on pre-existing networks created through neighborhoods, unions, political organizations, central labor bodies, etc. Although there have been many such acts of solidarity by groups of workers, they have not spread into real mass or general strikes in the United States since 1946.[24]

So the question arises: Why there have been no mass strikes since 1946? Not even during the labor upsurge of the 1960s and 1970s, despite nationwide strikes by postal workers and Teamsters, political strikes by coal miners, and widespread "wildcat" strikes, was there a general or mass strike involving joint activity by different unions. One reason may well be that the sorts of networks that existed in old working-class neighborhoods had disappeared; those within unions had become bureaucratized and central labor councils rendered moribund, while left political networks were no longer large or strong enough to make a difference. Another, of course, is that "sympathy" strikes were made illegal in 1947 by the Taft-Hartley amendments to the National

Labor Relations Act. To make matters worse, since that time (or even before) most unions have accepted no-strike clauses in their contracts—making a solidarity strike during the life of the contract doubly illegal and the union subject to lawsuits for damages. For most business-union leaders of the last few decades, these were enough to put the idea of a general strike permanently off the agenda.

Mass strikes and strike waves, however, are not respecters of the law or, necessarily, of union officials. They have frequently been opposed by union officials and almost always fought by the authorities, declared illegal by the courts, and confronted by the police or military in one or another form, and yet have still grown. Furthermore, as indicated above, in the US experience they are initiated from below, sweeping up conservative and radical union leaders alike in their wake. The wave of sit-down strikes that established the CIO unions in the mid-1930s was at first opposed by the union officialdom, was illegal, faced court injunctions, and was confronted by police again and again. Despite all of this, the great sit-down at General Motors in 1936 and 1937 inspired more than a thousand others in the following months.[25]

Even more important in assessing the likelihood of a mass strike in America is the question of the conditions that might produce such actions. As argued above, this is not a matter of business-cycle ups and downs. The strikes of 1877 and 1886 occurred in years of growth, while those in 1919, 1934, and 1946 took place in recessions or years of slow growth and high unemployment. The conditions that produced these upheavals had more to do with direct assaults on working and living conditions—efforts to increase the rates of absolute and/or relative surplus value through longer hours, reduced wages, and/or work reorganization and intensification. While a full-scale analysis of unfolding conditions affecting the majority of working-class people in the United States and elsewhere is beyond the scope of this chapter, two observations seem appropriate.

First, the attack on working-class working and living conditions now under way across much of the world appears more intense and permanent due to today's deeper and more enduring capitalist crisis in comparison, for example, to that from 1975 to 1982. Indeed, the current crisis is already deeper and approaching the last one in length, with no sign of serious revival. It is now evident, as McNally (2011), Shaikh (2010), and Moody (2012) have argued, that capitalism's relative growth from 1982 to 2007 rested in large part on a substantial devaluation of labor in the United States, through declining or stagnating real wages on the one hand and rising productivity on the other. For any level of recovery or even stability to be achieved, a much greater devaluation is required, and there is plenty of evidence that this is what both employers and governments are attempting today. The financial crisis has added to these pressures. A working-class reaction is already visible from Europe to China and there is no reason to believe that the United States will remain forever insulated.[26]

Second, many of the changes in capitalist production and organization that have disoriented workers and their unions for so long, such as lean production methods, extensive outsourcing, work reorganization, etc., have now become "normal." That is, they are now experienced by millions of workers in industries as different as manufacturing, retail, public service, and health care, with equally damaging effects. Furthermore, as mentioned earlier, the fragmentation of production and work has become embedded in a network of tightly organized just-in-time production or commodity chains highly vulnerable to disruption. This could provide the window to a mass strike if one key group disrupts the chain in support of another.

Taking the "Next Step"

What, then, are socialists and union activists to do if simply calling, or calling on union leaders to call, a general strike is unlikely to work?[27] The first most obvious task is to educate on this question: analyze our own past experience and those of other countries today, in more detail than I can do here, so that US workers become aware of this powerful weapon. Simply repeating demands or resolutions for a general strike are not the best ways to educate. Any possible impact they have is diminished, as they most likely come repeatedly from one tiny faction in the union and are routinely defeated. Group and one-on-one discussions with fellow workers are more likely to have an impact. Articles, pamphlets, perhaps even books on the subject would help as well. Resources such as *Labor Notes* or Labourstart.com can play a role in popularizing the idea. But education only takes us so far.

Socialists and union activists need to think about what they could do should the opportunity arise. That is, how could we best be prepared? How can our unions, at least at the local level, be prepared to take that *next step* that often makes the difference? The fight for union democracy is crucial because it empowers the ranks and minimizes the ability of conservative leaders to dampen any action. Strong grassroots workplace organization makes such action possible. Mobilization strategies employed in "routine" contract or grievance strikes offer another means of preparation through involvement. Cross-union actions and mass demonstrations short of a strike, like those in Wisconsin, Ohio, and elsewhere, can also have aspects of a rehearsal. The building of networks through union reform caucuses, political organizations, active central labor councils such as Madison's, or the informal national and local networks formed over the years though the publications, conferences, and schools of Labor Notes can help to enable the spread of strikes under the right conditions. At key moments the use of social networks can also expand a strike wave.

In this regard, for the first time in a long time, a new generation of union militants appears to be taking shape. We can see these primarily through the growth of the Labor Notes conferences in the last few years. The positive response of many unions to the Occupy movement and the explosions in Wisconsin and Ohio are other indications of changes taking place within organized labor, even if these have not impacted the highest levels. While these developments cannot create the conditions for a general strike, they have the potential to make the most of such conditions and in that way, perhaps, affect the possibilities of the moment as well as laying the basis for the type of consciousness that makes a mass strike possible.

The idea of a general strike does come up from time to time in the context of existing struggles, particularly those that go beyond the routine. The 2011 upsurge in Wisconsin is, of course, one such case. Mass demonstrations and the occupation of the Capitol suggested such a course and, indeed, the South Central Federation of Labor, the Madison-based central labor council, put forth the idea for discussion. A general strike did not happen, perhaps because even the exhilarating experience of the mass demonstrations, the sense of solidarity in action, was in itself so new. An inkling of how it *might* have happened, however, came up in the Wisconsin workshop at the 2012 Labor Notes conference.

It wasn't a suggestion, much less a "demand," that someone call such a strike. Rather it was an almost passing comment by a Madison firefighter concerning the actions of his union. He described the role of the firefighters in the capitol occupation, which was done by shifts so that no one missed work. Noting the "sick-in" stay-away action taken by a large number of teachers, he speculated that perhaps the firefighters, and maybe others, should have followed their example. What he suggested was a seemingly modest action. But it was a potential *next step*—and had they done this, isn't it likely that others would have followed? Isn't it possible that a mass "sick-in" might have become a mass strike? The network needed to spread it further was there in the streets, the mass meetings, and the occupation. Retrospection is easier than bold action at the moment. Nevertheless, this speculation reminds us that as the attacks on the working class intensify and more groups of workers resist, it becomes more likely that moments of opportunity will arise as they did in 1919, 1934, 1946, and in 2011 in Wisconsin. It is in these moments that the movement *calls us* to take that next step.

Part II

The Future of Unions in the United States

7

Beating the Union: Union Avoidance in the United States, 1945 to the Present

Kim Moody

Introduction

For much of the history of American capitalism, its owners and managers have fought trade unions to a degree unknown among their European counterparts. The nineteenth century was rife with employer-promoted violence against unions and unionists, much of it successful in preventing and defeating the implantation of worker representation and collective bargaining in rapidly growing industry until the twentieth century. In the 1930s, in the wake of an enormous labor upsurge, unionism was imposed on the very commanding heights of industry. Even then, with rare exceptions, employer resistance among those not yet unionized was the norm until World War II.

A version of this essay was originally published in 2013 in Global Anti-Unionism: Nature, Dynamics, Trajectories and Outcomes, *edited by Gregor Gall and Tony Dundon (London: Palgrave).*

Most analyses would agree with this sketch up to the end of World War II, but looking back on the 1940s and 1950s from the vantage point of the 1970s and 1980s many historians, economists, and industrial-relations academics saw a changed landscape. Often described as a "social compact" or "labor-management accord," the immediate postwar era was seen as a period of relative industrial peace and the general acceptance or tolerance, if not the enthusiastic embrace, of unions and collective bargaining by America's corporate managers and leading capitalists. The rise of management resistance to unionism in the 1970s was seen as a change.

Since then, a number of academics have questioned this picture of relative tranquility and acceptance.[1] Looking back to the 1970s and beyond to the end of World War II, they have seen a pattern of rising resistance to unions by American management that contrasts with the practice of most other developed industrial nations of that period as well as with the notion of an era of "social compact." This chapter will argue that American capital has, in fact, never accepted unions or collective bargaining. The means of union avoidance have changed with circumstances, but the fundamental opposition to worker organization by American capital, with only the rarest of exceptions, has been and remains a constant in US industrial relations. Even by the conventional measure of employer resistance to union growth, the rise in Unfair Labor Practice (ULP) claims filed against management with the National Labor Relations Board, the great acceleration begins not in the 1970s but, as we shall see, in the late 1950s.

In that period, management conducted the traditional fight over the division of the surplus, not over the wage bill per se, which did rise in the postwar years, but over the productivity that underlay profitability and the "boom." In this fight, less visible in the "black box" of the workplace, the union appeared as a threat to management's prerogatives via the "effort bargain" or what Selig Perlman called "job control."[2] As one union avoidance consultant warned management in the 1970s, "Having a union in your shop is going to affect how you operate in many personal areas. It will affect your ability to control promotions, transfers, job assignments, trial periods, discipline, discharge, retirement, layoffs, and recalls."[3] *This* American management was never prepared to tolerate without a fight.

The source of this abiding antiunionism lies in the deeply held "unitarist" ideology of America's industrial and managerial elite and the historical circumstances of its origins. Writing in the 1950s, business historian Thomas Cochran summarized a view that was, he argued, as likely to be held by an American businessman in 1850 as in 1950: "Business, he might argue, had to have a system of ideas of its own, such as physical efficiency, substantial rewards for unusual ability, and clear lines of authority based on sanctions of ownership."[4] All three business "ideas" ran against the notion of sharing the control of production with labor in any form. The last, "clear lines of authority," however, is key. Jacoby notes, like Cochran, that individualism, opposition to state interference (as opposed to subsidy), and antiunionism are linked in the "doctrine of 'freedom to control'—the right of management to control every aspect of business."[5] That is, in today's terms, management's right to manage or management's prerogatives. Related to this is management's "special responsibility for efficiency,"[6] something with which unions presumably could interfere. If the rise of industrial unionism in the 1930s appeared as a challenge to these prerogatives, the decisions of wartime boards and courts firmly established these management "rights" as one of the foundations of American industrial relations, while the Supreme Court would repeat and expand their scope in the years following the war.[7] And, indeed, almost every US employer forced to recognize a union has, to this day, refused to sign a collective agreement that did not include a management's rights clause.

The strength of this ideology is rooted in the unique development of capitalism in the United States. As both Jacoby and Lichtenstein argue, unlike in Europe, where strong states preceded "big business," in the United States the giant business corporation, from railways to steel mills, preceded the development of a strong central state.[8] Although the states and, at times, the federal government provided funds for canals and railroads, the state played a minimal role in the development of the US economy until well into the twentieth century. As Vogel argues, "Throughout the period of industrialization the critical decisions about the direction of economic development were in private hands." As a result, he writes, "the true meaning of freedom for the American bourgeoisie is the ability of those who own or control economic resources to allocate them as they see fit—without interference from either labor unions or government officials."[9] Polls taken in the 1970s, as union avoidance was accelerating, he reports, revealed these ideas to be alive and well.[10] More recently, one of America's leading business publications, *Fortune*, observed that most US employers "greet the prospect of unionization with the enthusiasm that medieval Europeans reserved for an outbreak of the Black Death."[11] Hence, American capital's ideology forms a key part of the background to the analysis of this article.

The Law and Management's Impact on Union Organizing

The National Labor Relations Act of 1935 (NLRA), which governs the official procedures of union recognition for most private-sector workers, has been shaped and reshaped by management practices, rulings of its own National Labor Relations Board (NLRB), and an ongoing barrage of court decisions that almost from the beginning invariably favored employer over employee.[12] No attempt will be made here to trace the details of this history. Its well-known asymmetrical but legal features include, among other things, management's exclusive right, during a recognition election campaign, to address its employees at work (the "captive audience" meeting) on the grounds of "freedom of speech," while union representatives are barred from company property during the election process on the basis of common-law property rights.[13] Furthermore, early on, the NLRB was denied the right to prevent management misbehavior. The Supreme Court ruled in the 1938 *Consolidated Edison* case that the Board could not move to prevent subvention of the law and that its remedies were "remedial, not punitive."[14] Hence employers are free to bend or break the law and the union can only hope for a later ruling against management. Here, however, some more basic points need to be made.

Born in the midst of an enormous labor upheaval, the act was meant to take the strife out of the union recognition process. As the Act itself states, "It is the purpose of this chapter, in order to promote the full flow of commerce, to prescribe the legitimate rights of both employees and employers in their relations affecting commerce, to provide orderly and peaceful procedures" for union recognition.[15] The Act, however, is pointed directly at nonunion employers functioning in competitive markets. As Gall argues, such orderly and peaceful procedures tend to "signal a hostile and aggressive act against capital and for labor" despite the pacific intentions of the legislators who created them.[16] For a capitalist class predisposed to resist unionism on ideological as well as economic grounds, the interpretation of employee actions as hostile is even more likely.

What is more, recognition elections conducted under this law by the NLRB are necessarily firm by firm. Unlike in countries where capital has until recently accepted industry- or sector-level bargaining that neutralizes the competitive wage side effects by negotiating standard wages and hours, under the NLRA each firm must face the prospect of higher labor costs than its nonunion competitors in the same industry or market. It is not simply, as Freeman and Kleiner argue, that an employer will decide whether or not to resist unionization on the basis of a cost-benefit analysis of the relative costs of resistance versus the "prospective loss of profits, which itself depends on the union wage differential."[17] It is also the prospect of permanently losing market share due to the competitive advantage the nonunion firms have gained should the union win and impose the "differential"—and, of course, the less flexible workplace regime described above. Furthermore, the simple cost-benefit approach of individual firms can hardly explain the general rise in union avoidance that characterizes the whole postwar period.

Analytical Framework and Outline

This article will argue that employer resistance is explained on longstanding ideological grounds, reinforced by the institutional framework of the NLRA, encouraged by the rise in labor militancy (and, perhaps ironically, later its rapid decline) and affected by economic circumstances, particularly those flowing from problems of productivity and profitability. In this analysis, both sides of the conflict are seen as actors. There is in this ongoing conflict a certain rhythm in which each side reacts to the aggression or retreat of the other. In analyzing management behavior in NLRB elections, Unfair Labor Practice (ULP) claims filed by unions or individual workers under section 8a of the NLRA dealing with elections and postelection bargaining will serve as a proxy for management's use of both legal and illegal means of defeating the union. There is, of course, no direct measure of management behavior. The 8a ULPs are labor's main counter to management's willingness to stretch or surpass such legal limits as the NLRA imposes. Hence, the use of 8a ULPs has become standard in gauging management resistance and will be used here.

Early studies of union success or failure in NLRB representation elections concluded that, at best,there was "uncertainty concerning the effects of campaign tactics on the election process"[18] or that illegal antiunion tactics in a representation election had little effect on workers' decisions on whether or not to vote for the union.[19] Not surprisingly, these findings were soon challenged. Eames found that even Getman, Goldberg, and Herman's data showed that illegal tactics had some impact.[20] Dickens found that "both legal and illegal tactics can affect how workers vote."[21] More recent studies are even clearer on the impact of management tactics and that the more tactics, legal or not, management uses, the greater the impact on the election outcome. In a similar vein, as will be discussed later, the actions of workers and their unions are also seen as making a difference in outcomes.[22] So difficult has the NLRB process become that some scholars have concluded that "the organizing process is broken."[23] To view the course of employer opposition to unionization, we will look at both NLRB outcomes and the context in which management tactics change and accrue.

The article will look first at the acceleration of union-avoidance activity in the 1940s and then the 1950s, as problems of productivity arose, and labor's reaction to management pressures in the 1960s. It will be argued that this in turn led capital to organize more effectively and management to intensify opposition to unionization, measured by a general increase in 8a ULPs, in the 1970s. The 1980s saw a rapid decline in union members as well as a general retreat in collective bargaining outcomes. This trend would be reinforced in the "neoliberal" 1980s and 1990s by the growing presence of union-avoidance consultants. As a result, union win rates fell and the number of NLRB elections sought by unions declined. In the 1990s and 2000s, illustrating the rhythm of industrial conflict, some unions developed new forms of organizing and new tactics that led to an increase in union win rates. Union membership rose in some years. Although recession would wipe out most gains, the relative decline in the effectiveness of union-avoidance tactics and improvement in union strategies holds the potential for a reversal of fortune.

The Opening Gambit: Change the Rules

With the end of World War II the government restraints on capital's behavior were removed. The unions that had forced recognition in the 1930s and early 1940s, whose position had been protected by the priorities of war production, however, were still there. Indeed, their presence was asserted in the massive national strike wave of 1945 and 1946 that opened collective bargaining on a scale never before seen.[24] Additionally, in 1946 general strikes occurred in five American cities as managers fought to restrain union power locally.[25] In addition, recession and falling profit rates in 1948 and 1949 called for action to undermine the power of these still-militant unions.[26] Although the postwar boom lay ahead, it was by no means a given in the mid- to late 1940s. The intensity of class conflict and the specter of economic uncertainty sent business off in two directions in the immediate postwar period in the hopes of weakening existing unions and avoiding them where possible.

First, to take on the unions and reduce their ability to grow, American capital moved in 1946 to change the NLRA, which they held responsible for union growth. With the Republican victory in the congressional elections of 1946, business had the means to do so. The outcome was the passage of the Taft-Hartley Act in 1947, which severely limited union actions and gave employers new "rights."[27] Despite this setback for labor, union win rates in NLRB elections continued to be high, remaining above 70 percent for several years while union membership grew by two million members from 1945 to 1950.[28]

A second, more effective way of avoiding unions and, indeed, leaving them behind in many cases was simply to relocate production, and this capital did on a large scale beginning at the end of the war. Some companies simply moved out of heavily unionized cities. General Motors, for example, built twenty-five new plants in the suburbs outside of Detroit from 1947 to 1958, soon to be followed by fifty-five other Detroit-based firms.[29] Other corporations, such as General Electric, "decentralized" production across the country away from the unionized Northeast.[30] But the major strategy was to move to the low-wage, mostly nonunion South. From 1947 to 1963 value added in manufacturing grew by 94 percent for the nation as a whole, but 163 percent for the South.[31] This was union avoidance on a grand scale, one that was very difficult for unions to resist. Nevertheless, union membership continued to grow into the 1950s from 14.3 million in 1945 to 17.5 million in 1956.[32] Employer attention would now turn toward stopping union growth in the arena meant to encourage it: the NLRB election.

A New Antiunion Offensive

By the second half of the 1950s, capital ran into additional problems with labor productivity and costs. The rate of productivity increases slowed down from an annual average of 3.3 percent a year from 1951 to 1955 to 2.4 percent from 1956 to 1959, while unit labor cost increases rose from 2 percent a year in the first period to 3 percent in the second.[33] Partly as a result, profit rates fell from 1956 through 1958.[34] This brought on what Mike Davis has called the "Management Offensive of 1958–63."[35] This was an offensive over union power in the workplace. Its most visible symbols were "Boulwarism," or take-it-or-leave-it bargaining, at General Electric (GE) and the attempt by US Steel to eliminate the contract clause that gave workplace representatives the right to bargain over "custom and practice." Capital's new aggressiveness led, in turn, to long strikes at US Steel in 1959 and GE in 1960.[36] At the same time a new generation of managers entered industry unwilling to accept the union status quo and ready to challenge union power.[37]

Alongside accelerated warfare in the workplace came a leap in management opposition in NLRB representation elections as more companies attempted to avoid unions when and where they attempted to organize. Between 1956 and 1959, while the number of elections grew by 14 percent, the number of 8a ULPs filed against management rose by 135 percent, or 33 percent a year, the largest annual increase in ULPs ever. At the same time, management made greater use of the new tool it had acquired under Taft-Hartley, the 8b

ULP, filed by management against the union. These rose from 1,145 in 1955 to 3,973 in 1959, an increase of 250 percent, an astounding 50 percent a year. The number of 8a5 claims, protesting management's refusal to bargain "in good faith" once the union has won recognition, also rose significantly, by 56 percent or a little over 10 percent a year, indicating continued resistance even after the union won recognition.[38] Both the number and the ratio of ULPs to elections were well below those of the 1970s and later, but the rapid increase is unmistakable and larger than any that followed.

A sign that not all businesses were facing the economic problems mentioned above with equal severity or, perhaps, were not yet armed with new "young Turk" managers, was that consent elections, in which both sides agree to the election and ULPs are absent, were still relatively common, at about 27 percent of all elections.[39] On the other hand, the antiunion consultants and lawyers, whose presence would explode in the 1970s and 1980s, made their initial appearance in the 1940s and 1950s, being uncovered by the 1958 congressional investigations that produced the Landrum-Griffin Act of 1959.[40]

Conflict Heats Up

As might be expected, the workplace employers' offensive of the late 1950s and early 1960s brought on a backlash from the nation's organized workers as work intensification took its toll. Beginning as early as 1964, the number of strikes began to rise year after year from 3,655 in 1964 to 5,716 in 1970, while the number of strikers doubled.[41] This was the beginning of the labor upsurge that would last through the 1970s. It was spurred by management's push for productivity on the one hand and, somewhat later, by soaring inflation on the other.[42] Management's response to the early phase of this increase in militancy in addition to the rise in both 8a and 8b ULPs was a precipitous decline in consent election, from 31 percent of all elections in 1963 to 18 percent in 1969, and a steady increase in decertification elections from about 150 a year in the mid-1950s to 300 in 1970.[43] In terms of decertification efforts, Georgine quotes a former NLRB lawyer who reported in the late 1970s: "In 1963, when I worked for the NLRB, we got a decertification petition in our office. No one had ever heard of it. Last year there were 600 decertifications and this year there will be more than 1,000."[44] Technically, employers are prohibited from organizing decertification petition drives. But as with so much else in American labor law, managers have found ways to encourage this sort of activity among pro-employer workers. As industrial conflict intensified in these years, management's union-avoidance repertoire grew.

The level of industrial action continued to rise unevenly during the first half of the 1970s, reaching a peak of just over six thousand strikes and nearly three million strikers in 1974. Even after this, the level of strike activity would remain high until it virtually collapsed in 1980 and 1981.[45] Furthermore, productivity fell off after 1969, while the rate of inflation doubled during the 1970s.[46] The ending of the Bretton Woods monetary system and, more than anything, the recession of 1974–75 spelled the end of the postwar boom.[47] Profit rates dropped throughout the decade until the early 1980s.[48]

In response to mounting economic problems and high levels of labor militancy in the 1970s, "business refined its ability to act as a class," as one journalistic study argued.[49] The leader in this refinement was the Business Roundtable, founded in 1972. It was composed of the leaders of 125 of America's largest corporations and represented the commanding heights of industry. The Roundtable was activist in orientation and set its sights on curbing inflation by reducing union power. This it did in 1977 and 1978 by defeating labor law reform, the unions' major political objective of the decade, at a time when the Democrats controlled the White House and both houses of Congress. In 1978, Doug Fraser, head of the United Auto Workers, aptly commented that organized business had waged a "one-sided class war in this country" during these years.[50]

It was in the context of this intensification of class conflict and growing economic instability that all 8a ULPs filed per year grew by 113 percent from 1970s to 1979, while the number of 8b ULPs per year grew by two-thirds, decertifications nearly tripled, and "consent elections" all but disappeared. By the end of the decade, workers and their unions were filing nearly 30,000 8a ULPs a year even as the number of elections fell from their 1973 high of 9,660 elections to 8,249 in 1979. Not surprisingly, the union win rate in NLRB elections fell steadily, from 56 percent in 1970 to 45 percent in 1979.[51] Business's increasing fortunes in discouraging and defeating union organizing drives were aided by a growing legion of union-avoidance lawyers and consultants.

Enter the Consultants

Looking back on the 1970s, Robert Georgine, president of the Building and Construction Trades Department of the AFL-CIO, observed that "union-busting is a rapidly expanding and growing industry itself." He reported that "out of 6,000 organizing campaigns of 10 or more workers, two-thirds involve some form of outside antiunion expertise," estimating that more than a thousand union-avoidance firms were engaged in "preventing unionization efforts" taking in revenues of half a billion dollars.[52] A year after Georgine's report, union-avoidance practitioner Woodruff Imberman attempted to refute Georgine's arguments about the effectiveness of consultants such as himself, mistakenly attributing the report to former AFL-CIO president George Meany.[53] What is interesting about this piece is not Imberman's arguments, which are mundane and self-serving, but the list of corporations he produced in order to show how poorly they do in NLRB elections. The list of sixty-eight corporations using consultants, many of them members of the Business Roundtable, included numerous firms engaged in longstanding collective bargaining relationships, such as Chrysler, Firestone Tire & Rubber, General Tire & Rubber, International Harvester, Kroger, Martin Marietta, Michigan Bell Telephone, National Can, Swift & Co., Uniroyal, US Steel, and Western Electric, to mention a few.[54] Union-avoidance consultants were active in preventing the spread of unions within companies thought to have underwritten the era of "labor-management accord" as well as those who had never faced a union.

Consultant is really shorthand for the triad of antiunion lawyers, industrial psychologists, and consultants. Each has a somewhat different role, even if they share the same goal. The union-avoidance lawyer helps the employer navigate and circumvent the legal labyrinth that has evolved as ULPs proliferate, the NLRB changes political complexion, and the courts open new possibilities. They advise on what is legal and what is not, generally leaving it to management to decide which route to take. The psychologist administers employee attitude surveys and, more recently, the "union vulnerability audit" to determine the roots of employee dissatisfaction. These are often concerned with heading off a union drive in the first place.[55] The consultant, however, is the chief strategist and drill sergeant in the fight with the union. They advise managers to get tough fast, to break the rules (as the consequences are minimal), to make maximum use of "captive audience" meetings, to make sure they have a consistent policy that prevents anyone from entering company property, to file complaints in order to delay the elections, to fire union activists, etc. In this fight, the supervisor is the frontline solider and is expected to hold regular face-to-face meetings with employees.

Private-sector union membership reached its high point in 1970 at almost seventeen million members, but by 1979, just before the recession set in, these unions had already lost nearly nine hundred thousand members.[56] As with later losses of union jobs, this decline is due mostly to industrial shift, technology, and in some cases trade policies. But management resistance to new unionization, increasingly guided by consultants, was one factor in preventing unions from making up for those losses by organizing among the millions of nonunion workers throughout the economy. During this decade unions managed to win representation elections covering just over two million workers, 40 percent less than in the 1960s and half that in the 1950s.[57] Had the win rate not fallen by more than 10 percent they might have at least held the line.

The Neoliberal 1980s and 1990s

The recession of 1980 to 1982 accomplished what the employers and their consultants could only dream of. Between 1979 and 1983 the unions lost nearly three million members in private industry.[58] In the same years, the number of strikes dropped by almost half, and, more significantly for this article, the number of NLRB elections collapsed by more than half, never to recover.[59] Despite an economic recovery beginning in 1982, union fortunes would continue to plunge into the twenty-first century as new forces set in. In the late 1970s, the United States saw its first major trade deficits, a signal of unfolding globalization.[60] Beginning in 1978, deregulation, first in transport and later in telecommunications, undermined or destroyed what centralized or pattern bargaining there was in those industries, soon to be followed by steel, coal mining, and other industries not directly affected by deregulation. The neoliberal era had arrived and unions responded, with some exceptions, by accepting concessions in wages, benefits, and working conditions and virtually abandoning the strike weapon. The 1980s and 1990s would see union decline and wage compression sustain economic recovery, with the usual ups and downs, for more than two decades. In its wake would come a new management-led offensive in the workplace, this time with the new tools of "lean production," with its extensive outsourcing and work intensification, new technology, and human resource management, itself often a "union substitute" program.[61] As union after union granted concessions in wages and working conditions, capital became bolder in encouraging further union avoidance.

The 1980s brought the acceleration of relatively new means of union avoidance. Outsourcing and subcontracting were central features of the "lean production" norms that spread across industry in the 1980s. There is no way to quantify the results of outsourcing, but we do know that union density in industries where this occurred, notably the automobile industry, fell significantly. The auto-parts sector, receptor of much outsourcing, was 76 percent nonunion by the end of the 1980s.[62] In construction and freight haulage, companies under union contract set up nonunion subsidiaries, a practice known as "double-breasting." This practice began in the late 1970s in construction and by 1983, 44 percent of the fifty largest US construction contractors had "double-breasted" operations. Although construction employment grew in the 1980s, union membership declined.[63] In the 1980s "double-breasting" also became widespread in freight haulage.[64] One indication of its impact under the new terms of deregulation was that the number of workers covered by the National Master Freight Agreements with the Teamsters union fell from more than 277,000 in 1979 to 160,000 in 1985, according to one estimate.[65]

In the realm of NLRB representation elections, the 1980s and 1990s were the "golden age" of the antiunion consultant. One study of NLRB elections from 1975 to 1982 found that "management consultants" had been used in 20 percent of the elections surveyed.[66] By the late 1990s, according to a study of 421 NLRB elections, three-quarters of employers had hired consultants.[67] The number of NLRB elections continued to fall, with only slight ups and downs, by 21 percent, from 4,533 in 1983 to 3,743 in 1999. Consent elections dropped from 2.9 percent of the total in 1980 to less than 1 percent after 1990. The ratio of 8a ULPs to elections, which indicates intensified management opposition, grew with each decade and the union win rate remained stuck in the mid-40 percent range in these two decades.[68] Labor, with few exceptions, continued its retreat as the level of strike activity fell from the already reduced 1981 level of 2,568 to 411 by 1999.[69] Doug Fraser's "one-sided class war" was still being waged two decades after he named it.

A look at the number of workers covered in representation elections where the union won will give us an idea of the state of union organizing in this period. The figures for the number of workers covered by elections won by the unions are net of those lost in decertification (RD) elections. However, not all of these workers would necessarily become or remain union members in "right-to-work" states where the union shop was outlawed or where the union failed to win a first contract, which can account of 26 percent of those in winning elections.[70] Nevertheless, the numbers provide a good indication of union success or failure. The ratio of 8a ULPs to elections gives us an indication of changes in employer resistance, while the win rate tells us of its effectiveness in defeating union efforts.

As Table 1 shows, the number of workers covered in successful representation elections and the rate at which unions won those elections has declined from decade to decade, while the ratio of 8a ULPs to elections rose. In the 1950s more than four million workers won representation, whereas in the 1960s it was 2.8 million, a drop of 32 percent, even though the number of elections contested increased by 37 percent. Part of this is explained by the drop in win rate from an average of 68 percent in the 1950s to 59 percent in the 1960s. The 1960s also saw a nearly 50 percent increase in the ratio of 8a ULPs to elections. We take this acceleration to be a reaction to the rise in worker resistance measured by increased strike activity in those years. The fall in the number of workers who won representation in elections from 1960s to the 1970s was 36 percent, again despite a rise in the number of elections. The decline is again explained in part by the fall in the win rate to 50 percent in the 1970s, most likely caused by another significant leap in the ratio of 8a ULPs to elections, which rose by 71 percent. By far the biggest drop in the number of workers covered in union-won elections was from the 1970s to the 1980s at 46 percent. This was due to a drop in the number of elections of nearly 40 percent and a further decrease in the win rate to 44 percent. This decade also saw the ratio of 8a ULPs to elections more than double, a sure sign of increased employer resistance.[71]

It seems reasonable to conclude that at least some of the drop in the success rate from 59 percent in the 1960s to 44 percent in the 1980s was due to the increasingly sophisticated employer resistance, enabled by the rising use of antiunion consultants and lawyers in those years. It is also possible that the fall in the number of elections was in part due to this, as unions saw their rate of success dwindle even as their resources became scarcer.

Table 7.1 Number of Workers in Won NLRB Representation Elections, Ratio of 8a ULPs to Elections, and Union Win Rates, 1950s–2000s[72]

Decade	Elections	Ratio of 8a ULPs to Elections	Percent Win Rate	Number of Workers
1950s	53,604	.9	68	4,159,028
1960s	73,419	1.4	59	2,818,255
1970s	87,218	2.4	50	2,076,164
1980s	53,074	5.0	44	1,122,135
1990s	38,127	6.4	45	934,085
2000s	25,395	7.4	55.4	908,755

Beginning in the 1980s, as globalization and free trade became centerpieces of US policy, employers once again expanded their repertoire of antiunion tactics. No doubt urged on by consultants, management increased the use of plant closing and relocation threats when confronted with a union organizing drive. Technically, such threats are illegal, but "predictions" of harm to the business that might lead to closings or relocations are not. Whether the threat is explicit or implied, proof is difficult to produce and the punishment for making threats minimal, as with most breaches of the NLRA. In the 1975–82 survey of employer tactics cited above, this threat was not even mentioned.[73] In the late 1980s, such threats were made in 29 percent of NLRB representation elections. By the mid-1990s, after the passage of the North American Free Trade Agreement, which made such threats even more credible, threats of partial or complete closing or relocation rose to 50 percent of all elections. A survey conducted between 1999 and 2003 showed that such threats occurred in 57 percent of recognition elections.[74]

From 1983, after the recession, to 1999, the unions lost another 2.5 million members in the private sector, a drop of 21 percent. Most of this, however, occurred from 1983 to 1989, with the decline slowing in the 1990s. The rate of decline in both decades had far more to do with the impact of globalization, technology, and industrial shift than with employer tactics in NLRB elections. Nevertheless, the ability of employers to slow down the rate at which unions grew through organizing, as seen in the figures in Table 7.1, was significant.

Unions on the Learning Curve?
If employers, advised by consultants, had expanded the variety of tactics used to defeat union organizing efforts, many unions had by the 1990s begun to respond by increasing theirs as well. The debate about the future of union organizing began in the 1980s around the duality of the traditional "servicing model" of unionism and a proposed "organizing model" in which resources would be shifted from older servicing functions such as grievance handling to carefully planned organizing efforts.[75] The organizing shot heard 'round the US labor movement, however, was the Service Employees International Union's (SEIU) 1990 "Justice for Janitors" victory in Los Angeles. This was a preplanned campaign with a worked-out strategy for organizing immigrant building cleaners employed by contract agencies. It employed a variety of tactics, including worker mobilization and community support, with an eye to organizing the entire relevant labor market.[76] Probably more than any

event, this put new organizing on the agenda. The election of SEIU president John Sweeney as president of the AFL-CIO in 1995 further promised a new era of aggressive organizing. The actual results would prove disappointing and even lead to a split in the US labor movement in 2005.[77] But some unions did pursue new organizing strategies and membership did grow in a number of years.

One new approach was simply to avoid the NLRB procedures altogether and, it was hoped, the reach of the consultants. Beginning in the late 1980s, several unions turned to winning agreements from employers to remain "neutral" during the organizing campaign and to use a simple and quick card-check procedure whereby the employer would recognize the union if a majority of workers signed cards. This voluntary approach had long been considered legal under the NLRA but had not been widely used. "Neutrality" agreements and "card-check" procedures became the preferred organizing method of several unions, including the SEIU, UNITE, HERE, CWA, UAW, UFCW, and the Teamsters, by the late 1990s.[78] Until 2005, the Federal Mediation and Conciliation Service (FMCS) published figures on the number of successful "voluntary" recognition campaigns, most of which would involve neutrality agreements, card-check procedures, or voluntary elections. Adjusted for win rates of 70 percent in these types of campaigns, these show an increase of 324 in 1988 or 9 percent of all union recognition efforts to 600 in 2001 or 18 percent of all campaigns, thereafter falling off to 369 or 12 percent in 2004.[79]

While neutrality agreements and card-check procedures tended to bring in larger bargaining units and more members than NLRB elections, they have not completely replaced the latter or become the common approach of most unions. One problem was that winning neutrality in the first place has proved very difficult outside of companies where the union has a prior bargaining relationship. Many of these campaigns stretch out as long as any NLRB election and absorb huge resources.[80] One commentator on these types of campaigns, writing of the SEIU's general growth, argues that it took the SEIU ten years and a billion dollars to win a net gain of six hundred thousand members. "To reach the same goal in health care, it would take upwards of thirty years, at a cost of three billion," she concluded.[81]

A broader approach that could be applied to both neutrality/card check and NLRB campaigns involves more mobilization and creative tactics in order to defeat or neutralize management resistance. Pioneering research by Bronfenbrenner and associates in the 1980s and 1990s found that the use of more "rank-and-file intensive" tactics was "associated with win rates 10 to 30 percentage points higher than win rates in campaigns that did not use these tactics."[82] Her research concluded that in NLRB elections "union tactics as a group play a greater role in explaining election outcomes than any other variables, including employer characteristics and tactics."[83] In the 1980s, however, only 3 percent of unions employed comprehensive campaigns using five or more rank-and-file intensive tactics. By the mid-1990s this figure had increased to 15 percent—still, however, a minority of unions.[84] If the idea that union tactics account for more than management tactics is truly astounding, the failure of more unions to take up this approach is even more so.

In the 2000s, the number of NLRB elections declined year after year, falling from 3,467 in 2000 to 1,619 in 2009. For its part, however, management did not let up its opposition. Although the number of 8a ULPs decreased along with the number of elections, the ratio of 8a ULPs to elections continued to rise, from 6.3 to 9.7 over those years, another indication of continued management hostility. Nevertheless, the union win rate rose steadily from 50 percent to 64 percent from 2000 to 2009, averaging over 55 percent for the decade, or 10 percentage points above the 1990s.[85] Management's enlarged arsenal was losing some of its impact. This increase can be partly attributed to the organizers' familiarity with consultant tactics and improved ability to inoculate members to them, the new rank-and-file intensive tactics, and, perhaps, to more union resources focused on fewer elections.

That the new union tactics were having some impact was seen in 2007 when union membership made a net gain of 311,000, 133,000 in the private sector. In 2008 membership grew by 428,000, 151,000 in the private sector.[86] However, the recession that began in 2008 rapidly undid these gains as unions saw a net loss of 834,000 in the private sector in 2009, followed by another drop of 339,000 private sector union members in 2010. In 2011 private-sector membership crept up by 110,000.[87] It was a roller-coaster ride with more descents than ascents. The new union tactics paid off, but not enough to overcome the impact of recession. With the failure of the Employee Fair Choice Act, by 2010, the chances of improving the NLRB procedures by making card check the legal standard evaporated. In April 2012, however, the Obama NLRB implemented new election rules that will reduce delays, a change that will make it slightly harder for consultants to employ all their tactics, though it remains to be seen just how effective the new rules will be.[88] It would seem that even bolder tactics by more unions are called for if unions are to grow fast enough to increase union density and power.

Conclusion

Following Kelly (1998) and Silver (2003), I have argued elsewhere that large-scale union growth comes in waves associated with a general increase in industrial conflict, union militancy, and new forms of organization.[89] This has clearly not been the case in the United States as yet. Labor upsurges, however, are neither automatic nor predictable. They are, like retreat or defeat, a product of the interaction of the agents in industrial conflict. If the efforts of business to defeat unions in NLRB elections seem to be losing steam, perhaps the improved tactics of labor, whether within or outside the NLRB procedures, will lead to a new confidence among the 53 percent of US employees who say they would vote for a union if they had the chance.[90] If that were matched by increased efforts by more unions employing new approaches, perhaps there could be a reversal of fortune.

8 Union Organizing in the United States: Why It Isn't Working and How It Might

Kim Moody

A 2005 survey by Peter D. Hart Research Associates showed that 53 percent of nonmanagerial employees in the United States would or probably would vote for union representation at their workplace.[1] This figure was up from 39 percent in 1996 and 30 percent in 1984.[2] Clearly support for unions has risen in the United States over the past two decades. As Robinson argues, the pressures of a quarter-century of "economic restructuring driven by neoliberal economic ideology" have moved more workers to view unions positively.[3] Yet union membership and density declined over these years, leaving more and more workers without union protection. This decline is most dramatic in the private sector, where losses account for almost twice the net decline since 1970. What is to explain this "representation gap"?

A version of this essay was originally published in The Future of Union Organising, *edited by Gregor Gall (London: Palgrave, 2009).*

Despite much rhetoric about accelerated organizing, new approaches such as "neutrality" and card-check agreements, and large amounts of money shifted from "servicing" to organizing, the results have been too meager to reverse the downward trend. Using academic, union, and government sources, this chapter will examine the course of this decline, the shift in organizing efforts from state-sponsored elections under the National Labor Relations Board to voluntary "neutrality" and card-check agreements, the extent and effectiveness of these new approaches, and the internal barriers to more rapid growth embedded in the American business-union model. The focus will be on the private sector, both because this is the location of the decline and because it is the heart of the US economy and, hence, the key potential source of labor's renewed power. It will conclude with a look at some of the alternatives, some of which are already practiced by some unions.

The Contours of Union Decline

Between 1970 and 2007, US unions lost just over five million members, while the proportion of union members in the workforce dropped from 27.3 percent to just 12.1 percent. In the private sector, however, the plunge was far greater: from 16.9 million members in 1970 to 8.1 million in 2007, a loss of more than 50 percent. Union density slumped from 29 percent in the private sector to 7.5 percent over those years.[4] Total US union membership continued to grow until 1980, reaching a high point of more than 20 million in that year. As Table 8.1 shows, however, union membership in the private sector began its descent after 1970. Between 1970 and 2006, when private-sector membership hit its lowest point so far, 8,997,000 union members disappeared. Not often noted is the fact that the biggest single slump in members came in the three years between 1980 and 1983, when 3.3 million members were lost. Another 1.4 million union members disappeared from 1983 to 1989, bringing the total loss for that decade to 4.7 million, over half of the private-sector loss to 2007.

Table 8.1 Private-Sector Union Membership[5]

Year	Membership	Decline/Increase	Density
1970	16,978,000		29.1%
1980	15,264,000	-1,714,000	20.6%
1983	11,933,600	-3,330,400	16.8%
1989	10,520,000	-1,413,600	12.4%
1991	9,909,000	-611,000	11.9%
1995	9,432,000	-477,000	10.4%
1996	9,415,000	-17,000	10.4%
1997	9,363,000	-52,000	9.7%
1998	9,306,000	-57,000	9.5%
1999	9,419,000	+113,000	9.4%
2000	9,148,000	-271,000	9.1%
2001	9,141,000	-7,000	9.0%
2002	8,652,000	-489,000	8.6%
2003	8,452,000	-200,000	8.2%
2004	8,205,000	-247,000	7.8%
2005	8,255,000	+50,000	7.9%
2006	7,981,000	-274,000	7.4%
2007	8,114,000	+133,000	7.5%

The fall in manufacturing that accounts for much of the drop in the number of private-sector union members came after 1980 but does not fully explain the loss of members. From 1980 to 1992, 1.9 million production jobs in manufacturing disappeared, 80 percent of them concentrated in three industries: primary metals, textiles, and garment.[6] But the number of union members lost in manufacturing in those years was over three million.[7] Shrinking membership in industries with growing employment can be partly explained by a geographical restructuring of several industries, notably automobiles, meatpacking, trucking, and construction. In these cases it was the unions' inability to follow the work to new sites, often in the South, that led to declining membership.[8] The rising opposition of employers to new unionization also explains some of the difficulty of organizing. Using back-pay awards due to Unfair Labor Practice claims with the NLRB as a proxy measure of employer resistance, Meyer and Cooke noted a dramatic rise in their incidence in the 1970s.[9] Similarly, they showed a four-fold increase in decertification elections.

While these external explanations for decline are relevant, Bronfenbrenner argues that "unions in the USA cannot simply blame external factors for their failure to organize. They themselves must take a significant share of the blame. In the 1950s and 1960s, when unions had the resources and power to launch massive organizing campaigns, taking on entire industries, they failed to do so."[10] It is certainly true that organized labor in the United States did not undertake any "massive organizing campaigns" following World War II, but beginning in the late 1950s and into the 1970s the number of certification elections rose significantly. It reached its peak in 1973 at 8,526, but remained well above seven thousand elections a year until 1980.[11] Then in a period of three years, from 1980 through 1983, the number of elections fell by more than half to 3,241, never to recover to earlier levels.[12] Suddenly, in the early 1980s, most unions all but abandoned new organizing.

By the 1990s, labor's decline and crisis could no longer be ignored. This gave rise to the 1995 campaign of John Sweeney for president of the AFL-CIO on the promise to make organizing a priority, urging affiliated unions to "organize at a pace and scale that is unprecedented."[13] As Fiorito and Jarely, Hurd, and others have argued, organizing decisions lie with the affiliated unions and not the federation, and the overall record of both organizing efforts and growth remained poor for all but a handful of unions.[14] Hurd showed that despite much talk and some effort by a few unions, private-sector union density continued its downward trend from 1995 through 2002, falling by 16.5 percent.[15] So too did density in all but one of the industries considered a major private-sector organizing target, hospitals. Similarly, in closely related occupational groups, only nurses and nurses' aides showed increases. Other well-known targets of active organizing, such as janitors, carpenters, and construction laborers, continued to show declining density from 1998 through 2003.

The Rise of Card Check and Neutrality Agreements

The number of NLRB representation elections held from 1999 to 2006 fell by 43 percent as unions downplayed this traditional approach to new organizing.[16] Not surprisingly, the number of workers organized through this method dropped steadily, from just over 100,000 in 1999 and 2000 to 67,468 in 2006. Beginning in the mid-1990s, in an effort to bypass the NLRB, several unions turned increasingly to non-NLRB methods of gaining recognition.[17] Most common are neutrality agreements and card-check recognition procedures. These are essentially voluntary forms of recognition upheld by the NLRB and by the Supreme Court since 1981.[18] Hurd breaks them down into two broad categories: those resulting from collective bargaining with a company the union already has an established bargaining relationship with, and those that stand alone.[19] The approach of extending recognition to nonunion units of already-unionized companies is sometimes called "bargaining to organize." Benz describes it as "the leveraging of existing contractual relations with a company in order to make it easier to organize other workers in the company, its joint ventures, or its suppliers."[20] Examples of this kind include the CWA's neutrality agreement with Southwestern Bell's Cingular Wireless, now part of AT&T, which brought it forty thousand new members between 1997 and 2007; UNITE-HERE's agreements with the Hilton and Starwood hotel chains, which netted six thousand members from 2004 to 2006[21]; and the UAW's eleven agreements with major auto-parts suppliers, which brought it twenty thousand new members between 2002 and 2006.[22] In a similar vein are voluntary agreements reached with employers in markets where the union has significant density or a pattern agreement.[23] The second, or stand-alone, type involves convincing or forcing an employer with whom there is no previous bargaining relationship to sign such an agreement. Most of these procedures include a neutrality agreement in which the employer agrees not to openly attack the union or use the extreme tactics associated with NLRB elections as well as a procedure to grant recognition upon verification of cards signed by a majority of the workforce.

It is, however, not only the employer who agrees to mute criticism of the union in most neutrality agreements. Three-quarters of the voluntary agreements studied by Eaton and Kriesky "set limits on the union's behavior." "Most commonly," they wrote, "the union agreed not to attack management."[24] Yet it is precisely "us versus them" and the "industrial conflict" that build the sense of solidarity required to build a strong union and display the power needed to win a first contract.[25] Furthermore, there is always a temptation to seek voluntary recognition by giving the employers much of what they want: low wages, bargain benefits, labor peace, etc. For example, a sort of quid pro quo that borders on a sweetheart deal has been criticized in the SEIU's deals with a California nursing-home chain. Hurd, who uses that example, goes further, stating, "There is no denying that most neutrality agreements are achieved through top-down methods; the bargaining, corporate campaigns, and political initiatives associated with neutrality are typically controlled by national union leaders and staff."[26] This does not mean that the various mobilization and "leverage" tactics that have become more widely used in recent years are not deployed. It does mean they are typically at the initiative and under the control of full-time organizers and high-level officials.

Bold claims are frequently made about the increased use of voluntary agreements. A widely cited figure from the AFL-CIO is that, between 1998 and 2003, 80 percent of the nearly three million workers organized by AFL-CIO affiliates were recruited outside the NLRB procedures.[27] This figure, however, includes public-sector workers who are outside the NLRB framework and for whom we have no figures. Similarly, it would include the four hundred thousand or so newly unionized home health and child care workers who are outside the NLRB's jurisdiction because they are either public employees or considered domestic workers. Another claim from the AFL-CIO is that in 2005 its affiliates recruited 150,000 private-sector workers outside the NLRB procedures.[28] In that year, AFL-CIO unions recruited some 70,000 workers through the NLRB for a total of 220,000 new private-sector members.[29] Clearly the non-NLRB approach was more effective. In terms of the number of elections, Martin found in his sample of seventy local unions that between 1990 and 2001 NLRB elections composed almost 90 percent of organizing drives, but 42 percent of the new members came from the non-NLRB campaigns.[30]

To get an overview of the frequency of voluntary recognition agreements and campaigns, I have used the Federal Mediation and Conciliation Service's figure for private-sector voluntary recognition, comparing them to the NLRB and National Mediation Board elections, the latter covering rail and airline employees under the Railway Labor Act. The FMCS requires unions that achieve recognition by whatever means to file an F-7 form in preparation for first contract negotiations. The recognition agreements reported to the FMCS would only be those that succeeded, so I have adjusted these numbers up to match the nearly 70 percent success rate in such voluntary agreements found by Eaton and Kriesky.[31] The results for the late 1990s are similar to those found by Martin.[32] Unfortunately, this breakdown of voluntary private-sector F-7 referrals was discontinued after 2004.

Table 8.2 Organizing Efforts by Type[33]

Type	1998	1999	2000	2001	2002	2003	2004
NLRB	3,339	3,162	2,983	2,694	2,604	2,797	2,565
FMCS/Voluntary*	227	260	381	420	273	240	258
FMCS adjusted	324	371	544	600	390	343	369
NMB/RLA	91	72	74	73	70	55	63
Total Efforts	3,754	3,605	3,601	3,367	3,064	3,195	2,997
Voluntary % total	9%	10%	15%	18%	13%	11%	12%

* Includes voluntary recognition under neutrality, card check, voluntary election, or some combination.

What Table 8.2 shows is that the frequency of voluntary recognition efforts doubled from 1998 to 2001, but slacked off thereafter. As a proportion of all organizing efforts in those years, voluntary recognition efforts never surpassed 18 percent and, for the years 2000 to 2004, averaged about 14 percent a year. Three things seem clear from these figures in terms of organizing efforts. First, NLRB elections remain the favored approach to organizing by far. In fact, with the exception of UNITE-HERE, even the unions that claim to bypass NLRB elections in favor of voluntary procedures still use the NLRB more frequently. The Teamsters claim to seek neutrality agreements in their national campaigns,[34] while the SEIU says it "infrequently uses legal mechanisms provided by the federal government," i.e., the NLRB.[35] Yet these two unions were the top two users of NLRB elections from 1999 through 2007, when these two Change to Win (CTW) unions accounted for more NLRB elections than all AFL-CIO unions.[36]

Second, the addition of voluntary recognition to the organizing repertoire has not been enough to replace the decline in NLRB elections. In other words, the declining use of NLRB elections is not simply the result of a switch to voluntary procedures. Furthermore, only a small number of unions use these with any frequency. A survey of the *Daily Labor Report* from 1997 through 2004 by Brudney revealed five unions as regularly pursuing voluntary recognition.[37] These were HERE with forty-six citations, CWA with twenty-five, the UAW twenty-one, SEIU fifteen, and the Steelworkers (USW) eleven. Bronfenbrenner and Hickey produced a list of the most frequent users of the NLRB procedure, which included the Teamsters, SEIU, USW, UAW, and UFCW.[38] Here again, with these unions the number of NLRB elections outstrips that of voluntary agreements significantly.

Third, the frequency of voluntary agreements is not great enough so far to produce the sort of gains that can sustain significant growth despite a high win rate, estimated at 67.7 percent by Eaton and Kriesky and 83 percent in Martin's sample.[39]

There are no figures for the number of workers recruited in this way, but Martin found that the average in his sample was 357 new members for voluntary procedures compared to only 83 for NLRB elections, more than four times as many.[40] This indicates the more general finding that voluntary efforts are almost always directed at larger targets. The question has to be asked: if voluntary procedures are so much more efficient a way to bring in new members, why don't more unions use them more often?

Why So Few Voluntary Recognition Agreements?

The problem with voluntary recognition agreements, outside of those negotiated with companies that already have an extensive bargaining relationship with the union, is simply that employers in the United States are intensely antiunion. Most see no advantage in accepting a union in their firm and, given the continued union premium in wages and benefits of about 28 percent for both, many disadvantages.[41] Those confronted with a union organizing campaign will deploy a broad repertoire of union-avoidance tactics. The SEIU estimates that 80 percent of employers hire union-busting consultants in NLRB elections, 91 percent engage in captive-audience meetings, and 31 percent illegally fire union supporters during a campaign.[42] As shown in the successful but long and hard-fought SEIU campaign for voluntary recognition and a first contract among five thousand building-service workers in Houston, Texas, such campaigns can drag out as long as any NLRB election. In Houston it took many months of mobilization, community support, and a ten-day strike to gain recognition, and then another year and a strike to win a contract.[43] Even where a prior bargaining relationship exists, it is not always a simple matter of gaining employer agreement. As Benz points out, the CWA's pioneering 1997 neutrality/card-check agreement with SBC "was the result of a long, hard won struggle."[44] She injects a tone of reality into the oft-cited ease of card-check procedures when she writes that "to evaluate the usefulness of the bargaining-to-organize strategy, we have to look at the process it takes to get *to* neutrality or card check agreements as well as the results from such agreements."

Employer resistance in voluntary recognition campaigns, as well as in NLRB elections, prolongs and raises the costs of such efforts. Bronfenbrenner and Hickey noted that "the utilization of a comprehensive union building campaign incorporating most, if not all, of the elements of our model has been critical to the success of many of the most significant non-Board victories."[45] In other words, voluntary recognition campaigns often require the same extensive effort as NLRB elections when we look at the entire process. Fine reminds us that it took SEIU ten years to organize nine hundred thousand workers for a net gain of six hundred thousand at a cost of one billion dollars. She notes that, at this pace, "to reach the same goal in health care, it would take upwards of thirty years, at a cost of three billion."[46] Thus, even such a fast-growing union as the SEIU, using many of the latest tactics including neutrality and card-check agreements, is unlikely to reach the sort of density goals it has set, even with above-average effort, using the current methods. Rendering things even more difficult, in September 2007 the NLRB delivered a blow to voluntary recognition when it ruled in *Dana/Metaldyne* that the "recognition bar" that prevented antiunion employees or employers from petitioning for decertification for a reasonable amount of time would no longer apply to card-check recognition.[47] This meant that 30 percent of the workforce could now petition for decertification soon after the employer had granted voluntary recognition. In the first test of this ruling, a CWA local in New Hampshire had to postpone negotiations for a first contract during the forty-five-day period granted by the NLRB for a decertification challenge and only became recognized in January 2008.[48] In April 2008, another CWA local in New York State won an NLRB election after its card-check recognition was challenged.[49] Prior to the *Dana/Metaldyne* decision, the UAW had won NLRB elections in three auto-parts suppliers in the South when a challenge to its card-check procedure by the antiunion National Right to Work Committee led to NLRB-ordered elections.[50] It appears unions can overcome this new barrier, but it is also clear it can add time and expense to voluntary organizing efforts, reducing the differential between these campaigns and NLRB elections somewhat.

A Closer Look at Progress

Table 8.3 shows the changes in union density in most of the major targeted industries and occupations from 2002 through 2007. Like Hurd's earlier assessment of the gains in density by those unions with the most aggressive organizing programs, these more recent figures show little progress outside of three industries—and there only modest gains.[51] The gains in health care may be the result of several unions' efforts in those industries and occupations. These unions include not only the SEIU, which is the dominant union in health care, but the California Nurses' Association/National Nurses' Organizing Committee and the USW, CWA, AFT, and UAW, among others. The same has to be said for the three occupational groups that showed increases in density: registered nurses, home health care aides, and security guards. All three are SEIU targets, but are also sought by other unions. The largest gains were in meat-packing, where the UFCW is the major player. After losing thousands of members during the restructuring of this industry in the 1970s and 1980s, the fortunes of the UFCW began to change in 2000 when it organized a number of plants in Omaha, Nebraska, with the help of a community organization and an immigrant workforce that was already organizing itself, a phenomenon noticed in this and several other industries.[52] According to Hirsch and MacPherson's figures, the industry has gained about eighteen thousand union members between 2003 and 2007, while the industry's workforce remained basically stable.[53]

Table 8.3 Union Density (%) by Industry and Occupation, 2003–2007[54]

Union	Industry	2003	2004	2005	2006	2007
SEIU	Hospitals	14.1	14.0	13.7	13.6	15.3
SEIU	Nursing care	9.4	8.7	8.4	8.4	9.1
SEIU	Home health care	7.6	10.0	9.8	7.9	10.2
SEIU	Building service	5.6	4.9	6.3	5.5	5.1
IBT	Trucking	12.2	11.0	10.9	12.0	10.6
UFCW	Grocery stores	24.0	21.8	18.2	19.1	18.9
UFCW	Meatpacking	16.1	16.6	18.8	18.8	20.1
CWA	Telecom (wired)	23.3	22.3	22.8	23.3	23.6
CWA	Telecom (other)	11.3	23.2	18.1	14.1	7.8
Union	**Occupation**	**2003**	**2004**	**2005**	**2006**	**2007**
SEIU	Reg'd nurse	16.9	16.7	16.6	16.7	17.4
SEIU	Nurse's aide	13.9	12.9	12.2	13.4	13.1
SEIU	Security guard	10.2	12.1	12.7	10.4	11.9
SEIU	Home care aide	8.2	9.6	11.4	8.9	9.1
UBCJA	Carpenter	17.4	15.2	13.4	13.2	15.6
LIUNA	Const. laborer	16.0	11.7	11.0	11.1	11.9
SEIU	Nurse's aide	13.9	12.9	12.2	13.4	13.1

Who Is Growing?

Despite this lack of progress in density, nineteen out of some fifty-six unions saw net gains in membership from 2000 through 2007. Table 8.3 looks at the membership of these unions based on their LM-2 reports to the Department of Labor. What is surprising is that a number of those unions usually designated as "organizing unions" are missing. The CWA, UAW, LIUNA, UFCW, and UNITE-HERE all failed to show net growth. Some of those that did make this list must be disqualified because their growth in this period was more than accounted for by mergers with or affiliations by other unions. The USW gained 291,000 members through two mergers in this period, while the IBT gained 125,000 with three mergers. The growth of the NEA must be modified, as it gained about four hundred thousand members in 2006 through the affiliation of the AFT-affiliated New York State United Teachers, now a joint affiliate of NEA and

AFT.[55] Its real gain would have been 237,612, or a jump of 9.4 percent.

Table 8.4 Unions with Net Gains, 2000–2007[56]

Union	2000	2007	Net Gain
SEIU	1,374,300	1,691,973	317,673 (23.1%)
IBT	1,402,000	1,423,038	21,038 (1.5%)
USW	612,157	722,545	110,388 (18.0%)
IFPTE	43,571	61,767	18,196 (41.8%)
CNA/NNOC	61,000	80,000	19,000 (31.1%)
ALPA	49,224	61,235	12,011 (24.4%)
IUOE	379,309	403,927	24,618 (6.5%)
OPCM	40,339	43,671	3,332 (8.3%)
PPF	307,454	332,205	24,751 (8.1%)
IATSE	100,000	108,386	8,386 (8.4%)
UWU	42,065	50,000	7,935 (18.9)
AFSCME	1,300,000	1,433,688	133,688 (10.3%)
AFT	706,973	832,058	125,085 (17.7%)
IAFF	241,933	283,932	41,999 (17.4%)
AFGE	197,096	235,678	38,582 (19.6%)
NATCA	13,682	14,648	966 (7.1%)
TWU	109,000	115,145	6,145 (5.6%)
ATU	170,466	183,781	13,315 (7.8%)
NEA	2,530,000	3,167,612	637,612 (25.2%)

Nine of the seventeen unions that grew other than by mergers were in the public sector: IAFF (firefighters), AFT, AFGE, ATU, TWU, AFSCME, NEA, and NATCA (air-traffic controllers). Most of those eight primarily private-sector unions with net gains seemed to defy the conventional wisdom that size and resources are what counts in the growth game. The fastest-growing union in the United States was not the SEIU, as it routinely claims, but the International Federation of Professional and Technical Engineers (IFPTE), which grew by 42 percent from 2000 to 2007. Other unions with high growth rates are also occupationally based—the three construction unions, Operating Engineers, Plasterers, and Plumbers, and the other professionally based unions such as the CAN/NNOC, IATSE (stagehands), and the Airline Pilots. Most of these growing occupational unions are quite small and even large percentage gains cannot turn labor's fortunes around. Clearly, something more and different is needed.

Business-Union Barriers to Growth

American business unionism has long been characterized by rigid hierarchical structures that mute debate and limit membership involvement, an ideology that denies a fundamental conflict between capital and labor, and an almost exclusive dependence on long-term, formal collective bargaining relationships. The original debate over the "servicing model" versus the "organizing model" (internal participation at the local level) in the 1980s and early 1990s attempted to address some of the problems that flowed from this form of unionism. With its emphasis on member participation, the original organizing model aimed to replace the dependence on top-down servicing with workplace self-organization and activity. By the late 1990s, however, the debate was transformed into the later duality of servicing the membership versus external organizing.[57] In this phase of the debate, the "organizing model" became, as Fletcher and Gapasin describe it, "focused on retooling existing unions to make them more effective *organizing machines*."[58] This later version of the "organizing model," they argue, "holds that organizing workers into unions is, in and of itself, a progressive, if not revolutionary, action." In this view, "one chooses to ignore the character of the union or unionism and proceeds with the conviction that things will work out in the end." This debate was well within the parameters of American business unionism.

Business unionism perpetuates a bureaucratic form of organization that both insulates leaders and breeds passivity among members. The "servicing model," which places power in the hands of officials and professionals, fosters the notion of the union as something other than the workforce it represents, while the new "organizing model" bypasses the current members. As De Turberville concludes, however, "the two models are not opposites."[59] Bureaucratic business unionism has always practiced both. The ultimate "organizing model" union, the SEIU, continues to provide services from above, recently carrying this practice one remove further from the membership by initiating a grievance servicing call center.[60] Now, however, the emphasis, deployment of resources, and tactical repertoire has changed significantly for some unions.

There are certain practices in the US business-union model that have arisen since the 1930s that were encouraged, though not required, by the legal framework of the National Labor Relations Act as it has been interpreted by most of the labor leadership. As a result, they are deeply engrained in both the mentality of most leaders and the daily practice of most unions in the United States. The broadest of these have been the structural and political limitations on union democracy and the participation of members in union affairs beyond the workplace or local union. Some unions (CWA, USW, UNITE-HERE, SEIU) have made various efforts in recent years to overcome the impact of this through mobilization tactics, while seldom addressing the structural problem. Hence, there is a tendency for mobilizations and member involvement in new organizing or contract campaigns to be tightly controlled by the officialdom. Lustig suggests that "increased activism and recruitment turn out to bear no necessary connection to decentralizing initiative, promoting internal debate or developing new organizational structures. Ironically, the multitude of new tasks mandated by the model . . . can actually provide a new rationale for centralization to coordinate it all."[61] Yet it was a great deal of spontaneity and grassroots initiative that created most unions in the first place. This is important and I will return to it in the discussion of alternatives.

Here I will focus on four structural features of business unionism:

- Defining the "membership" as those under a collective bargaining agreement
- Separating "recognition" and "representation" phases in organizing
- Making choices through cost-benefit analysis (money)
- Lack of horizontal communications within the union

Most US unions count as members only those already covered by a union contract. A few count those involved in winning a contract. Fewer still include those who choose to be members within a workplace where no majority or recognition has been established. Almost none open their membership simply to workers who are looking for a union, even if they are in an industry or occupation covered by that union. If 53 percent of nonmanagerial workers (fifty million employees) are willing to vote for a union, it is likely that a smaller number (perhaps one in ten, or five million) would be willing to actually join one at their workplace or in a geographic area that included their job. Such limits were in place prior to the Supreme Court's ratification of the NLRA in 1937, after the great upheaval of that year. Outside of rail workers, covered by the 1926 Railway Labor Act, there was no state-sponsored procedure nor any thought of "neutrality" agreements, though "sweetheart" deals by AFL unions in competition with more militant CIO unions were not uncommon.[62] By requiring workers to be part of a workplace or group already in the union's sights, organized labor is certainly limiting its potential growth.

For most unions the phase of "organizing," that is, seeking recognition, is a totally different function than "representation," which might begin with the negotiation of a first contract or even after that. Organizing is perceived as a specialized function or skill and negotiating and representation as another. In most organizing drives this separation is embodied by different staff personnel. When recognition is achieved, the organizers exit and the full-time negotiators enter. In their sample of unions, Jordan and Bruno found that "in most of the unions, organising and negotiations remain separate functions and seldom are they unified as a strategic plan."[63] Yet, summarizing the many studies of organizing she has led over the years, Bronfenbrenner argues that unions are most likely to achieve recognition "when they run aggressive and creative campaigns utilizing a grassroots, rank-and-file-intensive strategy, *building a union and acting like a union from the very beginning of the campaign*."[64] Acting like a rank-and-file-intensive union from the start also increases the chance of winning a good first contract. Jordan and Bruno point out that the choice between NLRB and voluntary procedures "is not as stark as some have suggested."[65] In both cases, pressure is required. Bronfenbrenner's call to act like a union from the start would end this dichotomy and engage the members from the beginning. But, as she points out, few unions follow this prescription.[66]

Another limit to organizing is the exclusive emphasis on cost-benefit analysis by most unions. Of course, unions have limited financial and staff resources and must make choices, as organizing is done under today's staff-driven model. On average, however, unions still spend only 10 percent of their resources on organizing, far less than the 30 percent Sweeney once called for or the 50 percent the SEIU spends. So even here there is room for greater effort.[67] There are, however, also alternatives to high-cost campaigning, mostly involving activating existing members. It has been argued, by Fletcher and Hurd for example, among others, that current members and even stewards resist taking on external organizing; this is no doubt a problem.[68] But the same authors found examples of local unions that had drawn members into organizing. Some local unions make this a matter of principle.[69] As long as US unions see new organizing as primarily a professionalized, budget-specific activity in opposition to "representation," Fine's point about the high-cost, decades-long trek to density will be valid.[70] To be sure, such ambitious and costly national campaigns as UNITE-HERE's "Hotel Workers Rising" are having an effect.[71] Ironically, this campaign also provides an example of how rank-and-file leaders can take over a campaign and reduce staff costs. Talking about the recent UNITE-HERE victory at a Hilton hotel in California, the leader organizer said "the [rank-and-file] leaders were in the forefront, training workers to be organizers. It got to the point where we didn't have a lot of staff on it because the leaders were pushing each other."[72]

Another barrier to organizing, if it is to become a rank-and-file-based activity, is the lack of horizontal communication between locals of the same union. Many cities will have several locals of the same union that could coordinate efforts on a geographic or industrial basis. But communications in most unions run from local to international and back—if, indeed, there is even a two-way dimension. There are, of course, some structures, such as Central Labor Councils, the AFL-CIO Union Cities program, and a number of Industry Coordinating Committees that bring together locals for organizing and campaign purposes.[73] But direct contact between locals of the same union is seldom encouraged. This, too, limits low-cost local organizing possibilities.

Alternative Approaches

If the NLRB procedures are, as AFL-CIO organizing director Stewart Acuff puts it, "broken,"[74] neutrality agreements and card-check procedures do not seem to provide a fast track to growth either. What is needed are institutional changes within the unions to enlist a broader layer of the membership in organizing new members. This would resemble the original "organizing model" of local member participation in both recognition and representation. Below are some alternative approaches that could expand and speed up the organization of the millions who say they want a union. Some of these are already practiced by a few unions in limited cases. The idea is to generalize them.

Alternatives:

- Open-source/nonmajority unionism
- "Federal" or local CLC charters
- End the separation of recognition and representation
- Activate and empower members

Richard Freeman and Joel Rogers argue for what they call "open source" or nonmajority unionism, not based exclusively on bargaining units recognized by majority vote or a show of cards. It is a unionism that would be open to "any worker, anywhere, everywhere in the economy."[75] It is a practice that could have brought many of the 366,000 workers who participated in lost NLRB elections between 2003 and 2006, those disqualified under *Dana/Metaldyne,* and those from the 30 percent or so of card check efforts that failed into the "house of labor." It could reach out to the 53 percent of nonunionized workers who say they would want a union if it were widely used and defended. The organizing process would typically be initiated by groups of workers seeking a union, who could be issued a charter by international unions, Central Labor Councils, or one of the two federations. The charter could be specific to a workplace, occupation, geographic area, or a partially organized industry. This is precisely how most unions in the United States were organized until after World War II. According to Cobble, between its founding in 1886 and the merger with the CIO in 1955, "the AFL chartered some twenty thousand federal or directly affiliated local unions."[76] The practice was abandoned after World War II in favor of the self-imposed model of growth exclusively through the international unions and NLRB channels. While such workers will certainly face intense employer opposition, Freeman and Rogers argue that nonmajority unionism is supported by Section 7 of the NLRA, which is supposed to protect "concerted activities" by any group of workers.[77] Reinstatement and back pay for workers fired for union activity through the NLRB are fairly common. More reliable support could come from CLCs, other unions in the area, or directly from the federations. Examples of this type of union in the United States today include the New York Taxi Workers Alliance, UE Local 150 at the University of North Carolina, and the CWA's Washtech at Microsoft, WAGE at General Electric, and Alliance@IBM.

Another self-limiting practice, described above, is the separation of the recognition phase from the representation phase. As cited above, Bronfenbrenner has found over and over in her research that unions are most likely to win recognition by "acting like a union from the very beginning of the campaign."[78] Further, the militancy and experience accumulated in the organizing phase needs to be carried over into the day-to-day practice of representation. All of this implies the activation and participation of the members in bargaining, representation, grievance handling, and more, not simply their occasional mobilization. This goes back to what Fletcher and Gapasin said about the purpose of the union. It cannot be just an organizing machine or servicing agent. It must be a workers' organization that defends and advances their interests and those of the broader working class in the workplace and society in general.

Conclusion

Unionism in the private sector remains in crisis despite some increase in effort by several unions. As neutrality and card-check efforts move beyond companies with previous bargaining relationships or areas with significant density, they run into the same intense employer resistance experienced in NLRB representation elections. The time, effort, and resources required to win in standalone situations are likely to increase in these cases. Neutrality and card-check agreements are not a panacea, despite their more efficient outcomes. Industry-wide campaigns like Hotel Workers Rising and Justice for Janitors are certainly part of the way forward, but labor needs to cast a still wider net if it is to regain power across the private economy. Some of the barriers to union growth inherent in the business-union model can be overcome if alternative methods of growth are more widely employed. More research into both organized labor's internal barriers and the alternatives to majority-bargaining-unit organizing could help advance the possibilities for union growth in the United States.

9 Striking Out in America: Is There an Alternative to the Strike?

Kim Moody

Introduction

"The strike is the essence of collective labor activity," wrote Craig Becker, former Clinton National Labor Relations Board (NLRB) recess appointee and legal scholar.[1] The National Labor Relations Act (NLRA) of 1935, which established the legal basis of collective bargaining for most of the private sector in the United States, unequivocally guaranteed the right to strike. Furthermore, Becker notes that the Supreme Court, as late as 1963, argued that the NLRA had upheld a system of collective bargaining "with the right to strike at its core." Yet, beginning in the 1980s, the use of the strike has declined from year to year. The number of strikes in the United States has fallen from an average of more than five thousand a year in the 1970s to an annual average of fewer than three hundred

This essay was originally published in 2013 in New Forms and Expressions of Conflict at Work, *edited by Gregor Gall (London: Palgrave).*

in the 2000s (see Table 9.1). How could such a huge decline in the use of labor's "only true weapon"[2] be explained? Were there alternative forms of industrial action workers and their unions could deploy to pressure employers in the process of collective bargaining?

This article will examine the various forces behind this decline as it relates to workers and unions in the private sector.[3] Following an analysis of the roots of the near-abandonment of the strike weapon, it will then discuss the various alternatives. It will argue that the central explanation for reduced strike activity lies not just in the US legal regime that severely limits workers' "self-help," as the NLRA terms industrial action, or in the "global" economic trends that disadvantage workers, but in the dynamics of class conflict that these trends have encouraged or enabled. Furthermore, in examining the alternative forms of industrial action developed by union members and leaders in the last couple of decades, the article will argue that the very forces militating against workers' withdrawing their labor in an industrial dispute present problems for the successful exercise of these alternatives.

International Trends in Strikes and Trade Union Upsurge
As a number of academic analyses have noted, strikes, labor unrest, and union growth and renewal come and go in waves.[4] Each of these analysts has a theory of just what brings about an upsurge or its abatement. Silver emphasizes shifts in production systems and geographic location as well as the rhythms of accumulation and the impact of world wars.[5] Kelly relates periods of workers' mobilization to the movements of long Kondratieff waves of economic growth and decline.[6] These theories and the criticisms of them are too complex to do justice to in this article. However, the empirical fact of waves of worker militancy is difficult to deny and the underlying changes in the economies of the developed countries in these periods are undoubtedly a major factor. The pictures painted by Silver and

Kelly differ somewhat, but both see the first labor upsurge in the major capitalist countries in the 1880s, followed by a slump in the 1890s, a rise before and after World War I, followed, in turn, by a downswing in the 1920s, another upswing in the 1930s and 1940s, and up again in the 1960s and 1970s. The upsurge of the 1960s and 1970s was the last to date.[7]

The international nature of the recent wave of decline in strike activity in the world's more developed economies since the late 1970s has been confirmed by two recent studies. An ILO study shows that strike activity in thirty-eight nations, measured by an index based on days not worked during strikes, fell by 80 percent from the 1970s to the early 2000s.[8] A similar study of strike trends by the European Trade Union Institute (ETUI) showed that the levels of days not worked due to strikes in the fifteen core countries of the EU fell by 40 percent from the 1990s to the 2000s.[9] As in many studies, the ETUI attributes this decline in part to the shift from manufacturing to service industries. However, it also notes that strike levels declined in both manufacturing and services since the 1990s in Western Europe, indicating that more than deindustrialization is at work.[10] The study speculates that such strikes as still occur may be defensive in nature as "workers resist wage restraint, job losses, work intensification and so on."[11] This would appear to reveal a strong change in the behavior of European capital in the vortex of European-wide market integration. This shift to neoliberalism in the EU has been noted and protested by the European Trade Union Confederation in its *Strategy and Action Plan, 2011–2015*.[12]

The notion of waves in strike activity, then, would seem to be confirmed at least in the negative. It is not difficult to discern that globalization and neoliberal marketization lie behind this trend. Two qualifications, however, must be made. First, the behavior of the parties to the employment relationship, perhaps especially that of capital, greatly influences whether strikes are viable. Great economic trends affect that behavior, but it is the actors in industrial or class conflicts who pick from available strategies and tactics in this ongoing struggle over the fruits of production. The second is the distinct context of labor in the United States, to which we now turn.

Undermining the Strike in the United States

It is difficult to make a precise comparison between the fall in strike activity internationally and that in the United States, because figures on days not worked during strikes have not been available since 1981. In 1982, the Reagan Bureau of Labor Statistics stopped counting all strikes, recording only strikes of one thousand or more workers.[13] The Federal Mediation and Conciliation Service (FMCS) does report all strikes, but does not report the days-not-worked measure used in the two recent international studies cited above. Nevertheless, a comparison of the average annual number of strikes in the 2000s to those in the 1970s in Table 9.1 shows a sharp drop of 95 percent. This is a much greater drop than that measured in Europe by the ETUI and significantly higher than the ILO measure of thirty-eight countries. It is also larger than the drop in union membership and density in the United States during those years.

Table 9.1 Average Annual Private-Sector Union Membership, Density, Strikes, and Duration in the 1970s and 2000s[14]

Decade	Members	Density	Strikes	Duration*
1970s	16,500,000	25%	5,254	27.7
2000s	9,074,000	8.7%	285	64.9
Percent change	*-45%*	*-65%*	*-95%*	*+134%*

*In calendar days

One explanation for this above-average decline in strikes lies in the legal environment that governs labor relations in the United States. The NLRA guaranteed both the right of workers to organize unions and to strike or engage in other "concerted activities." Section 7 of the Act specifically grants the right to "concerted activities for the purpose of collective bargaining or other mutual aid and activities," while Section 13 states that nothing in the Act "shall be construed so as either to interfere with or impede or diminish in any way the right to strike."[15] Yet no sooner had the Supreme Court upheld the Act in 1937 than it began the long process of whittling away the very rights Sections 7 and 13 spelled out. As these court decisions also impact the various alternatives to the strike, a closer look at them is necessary.

Concerning the major court decisions that would undermine worker rights to organize and strike, Pope argues that although it is generally accepted that federal statutes can only be trumped by the US Constitution, the judiciary has in fact elevated "the state common-law rights of employers over the federal statutory rights of workers."[16] These common-law rights were, above all, the right to possess and protect private property. The organization Human Rights Watch also concluded that "many of the features of U.S. labor law and practice that counter international norms result from court-fashioned doctrine, not just from statutory deficiencies."[17] Court-made law is, of course, initiated by one or another of the parties to a dispute covered by the NLRA. Most of the challenges to the various aspects of strike activity come, as one would expect, from the employers. In other words, the bulk of actual labor law in the United States has been initiated by corporation lawyers and crafted by the courts out of the reach of normal democratic practice and trade-union influence.

In the first such case, known as *Mackay Radio & Telegraph*, in 1938, the Supreme Court found that the employer had a right to hire permanent replacement workers during a legitimate strike, an act that meant the strikers had no guarantee of returning to their jobs once the strike ended. As early as 1936, one NLRB lawyer argued that if employers were allowed to bring in permanent replacements "it would destroy all unions, abolish all efforts at bargaining and emasculate all strikers."[18] While this may be somewhat of an exaggeration, *Mackay* has made the strike a highly risky proposition in most industrial settings.

The next Supreme Court decision limiting strike activity came in 1939 in the *Fansteel* case, which banned sit-down or sit-in strikes—again on the basis of common-law property rights.[19] Sit-down strikes, of which there had been more than a thousand in 1936–37, were the major means by which both the new industrial unions and older craft unions forced recognition on giant corporations and smaller employers alike.[20] *Fansteel* made sit-down strikes both illegal and "unprotected" under the NLRA, meaning that workers could be dismissed for engaging in such "unprotected" activity. In addition, it narrowed the definition of a strike to one where workers both stopped work altogether and left the workplace. *Fansteel* would also be used as a precedent for declaring other forms of industrial action such as slow-downs, intermittent strikes, and partial strikes "unprotected."[21] This has implications for some alternative, non-strike forms of "concerted activities."[22]

Mackay and *Fansteel*, along with all the court findings that followed, both narrowed the definition of "protected" strike activity and rendered the strike in a number of forms a dangerous venture for any union and its members. Yet from the end of World War II until the 1980s, employers seldom introduced permanent replacements.[23] Indeed, strike activity remained high in the 1950s and rose dramatically from the mid-1960s until the late 1970s. The collapse in the frequency of strikes came between 1979 and 1981, when they dropped by almost half, partly the consequence of the recession of those years.[24] By the mid- to late 1980s, however, managers increasingly said they would consider using permanent replacement workers in the event of a strike.[25] The downward drift in strikes would continue into the economic recovery of the 1980s as employers of all sizes grasped, for the first time, the weapons the courts had handed them four decades earlier.

Renewed Management Aggression

What had occurred was a change in the terms of industrial conflict as management altered its outlook and strategy. Even well before employing permanent replacements, management began responding to falling profit rates in what Davis has called the "Management Offensive of 1958–63."[26] This entailed management of the big corporations taking a harder position on wages and attempting to regain authority in the workplace. As Pope describes the change, "A new generation of managers had begun to replace those who had experienced the mass picket lines of the 1940s."[27] The management offensive would increase throughout the 1960s and 1970s, as profit rates fell sharply and international competition intensified. Yet, far from crippling the strike, management's aggressive actions in those years brought on an increase in both official and unofficial ("unprotected") strikes until the tide was broken in the wake of the 1980–82 recession and the wave of union concessions brought on by the 1979 Chrysler bailout—even before Reagan broke the PATCO strike in August 1981.[28] What the end of the strike wave of the "long 1970s" revealed, however, was the weakness of organized labor and the increased willingness of its leaders to grant concessions. Capital, for its part, had reorganized and regrouped both economically and politically during the 1970s to dramatically reduce the power of organized labor.[29] No doubt the era of neoliberalism that soon emerged encouraged the newer generation of managers to press the unions harder for concessions, but, perhaps ironically, it was the very weakness of the unions that encouraged the accelerating use of *Mackay* by the mid-1980s.[30]

Nineteen eighty-two saw a recovery and the return of profitability that would last, with the usual ups and downs, until the "Great Recession" of 2008.[31] Far from bringing a relaxation on capital's part, this encouraged a more aggressive stance. The secret of this prolonged recovery of profitability was that it was based largely on wage compression and an increased effort bargain extracted from a retreating labor movement.[32] From 1983 onward, American unions granted almost continuous contract concessions. Increased work intensification through the introduction of lean production methods, human resource management (HRM) techniques, labor-management cooperation schemes, and a long string of defeated strikes in which permanent replacement workers played a key role all accelerated in the 1980s. By the late 1980s it was not just financially desperate businesses that deployed permanent replacements but "financially successful firms that had provoked strikes by demanding sweeping reductions in wages and benefits established through collective agreements."[33] And while international competition no doubt pressured many companies into seeking concessions, the use of replacement workers had spread to "landlocked" industries such as newspapers, hotels, and retail.[34]

Table 9.2 Strike Threats, Strikes, Threats of Replacements, and Use of Replacements in Collective Bargaining, 1996, 1999, and 2003[35]

Year	Strike Threat	Strike*	Threat of Replacements	Use of Replacements
1996	N/A	8%	14%	1%
1999	39%	6%	13%	2%
2003	40%	4%	18%	3%

*Includes lockouts and other job actions

Three surveys of between 1,500 and 2,000 union and management negotiators, conducted by the University of Massachusetts for the Federal Mediation and Conciliation Service (FMCS) in 1996, 1999, and 2003, provide a look at the extent of the use of permanent replacements during collective bargaining. Answers given by union negotiators are summarized in Table 9.2. The actions referenced could have taken place in the two years leading up to each of the three surveys. According to union negotiators the threat of strikes remained fairly high, indicating that union negotiators still thought these threats credible. The actual use of the strike and other forms of job actions, however, declined in the period as would be expected. Management threats to deploy permanent replacement workers were less frequent than strike threats but grew somewhat over this eight-year period. The actual use of permanent replacements, though relatively uncommon in terms of overall bargaining, appears to be frequent and growing in proportion to actual strikes, rising from one in eight in 1996 to three out of four in 2003. If this survey reflects reality, it is no surprise that the number of strikes dropped from 372 in 1996 to 277 in 2003 and 159 in 2010. The intensification of capital's assault on unions is also suggested by the fact that not only had the duration of strikes become longer since the 1970s, but it also rose from an average of fifty-one days in the second half of the 1990s to sixty-four days in the 2000s.[36]

The Cost to Labor

The impact on collective bargaining was predictable. As union membership, density, and strike frequency all fell, so did the size of wage settlements. Median wage increases for the first year of negotiated settlements had ranged from 5.9 percent to 10.2 percent between 1949 and 1965, growing much higher in the 1970s as both inflation and strike levels rose. By the 1980s they were falling drastically, from a high of 9.6 percent in 1981 to 2.7 percent in 1988 and 3.4 percent in 1989. In the 1990s, they leveled off at 3 percent, falling from 3.8 percent in 2000 to 1.6 percent in 2010. Although it varied from year to year, from 2000 through 2010 an average of 22 percent of agreements, one in five, had no first-year increase.[37] Benefits, especially health insurance and pensions, also receded from 1979 onward. Those covered by any employer-provided health insurance fell from 69 percent of the workforce in 1979 to 55 percent in 2004, while those with employer-provided pensions fell by 7.8 percent from 1979 to 2006. The value of pensions also fell as those covered by defined-benefit, as opposed to defined-contribution, pension plans dropped from 39 percent in 1980 to 18 percent.[38]

These trends extended to the entire workforce, now largely bereft of the "threat effect" and wage spillover unions had once provided.[39] Despite some increases in the late 1990s and late 2000s, real average weekly wages in private, nonagricultural industries in 2010 remained 13 percent below those of 1973.[40] The result was a reversal of the long-term shift of national income toward labor. From 1959 to 1979, labor's share of US GDP had risen from 68.3 percent to 73.9 percent, but from 1979 to 2006 it fell to 70.4 percent.[41] Perhaps the clearest evidence that capital was getting its way not only in labor costs but also in the effort bargain was the enormous and growing gap between labor compensation and productivity. From 2000 through 2009, productivity grew at more than twice the annual rate of real hourly compensation.[42]

The Search for Alternatives—Outside the Workplace

Noting the dramatic decline in the incidence of major strikes since the 1950s and the simultaneous rise in the frequency of unfair labor practice (ULP) cases filed against employers with the NLRB, McCammon asked, given the "increasing difficulty of using the strike," whether "workers have substituted legal strategies for labor militancy in their attempts to organize and preserve unions."[43] After an extensive examination of the various circumstances that might lead to such a choice, including the changing economic circumstances that may lead employers "to act in potentially illegal ways to protect their profitability," she concludes that "workers are not choosing between striking and filing unfair labor practice charges."[44] Given that ULPs are a very blunt instrument subject to endless delays and mostly occur during organizing drives or first contract negotiations, it is unlikely that this form of "legal mobilization" could be seen as a substitute for the strike. The search for possible alternatives, however, has been going on for some time.

Facing increased employer hostility on every front, organized labor turned again and again to politics and the hope of labor law reform. Each effort, in 1977–87, 1993, and 2008–09, failed to win any legislative relief, including President Clinton's unsuccessful effort to ban permanent replacement workers.[45] In the 1970s, however, a different search for increased union power began in the unlikely setting of the US South. At Farah Manufacturing in Texas in the early 1970s and at J. P. Stevens in South Carolina in the late 1970s, Ray Rogers, working for the Amalgamated Clothing and Textile Workers Union, deployed what he called the "corporate campaign." One early study described the Stevens campaign as "a three-pronged effort consisting of legal changes of unfair labor practices, a consumer boycott of Stevens' products, and a corporate campaign designed to isolate Stevens from the rest of the business and financial community."[46] It was the latter aspect that was new.

The idea was to put public pressure on financial backers of the target company in order to force the company to recognize the union in the case of an organizing drive such as Stevens. The Stevens campaign was largely successful. When the Industrial Union Department of the AFL-CIO picked up the idea in 1985, it saw its version of the "coordinated corporate campaign" as reinforcing "a well-prepared and well-conducted strike when necessary." Based on his experience at Stevens, Rogers went a step further, suggesting that the "corporate campaign" could substitute for a strike.[47]

In the 1980s, the concept was broadened, but almost always involved pressure on the board members of related financial institutions and often an intervention at the target firm's stockholder meetings. This had been the case at Stevens, where Rogers had some success in that the CEO of New York Life resigned from the Stevens board.[48] When the same tactic was applied against the First Bank System (FBS) during the Hormel strike in the mid-1980s, however, it didn't work. As Rachleff observed, "FBS, of course, remained available to Hormel throughout the struggle."[49] Again in 1988, a Rogers-run corporate campaign failed to prevent defeat at International

Paper.[50] In the early 1990s at Tate & Lyle subsidiary A. E. Staley in Illinois, where Rogers picked State Farm Insurance as the target of the campaign, it had no apparent impact and most locked-out workers judged it a mistake.[51]

Many corporate campaigns also included a consumer boycott, but this approach could not effectively be applied to companies making producer goods. Farah and Stevens sold directly to the public, although only a third of Stevens products were sold directly to consumers; other targets of corporate campaigns such as BASF, Louisiana-Pacific, and Phelps-Dodge mainly supplied other businesses. There was also a potential problem with what amounted to a secondary boycott. The NLRB had ruled the FBS boycott an unfair labor practice. Later, however, in the BASF campaign, it ruled that "use of a corporate campaign by a union to assist in meeting its goals at the bargaining table does not violate the Act."[52] The 1980s also saw the increasing use of labor-community coalitions such as those at Morse Tool, the Van Nuys General Motors plant, the Tri-State Conference on Steel, the Austin United Support Group, and the New Haven Community-Labor Alliance. These were not really substitutes for strikes, however. The first three were attempts to stop plant closings, while the latter two were strike support organizations.[53]

Some corporate campaigns, such as that conducted by the Oil, Chemical and Atomic Workers (OCAW) at BASF, also made use of allegations of company lawbreaking in areas such as taxation, toxic materials, discrimination, etc.[54] In all cases, the "corporate campaign" was preceded by extensive and deep research on the financial and political vulnerabilities of the target firm. In this sense corporate campaigns are very different from the traditional union consumer boycotts.

Another corporate campaign that employed a wide variety of tactics was that against Ravenswood Aluminum Company. The workers at this West Virginia firm were locked out in 1990. Eventually, the Steelworkers union (USW), which rep-

resented the 1,700 Ravenswood workers, put together a multifaceted campaign to pressure the company to negotiate and
end the lockout.[55] Unlike Rogers's campaigns, the USW's
campaign at Ravenswood did not focus on the firm's institutional financial backers but rather on the consortium of individuals who had purchased the company from Kaiser shortly
before negotiations began. It also included an "end-users" campaign directed at aluminum companies where the USW had
members and at Stroh's and Budweiser beer companies; revelations of environmental damage; and, eventually, proof of financial wrongdoing by one of the major owners. Unlike most
earlier corporate campaigns, this one went international, organizing union demonstrations across much of Europe. The
strike ended in 1992 after eighteen months, in a settlement
that included some concessions but was deemed at least a partial victory by the USW. This partial victory owed much to the
unusual fact that the major figure behind Ravenswood, Mark
Rich, was wanted by the US government on several counts of
illegal trading. The union managed to discover his hiding place
in Switzerland and, with the help of European unions, to
demonstrate in his "own backyard."[56]

It is doubtful if the corporate campaign can be seen as a
substitute for the strike. For one thing, several of the best known
examples occurred during and often as a response to strikes or
lockouts, including BASF, General Dynamics/Electric Boat,
Louisiana-Pacific, Hormel, Ravenswood, Detroit Newspapers,
and Staley. Nor have most of them ended in clear-cut victories.
Indeed, the record of falling real wages and contract concessions
cited above are an indication of the limits of these strategies. For
one thing, as a recent commentator on union tactics argued, "an
employer is able to continue operations during the corporate
campaign."[57] The company is free to hire permanent replacement workers, thus undermining the impact of the strike, while
the campaign can do little more than harass the employer. It is
for this reason that these campaigns often fail, as they did at

Hormel, Detroit Newspapers, and Staley. Another problem is that the more sophisticated and elaborate the corporate campaign, the more it becomes controlled by professionals or high-level union officials. The Ravenswood campaign was run by the team assembled by the USW leadership, not by local union leaders or members. As Juravich and Bronfenbrenner point out, "The local leaders remained in Ravenswood. In the Steelworkers' tradition, strategic bargaining decisions remained an international prerogative."[58] The research the USW did on Ravenswood and its various owners, practices, and connections, as well as its international dimension, however, probably raised the standard for future campaigns.

By the 2000s outside pressure had evolved far beyond the early corporate campaigns to include research into the global connections of target firms, pressure on a variety of corporate decisionmakers, international coalitions of unions and other social groups, and focused pressure on specific segments of the business as well as the more traditional financial bankers. As Juravich summarized the research behind what were now called comprehensive or strategic campaigns, this research was "directed both at understanding how power flows in firms and identifying vulnerabilities and potential points of leverage," which was to be "the first step in developing the kinds of multifaceted strategic campaigns that are necessary to win today."[59] The global reach of many of the strategic campaigns of this sort, however, has seldom been seen in the United States as a substitute for striking so much as a way for unions representing workers in the same multinational corporation to lend each other support in bargaining or organizing through pressure tactics. Furthermore, as strategic campaigns get more elaborate they become very expensive and time-consuming, so that they can only be used sparingly even by most large unions. With more than twenty thousand union agreements expiring each year,[60] it is unlikely that these sorts of complex campaigns could be mounted often enough to make a difference. In this sense, they cannot serve as an alternative to the strike in most bargaining settings.

The Search for Alternatives—Back to the Workplace

In 1981, Jerry Tucker, a staffer for Region 5 of the United Auto Workers, was assigned to help the five hundred union members at Moog Automotive negotiate a new contract. Like so many companies at that time, Moog management was demanding deep concessions; with the recession still on people's minds, a strike seemed too risky. Tucker devised what he called the "in-plant strategy," later known more generically as the "inside strategy." As most of the tactics involved, such as work-to-rule, are "unprotected" during the life of the contract, the union let the old one expire. It was a collection of old and new tactics from the work-to-rule at the center of the strategy to wearing union T-shirts and buttons, singing labor songs during breaks, filing grievances en masse, demanding meetings between large contingents of workers and management, and more. The object was reducing production or, as Tucker put it, "running the plant backwards." After almost six months, management gave in and negotiated a concession-free agreement. The strategy was a success and Tucker went on to apply the same approach in 1983 at Schwitzer Manufacturing, a small auto-parts company, and in 1984 at Bell Helicopter and LTV, both major corporations.[61]

The inside strategy had great advantages. It activated the membership and built strong solidarity. And while slowdowns and other "partial strikes" are not protected by the NLRA, the legal status of work-to-rule campaigns is more ambiguous. The NLRB looked at the "difficult issues raised by work-to-rule" and left them undecided in 1996, 1997, and 1998. The Supreme Court had done the same in 1960 and 1976.[62] This is probably because there is no refusing of direct orders or company policies in a work-to-rule campaign. Indeed, the point is to follow management direction to the letter, a practice certain to reduce production. Only voluntary tasks, such as optional overtime, are refused. Like the "corporate campaign," however, the in-plant strategy has limitations.

In 1992 Tucker organized an in-plant campaign for Allied Industrial Workers Local 837 at A. E. Staley in Decatur, Illinois. After nine months of "running the plant backward" successfully, Staley locked the workers out.[63] The lockout, of course, completely changed the terms of engagement, as replacement workers entered the plant and resumed production. The local union, now part of the United Paperworkers International Union due to a merger, had to fall back on two "outside" campaigns: Ray Rogers's corporate campaign against State Farm, which was not working, and Tucker's campaign against two of Staley's most important customers: Miller Beer and Pepsi. Miller did, in fact, refuse to renew its contract with Staley—no doubt worried about its largely blue-collar customer base. Before the Pepsi campaign was able to produce a similar victory, however, the International Union pulled the plug on a fight the local union activists felt could have been won.[64] As in the case of the corporate campaign at Hormel in the 1980s, the inside campaign at Staley made clear that such campaigns require the support of the national union.

The application of various innovative tactics on the job is not limited to highly coordinated efforts such as Tucker's "running the plant backward." For some unions the various tactics association with the inside strategy have become almost normal ways to conduct a contract campaign, whether it ends in a strike or not. T-shirt days, brief in-place work stoppages (too brief to be illegal), lunchtime rallies, community support, bans on voluntary overtime, etc., have become part of the repertoire of a number of unions. Most notable in this respect, perhaps, is the Communications Workers of America (CWA). Facing an expected assault on its terms and conditions by the East Coast telecom giant NYNEX, the CWA began a "mobilization" program a year before the contract expired in 1989. This involved months of workplace meetings, wearing anti-concessions buttons and red T-shirts on the job, lunchtime picketing, working-to-rule, and confronting NYNEX executives at their annual shareholders' meeting. This vigorous campaign, however, was not enough to head off a strike—and when the strike came it would last four months before beating the company's demands for "cost-sharing" on health insurance.[65]

In 2003 the CWA did use an inside strategy as a substitute for a strike. This time, well before the strike deadline, the company, now larger and known as Verizon, spent millions of dollars and recruited thousands of managers from around the company to act as temporary replacements in the event of a strike. The union surprised management by letting the traditional deadline pass and the contract lapse, but refusing to strike. Workers engaged in carefully planned work-to-rule efforts, carried out prolonged safety checks of all company vehicles day after day, did all the "five points of contact" with customers, and followed company rules and procedures to the letter. The union also organized community support and demonstrations. After a month of this, the company abandoned its most onerous concessionary demands and the union settled for a contract with some concessions, which it termed a "defensive victory."[66]

Is There Really a Substitute for the Strike?

Despite the example of the CWA's 2003 Verizon inside campaign, the evidence on the effectiveness of the potential alternatives is mixed at best. Outside campaigns often supplement rather than replace a strike or lockout, while inside campaigns often lead to one or another of these. Furthermore, the general rule that the threat or deployment of permanent replacements is sufficient to kill the strike weapon altogether has numerous exceptions. For one thing, in some cases, as at Verizon with seventy-eight thousand workers or at UPS in 1997, where nearly two hundred thousand workers struck, the use of permanent replacements on the scale required with the skills needed is not practical. Indeed, many large corporations, such as GM, Ford, and GE, have never used permanent replacements despite their efforts to wring concessions from their workers. For those more vulnerable it is sometimes possible to initiate a strike as an unfair labor practice strike, in which case permanent replacements cannot be used. Although exceptional, it is also possible in some cases to convert an economic strike into an unfair labor practice work stoppage.[67] Teamsters at US Foods took advantage of an unfair-labor-practice strike of only two workers in 2011 to conduct rolling strikes by more than two thousand workers using a contract clause that allowed them to decline to cross a picket line—an admittedly unusual contractual feature.[68] Additionally, Becker has argued that repeated grievance strikes are not "intermittent strikes" and are protected under the NLRA.[69] He suggests that such repeated grievance strikes can be used to pressure management on other issues. Nor does the "unprotected" status apply to those workers on railways and airlines who are covered by the Railway Labor Act. Dubbing their strategy CHAOS, for example, flight attendants at Alaska Airlines and Midwest Express Airlines conducted a series of unannounced one-day strikes at different facilities in 2002.[70] For the majority who are covered by the NLRA, there is the additional problem of the self-imposed no-strike clause that most union agreements include. The nearly universal existence of no-strike clauses was initiated decades ago as a tradeoff for recognition. These clauses mean that the union cannot strike during the life of the agreement unless it specifies otherwise, as do the UAW contracts at the major US auto-assembly companies. Between 1994 and 1998, more than twenty UAW local unions at various GM plants conducted grievance strikes during the life of the contract. Though these were technically over issues such as health and safety allowed by the contract, they were mostly directed at relieving the intensity of work by hiring more workers. Most, in fact, were successful in increasing the workforce, at least for a while. More

recently, members of the CWA, whose contract allows grievance strikes during the term of the contract, struck a silicone
plant three times in 2010 and 2011.[71] Unless the contract
specifically allows for grievance strikes during the life of the
contract, they can only be conducted when the agreement ex-
pires. In 1974, the Supreme Court took this even further when
it ruled that strikes during the life of contracts with arbitration
of grievances could be enjoined even where there was not a no-
strike clause.[72]

For all the difficulties of striking, there does not appear to
be an alternative that is viable for the labor movement as a
whole. As I observed in the beginning of this chapter, both
union growth and strikes tend to come and go together in
waves that are often brought on by significant changes in the
economy, a circumstance that certainly holds today. In addition,
these labor upsurges are seldom respectful of the law. The
thousand or so sit-down strikes that made the rapid growth of
the CIO possible in 1936 and 1937 were illegal on the grounds
of trespass law well before *Fansteel.*

Even in the period of relatively low strike activity, defiance
can win. The plant occupation of Republic Windows and
Doors in Chicago in 2008 was both illegal and unprotected,
but with support from other unions and even some politicians
was nevertheless successful.[73] Even more dramatic was the occupation of a coal-processing plant by ninety-nine miners and
one "preacher" during the long 1989 strike by the United Mine
Workers at Pittston mines in Virginia. Backed by thousands
of members from unions around the country who descended
on Virginia, the UMW defied court orders to vacate, facing
millions in fines when it didn't. In the end, the union and its
allies beat Pittston's attempt to break the national master contract.[74] In 1970, some two hundred thousand postal workers
struck illegally and defied Nixon's attempt to end the strike by
using the National Guard. When in 1978 President Carter
tried to enjoin the coal miners' strike under the provisions of

the Taft-Hartley Act, the miners successfully disobeyed, chanting, "Taft can mine it, Hartley can haul it, and Carter can shove it."[75] Social upsurges, after all, tend to be disrespectful of the status quo and its rules.

Is Another Upswing in Strike Activity Likely?

The various theories concerning the waves of labor insurgency may offer some insight into whether or not another upsurge in militancy and union growth is likely. Looking at the strike waves of the late 1800s, 1910 through 1920, and 1964 through 1974, Kelly observes, "These three waves have one vital feature in common, which is that all of them occurred at or near the peak of Kondratieff upswings as the world economy passed from a period of sustained economic growth into a long period of recession."[76] We have certainly seen the end of the period of growth that began in 1982; predictions of prolonged stagnation and austerity, even "a decade of pain," abound.[77] As yet, however, there is no evidence of an upsurge in the United States. Indeed, the raw data for fiscal 2011 from the FMCS indicate a slight fall to 153 strikes.[78]

The theory, however, does not predict that such strike waves will begin in any particular country. Certainly in 2011 and 2012 strike activity has picked up in the EU as a result of the crisis-induced austerity being imposed there. As the European Trade Union Confederation recently noted, "Strikes and demonstrations are growing both in terms of frequency and intensity."[79] Silver argues that strike waves rooted in manufacturing, as most have been, will begin where new production is increasingly concentrated. Recently, that has been primarily in low-wage developing countries. So, she argues, "The epicenter of world labor unrest in the twenty-first century is thus likely to be concentrated in these same countries."[80] Here too there is some evidence that this is happening in the new manufacturing locations, above all China, where strikes were on the rise in 2010 and 2011.[81]

Whether this rising tide of international strike activity will wash onto the shores of America remains to be seen. One observation Silver makes, however, deserves comment in the light of what has been written above. Using a distinction made by Eric Olin Wright, Silver notes that the weakening of labor's "structural bargaining power" in the market or workplace, brought on by vertical disintegration in production, has led to the deployment of "associational power" that flows from organization and broader alliances. She concludes that "links between contemporary labor movements and other movements need to be traced."[82] Many of the more recent versions of "outside" strategies analyzed above involve alliances with other unions or social groups and can be classified as associational forms of power. But, as we have seen, by themselves they do not necessarily guarantee victory or even head off defeat. They are likely to work best precisely when they supplement, rather than replace, a strike. The problem of "vertical disintegration" of production, whether of goods or services, is primarily a problem for conventional collective bargaining and can be overcome, as it has in the past, if a new strike wave sweeps from one industry or location to another in defiance of the status quo. As Burns concludes, "Unions did not expand one shop at a time during these surges, but rather ballooned up in large bursts as the result of ordinary working people taking it upon themselves to organize and fight for change."[83]

Yet the problem, almost unique to the United States, of permanent replacement workers remains. For this obstacle to be overcome, the unions and their allies must be willing to challenge and, if necessary, break a "law" that appears in no statute, is contradicted by the wording of the NLRA, and fails to meet international labor standards. Sit-in strikes or occupations remain a strong way to prevent the use of replacement workers. Aside from local trespass laws, the ban on this tactic, too, is found in no statute and has often proved unenforceable, as in the 1930s, at Pittston in 1989, and in Chicago in 2008.

In American politics, changing unjust laws invariably requires a massive challenge in the streets well before the lawmakers act. This was the history of the early unions, the African American civil rights movement, the women's movements of different eras, and more recently the struggle for immigrants' rights. The greatest show of power by immigrant workers to date occurred on May 1, 2006, the "Day without Immigrants," when millions left their jobs to protest and eventually defeat a draconian law then being proposed by Republicans in Congress. Although not called a strike, this demonstration crippled several key industries for a day. Insofar as it was a political strike, of course, it was illegal.[84]

The power to stop production, whether of goods or services, remains the central source of power for workers of all kinds. In the final analysis, the search for alternatives to the strike leads us inevitably back to the strike itself.

10 Competition and Conflict: Union Growth in the US Hospital Industry

Kim Moody

Introduction

Decline in trade union membership and density, punctuated by only occasional spurts of growth, has been the most notorious fact of private-sector employment relations in the United States for decades. Yet America's hospitals stand out as a major exception as health professionals, technicians, and support workers join unions in growing numbers. Union membership in the private sector fell from 9.2 million in 2000 to 7.1 million in 2010, while density dropped from 9.1 percent to 6.9 percent in that period.[1] In the same period, however, union membership in US hospitals grew from 689,416 to 889,006, while density rose from 13.8 percent to 14.3 percent in those same years.[2] Although the growth in density might seem modest, it

A version of this essay under the same title was published in Economic and Industrial Democracy 34 (November 2012), no. 3.

was nonetheless significant, as union density in hospitals was twice that for the private sector workforce as a whole.[3]

This chapter will examine the transformation of the hospital industry in order to provide a context for analyzing recent developments in unionization and collective bargaining across this industry. It will draw on both theoretical and empirical studies to examine the changing objective and subjective conditions that lead many hospital workers to choose unions as a means to dealing with these conditions.

In order to construct an overview of the development of unionism in hospitals, this article draws upon a wide range of secondary data sources. These comprise National Labor Relations Board (NLRB) reports and the US Department of Labor file of collective bargaining agreements for the industry/sector, as well as coverage by the specialist independent publication *Labor Notes*. In turn, these were supplemented by union and industry sources, material from the Bureau of National Affairs (the major agency compiling detailed data on collective bargaining), previous opinion surveys, and coverage by the daily press, revealed through LexisNexis searches. The main strength of deploying these secondary sources is their breadth of coverage of developments across a sector comprising four thousand private profit and nonprofit hospitals employing around four million nonsupervisory staff across the fifty states of the United States. The main weakness of using such sources and materials is that the questions, issues, and approaches underpinning them were not determined by the researcher, as would be the case where primary data were generated specifically for the purpose of analysis. That said, the extent and variety of sources deployed from union, industry, government, and policy groups lessened the significance of this weakness to some degree.

Theoretical Framework

Since the end of the Second World War until recently, union growth was achieved primarily through representation elections held under the terms of the National Labor Relations Act (NLRA) and administered by the NLRB. Under the NLRA, unions in the private sector (other than railways and airlines) are granted exclusive representation for purposes of collective bargaining in those units in which they are recognized. Hence the importance of NLRB elections. Consequently, much of the research about union growth has been based on the results of these elections, on the one hand, and attitudinal surveys that provided a basis for predicting who would vote for the union, on the other. From the 1970s onward, a debate flourished around the work of Getman, Goldberg, and Sage and their critics concerning what sort of opinions determined how workers voted in NLRB elections.[4] As useful as these studies are, they tend to overlook the impact of changes in work on the willingness to vote for and join a union, treating job satisfaction as a static opinion. More recently, the debate among academics and practitioners has centered on the resistance of employers and on union tactics to "inoculate" members to management's message and neutralize such opposition through mobilization.[5] These, too, are valuable in understanding the evolving tactics of both sides in this perennial conflict, but still say little about the underlying dynamics that determine the decisions and actions of workers, unions, and management.

A more dynamic look at work and changes in work as a factor in motivating workers to vote for a union was taken up by Wheeler in what he termed an "integrative" theory.[6] In this theory a worker's decision on whether or not to support a union was shaped by a number of factors, including: deprivation of pay or other conditions, including respect; "recent decrease" or the threat of a decrease in conditions; lack of "voice" in remedying deprivation or decrease; and the "calculation" that the benefits of unionization outweighed the costs, which are all "positively related to a pro-union vote or action."[7] More recently, Clark applied a survey-based "model" using three factors—job dissatisfaction, dissatisfaction with management, and attitudes toward unions—as determinants in how workers would vote in an NLRB election. Clark writes, "The study found that it was dissatisfaction with working conditions, rather than the nature of the work itself, that led to an interest in unionization."[8] This is an important distinction that applies to nurses in particular.

Refining this sort of approach further with a focus specifically on hospital-based nurses, Clark et al. examined the impact of the changes in health care work driven by "market reforms" that accelerated in the 1980s.[9] Their "partial model" saw the shaping of pro-union sentiment in the process of market-driven work reorganization and the impact it had on the "climate for patient care," arguing that "the more negative the perception of the climate, the more likely the nurse would vote for a union."[10] Indeed, their survey of 483 nurses in Pennsylvania revealed a very high correlation between those who expressed dissatisfaction with the "climate of patient care" and those who said they would vote for a union. Further support is found in Jarley and Fiorito, who showed that noneconomic issues such as autonomy and the content of work played a growing role in workers' assessments of unions.[11] Space prevents a thorough discussion of the role of gender in hospital unionization. But it is important to bear in mind that women have made up the majority of all new union members in the United States for over two decades.[12] They have risen from 37 percent of union members in 1991 to 46 percent in 2010.[13] Some 88 percent of health care support workers are women, as are 93 percent of registered nurses, while unions with large female memberships have higher-than-average NLRB win rates.[14] Thus, if the past two decades or more are any indication, unionization benefits from the predominant role of women in hospital work. It should also be noted, however, that as the number of NLRB elections has declined both generally and in hospitals, the success rate has risen across the board. This increased success may well indicate a more planned and strategic approach to representation elections, as Bronfenbrenner and Juravich have argued.[15]

The analysis in this chapter will draw on the dynamics of changing work as a factor in the above-average growth of unions in hospitals in the past decade. It will accord with Clark et al. that these changes are the result of market-driven forces.[16] It will go a step or two further in analyzing both the roots and impact of increased competition in the political economy of the US hospital industry. The study will first look at the changes in the health care market that began in the 1970s and the impact this had on hospitals as organized businesses. It will then examine the major consequences of increased competition and consolidation as hospital managers turned toward capital-intensive strategies, the introduction of new technology, cost-cutting, and work reorganization. Employing the more dynamic aspects of the theories examined above, it will then make the link between these changes and the growth of unionism in hospitals. Following this, it will discuss the nature of collective bargaining as it has evolved under these circumstances and the varying types of unionism that have emerged. Finally, although space precludes a discussion of the broader economic and political circumstances in which these developments unfold, it should be noted that the transformation of the US hospital industry occurs in the context of the neoliberal era, with its continuous economic restructuring and work reorganization. Partly due to this, the chapter will suggest that the approach of this study, with its emphasis on changing conditions of work, may well apply to other industries and unions.

Growth, Competition, and Consolidation

Following the final defeat of national health insurance legislation in the United States in 1947, unions turned to negotiating employer-provided health insurance for their members. The number of workers with health insurance as part of their collective agreement rose from one million in 1946 to twelve million by 1957.[17] Private health-insurance expenditures grew from six billion dollars in 1960 to fifty billion dollars in 1970. This was followed by the growth of government spending in health care, boosted after 1965 by Medicare and Medicaid payments, from $28 billion in 1970 to $256 billion by the end of the 1980s. In a matter of two decades, a massive market for health care of all kinds was created, with expenditures for hospital care growing by two and a half times in the 1970s and one and a quarter times in the 1980s before leveling off in the 1990s and 2000s.[18] As Stevens argues in her economic history of American hospitals, it was these new sources of government money that drove competition among the privately owned hospitals that dominate US health care and accelerated new construction, which, in turn, shifted the financial dependence of not-for-profit hospitals from philanthropy and the "community" to the bond market and profitability.[19]

As managed care—prepaid insurance with stringent cost controls—replaced fee-for-service payments beginning in the 1980s, it put pressure on revenues, further accelerating competition, cost-cutting, and consolidation in the industry as hospitals sought to increase revenue by trimming costs and increasing market share through expansion or acquisition. As one of the pioneers of managed care, Paul Ellwood, wrote, managed care would bring aspects of the Industrial Revolution, in particular "conversion to larger units of production, technological innovation, division of labour, substitution of capital for labour, vigorous competition, and profitability as the mandatory condition of survival."[20] This is substantially what happened, as Health Maintenance Organization (HMO) coverage, the most common form of managed care, accelerated from thirty-three million people to eighty-one million in 2000. Managed care helped intensify cost-cutting and competition, but it became a fixture of the industry by 2000, with competition becoming the dynamic factor in change.[21]

Competition between hospitals and hospital systems tends to be specific. As one study put it, "Hospitals compete with each other not for the entire clinical continuum but for each service separately."[22] While competition occurs between all systems in a given geographic area, the entrance and proliferation of for-profit hospitals specializing in specific types of surgery, the so-called "focused factory" model, has intensified competition even further, particularly in large urban areas. As Kumar argues, "Since general hospital managers often subsidize less profitable departments using profits from surgery, they complain that specialty hospitals represent a threat to their viability."[23]

Competition has been most intense in major urban markets, where the majority of large hospitals are located. Brooks and Jones describe the transition:

> The landscape of hospital ownership and affiliation before the 1980s stands in sharp contrast to that of the early 1990s. In the pre-1980s era, the terrain was marked by large numbers of freestanding hospitals, independent of but coexisting with other hospitals. By the early 1990s, many of these hospitals had merged with others, had rationalized operations, and had entered into networks of hospitals, insurers, and physician groups.[24]

By 2009 three-quarters of private hospitals were consolidated in mostly urban-based corporate systems.[25]

The Consequences of Competition

Increased competition brought about four major interrelated changes in the structure and functioning of the industry: the consolidation of formerly free-standing hospitals into privately owned corporate systems, as discussed above; the rising importance of profits for all private hospitals; the increased capital intensity of the industry; and the introduction of work reorganization and "lean production" norms in hospital work.

In this increasingly competitive atmosphere, the "not-for-profit" classification has become little more than an official tax-free status, albeit with a requirement to provide some "community benefits."[26] Much like their for-profit rivals, these once-upon-a-time charities calculate their profits as profit margins and return on assets or capital.[27] Indicating the general shift among hospital executives toward a more businesslike mentality, a survey of the priorities of hospital executives published in 2008 showed that the highest mean score (4.58 out of 5) on a Likert scale was for "Operating Profit Margin."[28] Also like their for-profit competitors, the "not-for-profits" are run by CEOs on a business model. Compensation for these CEOs, while more modest than those of for-profit chain CEOs, can run from six figures to the eight million dollars received by Kaiser's CEO in 2009.[29] Even the juridical distinction between for-profit and not-for-profit hospitals is often rendered meaningless by overlap. All physician services for Kaiser Permanente, the nation's largest "not-for-profit" HMO, for example, are supplied by affiliated for-profit Permanente Medical Groups.[30]

In taking on the competition, consolidation has been matched by accelerating capital intensity. Measured in real, inflation-adjusted terms, the value of the net stock of fixed private assets in US hospitals rose by 40 percent from 2000 to 2009, compared to 21.5 percent for the US economy as a whole. The real net stock of private equipment and software, an indication of increased application of new technology, rose by an extraordinary 92 percent, compared to 28 percent for the economy as a whole in those years.[31] Much of this was due to the need to provide advanced equipment within each hospital in a given market. This has led US hospitals to have a much greater frequency of MRI units and CT scanners, used to detect internal medical problems, than hospitals in other countries: 25.9 MRI units per 1,000 population in the United States compared to 11 for OECD countries; and 34.3 CT scanners per 1,000 compared to 22.8.[32] In fact, 91 percent of US community hospitals have CT scanners and 68 percent have MRI scanners.[33] As a consequence, the real net stock of assets per worker in hospitals grew from $28,056 in 1980 to $32,863 in 1990, $53,878 in 2000, and $81,290 in 2009. While this ratio grew by an annual average of 1.7 percent in the 1980s, in the 1990s, as competition accelerated, it grew by an average of 6.4 percent a year. It leveled off at about 5 percent a year in the 2000s, due in part to the recession.[34]

The pressures of competition and the expense of capital investment also led a growing number of hospitals to attempt cost-cutting through work reorganization. Among other things, this has meant the adoption of "lean production" and "operations management" techniques borrowed from manufacturing. Some hospitals, like the Seattle Children's Hospital, have been quite explicit that what they were imitating was the Toyota Production System (TPS), with its "checklists, standardization and nonstop brainstorming."[35] The trend, however, has come to cover much of the industry. Kumar summarizes the trend: "Over the years, they have adapted Lean Manufacturing, Six Sigma and supply chain strategies in order to become more efficient as well as improving patient care and satisfaction."[36]

Much of lean production as applied to hospitals involves workflows, but just as in a factory, it usually means more output with the same or fewer people. For example, a 2010 article in the *Boston Globe* reported, "Cincinnati Children's Hospital estimates efficiency measures will allow the hospital to generate an additional $137 million in revenue this year from treating more children with the same staffing levels in surgery and other departments."[37] While some of these measures do contribute to greater efficiency, they also tend to increase the workload and effort. One aspect of lean production related to this is outsourcing—that is, "supply-chain strategies"—which has been done extensively not only with ancillary services, but even with nursing staff. While lean measures apply to the entire workforce, the use of temporary and part-time nurses has increased, playing havoc with nurse–patient ratios, which have become a central issue in collective bargaining.[38]

Lean production or operations management relies on standardization, and this has been accelerated by the application of digital technology that also serves as workforce surveillance. Nurses and other workers in some US hospitals must now wear badges containing GPS tracking devices.[39] Electronic health records (EHR) clearly improve clinical performance, but they also have negative side effects on the work of registered nurses. In particular, "the standardization required by computer technology deprives caregivers of the opportunity to tailor treatment to the needs of their patients."[40] In addition, EHR can include a nurse schedule function that automatically sets staffing patterns, which has meant the increased use of "nurse extenders" who are less trained than registered nurses.[41] Another innovation that affects treatment and threatens skill is the Clinical Decision Support System (CDSS), derived from critical path analysis used in manufacturing. CDSS recommends standard treatments on the basis of studies that "systematically exclude women and minorities," according to one union-backed study.[42] By 2009, the study reported, CDSS was in use in 68 percent of US hospitals. All of this has decreased nurse autonomy and increased pressure on the entire hospital workforce, altering the "climate of patient care" substantially.

The impact of President Obama's Patient Protection and Affordable Care Act of 2010 is likely to be complex, but what is certain is that by providing billions of dollars and millions of newly insured patients, it will increase competition for these funds. At the same time, it will introduce reductions in Medicare payments and require hospitals to make cost-cutting and efficiency gains that will be difficult to meet.[43]

From Impact to Action

That there is a strong link between the enormous pressures on the workforce and changing working conditions, on the one hand, and the willingness to join a union, on the other, is indicated, for one thing, by the much higher percentage of union win rates in NLRB elections in hospitals. Union win rates from 2001 through 2009 averaged 60 percent for all industries, but 68 percent for hospitals. By 2009 they had risen more or less steadily to 80 percent, compared to 69 percent for all industries.[44] Furthermore, a study by Clark et al. found that nurses who had experienced job reorganization had a more negative attitude toward work, were more concerned with "voice" and administrative support (or lack of it), and, as a result, were more likely to see unions as effective and vote for them.[45]

Further survey data show that during the 1990s the perception was that working conditions had degenerated. A survey by the polling company Peter D. Hart Research Associates showed that 63 percent of current nurses and 78 percent of those who had left their jobs believed "the situation facing RNs has been getting worse."[46] Sixty-six percent of current nurses believed patient load was a problem, while 79 percent reported that the acuteness of patients' conditions was more severe. Understaffing, stress, and the physical demands of the job rated high as problems, while concern with pay was very low. In identifying the causes of degenerating conditions, 69 percent of current nurses saw managed care as the major cause.[47] More recently, a 2006 survey of more than twenty-two thousand nurses in California, New Jersey, and Pennsylvania revealed that many nurse still felt that staffing was too low. When asked if there was "enough staff to get work done," only 40 percent in New Jersey, 44 percent in Pennsylvania, and 56 percent in California said yes. California's higher "yes" rate was due to the state-mandated nurse–patient ratios won in 2004 through the efforts of the CNA.[48] As Table 10.1 shows, these views are consistent with the findings of Clark and Clark et al. linking working conditions and reorganization with the "climate of patient care" and pro-union attitudes.[49]

Table 10.1 Climate for Patient Care and Inclination to Vote for a Union[50]

	Vote for a Union	
	Yes	No
Report negative climate	62%	38%
Report positive climate	28%	72%

The link with pro-union attitudes and patient care is further confirmed by experienced observers. National Nurses United (NNU) organizing director David Johnson says of the union's effect on work standards, safety, and patient advocacy: "NNU's track record in achieving gains in all these areas is a reason for our explosive growth."[51] As Benson summarizes it in his survey of nurse unionization, "They are won over to unionism as a curb on the authority of imperious management."[52]

While hospital managements do resist unionization, they seldom have the threat of workplace closure to intimidate the workforce as a credible tool.[53] In an earlier study, Bronfenbrenner noted that while the frequency of plant closure threats went as high as 75 percent in many manufacturing, communications, and utility organizing efforts, in health care it was 31 percent.[54] This figure includes several health care industries as well as hospitals; it is likely that today's hospitals, with their far greater intensity of "sunk capital" than nursing homes, are even more immune to plant closure threats during representation elections.

More credible, from management's point of view, is the argument that unions imply a self-interest that may conflict with professionalism and patient care. The unions counter that it is, in fact, management attacking the quality of care through cuts in staff, "gag" rules, and technology that limits the personalization of care. The question of the interests of nurses versus patients is, of course, more difficult when the question of strikes arises. One study of the impact of nurses' strikes in New York State did indeed find an increase in in-hospital mortality during strikes.[55] The NNU answered this study with one of its own, conducted by University of Pennsylvania researchers who surveyed twenty-two thousand nurses in California, Pennsylvania, and New Jersey. The results showed that California nurses, who have the highest nurse–patient ratio at an average of one to five, have more time with patients than those with lower ratios. It also estimated that New Jersey hospitals would have 14 percent fewer deaths and Pennsylvania 11 percent if they had the California ratio.[56]

In other words, it is the fight for improved ratios and other patient-related union goals that saves lives. As one representative of the Minnesota Nurses' Association commented, "Our nurses said it was the most difficult decision of their lives to authorize this open-ended strike vote. But they truly feel that the unsafe staffing issue is that important, and if they don't stand up for their patients now, who will?"[57] In any event, the unions' consistent advocacy of improved patient care has been sufficient to counter the management case more often than not.

Although space prevents a full discussion of the other, more traditional, factors in union success or failure, most point to a positive organizing environment in US hospitals. High rates of union success are associated with an urban setting, with 92 percent of hospitals with two hundred or more beds located in urban areas.[58] Small bargaining-unit size is another well-known factor in union success, the 1991 NLRB decision to divide hospitals into eight bargaining units has provided this advantage.[59] Finally, workplaces with high injury and illness rates have been shown to be sites of union success.[60] The injury and illness rate for hospitals is one of the highest at 7.7 per one hundred full-time workers, higher even than construction or mining at 5.4 and 5.2 respectively.[61] Finally, as mentioned earlier, the dominant role of women in hospital work has been a distinct advantage in organizing as, going by the results of the past two decades, unions with a high proportion of women members tend to have a higher win rate than others in NLRB elections.[62]

It can reasonably be asked, then, if hospitals and their workers betray all the aspects of pro-union success, why are 85 percent of these employees still nonunion? As argued above, while management resistance undoubtedly affects some workers' choices, the largely immobile nature of hospitals denies management the opportunity to threaten closure or relocation. Management, of course, does try to appeal to the professionalism of nurses in particular. Again, however, this runs up against the fact that even the major professional association, the American Nurses Association, has engaged in collective bargaining and even industrial action for decades.[63] Furthermore, the nurses' unions have themselves captured the mantle of professionalism with their embrace of patient advocacy.[64] A 2009 "global" survey of eleven countries found that 72 percent of US nurses surveyed thought unions were supportive of nurses and their concerns, exactly the "global" average.[65]

A more plausible explanation for the 85 percent still not represented by unions lies in the "fight or flight" dilemma. Staff turnover is extraordinarily high in US hospitals. One study found that turnover among support staff of a major urban hospital was 47 percent, while that for "allied health personnel," notably nurses, was 49 percent.[66] Another calculates the turnover rate for support workers as high as 100 percent in some hospitals, while rates in excess of 50 percent are common.[67] In addition, there are at least a quarter of a million qualified nurses who are not practicing their profession due to poor staff–patient ratios, lack of voice, and overwork.[68] Along with the surveys cited above, these studies show that the reasons for leaving the job are substantially the same as those for joining a union. It does seem clear that large numbers of nurses and support workers chose "flight" as the most practical course in many circumstances. The choice of flight over fight, however, is due in part to the limited ability of unions to reach the nation's four million nonsupervisory hospital workers.

A credible, if still partial, explanation for the level of "flight" and the unorganized 85 percent lies, therefore, in the limited, often dwindling resources of American unions. Most US unions are financially strapped and face rising real staff costs. They spend more than they receive in membership dues. In 2009, for example, the Service Employee International Union (SEIU), a major player in health care, drew only 83 percent of its revenue from member dues.[69] Partly for financial reasons, the SEIU has chosen the more cost-effective route of organizing public-sector home health care and child care workers, largely through political deals with state governors.[70] Like the SEIU, other unions that organize hospital workers, such as the American Federation of Teachers, have other jurisdictions that often take precedent. The new nurses' unions, although aggressive organizers, are as yet small. The fact is, the number of NLRB elections in hospitals has fallen in the last decade from an average of 166 a year from 2000 to 2003 to a little over 100 a year in 2007 to 2009, despite very high rates of success.[71] It will take a much greater focus and effort to realize the full potential for unionization as an alternative to "flight." At this point, it is appropriate to look at the state of unionism in recent years.

Hospital Unionism in the Early Twenty-First Century

About a dozen unions claim a significant number of members in US hospitals. The large number of unions is explained in part by the 1991 NLRB decision to split hospitals into eight bargaining units, three for professionals and five for nonprofessionals, the latter of which include maintenance workers, housekeeping staff, clerical workers, and laboratory technicians.[72] Thus, the presence of professional and technical engineers, office employees and professionals, Teamsters, and operating engineers reflects unionization of the different professional and nonprofessional units. By far the largest unions in the private sector of the industry are the SEIU, with 400,000 to 450,000 members in hospitals, and the recently formed National Nurses United (NNU), formed in 2009 through the merger of the California Nurses' Association (CNA), the Minnesota Nurses' Association (MNA), and the United American

Nurses (UAN), claiming 160,000 members.[73] The American Federation of Teachers (AFT) claims 70,000 members, the "majority" of whom work in hospitals.[74] The National Federation of Nurses (NFN), a loose confederation of eight state associations formed in 2007, claims 70,000 members.[75] The United Food and Commercial Workers (UFCW) and the United Steelworkers (USW) also claim health care members, but offer no breakdown of hospital members.[76] Various state affiliates of the American Nurses Association (ANA) also engage in collective bargaining.[77]

A final union must be included despite its currently small size. This is the National Union of Healthcare Workers (NUHW), which was founded in 2009 after the leaders and thousands of members of SEIU–United Healthcare West (SEIU–UHW) left SEIU when SEIU president Andy Stern put that local into trusteeship. As SEIU–UHW members were formally under contract with the SEIU, under US labor law the NHUW could not automatically take UHW's 150,000 members with them, despite the fact that about 100,000 UHW members signed petitions supporting the NUHW.[78] Although the NUHW signed up a majority of Kaiser's 44,000 workers in 2009, it was defeated in a 2010 NLRB election contest with the SEIU, at great expense to the SEIU and some say with a good deal of help from Kaiser management. Nevertheless, the NUHW has succeeded in winning a number of bargaining units in Kaiser, Sutter, and elsewhere in California, bringing it close to 10,000 dues-paying members in 2010.[79]

The ninety-three collective bargaining agreements concluded in hospitals in 2009 and the first three-quarters of 2010 provide a picture of the ranking of unions in hospital collective bargaining.[80] The SEIU comes in first with forty-five contracts, or nearly half of the total. The NNU is next with eighteen contracts, or just under 20 percent. The AFT, which includes some nurses' agreements, had thirteen in this period, or 14 percent, and the UFCW eight, or 9 percent. The remaining 8 percent was divided among the three independent nurses' unions, the Teamsters with two, and one each for the Office and Professional Employees International Union (OPEIU), the USW, the Communications Workers of America (CWA), and the American Federation of State, County, and Municipal Employees (AFSCME). Occupationally, forty-two contracts represented nurses alone and forty-five technical and support staff, sometimes including nurses, while six covered doctors. As Table 2 shows, efforts at new organizing through NLRB elections showed a similar distribution, with the SEIU holding forty-two elections, nurses' unions (listed as independent unions by the NLRB) eight, the AFT seven, IUOE six, the UFCW three, and the remaining twenty-eight held by a broad variety of unions. The NLRB figures in Table 10.2 also show the concentration of hospital unions in coastal states.

According to the Current Population Survey figures cited at the beginning of this article, union membership in hospitals grew by 199,590 from 2000 through 2010.[81] The total number of hospital workers who gained representation rights through NLRB elections in this period was 149,110.[82] Some of these units may have faced later decertifications, while not all those in these units, particularly in right-to-work states, necessarily became union members. The remaining fifty to perhaps seventy thousand are most likely explained by "organic" growth, on the one hand, and organizing by means other than traditional NLRB elections, on the other. ("Organic growth" refers to the growth of facilities or systems already organized.) The rest may have organized through "neutrality" agreements such as the SEIU has with Kaiser, Catholic Healthcare West, and Tenet.[83]

Collective Bargaining Trends

The recent state of collective bargaining in hospitals reflects the pressures on the workforce resulting from the industrial re-structuring and work reorganization described above. The first thing that stands out in this regard is the comparatively high

Table 10.2 Distribution of NLRB Elections, Hospitals (622) 2010, by Union and Region[84]

Union	Number of Elections	Percent of Elections
SEIU	42	44.7
Nurses	8	8.5
AFT	7	7.5
IUOE	6	6.4
UFCW	3	3.2
Others	28	29.8
Total	94	100.0
Region		
East Coast	40	42.5
West Coast	32	34.0
Coasts	72	76.6
Rest of country	22	23.4

number of strikes in recent years, a fact that not only indicates that intensified pressures on the workforce are a major factor in union growth, but also implies increased militancy among union members. A LexisNexis search (2010) for 2009 and 2010 revealed thirty strike threats and ten actual work stoppages out of the approximately one hundred contracts negotiated in those years. This is a rate of 10 percent, compared to 0.06 percent for all strikes and contract negotiations reported by the Federal Mediation and Conciliation Service (FMCS) for those years.[85] Three of the hospital strikes were conducted by SEIU locals and seven by nurses' unions, mostly affiliates of the new National Nurses United (NNU). Most of these strikes were not primarily over wages, but over issues related to the "climate of patient care," which will be discussed below.

Overall, real wage growth in hospitals has run a little ahead of the economy as a whole, 7.2 percent from 2005 to 2009, compared to 5.1 percent, or 1.4 percent and 1 percent annually.[86] In terms of collective bargaining, hospital-based unions did better than the hospital industry averages and slightly better for all industries in the United States in 2009 and 2010 when measured by first-year increases, according to the Bureau of National Affairs (BNA) reports.[87] In 2009, the average first-year wage increase rose by 2.4 percent for hospital unions, compared to 2.3 percent for the United States as a whole. For the first three-quarters of 2010, first-year increases in hospitals averaged 2.1 percent, compared to 1.7 percent across all agreements. In 2009, 14 percent of hospital contracts had no increase in the first year compared to 24 percent for all industries, while in 2010 the gap narrowed with hospitals seeing no first-year increase in 30 percent of all new contracts, compared to 35 percent for all settlements reported by the BNA. There was, however, a considerable range of first-year increases. The average for NNU affiliates was 3.6 percent and that for the SEIU was 2.5 percent, with AFT hospital locals averaging 0.6 percent. The increases also varied by occupation. In 2009 and 2010 combined, average first-year increases covering nurses were slightly below those for all hospital workers, 1.92 percent compared to 2.25 percent, largely because of the low increases for AFT hospital locals. Not surprisingly, these recession period wage increases are significantly smaller than some of the major collective agreements signed earlier in the decade at some of the trendsetting hospitals, which averaged 3.4 percent.[88]

Like virtually all unionized workers in the United States, hospital workers have faced concessionary demands on pensions, medical benefits, and working conditions. *Modern Healthcare* reported that some hospitals and hospital chains were freezing pension benefits as the recession hit their pension funds.[89] This was an issue at the fourteen Minneapolis hospitals struck in 2010 by the Minnesota affiliate of the NNU.[90] Health care benefits were also an issue in disputes in Massachusetts, Maine, Pennsylvania, Minnesota, and New York in early 2011.[91] These were also among the major issues in the strike of twenty-one thousand members of the NUHW and CNA in September 2011.[92]

The most critical issues, above all for nurses, however, involved staffing levels, nurse–patient ratios, mandatory overtime, and "floating," all issues associated with "the climate of patient care." All of these issues have been enabled to one degree or another by the new technology and "lean" practices discussed above. The conditions faced by support workers necessarily follow those of nurses, only at much lower wages. As a result, turnover rates for these occupations often run more than 50 percent to 100 percent, as reported earlier.[93]

Not surprisingly, as the findings of Clark (2009) and Clark et al. (1999, 2001) would predict, a major goal of nursing unions has been the "climate of patient care."[94] For over a decade, nurses' unions have sought to negotiate contract language on staffing levels and patient ratios, with some success. Examples of specific nurse–patient ratios are found in the agreements negotiated by the New York State Nurses Association (NYSNA) with New York's Voluntary Hospitals and the AFT-affiliated Health Professionals and Allied Employees at New Jersey hospitals in 2004. The CNA, MNA, SEIU, and other unions representing nurses have dealt with staffing issues through joint committees to oversee staffing matters and patient care in general.[95] All of the 2009 and 2010 strikes by nurses involved staffing issues and most won contract language giving them some control over this.[96]

Another key issue related to staffing is mandatory overtime. Here NNU affiliates and SEIU locals have succeeded in negotiating contract language that limits this. The MNA won contract language stating that "no nurse shall be disciplined for refusal to work overtime" in 2004 and again in 2007.[97] The NYSNA version reads, "Employees will not be required to work involuntary overtime except in a disaster/emergency," with "emergency" clearly defined.[98] The SEIU has also won limits on forced overtime in Miami and Boston.[99]

"Floating" or the allocation of nurses out of their usual unit and specialty is another important staffing issue. Seeking greater "flexibility" to cut costs, hospital managers tend to fill vacancies without hiring more personnel by simply moving nurses around. It often means that nurses must work in areas they are not familiar with and that overall staff shortages remain unaddressed. It is a relatively new practice, creating "just-in-time" nursing.[100] Nurses' unions have attempted to negotiate contract language to limit the practice. The NYSNA language at Mount Sinai Hospital, for example, reads, "An RN shall not be floated inside or outside her/his area of clinical practice . . . unless the RN has appropriate orientation."[101] All of these staffing issues affect working conditions for nurses and those technical and support workers working with them, as well as challenging management prerogatives on workforce deployment. But they also affect the quality of health care. Thus, staffing concerns have become one of the important aspects of the NNU's "patient advocacy" approach to collective bargaining.

Divergent Directions of Hospital Unionism

In the last decade or so, there has been an increasing divergence in the practices and structures of unionism most clearly articulated between CNA/NNU, on the one hand, and the mainstream of the SEIU's leadership, on the other. The pressures of the hospital industry on its workforce and the response of many of the unions have both given rise to changes that are, perhaps, clearest and most thorough in many of the nurses' unions. The change of nurse organization from management-dominated associations to more assertive and oppositional unions has been a long one, but it has accelerated in the last decade or so.[102] The NNU and others have adopted a modern-day version of "social unionism," a term NNU director Rose Ann DeMoro uses to mean patient advocacy as a central theme of unionism.[103] The 2010 twenty-eight-day strike of 1,200 nurses and technicians against Temple University Hospital in Philadelphia not only sought action over staffing issues, but successfully rejected company demands for a "gag rule" that would prevent nurses from criticizing hospital practice even where it was endangering nurses and patients.[104] In a similar vein, the CNA rejected participation in the labor–management cooperation program at Kaiser Permanente on the grounds that one of the requirements was confidentiality, meaning the union could not publicly criticize Kaiser.[105]

SEIU president Andy Stern, on the other hand, was a strong advocate of labor–management partnerships, or what he called "value-added employer relationships."[106] The SEIU not only has its Labor–Management Partnership (LMP) with Kaiser Permanente, but a similar arrangement is in place between the SEIU–United Healthcare Workers–East and the League of Voluntary Hospitals in New York City.[107] The CNA and NNU reject such cooperation in favor of a more independent and adversarial approach to unionism. Indeed, the CNA was one of the only unions to remain outside the Kaiser Permanente Labor–Management Partnership.[108] In the late 1990s the Minnesota Nurses' Association, one of the founders of NNU, left a labor–management cooperation scheme that had begun in the mid-1980s and covered more than a dozen hospitals in Minneapolis–St. Paul.[109]

Equally, if not more, important are the trajectories of the two unions on matters of workplace organization and power. The SEIU, though its locals still possess workplace organization and shop stewards, has moved away from face-to-face organization on the ground toward the introduction of Member Resource Centers (MRCs), that is, call centers meant to handle workplace problems at a distance. Stern described this approach as "a new model less focused on individual grievances, more focused on industry needs."[110] The approach to grievances implied by the MRCs was controversial within the SEIU. SEIU–United Healthcare Workers–West delegates to the 2008 convention criticized the call-center approach. One argued, "A union is not about long-distance representation from someone who's never set foot in your workplace, who doesn't know you or your manager, and who doesn't have any understanding of what goes on where you work." For nurses' unions focused on patient care, staffing matters, and work organization generally, such a new "model" was unlikely to be attractive. While the SEIU and CNA agreed to end their feud in 2009 and the aggressive Andy Stern was replaced as president of the SEIU by the "more collegial" Mary Kay Henry in 2010, the differences in orientation remain.[111]

The differences in outlook and practice that emerged in the 1990s and 2000s did not exist only between the SEIU and CNA/NNU, but within the SEIU as well. California SEIU affiliate United Healthcare West (UHW) became a severe critic of the Stern leadership in the 2000s, primarily due to what UHW leaders saw as the evolution of Stern's increasing accommodation to employers and his top-down internal regime. The UHW was part of the Kaiser LMP, but saw things differently. As then UHW president Sal Roselli put it, referring to the strikes of the 1980s and 1990s that led to the LMP, "The Kaiser 'partnership'—and the Kaiser contract—exists because of struggle, not because Kaiser is some benevolent employer."[112] The UHW had fought hard to produce some of the best labor agreements in the industry. In matters of workplace organization and power, it shared views more like those of the CNA than the SEIU leadership. That is, despite its statewide structure, it maintained a democratic chapter structure and a very strong stewards' organization. As one pro-NUHW study described the UHW before it left the SEIU: "UHW was democratic, certainly by trade union standards. There were elections at every single level. Its structure was egalitarian—from its universal system of elected shop stewards, stewards' councils, and divisional bodies to its elected executive committee."[113]

The UHW leadership, with support from much of the membership, left the SEIU in 2009 to form the independent NUHW after a long and bitter fight with the national leadership, culminating in the trusteeship of UHW.[114] They took with them the democratic tradition of the UHW, along with its advocacy of strong workplace organization and a willingness to combat management prerogatives on questions of staffing and work organization. In March 2011, for example, the new NUHW led a strike of one thousand Kaiser nurses in Los Angeles over the issue of staffing levels.[115] Although it is beyond the scope of this study, there are differences in approaches to political influence. For example, the NNU and NUHW are committed to fighting for a single-payer health care system, which the SEIU leadership has opposed.

Despite these divergent approaches to unionism, the one thing the NNU, NUHW, and SEIU have in common is that they are aggressive organizers. The SEIU has a reputation as an "organizing union" and has grown from 981,331 members since 1995, just before Stern took the helm, to 1.9 million in 2009.[116] A good portion of its growth among hospital workers is explained by the absorption of some 125,000 members of Local 1199 in 1998. The SEIU, however, grew by about 65,000 in California and has had a number of successful recent hospital organizing drives. In 2009, it brought in nearly 8,000 hospital workers through NLRB elections alone.[117] CNA's membership grew from 35,000 in the 1990s to 85,000 in 2006, when it affiliated with the AFL-CIO.[118] It then led the formation of the NNU, which immediately began organizing nationally. Even the as-yet-small NUHW has shown organizing ability not only in its UHW past, but since its independence, growing to about 10,000 members in little over a year.[119] The unknown piece of the future puzzle is the degree to which the more workplace-based organization and democratic style of the NNU and NUHW will affect the locals of the SEIU. In any case, union growth in this industry seems a certainty.

Applicability to Other Industries and Its Limits
The findings of this study certainly have applicability to other sections of the US health industry partly, as noted toward the

beginning, because they provide an example of the sort of re-structuring typical of the neoliberal era. More specifically, this analysis is of direct relevance to work in nursing-care facilities, where many of the same conditions, economic pressures, and unions are at work. These facilities employ 1.7 million workers, but union density remains a low 8 percent.[120] The hotel industry is another one that exemplifies the relationship between change in the industry, work reorganization, the potential for unioniza-tion, and what this says for the union's message. The full-service hotel sector is a primarily urban industry that has faced sharp competition and consolidation into large chains, and its demo-graphics are similar to those among hospital support workers. Its high turnover rate of 152 percent reflects a "flight" response to work intensification and "flexibility" similar to that in hospi-tals.[121] An obvious difference is that hotels lack the large pro-fessional workforce represented by nurses, the emotional content of the work, and the likely differences in the implementation of lean production norms. Nevertheless, the pressures on the work-force have been substantial. Additionally, the major union in the industry, UNITE-HERE, is an aggressive organizer with a style and outlook similar to that of the NUHW and the NNU that has turned around a slumping union density in the 1980s to achieve a national density of 19 percent in the full-service hotel sector, with much higher levels in many major cities.[122] Finally, all of these industries have a high proportion of female workers, a positive factor in unionization for over two decades. Further research following this approach may find application in other service industries as well.

Conclusion

The dramatic changes in the hospital industry and the enor-mous workplace pressures on its workforce have been major factors in the growth of hospital unionism in the past decade, while the relative immobility of hospitals has undoubtedly en-abled the process. The leading force has been among the nurses' unions, with the NNU now forming something like a vanguard. The major gains of the last decade have been less in wages than in contract language that has challenged management prerogatives on important issues. Two distinct approaches to unionism have taken shape in the course of the struggles for these gains and the growth of these unions. Though the terrain of unionism in America's profit-seeking hospitals is a patchwork of rivalry and cooperation, organizing competition between differing approaches may boost the growth of unionism in this industry, as it once did in basic industry in the 1930s. The continuation or even acceleration of the pressures on the workforce will almost certainly spur more hospital workers to seek union protection. Furthermore, the theory that work reorganization, brought on by increased competition and industrial restructuring, particularly in an urban setting, offers the potential for union growth as the "fight" alternative to "flight" may well have an application beyond the nation's hospitals in this neoliberal world.

11 Immigrant Workers and Labor in the United States

Kim Moody

On May 1, 1886, hundreds of thousands of workers, many of them immigrants, struck across America for the eight-hour day, creating what would become International Workers' Day almost everywhere in the world except the United States. One hundred and twenty years later, on May 1, 2006, millions of immigrant workers struck and demonstrated for the right to work without harassment in the United States. It was called "A Day without Immigrants," and many of the nation's worst-paying jobs would go unperformed for all or part of the day. If the estimates of five or six million participants are right, then perhaps as much as a quarter of the country's twenty-one million foreign-born workers took action of some sort. Unlike May 1, 1886, unions did not call this action and played only a supportive role in it. Along

Versions of this essay were originally published in Jo McBride and Ian Green-wood, eds., Community Unionism: A Comparative Analysis of Concepts and Contexts *(London: Palgrave, 2009) and in Leo Panitch and Colin Leys, eds.,* Socialist Register 2007 *(New York: Monthly Review, 2007).*

with a series of ad hoc coalitions that called each of the demonstrations leading up to May 1 in March and April, a network of some six hundred advocacy and community organizations with strong backing from the Catholic Church served as the organizational backbone for May 1.[1] The turnout was all the more impressive because the organizers in different cities had different approaches. Some called for a boycott or stay-at-home, but others, like L.A. cardinal Roger Mahony, warned potential demonstrators not to risk their jobs.[2] Still, they turned out by the tens and hundreds of thousands in cities across the country.

Unions did play a supporting role in the events of May 1. In Los Angeles, for example, they put up more than eighty thousand dollars and handled much of the logistics. SEIU and AFSCME leaders acted as liaison to the immigrant organizations and the Teamsters provided two eighteen-wheelers to lead off the march.[3] Labor support was aided by a dramatic change of policy by the AFL-CIO in 2000, when it embraced amnesty for undocumented workers. This, in turn, was preceded by a demonstration of fifteen thousand in Washington, D.C., called by the National Coalition for Dignity and Amnesty. Indeed, this coalition had been holding demonstrations on May 1 since 1999.[4] The growing interaction between immigrant groups and unions reached a new level when several unions went on to play a key role in the 2003 Immigrant Workers' Freedom Ride, a caravan that crossed the country and ended in a mass demonstration in New York. This high-visibility event helped to build self-confidence in going public with the issue of immigrants' rights.[5]

The actions on May 1 also revealed the often-overlooked strategic position that immigrant workers have in some industries. The Mexican and Central American waterfront truckers in the nation's largest port, Los Angeles/Long Beach, brought 90 percent of that port's activities to a standstill on May 1. The meat and poultry processing industry reported that 50 percent of its operations across the country had been halted on that day. The American Nursery and Landscaping Association said that 90 percent of its workers struck, as did a similar percentage of workers in garden supply warehouses. Construction was also heavily hit in many areas as immigrant workers, like the California drywall hangers, walked out for the day.[6] Thus, May 1, 2006, showed not only the willingness and ability of immigrant workers to act on their own despite the high risk of job loss or even deportation, but also the strength of the immigrant workforce in significant parts of the US economy.

Harvest of Empire

The 1965 Hart-Cellar Act ended the highly discriminatory national quota system and opened the door, within limits, to Third World immigration, particularly for those with relatives in the United States or sought-after skills. In the United States, where the immigrant population had declined in the 1950s and remained stagnant in the 1960s, the foreign-born population rose from 9.7 million in 1970 to 34.2 million in 2004, 21 million of whom were not yet citizens. By 2004, the employed foreign-born workforce had risen to over 20 million, composing 14.5 percent of those employed in the United States. Of these, 12 million were not citizens.[7] By 2004 there were 11.6 million legal permanent resident immigrants in the United States, according to the Department of Homeland Security. Legal permanent residents are those with "green cards." Of these, 3.1 million were of Mexican origin, by far the largest group. The next largest groups were from the Philippines and India with half a million each, followed by China, the Dominican Republic, and Vietnam, each at about four hundred thousand.[8] In addition, according to estimates by the Department of Homeland Security, which replaced the Immigration and Naturalization Service in tracking and regulating immigration after 2002, there were 10.5 million "unauthorized" or undocumented immigrants in the United States as of January 2005. More than 80 percent of these undocumented immigrants had arrived since 1990.[9] Some, however, put this "unauthorized" immigration as high as 20 million by 2007.[10]

The list of major countries of origin is suggestive of the most basic causes of such growth in immigration in recent years. With the exception of India, all of these countries have established trails of immigration that go back to US economic and/or military involvement in these nations. Mexico, China, Cuba, and the Philippines go back to the initial period of US empire-building just over a hundred years ago but also reflect, with the exception of Cuba, the deep contemporary involvement of US business in these areas. Korea, of course, entered the US orbit during the Korean War in the early 1950s. Vietnam and the Dominican Republic trace back to US military interventions, albeit on a very different scale, in the 1960s. El Salvador, Korea, and Cuba, with three hundred thousand each, are all sites of US intervention within the last half-century. In the cases of Mexico, the Dominican Republic, and El Salvador, the correlation between the impact of globalization, US foreign policy, and accelerated emigration from those countries to the United States is all too clear.

Like the Caribbean, Central America became part of the US "backyard" after the Spanish-American War. By the 1920s, US business had more invested in all of Latin America, mostly in Central America and the Caribbean, than in Europe. In the 1920s and 1930s, the US military intervened throughout the region scores of times to protect American business interests there. As Sidney Lens wrote some years ago, "There was never a day from 1919 to 1933 when American marines did not intervene in or occupy the sovereign territory of another country."[11] After World War II this practice was resumed, with interventions in the Western Hemisphere, sometimes covert, in Guatemala (1954), Cuba (1960), Brazil (1964), the Dominican Republic (1965), Chile (1973), Grenada (1983), and Panama (1989).[12] In all but one case, Cuba, they were directed against elected officials or governments.

It wasn't just military intervention, overt or covert, that pushed millions of Latin Americans from their homelands. It was that other favorite policy of corporate America and virtually every administration of the last half-century or more— free trade. "Free trade," as a policy, isn't just about trade: it's about opening nations, all nations, to investment by the big corporations. Because many nations developed their domestic industry by protecting it from imports and foreign ownership, free-trade policy required that these nations abandon that development strategy. US capital first found an opening through the development of free-trade zones (FTZs). The FTZs suspended government regulations and gave the corporations a free hand. Next came the border development program in northern Mexico, with its *maquiladora* plants, in principle similar to an FTZ. In 1985, the Reagan administration negotiated the Caribbean Basin Initiative, which opened countries in the region to this type of investment. By 1992, there were two hundred FTZs in Mexico and the Caribbean, housing more than three thousand plants employing 735,000 workers. All of this was only a rehearsal for NAFTA, which did more of the same as we saw earlier.[13]

This, however, was only one side of "free trade." The other was investment by the banks in New York, London, and the Third World. In Latin America this meant, above all, the New York City banks—Wall Street. When oil money poured into these banks in the early and mid-1970s, they promoted low-interest loans to Third World countries. But then inflation and high interest rates took hold and by the early 1980s, countries throughout Latin America were increasingly unable to pay even the annual interest. This became the Third World debt crisis. The debt became the lever by which the United States and other industrial powers, with the help of the International Monetary Fund, not only ended barriers to their investment but literally forced the redesign of many Third World economies. Mexico is a prime example.

As a result of the neoliberal restructuring of the Mexican economy in preparation for NAFTA, average real wages dropped by 67 percent from 1982 to 1991, and those of Mexico's slightly better-paid industrial workers by 48 percent. Four dollars a day became the wage along the Mexican border as well as in the Dominican Republic.[14] Foreign investment in agribusiness and plantation farming, another side of "free trade," also served to drive millions off the land in Mexico, Central America, and the Caribbean with no hope of work in their own countries. So Mexican legal immigration into the United States rose from 640,294 in the 1970s to 1,655,843 in the 1980s, 3,541,700 in the 1990s, and then dropped to 876,823 from 2001 through 2005.[15]

Economic Impact

The economic importance of immigrant labor to the US economy is beyond doubt. Former secretary of labor Ray Marshall recently wrote:

> Immigrants are particularly important to the US economy, accounting for over half of the workforce growth during the 1990s and 86% of the increase in employment between 2000 and 2005. Because there will be no net increase in the number of prime-working-age natives (aged 25 to 54) for the next 20 years, the strength of the American economy could depend heavily on how the nation relates immigration to economic and social policy.[16]

Immigrant workers in the official economy are more heavily concentrated in services, construction, transportation, and factory work than native-born workers. On average they make 76 percent of what natives make.[17] This figure, however, is high, as it includes a significant number of white and Asian professionals. But millions work on the edges of recorded employment and in the growing informal economy for much less. So it is likely that wage levels in these industries were lower than if there had been a severe labor shortage pushing up the wages of native workers. While there is no way to measure this, the cost savings in industries such as food processing, consumer services, and construction probably lowered the relative cost of living to some degree and rendered some industries more globally competitive than might otherwise have been the case. As in the last great wave of immigration from 1870 through 1920, the recent wave has no doubt contributed to the accumulation process within the United States.

The question is raised, then: Did this immigration have a negative impact on the wages of employed native-born workers? In any overall sense, the answer has to be no, because the timing is wrong. Real weekly wages of production and nonsupervisory workers began their descent in 1973, well *before* the major upswing in immigration numbers that occurred in the 1980s and 1990s. The causes of that fall in wages were the recession of 1974–75, the "stagflation" that followed into the 1980s, and the wage concessions that began nationally with the 1979 Chrysler bailout and spread throughout industry from the early 1980s onward. Furthermore, if there was to be an overall negative impact on wages, one would expect it to come in the wake of the enormous increase of immigration from the mid-1980s through the 1990s and beyond. This would presumably raise unemployment and depress wages. But, in fact, real weekly wages rose after 1995 through 2000. After that they did fall somewhat, then rose again by 2010.[18] The pattern follows the contours of the economy rather than that of immigration. It is possible that the huge proportion of immigrant workers in the growth of the workforce after 2000 had the statistical effect of flattening the overall average wage level, even if it did not affect the wages of already employed workers.

Competition for jobs between immigrants and natives is blunted by the "ethnic niche" or "queue" phenomenon described by sociologist Roger Waldinger.[19] That is, immigrant and other low-wage workers are entering jobs abandoned by other groups, often as a result of industrial or occupational restructuring, so that competition is minimal. Janice Fine summarized this argument as it relates to African Americans:

> Nelson Lim's analysis of significant African American labor market niches in New York, Los Angeles, Miami, San Francisco, and Chicago in 1970 and 1990 showed an overall pattern of succession, as opposed to competition between African Americans and immigrants. Roger Waldinger also concludes that there is no direct evidence to show competition between African American and immigrant workers.[20]

It would be naïve, however, to deny that there is some level of competition between newer immigrant groups and other working-class people. Like jobs, space in cities is finite and the transition from one group to another in a given neighborhood is full of friction. An organizer for the workers' center Carolina Alliance for Fair Employment (CAFE) said of his mainly African American members, "What I kept hearing was that Hispanics are taking over the neighborhood." While he stated that they exaggerated, there was a problem of friction.[21] While employment levels are more flexible, there can be friction here too. Yet what appears to be the case is that there is a strong tendency today, as there was over a hundred years ago, for the various ethnic immigrant groups to concentrate in particular occupations or industries in a given geographic region where jobs were being or had been abandoned by native-born workers. So, in L.A., for example, the building maintenance workers are heavily Mexican and Central American, as are the drywall installers and the truckers on the waterfront. In New York, Latino immigrants are found in greengrocers' stores and restaurant kitchens but also construction, while Indians and Pakistanis are found driving cabs, Chinese and Latino women in garment sweatshops in New York and L.A., and so on. In these cases, there is little evidence of competition with other groups of workers.

Immigrant Workers and Trade Unions

According to the Migration Policy Institute's estimate, 1.8 million foreign-born workers belonged to unions in 2003, up from 1.4 million in 1996, increasing as a proportion of union membership from 8.9 percent to 11.5 percent in that period. The rapid increase in the proportion of foreign-born union members was due in part to the decline inmembership among native-born workers.[22] Ruth Milkman, in the introduction to a recent study of immigrant organizing, reached the following conclusion concerning the unionization of immigrant workers:

> A key finding from this analysis is that recent immigrants (those arriving in 1990 or later) are the least likely to be unionized, whereas those who have been in the United States the longest (arriving before 1980) have unionization levels roughly double those of newcomers, and in California over four times as great.

She goes on to say, "In fact, for the nation's most settled immigrants, union membership is as likely—and for most subgroups more likely—as for native workers."[23] In other words, as time goes on and immigrants become more accustomed to their new homes, establish documented status, or become citizens, they are as or more likely to join or organize a union than native-born Americans. The outpouring of millions of immigrant workers on May 1, 2006, was certainly a signal that they will fight for a better life even in the face of repression and possible job loss. These signs are extremely important as they can lay the basis for current and future organizing. Although US unions have a history of anti-foreign attitudes and practices, that has begun to change. In addition, immigrants are already attempting to organize in a variety of ways. The question is, are the strategies and structures of today's unions fit for the job? Are they even looking at some of the immigrant groups with the most potential bargaining power?

If the carefully planned and centrally directed 1990 Justice for Janitors strike was one of the first strikes by nonagricultural immigrant workers to capture public attention, the 1992 strikes by some four thousand drywall hangers in Southern California pointed to something new. The strike was initiated and sustained by the immigrant workers themselves. While they would receive support from the Carpenters and eventually join that union, the immigrant construction workers organized and led the strike on their own terms, closing down the residential construction industry in much of Southern California for five months. This was a piece of the residential construction industry that had gone nonunion, like that in the rest of the country. In 1992, striking on their own, these drywallers would bring back the union—a union that had given up organizing this industry years before and was at first reluctant to bring the drywallers under contract. The organization of the strike initially came from immigrants from the town of El Maguey, Mexico, several hundred of whom worked in the industry. This pattern would be repeated in countless strikes and organizing drives.[24]

The uniting of workers from the same place in new communities and in the same work had reestablished links long broken for many native-born workers. The connection of common origin, shared neighborhood or community, and work provides a source of strength for immigrant organization in many cases. It had been a factor in the 1990s Justice for Janitors campaign.[25] It also helps explain for much of the self-organization that has taken place among immigrant workers. A survey of efforts by immigrant workers to organize unions is beyond the scope of this study. But to get at the potential and dynamics of this key sector of the workforce, we will look at a few examples.

Like building services and construction in Southern California, waterfront trucking there had gone through a major restructuring in which Teamster members had been replaced by independent owner-operators and declining conditions in the 1980s. Once again, Latino immigrants filled the void. In 1988 and again in 1993, the Latino truckers had struck with only informal organization. Though further organization was largely initiated by the workers themselves, Communications Workers of America (CWA) Local 9400 offered to help. As owner-operators and independent contractors, the truckers had no statutory rights to unionize or strike. Together, however, they planned a complex strategy that involved the creation of an "employer" and, in 1996, a strike. Unlike the drywallers' strike, the truckers' efforts failed, largely due to the massive efforts of the truck contractors and extensive legal barriers, but the potential of self-organization had shown itself once again.[26] The fight of the waterfront truckers, however, didn't end in the 1990s. In 2004 and 2005 they would strike again over government harassment and fuel prices. Then on May 1, 2006, the "Day without Immigrants," they struck along with millions of others, once again closing the port of Los Angeles/Long Beach.[27]

This transformation from formerly unionized workers to owners or drivers who leased their equipment was common to other areas of transportation as well. Across the country in New York, both the taxi and "Black Car" or limousine services had been reorganized so that the fleet drivers ceased to be employees and became independent contractors who now had to lease their cars. In both cases, the immigrant drivers who filled these new contracted positions organized themselves to resist the near-poverty earnings they made and the long hours they worked to make them. Taxi drivers who had been employees earning a percentage of "the meter" until the 1970s now had to lease their cabs and pay for their own fuel. They literally spent the first few hours of each day working off their daily lease fee. Most of the drivers were now mostly Indian or Pakistani. In 1998, they transformed an older, ethnically based group into the New York Taxi Workers Alliance, open to all yellow cab drivers. In May 1998, the new organization surprised the city when virtually all twenty-four thousand working cab drivers struck for twenty-four hours. Although as independent contractors they have no collective bargaining rights, they have functioned as a union ever since, with about five thousand actual members. They scored an enormous victory in 2004 when they negotiated a fare increase with the city, with 70 percent of the increase going to the drivers.[28]

The city's twelve thousand "Black Car" drivers worked for fleets that serve corporate customers who want the elegant cars for their executives and clients. But, like the taxi drivers, they were independent contractors who had to lease these cars. After paying their lease fees and other expenses they make between four and six dollars an hour. Most are South Asians but there are also East Asians and Central Americans. In 1995, they began organizing themselves. In this case, through an acquaintance, they approached District 15 of the International Association of Machinists, which allowed the drivers to organize and lead their own local, Machinists' Lodge 340. In an unusual turn of events that does not seem to have been picked up by other unions, the Machinists won a National Labor Relations Board case in 1997 declaring the drivers employees. In 1999, Lodge 340 won its first contract with one of the major companies. Resistance from employers was intense and, because many drivers were Muslims, so was harassment by the federal government after 9/11. Nevertheless, by 2005, Lodge 340 had one thousand dues-paying members. The effort to organize the whole industry continues.[29]

Unfortunately, unions are not always this attentive to those who try to organize themselves. When the mostly Mexican workers in New York's green grocery stores began to organize themselves in the 1990s, they were at first helped by UNITE Local 169. In a jurisdictional dispute, however, they were passed on to United Food and Commercial Workers (UFCW) Local 1500, which, by most accounts, was not particularly attentive to the needs of these immigrant workers. A similar case occurred with UFCW Local 338 in New York with African grocery-store delivery workers, who had also organized themselves before approaching the union.[30]

The phenomenon of common origin, community, and work doesn't only occur in big cities. The example of the Guatemalan workers at the Case Farms poultry plant in Morganton, North Carolina, shows that it can work in a semirural area as well. These workers, Mayas from the same areas of Guatemala, composed the majority of the five hundred workers in this plant. As in most poultry plants, the conditions were horrible and unsafe, and in 1993 these workers staged a brief strike. The Laborers' International Union would help them through another strike in 1995 and on to union recognition. What was clear, however, was that the union found an organized group of workers. As one union representative put it, "We didn't organize anybody. There was a union there before the union got there." Unfortunately, neither the workers nor the Laborers' Union were able to force a first contract on the company. Rather than simply abandoning the Case workers, the Laborers agreed to fund the formation of a workers' center that would address the problems of the many Central American workers in that part of North Carolina.[31]

If it is true that union organizing among immigrants is often enabled by the overlap of place of national or ethnic origin and shared neighborhood or community as well as common work, it should come as no surprise that much of the organizing that goes on among immigrants is community based. This includes a very broad range of organizations providing services, advocacy, legal rights, education, political mobilization, and policy development. As we saw above, hundreds of such organizations were involved in the massive mobilization of May 1, 2006. Many of these organizations serve or "do for" immigrants and are run by middle-class professionals focusing on broad issues of immigrant rights or social welfare. What concerns us here are those organizations that actually organize immigrant workers with a focus on their work.

Workers' Centers

Workers' centers differ from other community-based organizations in that they focus mainly, though not exclusively, on workplace issues. Most of them engage in a combination of service delivery, advocacy, leadership training, and organizing. All four tend to focus on issues related to work: pay and failure to pay, health and safety, immigration status, various employment rights. It is the organizing and leadership development functions, however, that give workers' centers the potential to play an important role in the development of unionization and a broader social and political movement. As community-based organizations they are geographically bound. Most of the workplaces or jobs in which their members are employed are within or near the communities. In some cases, like those of day laborers or farmworkers where the work itself may be distant, the center focuses on sites where workers obtain jobs (street corners, contractors, or agencies). In almost all cases it is the employer-employee relationship, the reality of exploitation, that gives the workers' center its significance.[32]

The workers'-center phenomenon grows out of many of the changes in work itself that have taken place in the last thirty or so years, some of which were described earlier. Subcontracting, sweatshops, exploding food-service and hospitality industries, relocated/deunionized industries, new retailers giant and small, and the growth of "off-the-books" work in the informal economy. All of these sources of employment have in common low wages, poor benefits, and workers of color. Increasingly the latter are also immigrants. By 2005 there were by one count 137 workers' centers, 122 of which dealt specifically with immigrant workers. In terms of the regions of origin of those immigrant workers who participate in workers' centers, about 40 percent come from Mexico and Central America, another 18 percent from South America, 15 percent each from East Asia and the Caribbean, 8 percent from Africa, 3 percent from Europe, and 1 percent from the rest of Asia.[33] In terms of their region of settlement in the United States, workers' centers reflect concentrations of immigration: forty-one are in the Northeast; thirty-six on the West Coast; thirty-four in the South; seventeen in the East North Central region, and the rest scattered around the West. Almost 80 percent of the workers involved are immigrants. The relatively large number in the South tells us something about the geographic distribution of reorganized and subcontracted industries such as food processing and automobile-parts production.

The rise of workers' centers has followed the rhythm of both work reorganization and of immigration and has come in three waves. The first group began in the late 1970s and early 1980s, initiated by politically minded activists with some connection to union organization. One of the first was the Chinese Staff and Workers' Association (CSWA) in New York City's Chinatown. CSWA was born out of a 1978 drive by HERE Local 69 to organize the city's Chinese restaurants. Workers joined Local 69 but became disillusioned with the neglect they experienced. In 1979, those at Chinatown's huge Silver Palace voted to form their own union with the support of what became the CSWA. Others soon followed suit. CSWA organizers linked the independent unions to the community and went on to help workers not in unions as well and to deal with other neighborhood issues such as housing. One of their organizers explained their view of organizing: "By organize, we don't just mean joining the union. We see the union as a means to organize something greater. . . . We organize where we live and work."[34]

At least two other workers' centers were formed around this time. La Mujer Obrera (the Woman Worker) in El Paso, Texas, grew out of a garment workers' strike at Farah Clothing. Formed in 1981, it focused on women in the small garment shops on the border after the big outfits like Farah folded up or moved across the border and the unions left the area. Not all of these women workers are immigrants. Many are citizens. Families often overlap the Rio Grande (or Rio Bravo on the

Mexican side), which forms the border. Black Workers for Justice, based in Rocky Mount, North Carolina, came out of a fight against discrimination at Kmart. This is an African American organization in an industrializing area of the South's "Black Belt." It brought together workers from many of the plants in and around Rocky Mount on a community-wide basis.[35] Black Workers for Justice, CSWA, and La Mujer Obrera set the pattern of community-based worker organization for most of those who came after. Another organization that began as part of the first wave was the Committee Against Anti-Asian Violence (CAAAV) in New York City, formed in the 1980s to defend Asian women in particular. In addition to that work, CAAAV spun off at least two other organizations that would form part of the third wave of workers' centers: the Lease Driver Coalition, which became the New York Taxi Workers Alliance, discussed above, and Domestic Workers United.[36]

The second wave came from the late 1980s through the mid-1990s. Much of this was driven by the wave of immigration from Central America as people fled the wars, death squads, and counterrevolutions that were largely the result of US foreign policy in the region.[37] One of the earliest second-wave workers' centers was the Workplace Project, based in suburban Long Island, New York. Founded in 1992, the Workplace Project was a spinoff of a Central American immigrant service organization. The Workplace Project organized among those working in this area's restaurant, construction, landscaping, and housekeeping jobs. Many of these workers were undocumented and were being paid well below the minimum wage. Often they worked as day laborers, gathering on street corners to be picked up by potential employers. The Project began by taking legal cases to gain unpaid wages, a common problem for immigrants. But founder Jennifer Gordon realized this was not increasing the power or security of the workers. So the Project hired Omar Henriquez, a Salvadoran, to help the workers organize to press their claims collectively, learning from CSWA and La Mujer

Obrera. In particular, day laborers who gathered on certain street corners organized and demanded a common wage and succeeded in increasing their earnings significantly.[38]

Another second-wave workers' center is Make the Road by Walking, located in Brooklyn's Bushwick neighborhood, historically one of New York's poorest. With new waves of immigrants in the 1980s and 1990s, Bushwick became a predominantly Latino area. Make the Road is a multi-issue organization dealing with housing, education, community development, and gay and lesbian issues as well as workplace problems.[39] The heart of its organizing program is Trabajadores en Acción (Workers in Action), which focuses on local garment sweatshops and the area's retail stores, which employ mostly immigrants at notoriously low wages. Like other workers' centers, one of its main activities is recovering unpaid wages. In one year, they recovered two hundred thousand dollars in back wages.[40] At one store, MiniMax, organizer Deborah Axt explained, "We won $65,000 in back wages. More importantly, though, was that the women were organizing to change the conditions of the workers who are there now. We were able to win paid sick days, an FMLA [Family Medical Leave Act] kind of coverage, and public posting of legal and workplace rights."[41] Make the Road also worked with the Retail, Wholesale and Department Store Union to successfully organize a small athletic shoe chain, Footco, winning their first contract in January 2006.[42]

The third wave of workers' centers came after 2000. According to Janice Fine, more of these were connected to unions than in the past.[43] One example is the Restaurant Opportunities Center (ROC), set up in the wake of 9/11 by workers from the Windows on the World restaurant in the World Trade Center. Under pressure from displaced workers, HERE Local 100, to which the workers belonged, asked former workers to set up the ROC as a self-help effort in 2002. Soon, however, it became an organizing project willing to work with those in restaurants the union hadn't approached in the past. Like other workers' centers, it helped nonunion workers win back pay, paid days off, lunch breaks, and other improvements. ROC has its own board, composed mostly of immigrant workers, but still maintains a relationship with HERE Local 100, which acts as ROC's fiscal sponsor.[44] In part, ROC sustained itself by acting as a catering cooperative, but in 2005 it set up its own full-service restaurant, Colors. Another third-wave organization is Domestic Workers United, based primarily in Brooklyn among a very broad base of immigrant groups. In 2003, DWU succeeded in winning a Domestic Workers' Bill of Rights from the New York City Council, requiring agencies to spell out terms and conditions of employment and the actual employer to sign an agreement to those terms.[45]

While we cannot attempt a total survey of workers' centers, no account would be complete without reference to the Coalition of Immokalee Workers (CIW). Founded in 1995, the CIW is a second-wave workers' center. CIW differs from most workers' centers, however, in that it is rural and based mostly on farm labor, though workers from other low-wage industries also belong. Immokalee is a dirt-poor town in the midst of Florida's tomato fields. CIW members come mostly from Mexico, Guatemala, and Haiti. Although it is not affiliated with the United Farm Workers or the Farm Labor Organizing Committee and does not regard itself as a union, it has used the same tactics as those unions to make its major gains: the boycott. In fact, CIW has used a number of tactics in its efforts to get Taco Bell, purchaser of most of the tomatoes they pick, to pay a penny more per pound—enough to double their wages.

They have organized three strikes in the area, held a thirty-day hunger strike in 2003, and marched 240 miles across Florida to make their point. Some of these actions produced wage increases. It was, however, the boycott that finally won the amazing victory of several hundred farm workers over Taco Bell and its parent, fast-food giant Yum Brands, which also owns Kentucky Fried Chicken, Pizza Hut, Long John Silver's, and A&W. Like the UFW and FLOC boycotts before it, the CIW's Taco Bell boycott got widespread support from other organizations, including Jobs with Justice, church groups, and unions. Student "Boot the Bell" campaigns got Taco Bell kicked off of twenty-two campuses by the time of the victory. Key to going national with their campaign was the network of other workers' centers around the country. This reminds us that workers' centers are becoming a nationwide force. What CIW won with this support would affect more than their own members. Yum agreed to double the percentage of the tomatoes' price going to the workers by a "pass-through" increase in what it pays. Taco Bell agreed to buy only from growers who agree to the "pass-through." An enforceable code of conduct for fast-food-industry suppliers, with the CIW as a monitoring organization, was also part of the agreement. With the victory of the Immokalee workers and others that came before, like the Asian Women's Immigrant Association's victory at Jessica McClintock in the 1990s, workers' centers have staked a claim as part of the American labor movement.[46]

Workers' centers are an important addition to working-class organization in the United States, but like the unions, they have their limits and structural problems. First, they are small. Most of those that are membership groups have five hundred or fewer members. Perhaps more important is the matter of social power. Steve Jenkins, who was an organizer for Make the Road, argued that shared injustice does not necessarily mean shared social power. Unlike unions, the centers cannot stop production. They can exercise social power through rent strikes or civil disobedience, but their power over workplace issues, which is a major focus and purpose, is limited to appealing to governmental units or agencies and other elite institutions. Whether lobbying City Hall for housing improvements or going to the courts or state agencies for back pay, there is a strong tendency for the workers to be dependent on professionals—organizers, lawyers, etc. Most of these centers are also dependent on foundation grants, which means dependency on the priorities of foundation officials and boards and on those who are best at writing grant proposals. Thus, community-based groups tend to be dependent on staffers who are frequently, though not exclusively, drawn from the educated middle class.

Viewed only in the terms in which workers' centers and similar community-based groups define themselves and act today, these limits are real. But it is possible that in a period of more general social upsurge they can become a source of broader mobilization. The power of the poor, as most past upheavals show, lies in three areas: the disruption of business as usual; organization into and/or alliance with other working-class organizations, notably unions; and political action by virtue of numbers. The first, analyzed by Piven and Cloward, is the traditional recourse of the poor, whether in the form of urban disorder, concerted civil disobedience, rent strikes, or even mass workplace strikes. The 1960s provided many examples of this.[47] The second, unionization or alliances with unions, is trickier. There is a history of tension between many workers' centers and unions with which they have tried to work. As one ROC leader put it in terms of the HERE, the union "seems to have trouble letting go."[48] Unions as bureaucratic institutions don't like sharing power with risky or unfamiliar groups. Yet there are also many examples of cooperation between the two. And while many unions prefer to ignore low-wage workers, many of the recent gains have in fact been among low-wage workers with no central workplace, such as home health care workers in New York as well as in California. Once again, the context is crucial and periods of more general resistance and upsurge offer greater possibilities, as do changes in union practices and perspectives. Jenkins, despite his criticisms, also notes:

> Workers' centers are an oasis of support and useful services for workers facing inhumane working conditions and [who] have few other resources available to them. Many are playing a central role in developing linkages

between progressive unions and community-based organizing efforts that have the potential to strengthen both organizing arenas. It is possible that this will open up new strategies for organizing workers that improve upon traditional union-organizing models by broadening workplace struggles to involve the working-class communities.[49]

A good example of just that was the successful campaign to organize four big meatpacking plants in Omaha, Nebraska. The meatpacking industry had been drastically reorganized, the unions broken, and its new plants filled by recent immigrants from Mexico and Central America. It was the Omaha Together One Community (OTOC), a faith-based community organization affiliated with the Alinsky-inspired Industrial Areas Foundation, that first took notice of the plight of the packing-house workers. In 1999 they held a mass demonstration of 1,200 people to protest these conditions. The OTOC, as a workers' center, could spread the word and protest, but by itself it lacked the power to change things. Eventually, they decided that a union was needed and a joint plan to organize four thousand workers was announced in June 2000. With OTOC mobilizing the community as well as recruiting workers, the campaign was a success. This was a huge boost for the UFCW and a demonstration that this sort of alliance can bear fruit. There were, however, problems once the union began negotiating the contract. Basically, as we have seen before, the union officials didn't really listen to the workers. The contract they negotiated neglected many of the workers' most heartfelt workplace issues as well as the question of immigration status.[50] There is a gap between the cultures of most unions and many workers' centers that needs to be addressed. In particular, union officials and staff need to see workers' centers as part of the same movement, but with unique functions.

Perhaps the UFCW leaders have learned something from this. In 2003, they set up a workers' center in North Carolina as part of their long-term effort to organize the 5,500-worker Smithfield hog-processing plant in Tar Heel, North Carolina. About 60 percent of the workforce are Latino immigrants and the UFCW has made a long-term commitment. Drawing on community leaders and activists, the union called a May 1, 2006, rally; five thousand people from many plants and communities showed up. Most plants had to shut down production for the day. In June, rallies were held in seven cities around the country. Here is where the union, the workers' center, other community-based groups, and the national upsurge of immigrant workers came together.[51]

In August 2006, the AFL-CIO took a significant step toward greater unity of trade unions and workers' centers when it reached an agreement with the National Day Laborer Organizing Network, a nationwide network of community-based day laborer organizations, that would allow workers' centers to affiliate with state and local labor councils. In late 2006, the New York Taxi Workers Alliance announced that it would affiliate with that city's Central Labor Council. These moves follow on other local efforts at cooperation between unions and workers' centers, such as those described above, and that between the Koreatown Immigrant Workers Alliance and the building trades' Ironworkers Local 416 in Los Angeles in order to bring more immigrants into the union.[52] These recent developments represent a new direction in the way at least some of organized labor in the United States sees itself.

Workers' centers, in other words, are best understood in the context of a broader *labor movement,* of which they are one piece. Like unions trying new ways to organize and still not making huge breakthroughs, they need to be seen for their potential as much as for their current achievements and limitations. They are a potential training ground for groups of workers who are finding their own leaders and voicing their own demands and concerns. One measure of their potential is their survival rate as organizations. In a political atmosphere where most of the mass social movements have faded, unions have lost members and power, and politics has largely been unfavorable to working-class people in general and immigrants in particular, even the oldest of the workers' centers have survived and thrived, while new ones have arisen to challenge this atmosphere.

State of the Movement

The organization of the "Day without Immigrants"—or, as it was also called, the "Great American Boycott"—was done largely city by city, town by town, by local coalitions of advocacy and grassroots organizations, with the Catholic Church playing a key role in many places and unions in some. Even "the" Church was divided between the hierarchy, which cautioned against strikes and consumer boycotts, and the parish priests in the immigrant communities, who were caught up in the spirit of resistance. The calendarized coalitions (March 10, March 25, April 9, May 1) that called the national actions and the coalition's six hundred organizations that met just before May 1 were held together in part by the Republican Congress, whose Border Protection, Antiterrorism, and Illegal Immigration Control Act of 2005 was a massive threat to all immigrants. The May Day outpouring killed that bill.[53]

Success, however, soon brought new problems. For one thing, the Department of Homeland Security's Immigration and Customs Enforcement agency (ICE) waged a fierce crackdown on undocumented workers. For another, the movement lost the single focus of 2006. With softer bills appearing even before the newly elected Democratic Congress convened, the movement began to divide over support for new legislation. We Are America, led by the SEIU, UNITE-HERE, and several liberal advocacy groups, supported the Kennedy-McCain bill with its guestworker provisions. The National Alliance for Immigrant Rights (NAIR), formed in August 2006 by mostly grassroots organizations, opposes any guestworker program or repressive immigration enforcement. Along with older rights groups, such as the Network for Immigrant and Refugee Rights, it will continue to fight for the legalization of all immigrants.[54] Lacking a national focus and organizational push, the turnout on May 1, 2007, was much smaller. The biggest turnout was in Chicago, where estimates ran from one hundred fifty thousand by police to two hundred fifty thousand by the organizers. Los Angeles saw two separate demonstrations draw one hundred thousand, while in New York two feeder marches brought an estimated twenty thousand to Union Square. Altogether, the L.A.–based Immigrant Solidarity Network estimated that about half a million people in more than a hundred cities and towns across the United States demonstrated on that day.[55] Had this been the first such demonstration, it might well have been seen as a remarkable turnout, but it was dwarfed by the long shadow of 2006. Nevertheless, it is clear that immigrant workers will play a major role in the revitalization of organized labor in the United States.

Epilogue

Civil War, the "Great Recession," the Aftermath, and Beyond

Kim Moody

Only a few years after the split in organized labor that created the Change to Win (CTW) federation, a veritable civil war broke out among several of America's leading unions. At a time when more than eight million jobs were disappearing, unemployment was reaching highs unseen for nearly three decades, home defaults and foreclosures were hitting all-time records with no end in sight, and labor's major legislative goals were being defeated, some of the country's biggest, most aggressive unions went to war—not against capital or Congress, but against one another. At the center of this high-profile conflict was the Service Employees International Union (SEIU), or more precisely its controversial president, Andy Stern. Yet despite a battlefield cluttered with larger-than-life personalities, this fratricidal conflict was not really about egos. It was about failed strategies, tactics, organizational panaceas and dead ends, financial problems, and a growing loss of real social, economic, and political power. Ultimately, it was about the failure to grow.

The Bureau of Labor Statistics tells us that between 2006 and 2008, before the civil war became public, unions saw a net gain of 768,000 members. The private sector, however, gained only 314,000. At this rate it would take fifty years to reach the 1980 level of just over fifteen million private-sector members. In fact, things may be worse than the government figures show. In 2008, both the AFL-CIO and the rival CTW, formed in 2005, showed a net decline in members in fiscal year 2008 in their LM-2 reports to the Department of Labor. The AFL-CIO reported 146,939 fewer members, while CTW reported a disastrous drop of 458,083.[1]

Furthermore, the efforts of most of the big "organizing" unions in the private sector have either failed to achieve net growth (excluding growth from mergers) or have seen their efforts bring in fewer new private-sector members. About fifteen unions, based primarily in the private sector, reported growth between 2000 and 2008. For some years, notably, the Teamsters', Steelworkers', and Communications Workers' growth through mergers or absorptions of other unions accounted for all of the net gain. This is not to say that these unions didn't organize anyone in that period, but that without the gains from mergers they would have shown a net decline. In the numbers game, the big winner is the SEIU, the only CTW union to show a significant net gain through new organizing. But most of its nearly four hundred thousand "new" members were from the public sector, some through political deals with state governors who received SEIU campaign donations. If one examines the figures carefully, even the SEIU's growth machine ground to a near halt in 2008.[2]

In fact, some of the fastest-growing unions in this period from 2000 through 2008 were smaller, mostly occupationally based unions. The two star performers over this period were the California Nurses Association, which grew by 31 percent (even before its 2009 merger with two other nurses' unions to produce the new National Nurses United), and the Professional and Technical Engineers, by 44 percent. While the numbers are relatively small, this appears to put a dent in the conventional wisdom that only big unions with big treasuries and staffs can grow.

It also appears that another of the underlying causes of labor's civil war is that several of these big unions are in danger of going broke. A longstanding problem that affects many big unions is that they spend more than they take in from members, the difference being covered by loans and income from or sales of investments. In 1979, member-based income accounted for 89 percent of expenditures of the 10 biggest private sector unions. Today, member-based income is down to 75 percent for the same unions, despite many mergers and much organizing activity—or maybe because of it, as the current resource/staff driven approach of most unions is both slow and very costly.[3] The SEIU's percentage of member-based income shrank from 85 percent in 2000 to 77 percent in 2008, and in that year SEIU reportedly took out a hundred million dollars in loans. UNITE-HERE saw less than two-thirds of its income come from members. Others, such as the Teamsters, did better by raising dues—a lot. Some, like the UAW and the IAM, did worse as membership dropped. And while many of the bigger unions appear to have huge assets, almost none had a surplus of assets over liabilities in 2008 big enough to cover more than a year's expenditures.

Despite labor's dazzling mobilization for the 2008 presidential election, its waning power showed itself in the gutting and subsequent defeat of the Employee Free Choice Act. This was followed by the utter destruction of meaningful health care reform. Obama's health care plan was wrongheaded from the start, embedding the insurance industry in the plan and leaving the details to the world's most corporate-financed, lobby-ridden institution, the US Congress. There it was stripped of the public option meant to provide a "cheap" alternative to private insurance. Of course, the mobilization of the right and the three hundred million dollars the industry spent on killing the public option explain much of this defeat. But labor's disarray, political confusion, and inability or unwillingness to reprise the mobilization of 2008 allowed conservative Democrats to join forces with Republicans to thwart labor's (and many others') political hopes. Neither federation nor any major union fought for single-payer or in any way attempted to alter the terms of debate or up the ante. Most said the public option was the bottom line, though SEIU's Andy Stern said even that wasn't a "dealbreaker." And so, along with card check, it's gone.

A Brief History of the Civil War

By 2009 the failure to grow, particularly in the private sector, had led to frustration, finger-pointing, splits, and growing raids. The immediate origins and details of this internecine conflict are far too complex and Byzantine to relate here. An outline will have to suffice.[4] Here we can root the origins of the recent civil war in two important trends in addition to decline itself. The first was the radical reorganization and centralization of the SEIU that began in 2000 and intensified at the 2008 convention. This established the SEIU as the top-heavy, by-any-means organizing machine we know today. With this came the drive to merge local unions into huge statewide or multistate "locals," the "innovation" of long-distance grievance handling via call centers, and the move to employer-friendly organizing via partnerships and sweetheart deals. These moves would ultimately lead to internal opposition, especially from California's 150,000-member SEIU affiliate, United Healthcare Workers–West (UHW–W). Later—some would say in retaliation for its criticism—Stern proposed to remove sixty-five thousand home health care workers from UHW without a vote. When UHW resisted, this in turn led to the trusteeship of UHW–W and its split from SEIU to form the new National Union of Healthcare Workers (NUHW). Unfortunately, the NUHW was blocked twice in elections from winning back a good deal of its 150,000-member base by well-financed, management-supported efforts of the SEIU. It has since affiliated with the California Nurses' Association.

The new direction of SEIU involved more than internal centralization and deal-based organizing; it included an aggressive effort to affiliate (by any means necessary) existing organizations with SEIU. As part of its big-is-best drive, beginning in 2002, the SEIU staged a series of raids on and interventions in some seven other unions, many in jurisdictions in which the SEIU had no previous presence and none of whom welcomed the advances.[5] The tactics included robocalls, visits, and mailings to members, efforts to decertify, setting up front groups, and even intervening in internal officer elections. All failed except one: UNITE-HERE. Along with the formation of the NUHW, the raid on UNITE-HERE was the hot story of 2009.

This brings us to the second trend underlying labor's civil war: the secession of 2005, when six unions left the AFL-CIO to found the Change to Win Federation.[6] This sleek new federation, led by the centralized SEIU, was to do the organizing the old federation had failed to inspire in its affiliates. As argued above, it failed to do so. Between 2006 and 2008, only the SEIU grew significantly, three lost members, and the others grew only slightly. UNITE-HERE was the big loser in those years, with a net loss of more than ninety thousand members.

UNITE-HERE had been formed in 2004 by a merger of the two unions that make up its name. Apparently, the merger never took and the two major leaders came into open conflict in 2008 with UNITE chief Bruce Raynor complaining that HERE's organizing was too slow and too costly.[7] Somewhere in the process the SEIU's Andy Stern, who was already raiding HERE in its casino jurisdiction, intervened with one of the most outrageous raids in US labor history and by mid-2009 Raynor had taken most of his hundred thousand or so members out of UNITE-HERE and into SEIU.

This brought a strong reaction from the leaders of many unions in both the AFL-CIO and CTW. By late 2009, Rich Trumka, new head of the AFL-CIO, was denouncing the SEIU's raids. For its part, the SEIU, which had laid off seventy-five organizers earlier in 2009, now had tens of thousands of new members, a new jurisdiction, and a piece of the UNITE-HERE treasury. The rest of UNITE-HERE retained the full name, returned to the AFL-CIO in September 2009, and continued one of the more hopeful organizing efforts with its Hotel Workers Rising. The CTW had been a false start.

The Aftermath of the Great Recession

By 2010 labor's civil war had drawn to an end. National Nurses United and UNITE-HERE had signed truces with SEIU and the volatile Andy Stern had left office to be replaced by Mary Kay Henry. As the Great Recession unfolded, however, union fortunes worsened dramatically and in many cases, the gains of 2006 through 2008 were wiped out. By 2012 union membership had plunged by 1,731,000 from its new high in 2008. In 2011, it was the public sector that saw losses, reflecting the new offensive against public sector unions, while private-sector membership actually rose slightly by 110,000 members, according to BLS figures. In 2012 both sectors lost members. Most of this gain came in hospitals, where union membership had been growing for some time until 2012, when it fell somewhat.

Not surprisingly, member loss and the recession turned poor collective bargaining performance into a near rout. As Table E.1 shows, negotiated wage increases for union members plunged from an average of 3.4 percent, with even that gain wiped out by inflation, to average of 1.8 percent from 2009 through the first half of 2012, with that more than wiped out by inflation. What is more, the percentage of contracts containing no first-year increase rose significantly in those years.

Table E.1 Average Annual Negotiated Wage Increase, CPI-W, and Strikes 2006–2012[8]

Sector	Average, 2006–2008	2009	2010	2011	2012[9]
All	3.4%	2.6%	1.8%	1.8%	1.9%
No first-year increase	11% (2006–07)	24%	26%	41%	33%
CPI-W +	3.4%	-0.7%	2.0%	4.0%	n/a
Strikes	201	103	159	152	n/a
Cost of strike (in thousands)	$1,415.1	$1,359.3	$488.7	$703.2	n/a

According to the BNA, in 2009 59 percent of contracts saw "measures to control health care costs," that is, cutting benefits and shifting costs to workers. By 2011 such cost-cutting measures hit 79 percent of all contracts negotiated that year.[10] Underlying this worsening performance was the continued decline in the use of the strike, as seen in Table E.2.

Looking at all this from the point of view of capital, things went pretty well. As Table E.2 shows, employment costs, as measured by the Employment Cost Index (ECI), for all private-sector workers rose slightly in 2009 and 2010, but then fell back to their 2006 levels. Union workers were only a little more costly, but when productivity increases are figured in, capital came out on top all around. This almost certainly means a continued increase in the rate of surplus value, discussed earlier in this volume, as productivity outstrips labor costs. Indeed, from 2009, in the depth of recession, to the first half of 2012, domestic nonfinancial corporate profits grew handsomely by 64 percent. And, of course, as Table E.1 shows, the cost to employers of strikes had gone down significantly.

Table E.2 Real Employment Costs (Total Compensation) and Productivity Indices, Nonfinancial Private Sector, 2006–2012[11]

	2006	2007	2008	2009	2010	2011	2012[12]
ECI All Private (Sept.)	99.4	99.7	97.7	100.2	101.0	99.4	99.4
ECI Union	99.3	98.5	96.6	100.7	103.2	101.8	102.2
Productivity	101.9	102.6	102.9	103.4	109.4	110.9	112.3
Nonfinancial Corporate Profits (in billions) *(2005=100)				$660.6	$917,1	$1,007.1	$1,082.2

Despite the key role of organized labor in the election victory of President Obama, little relief appeared on the political front. Indeed, the Republicans, funded again by the Tea Party billionaire Koch brothers, extended their attack on public-sector collective bargaining to unions in the private sector. In one of the most alarming setbacks for organized workers, Governor Rick Snyder pushed through a right-to-work law in Michigan— long regarded as a labor stronghold. This was not the surprise that some thought. To head this off, Michigan unions, headed by the United Auto Workers, pushed for a state constitutional amendment, Proposal 2, on the November ballot, enshrining collective bargaining. It went down to defeat 42 percent to 57 percent.[13] This apparently encouraged Snyder to rush his right-to-work bill through the state legislature in December 2012. No doubt this will be a rallying cry for more of the same in other states.

Resistance and Beyond

This gloomy picture does not mean there has been no resistance. As always, there are examples of successful struggles others might do well to emulate. In fact, there seems to be an increase in new ways to organize and new or revived tactics to deploy— all in the context of continuing economic crisis. While many could have been picked, I will briefly look at a few struggles in the recession period for the innovative and often daring tactics they employed. The first was the December 2008 factory occupation at Republic Windows and Doors in Chicago. This action, by 250 mostly Latino workers represented by the United Electrical Workers (UE), is significant from the point of view of this collection not only because these workers had revived one of labor's most effective tactics and broken the law in order to win the pay owed them, but also because they had taken it upon themselves to throw out a useless union, the Teamsters' Central State Joint Board, in favor of the more militant and democratic UE. Both were clear examples of worker self-activity and rank-and-file rebellion. In addition, of course, they had directly challenged capitalist property rights by their occupation.[14]

In late March 2010, one thousand nurses and five hundred technical workers walked off the job at Temple University Hospital in Philadelphia. Members of the Pennsylvania Association of Staff Nurses and Allied Professionals, they were fighting concessions and management's attempt to impose a gag rule that would have prevented them from criticizing hospital practices. Like many other nurses' unions' fights in recent years, this strike challenged management prerogatives. Nurses have been striking more often than most other workers these days. But normally their strikes are of short duration. These hospital professionals showed that a prolonged strike is possible and can bring victory and that management's authority can be pushed back.[15]

For more than six months, until early 2012, members of the International Longshore and Warehouse Union (ILWU) faced arrest in order to stop nonunion grain shipper EGT from winning a foothold in Washington State. In the fall of 2011 ILWU blocked trains, invaded EGT's terminal, and dumped grain shipments. The ports of Tacoma and Seattle were shut down for a time. Shortly before EGT agreed to a settlement, ILWU members, joined by Occupy activists, prepared to block the loading of a major grain shipment escorted by the Coast Guard. Jobs with Justice organized community support. The potential for violence and further strike action led Washington's governor to broker a settlement. Apparently the ILWU leadership called off the action at the last minute. Nevertheless, this was direct action at the workplace, as well as a challenge to both capitalist property rights and state authority.

Perhaps the crowning example of successful recession-time strikes and public-sector resistance was the 2012 Chicago teachers' strike. This action came directly as the result of a rank-and-file rebellion that put the leaders of the Caucus of Rank-and-File Educators (CORE) into the top offices of the thirty-thousand-member Chicago Teachers Union in 2010. Pulling together the main opposition elements in the CTU and reaching out to students and parents, CORE defeated the reigning United Progressive Caucus, which had ruled the union for most of four decades. At the center of their program was resistance to the city's austerity plan, including its threat to raise class size to thirty-five, increase working hours by 20 percent, and lay off thousands of teachers. The strike against these was a direct challenge to Chicago mayor Rahm Emanuel, a close associate of President Obama. The new leadership used the fight to deepen rank-and-file involvement and workplace organization and develop confrontational tactics. The Illinois legislature had passed a bill requiring a 75 percent majority of all members to make a work stoppage legal. When the strike vote came, 90 percent of the members (98 percent of those who voted) voted in favor. The strike lasted seven days, becoming a major political event in the Windy City and a clear-cut victory for the union.[16]

Struggles in the midst of the economic crisis were not limited to collective bargaining situations. For one, there was of course the inspiring uprising of Wisconsin public workers in 2011 against Governor Scott Walker's attempt to strip them of bargaining rights. For weeks they occupied the state Capitol Building, with occasional demonstrations exceeding a hundred thousand. In the end it was not enough to win, but the mobilization seemed to tell us something of future possibilities. The idea of a general strike was discussed but not launched. Instead, the movement attempted to recall the governor and others. Despite this, the Wisconsin Spring was a rebellion from below, an uprising that went well beyond what union leaders had initially imagined.[17]

After years of agonizingly slow organizing, whether by NLRB elections or "neutrality" agreements, some new and less conventional signs of hope have emerged. In particular, warehouse workers in three of the major warehouse centers that service Walmart have begun to organize along these lines and take action. Inland from Los Angeles, Warehouse Workers United (WWU) has begun to organize among the hundred thousand warehouse workers in that area. WWU is backed by CTW and linked to the United Food and Commercial Workers' "OUR Walmart" organization of Walmart retail workers. Outside of Chicago, UE is backing a similar organization called Warehouse Workers for Justice (WWJ). In New Jersey, a workers' center calling itself New Labor has set up warehouse workers' *consejos*, or workers' councils, in three cities. What is particularly significant in all three cases is that many of these workers work for temporary or workforce agencies rather than Walmart but are part of Walmart's supply chain. They are avoiding the traditional route to organization, for now, in the hopes of mobilizing something like a movement that can impact Walmart as a whole. Most of these workers are Black and Latino, many are immigrants—which points to another important feature of today's working class.[18]

If the observation I made in chapter 5, "Updating the Rank-and-File Strategy," that a new layer of local union leaders appears to be taking shape is accurate, there is certainly a growing number of examples of ways to fight and win for them to draw on—even in the epoch of capitalist crisis.[19] All these point to mass mobilization, most to the importance of union democracy, and many to the need to challenge laws and norms designed to keep working-class people down. It is also worth noting the leading role of women and immigrants in many of these struggles, as well as unconventional alliances with activists from Occupy for a time.

Perhaps most crucial is the workplace as the center of power. Each of the four struggles described above were possible because either the workers themselves or a new leadership had created strong workplace organization. This organization could be extended to effective strike action or even to a workplace occupation, as at Republic, or an invasion of the property of a nonunion company like EGT. Yet the challenges to capitalist power and state authority could hardly have been conducted successfully without prior on-the-job organization. This sort of workplace power is not only the foundation on which effective action and leadership accountability can be based, it is in some small way a prefigurative element of workers' or workplace councils that typically arise in revolutionary situations.[20] It is what Marx saw in the ten-hour legislation of the nineteenth century—a piece of the "political economy of the working class" imposed on capital.[21]

The inability of the Wisconsin uprising to defeat Governor Walker might well lie, at least partially, in the failure to use the workplace power inherent in the situation. A general strike was discussed but no action was taken. It was not something any one group or leadership had the authority or membership backing to simply "call." Nevertheless, as I point out in chapter 6, the sick-in by teachers could have been extended into a de facto mass strike by other groups of public workers, had some key group taken similar action. Although we can't know for certain, it is at least possible that this could have made a difference in the outcome.

The new organizing efforts by warehouse workers underline another way in which workplace organization is critical to success. It is often argued these days that the fragmentation of the workforce by various forms of subcontracting, outsourcing, and the use of "temporary" agency workers has rendered unionization extremely difficult or even impossible, and that it does not fit the "New Deal" collective bargaining setup, etc.[22] What can you do when the place where you work is owned by one company and your employer—e.g., a temp agency—is another legal entity? Or, worse still, what can the union do where there are multiple employers, agencies, etc.? This all seems very new, but it isn't. Think of the waterfront docks, urban construction or haulage markets, or Hollywood film sites. All involve multiple employers. All have been successfully unionized at one time or another.

The fact that the actual employer of some of these warehouse workers might be called Big Temp, Inc. (for example), instead of Walmart or Big Box, Inc., may be important to whatever final bargaining arrangement is set up, but it is secondary to the organizing process. When the docks, the actual workplaces of thousands, were organized in the 1880s and 1890s, they were a jumble of companies performing different operations. In some places, like New Orleans, they were organized by craft unions that united in the Workingmen's Amalgamated Council and the Triple Alliance, which included both Black and white workers and led the 1892 general strike in that city.[23] On the Great Lakes docks, workers organized on an industrial basis, although locals might be based on specific occupations, and ended the contractor system there. The East Coast was a mixture of craft unions, but these eventually entered the International Longshoremen's Association, which negotiates its agreement on an industrial basis.[24] In all cases, all the workers, regardless of employer, were unionized on the job. This appears to be the long-term objective of the three warehouse organizations discussed above.

Furthermore, like so many workers today, these warehouse workers are part of a logistics chain that runs, in this case, from the docks to the retail stores. As Jane Slaughter points out in her *Labor Notes* analysis of this effort: "A work stoppage in any section of the interlinked network—dock workers, railroad workers, truck drivers, warehouse workers, store workers—could shut off the spigot of goods that keep consumers happy and keep profits churning through the supply chain."[25] So the potential power of these low-paid, as-yet-nonunion workers is enormous. If solidarity can be organized and exercised between the unionized rail and truck workers and as-yet-nonunion warehouse and retail workers, their workplace power will be, to borrow a phrase, "magnified a thousandfold."[26]

Unfortunately, the workplace was not to be the major focus of the AFL-CIO's latest effort to renew itself at its 2013 convention. This was more a gathering of "solidarity partners," a wide range of community-based groups, from workers' centers to the Sierra Club and the AFL-CIO's own well-subsidized 3.2-million-member Working America, for those who aren't in a union. The idea, apparently, is to bind together more closely, even formally, a grand progressive coalition capable of influencing politics and policy. No doubt this is a worthy goal, at least if it goes beyond the usual (e)mailing-list coalitions. Within this coalition, it is organized labor that has the greatest potential social and economic power due to both its numbers and its position in the production of goods and services. But not only is the roof of the house of labor leaking badly, its very foundations, the ranks in the workplace, have too long been neglected. As experienced labor organizer Steve Early observed about the convention, "Fighting give-backs and speed-up, organizing strikes, mobilizing members on the job, creating a 'stewards' army' face-to-face (as opposed to online) were all given little play."[27]

Clearly, given this vacuum, a socialist approach to unions that emphasizes the independence of the union from capital, the democratic accountability of leaders, the power that flows from strong workplace organization, and solidarity across union or occupational lines has a great deal to contribute to today's struggles and tomorrow's possibilities.

Socialists and the Future

The cases examined above, as inspiring and instructive as they are, remain isolated events or struggles, and the power of the US working class as a whole remains limited as the second decade of the twenty-first century unfolds. As I have argued in a number of places in this collection, working-class up-heavals, union growth, and radical possibilities come in waves like those of the 1930s, 1960s, and 1970s. They cannot be created at will. Nor does the accumulation of a number of important struggles in recent times necessarily mean an upswing in class conflict is imminent. Furthermore, even capitalist crisis is not an inevitable springboard to such an upsurge, although it may well be laying the basis for one. The course of class struggle, in other words, cannot be predicted. It can, however, be prepared for. On the one hand, mobilized workers, with stronger workplace organization and accountable leaders, will be better placed to win in the context of an upsurge. On the other hand, socialists rooted in today's struggles will have a far better chance of influencing events and people than those who jump on board at the last minute or simply preach from the sidelines. That is the point of revolutionary socialist work and organization in the unions today.

Furthermore, it matters a great deal how that work is con-ducted. Socialists are not active in the unions or other working-class organizations simply to recruit or propagandize. The first task is to build the broader movement. Socialist union work has to be rooted in the actual struggles and experiences of working-class people. By now, one hopes, most would agree that socialists need to do more listening than preaching, more learning than teaching about the realities of class struggle. As revolutionary so-cialists we have a great many positions on a great many things— issues of race and gender or war and peace, for example. But engaging workplace conflict with some prepackaged "program" of demands not only reeks of arrogance, but is bound to prove irrelevant to workers who already understand their grievances perfectly well. In explaining what he and other members of the Socialist Workers' Party did in a shipyard where he worked during World War II, Hal Draper explained: "[We] didn't have to invent the issues. There was no problem of program—unless, of course, you invented the problem for yourself. The issues were there. As a result of the war, and of the positions taken by the entire union bureaucracy, the workers' conditions were being cut right and left."[28] In the fight for better conditions, with workers in motion, other ("bigger") issues will emerge. But it is the existing issues and struggles that are the starting point.

In the introduction to this collection I said that socialist work involves more than union work. While many levels of organization, such as "factory" or workers' councils, are likely to be involved in any unfolding revolutionary situation, virtually all revolutionary socialists believe that some sort of explicitly socialist organization or organizations will be necessary for socialist revolution, however one might view that process. Most would probably agree that it cannot simply be the sorts of small organizations and sects that exist today. Similarly, at least in theory, most would also agree that the socialist organization(s) or party/parties of the future must have a mass working-class base.

There is much to discuss and debate about what such organization(s) might look like. Many newer activists are suspicious of socialist groups because of their track record of sectarianism, authoritarian organization, ideological rigidity, and, in some cases, attempts to "take over" movements. The burden of "proof" lies not with the doubtful activists, but with the socialists. Can we project organizations that are democratic, multitendency, tolerant of differences, open to new ideas, and hospitable to working people? On top of this, the question of how to get to such a mass organization rooted in the class remains unclear. It seems obvious to me that linear growth through recruitment to the sect or tendency organization of today is not an option and never really has been.

In my own view, the revolutionary socialist organization(s)

of the future will most likely evolve from some sort of fusion between the best socialist currents active in the class (that status being earned in the struggle, not proclaimed in advance) and a new layer of radicalized worker-activists and leaders forged in the intensified struggles of tomorrow—be that sooner or later. If this admittedly very general picture has any validity, it speaks once again to the need to be involved in the primary organizations of the class and the actual existing struggles in which this new layer is forged. The issues are there: not only wages, benefits, work intensification, or even the broader social issues, but the challenges to management prerogatives, property rights, and state authority—pieces of the "political economy of the working class" that point toward the future. The question is: Will the socialists be there?

Appendix

Toward the Working Class: An SDS Convention Position Paper

Kim Moody, Fred Eppsteiner, and Mille Flug

Why do sociologists view the working class as a potentially revolutionary force? Is it not true that the AFL-CIO actively supports and participates in America's imperialist policies? Isn't it even true that the white mobs that have attacked civil rights demonstrators in Chicago and beat up Negro youths in Baltimore were composed of working-class teenagers and adults? The answers to all of these questions and many more like them must be, Yes! Well, then, what is so revolutionary about the working class?

First of all, it must be pointed out that socialists do not identify with the working class because they "idealize" workers. Much less do socialists entertain illusions about the trade

This essay was originally published in 1966 as a position paper submitted by the International Socialist Committee (Berkeley, California) to the Students for a Democratic Society (SDS) convention in Clear Lake, Iowa. It is presented here unedited, in its original form.

union movement and its well-entrenched leadership. White workers in racist mobs are not excused because they are workers, union bureaucrats who attempt to "educate" Latin American workers in the glories of the American way of life are not excused because they function as labor leaders. Socialists, like any radical worth his salt, struggle to defend the Negro community from white racists and to build a revolutionary workers' movement in Latin America. In fact, the socialist view of the working class is not based on any set of purely moral positions; it is approached from a different point of view.

To begin with, the socialist view of the working class as a potentially revolutionary force is based upon an analysis of the social position of the working class. The most obvious fact about the working class is that it is socially situated at the heart of modern capitalism's basic, and in fact defining, institution, industry. Industry, be it production or service, is so much the heart of American society that you can say it is what defines the structure of society, that is, what decides who is rich, fair to middling, poor. This sounds so obvious to any radical that you might wonder why we have even mentioned it. The point can be made by way of a comparison. If welfare recipients organize and create an insurgency in the welfare system that is highly successful in the end, they have only helped about 8 million people. It would be an important fight and a great victory for those who are on welfare, but it would hardly scratch the surface of American society. On the other hand, if there were a general insurgency in industry, wages, etc. were raised, workers were given democratic control over their jobs, etc., tens of millions would be affected, the whole basis of the American economy would be changed. The point is not that welfare recipients or Negroes should not struggle, they should and must; the point is that the working class has a uniquely strategic position in American society—they are at the root of the economy. They are at the root of the same economy that causes poverty and creates welfare institutions. The working class is not the only group that must struggle to revolutionize American society, but it is a group that cannot be left out of this struggle.

There is another social fact that gives workers a unique place in any movement that would revolutionize society. For the most part, workers do not need to be organized in the same rudimentary way that poor communities must be organized. Workers are already organized. They are organized by the very conditions under which they work. They are organized in factories, warehouses, giant stores, mass transportation, offices. Every day they are brought together by their employer. Furthermore, they are brought together under circumstances which they do not control. Workers are not allowed to forget "their place." For nearly half a worker's waking existence the conditions of his work struggle against those things that divide him from other workers, race, religion, politics, etc. In short, the collective conditions of employment under which most workers work provide a cohesion greater than any neighborhood. This is why, when the working class does move, as it did in the 1930s and '40s, it moves in a massive way.

All right, these are advantages that workers, if they ever move in a progressive way again, have over other sectors of society, but what is to guarantee that the workers will ever move? In fact, workers, or at least some sections of the working class, are always struggling and moving. For the most part, the continuing struggles are visible. Later we shall discuss the existence and extent of these struggles; for now it is necessary to point out why workers are compelled to struggle. First of all, there is just plain old economic necessity, bread and butter. Everyone knows that the bosses do not usually just grant raises to workers. In one way or another, usually through unions, workers must fight for what they earn, be that a lot or little. One of the greatest snow jobs done on the American people has been convincing them that most workers have "made it." "They're not rich, of course, but they have a home, etc., etc." Many workers do have homes, etc., etc., but the fact remains that the basic condition of life for most workers is one of insecurity. The average worker in manufacturing now makes about $95 a week, which isn't much if you have a family, as most workers do. In transportation it is a little higher and in the service industries it is lower. As the cost of living rises workers must struggle harder to meet their bills, to feed their kids. In their struggle to maintain a decent existence, workers must fight not only the bosses, but today also the government. Workers face not only the resistance of corporations, but the 3.2 guidelines and the threat of injunctions from the federal government. For those who have doubts about the willingness of workers to struggle for progressive ends, take a look at the recent airlines strike of the International Association of Machinists. Not only did this strike hold out against the threats of a congressional injunction, but the rank and file had the guts to flatly reject a settlement pushed by Johnson himself. What other organized group of 30,000 has so clearly flaunted the president's will in recent months? An interesting political side light to this strike is that four IAM locals have recently called for a break with the Democratic Party and the formation of a third party. Keep in mind that this was a struggle that occurred without the benefit of radical organizers; it was, in a way, a spontaneous act.

There is another area of insecurity that workers face that most people are not aware of. That is the fact that a worker's job is still not a completely secure thing. The layoff and hiring systems of most manufacturing corporations is still such that a worker, unless he has a great deal of seniority, is not sure what he will be doing next year. In some industries, such as shipping and longshoremen's work, a man may seldom find a full week's work. Construction is, of course, seasonal, so that the relatively high wages paid are usually diluted by unemployment or the need to take a lower-paying job or travel long distances to find work. Added to these longstanding problems is the fact of automation. In addition to such unemployment as automation has caused, it has begun to transform the structure of the workforce.

This has meant that many workers are forced into new jobs, usually paying less. Employment in manufacturing has remained static, while public and service employment has grown. Service employment is lower-paying and even more degrading than manufacturing work. The fastest-growing areas of public employment are, because of educational requirements, close to most workers. It should be pointed out, even though it will be mentioned later, that this situation goes a long way to explain why in the absence of a program for revolutionary struggle, some white workers have turned their frustration on the Negro.

In addition to the worker's economic problems and situation, there is his position at the point of production. Much has been said on the left about "alienation." Historically this concept referred to the alienation of labor, the fact that the worker found himself to be an appendage of the machine. This idea was formulated by Marx and others in the nineteenth century, but it has even more meaning today. Today's worker in no sense controls the conditions of his work. In production, the very motions and speed of the worker's activity are determined by the machine he faces. Automation, far from curing or alleviating this situation, has exacerbated it. There is, today, a tremendous speedup on America's production lines which makes greater and greater physical demands on the worker—and incidentally, also decreases his relative share of the national wealth. A great many wild-cat strikes have occurred over the speed-up. Related to this point is the necessity of the worker to struggle for greater control over the conditions of his work. Since the early days of the Industrial Revolution, workers have struggled to gain a say in the work process, but automation has made this struggle even more crucial. Not only has automation produced a speed-up, but in many industries it has actually made the workload heavier. Pro-automation contracts such as the International Longshoremen's and Warehousemen's Union (ILWU) has signed have caused greater job insecurity for many workers and heavier physical labor for those with security. For signing such a contract, Harry Bridges and the ILWU official-dom faced a rank-and-file insurgency of Negro workers. In summary, it should now be clear that workers have reason to struggle against the status quo. What is most important is that these reasons for struggle are the defining characteristics of the worker's everyday life. If he is to maintain his dignity, his economic security, and even his health, the worker must struggle. Furthermore, the conditions of his work and his social position are such that he must struggle collectively, in concert with those of his class. His struggle involves not only "bread and butter" but also the struggle against a government which is dead set against the worker gaining "too much." In fact, as we shall see, the worker does struggle constantly.

Well, if the worker is always struggling, then why is the AFL-CIO almost never struggling? Historically, in America, the unions are the organizational form through which workers have struggled. Unlike most countries in the world, labor has never developed its own political arm—a labor, social-democratic, or revolutionary party. Workers, to a greater extent than any other social grouping besides the ruling class, have shown an enormous capacity for self-organization on a democratic basis. The initial organization of any industry has almost always been done by the workers themselves. In some cases they have gone on to form their own unions, in others they have called in or been approached by already existing unions—as in the 1930s. Whatever the case, there has not been, and will not be, any guarantee that over time such mass organizations will not become bureaucratic. Without going into the complex history of the bureaucratization of American labor unions, suffice it to say this is what happened to virtually every union in the country. To a certain extent this was due to the relative prosperity of the 1950s when the level of workers' struggle and therefore participation was rather low, but even here there are important exceptions. For instance, one of the most massive rank-and-file struggles against bureaucracy and for a militant fighting policy was waged in the 1950s in the United Steel Workers—the so-called Dues Protest Committee and the Organization for Membership Rights. Nonetheless, by the time our generation of radicals arrived on the political scene, the unions had become highly bureaucratized institutions. Specifically, this has meant that well-entrenched officials have had all the decision-making powers. It is important to understand that a group of bureaucrats that have held high office in large organizations such as unions for years and years—as is the case in most unions—no longer have the same experience as workers in the shops. The union bureaucrats function in a different social milieu than workers. They live with the upper-middle classes, they hob-nob with leaders of industry, they visit the White House. Workers, of course, do none of these things. The result is that the union "leaders," those who make the policy, lean not toward the workers, but toward the rulers of the nation. Since most unions are rigidly bureaucratic, there is little opportunity for the workers to make their voices heard under normal circumstances. Hence, there have developed in the last few years insurgencies of rank-and-file union members to regain control of their unions, or at least make their wishes known. Occasionally, this pressure from below forces the bureaucracy to wage a good fight and call a big strike, such as the transport workers' strike in New York or the recent airline strike. Generally, the struggle of the workers against the labor bureaucracy goes without public attention and without press coverage. Even a dramatic event like the murder of the Painters' rank-and-file leader, Dow Wilson, is able to find only small coverage in one or two papers—and then only as a result of the determined efforts of serious labor reformers.

Yet, invisible or not, this struggle goes on, day in and day out. What is most important here is that this struggle defines, for a socialist, what "orienting toward the working class" means. When workers, to advance their interests and build a militant struggle, are fighting the bureaucrats of their own unions as well as the bosses and the government, it is clear that we, socialists and radicals, look to the rank-and-file workers as our potential allies. So here it is, we do not mean orienting toward the labor officialdom—Reuther, Meany, Wurf, Bridges, or even Helstein. We wish to dissociate ourselves, and we hope SDS as a whole, from the bankrupt, coalitionist notion that rubbing shoulders with Walter Reuther is "orienting toward the working class." The labor officialdom, as a social grouping, is neither capable of nor interested in social revolution and participatory democracy. We are far less impressed with the liberal posturings of certain labor officials than we are with the relatively inarticulate struggling of rank-and-file workers. When we speak of looking to organized labor, we mean the struggling rank and file. Our attitude toward the bureaucracy is that they should be kicked out of office and the unions remade into democratic workers' organizations. We do not reject the unions, because they are the only mass organizations of workers today, but the function of the radical in the unions is to change them—to fight to make them truly democratic and militant.

We have already mentioned rank-and-file struggle in the unions. To support the contention that they exist we will refer to a few of them. In the United Auto Workers, regarded by some liberals as a model of democracy, rank-and-file insurgency is nearly universal. Every election year there is a tremendous turnover of local leadership—the union's structure makes it nearly impossible to throw out the International leadership. In the last couple of years there have been countless wild-cat strikes in the UAW. The issues involve contract sell-outs, greater job control, and union democracy. Reuther and his staff have consistently attempted to absorb or simply crush these insurgencies. In the UAW, militant rank-and-file activity is regarded by the leadership as "irresponsible." In the United Steel Workers, the rank-and-file fights of the 1950s have continued to this day. Although I. W. Abel's victory over McDonald was meaningless in itself, it was a reflection of the wide-spread discontent among the workers. The hottest area of revolt in the USW is in the Pittsburgh-McKeesport area. A long-standing revolt in the Paper Workers has resulted in the formation of an independent union, the Western Federation of Paper Workers, and a bolt to the Teamsters on the East Coast. There have been, in the last couple of years, countless insurgencies in the Machinists' Union (IAM). Until recently, the president of the IAM was Al Hayes, chairman of the AFL-CIO Ethical Practices Board and a member of the LID. Hayes, the liberals' liberal, expelled workers from his union and has placed dozens of locals under trusteeships, refusing any basic democratic rights to union members. Philadelphia teamsters carried out a bloody wild-cat strike against the opposition of Hoffa. (Most rank-and-file struggles have involved both Negro and white workers.) In virtually every union they are allowed in, Negro militants have struggled for equal rights as union members. Literally hundreds of examples could be given to support the idea that the workers continue to struggle, but there isn't space here for that. The fact remains that every major union has experienced, in the last few years, significant rank-and-file struggle. The class struggle has not disappeared, it has simply been forced to take on a new set of enemies, the labor bureaucracy.

A corollary to rank-and-file struggle in existing unions is the growth of an independent union movement. In California, the militant Grape Workers have formed the National Farm Workers' Association, which is now spreading to other states. The Grape Workers have placed their militancy above affiliation with the AFL-CIO and have had to fight attempts by the Teamsters to get sweetheart contracts. In Mississippi, SNCC attempted to set up the Mississippi Freedom Labor Union for farm workers. Although this attempt has not been very successful, it did produce some militant struggles. In Baltimore, the Maryland Freedom Union has been organizing low-paid Negro retail workers with great success. The MFU has won contracts that AFL-CIO unions said were impossible to win. Across the country, social workers (believe it or not) have organized independent unions that have waged unusually militant struggles and linked up with welfare recipient organizations to fight for the transformation of the welfare system. All of these independent unions are militant and democratic. They serve as an important example for rank-and-file workers in bureaucratic AFL-CIO unions. These independent unions have come about because the AFL-CIO has refused to organize these areas of employment. They are not dual unions in the traditional sense. But they are militant workers' organizations that are developing progressively more radical political ideals.

So, the working class is impelled to struggle and does struggle. But there is still a major question to be dealt with. What is the political outlook of these struggles? Do they have a political outlook? The fact is that generally rank-and-file insurgencies do not have a consistent political outlook. Like movements of the poor or of students, they grope around for political answers: When workers are struggling collectively for their interests the thrust of the struggle is progressive and they are responsive to radical ideas. Historically, socialists in the shops have found it easy to relate their ideas, or at least some of those ideas, to these struggles. Very seldom do political ideas come from a vacuum. Workers, like anyone else who is frustrated, will look around for ideas that make sense to them. When they are struggling they are open to radical ideas, when they are not struggling, or when there are no radicals around, they may listen to others. This is why certain groups of white workers in southeast Chicago turn into racist mobs and a few of the most frustrated turn to right-wing groups. The right-wing groups appeal to the workers, in a distorted way, on the basis of their experience in their neighborhoods. The neighborhood experience of workers is not necessarily radicalizing; their frustration can be turned against the Negro. In the shop or in the union it is somewhat different. Right-wingers have very little to say about militant unionism. Radicals, on the other hand, have a great deal to say about it. All of this leads to two points. On the one hand, radicals must relate to the working class and to workers in the shops.

The union movement was the stomping ground of the Old Left, and look where it got them. It's not too hard to see why the Old Left failed to radicalize very many workers. The failure of the Socialist Party to gain a following in the working class from the 1930s on stemmed from the fact that the SP never really oriented toward the rank-and-file workers. It is no accident that the SP and its various subsidiaries, such as the LID, have coalitionist politics. These are the politics of the labor official-dom. Such workers and left-wing socialists as do exist in the SP come from a different tradition entirely and do not play much of a role in party policy making. The SP is conservative and coalitionist because it has no other hope for survival. The Communist Party is a somewhat different problem. Although it is also true of the CP that its primary orientation was toward the labor leadership, this was true in a different way. From 1936 on, when the CP had some influence in the labor movement, the Party's primary tactic was to wrangle its members and sympathizers into positions of power in the unions. This was done under cover—"ain't nobody here but us progressives"—and through manipulation. When it adopted the Popular Front line, CPers, being politically indistinguishable from any good liberal, were able to gain some control in a number of unions. But they did not educate the workers in radicalism. Indeed they could not do this as they did not function as radicals themselves. Furthermore, the CP tended to act on the basis of Soviet foreign policy requirements rather than on the basis of the needs of the workers. Hence, after Hitler invaded Russia, the CP became super-patriots and pushed such anti-labor policies as no-strike pledges. Needless to say, you cannot work effectively with workers if you are obliged to follow the abstractions of one or another nation's foreign policy. In fact, Communist "internationalism" is really a form of nationalism—at that time Russian nationalism.

Following the war, the CP argued for a while for the continuation of wage restraints—not very popular among workers. Finally, in 1948, CP unionists pushed the socially abstract, classless campaign of Henry Wallace. Wallace, who always made it clear that he was for "progressive capitalists," did not run a radical campaign. In fact, his whole message was a sort of mushy call to Soviet-American friendship. Needless to say, this did not attract many working-class votes. By the end of all of these fiascoes, the CP union leadership had no real rank-and-file support, which made it rather easy for McCarthyism to destroy many of the CP-controlled unions. One could drum up the old failures and crimes of certain Old Left groups for pages, but the point is made. You cannot organize workers for radical politics by manipulation or flirtation with the bureaucracy. Participatory democracy is just as viable for workers as for anyone. In fact, it is absolutely the best way to organize workers, because it is the only way that actually builds revolutionary consciousness.

From the point of view of revolutionary socialists, consciousness is the most important element of workers' organization. By and large American workers have economic class consciousness and trade union consciousness. They can and do organize their own struggles for limited specific ends. What American workers lack most is political consciousness: the realization that they can organize politically to change the entire structure of society in a way that will benefit them and almost everyone else—except perhaps the capitalists and their politicians. This sort of consciousness does not develop automatically—not for workers, welfare clients, the poor, or anyone. Much of it must be taught. This is the primary job of radicals. But, let us stress again, political consciousness cannot be imparted by manipulation. The radical that seeks to bring a political message to workers must share the in the experiences and struggle of the workers. It is not enough to be the best radical, he must also be the best rank-and-file unionist. This brings us to the practical point of this paper.

SDS, as an organization, and SDS members should orient toward the working class as the decisive social sector in bringing about the transformation of American society. This should be true both of our intellectual analysis and our action programs. In addition to organizing the poor, SDS should begin seeking ways to politically organize workers as workers, that is, in the shops. Now that the Black Ghetto movement has raised the slogan of Black Power and decided that the Black Movement should be led by Blacks, white radicals should accept their responsibility to organize whites. As radicals who support the concept of Black Power, we are forced by the logic of this position to turn our efforts toward the white community. It should be obvious that the writers of this document believe that this must mean organizing in the white working class. There are, of course, other possibilities, but we feel that this would be the most fruitful. Our responsibility in this matter is enormous, for given the racial polarization that is occurring, it is clear that if we do not organize white workers there are others who will—with disastrous results.

In the last year or so there has been a growing orientation among SDSers to work in the labor movement in one way or another. Some students have organized university employees on their campus. Others have supported strikes or leafleted workers. Still others have taken jobs on union staffs as organizers. We believe that supporting strikes and organizing workers for independent unions or even existing unions is good, but it is not enough. Furthermore, there is a sort of hierarchy of value in these activities. Working on a union staff may provide good experience for a student or ex-student, but it cannot be a place from which political work can be done. The type of political work expected of union staff members is quite different from what we are talking about—that should be obvious to all. As a union staff member, your primary loyalty, whether you view it that way or not, is to the bureaucracy. You will, in that situation, find yourself doing coalitionist political work, even if you are allowed to do the more or less radical end of that work. The point is not that being a union organizer is selling out, it is not; but that you cannot do serious radical political work from that position. Participating in organizing drives, particularly militant, independent ones like the Grape Workers' drive, can also be a good experience for students. It is preferable to actually being on the union staff since you can, as a volunteer, maintain your independence and be more open about your politics. But obviously, as a student volunteer your position is different from that of the workers and your involvement more peripheral. As with supporting strikes, that amount of real political work you can do is strictly limited. Such activity does, however, serve one good purpose: to show the workers that those demonstrating students they see on television happen to be on their side. This is worthwhile, but it still is not enough. Eventually, if the radical movement is to make a serious impact, radicals must go into the shops in the same way they have gone into poor communities.

We want to make it clear what we think working in the working class involves. First of all, it cannot be done lightly. It is an extremely serious thing to decide to devote a good portion of your life to working in industry. There can be no romanticizing this, because it simply is not romantic. Not everyone is suited to do this sort of thing and it should not be made into some sort of moral virtue, excelling all other virtues to be "in the shops." More concretely, the person who plans to enter the working class must have an ideological commitment to the working class. Those who believe that workers are fat cats, or that the revolution will be made by peasants who must encircle the rich industrial nations, had better stay away from the workers. We already indicated some of the mistakes of the Old Left; it should be pointed out that not only the Old Left is guilty of these mistakes. There are groups today whose primary political considerations are based on the ideas and needs of various foreign ruling classes. Zengakuren activists in Japan have a wealth of stories to tell about how the Maoist Japanese Communist Party has helped to put down strikes because they viewed Japanese-Chinese trade agreements as more important than the interests of the workers. We must be clear that our politics are in line with the interests of the workers and that our internationalism is genuine and revolutionary for all workers. Again we want to stress that the role of radicals is to build consciousness, self-realization of one's power and potential, and not simply transplant slogans. We believe that radicals are to relate to or help real struggle. The first job of radicals is to relate to or help organize rank-and-file struggle and to bring a program to that struggle. For the radical movement today, this means that we must have such programs and the understanding to formulate them.

What we propose, then, is that SDS begin to work toward organizing in the working class. We do not propose that people go into shops without planning or discussion. To be effective we must know the history and structure of the labor movement, we must know what shops to go into, which ones are politically important and which are not. We will have to be clear in our break with coalitionism, and that means breaking completely with the Democratic Party. People will have to plan their lives for this sort of work and perhaps even learn skills that will get them the right jobs. All of this cannot be done at one convention, it cannot simply be voted on. But there is something that can be done.

We propose that the SDS Labor Committee be enlarged and transformed. Although the labor committee should continue to publish its newsletter, it should take on the serious task of educating SDS members in the history and structure of the labor movement.

Even more importantly, the Labor Committee should take on the responsibility of doing serious research into the internal politics of unions today. This should be done both on a national level and on the local level. Research groups in industrial areas should be set up, under the coordination of the Labor Committee, to determine what struggles are going on in their locality, what significance these struggles have politically, how they relate to other struggles elsewhere in the same union. This research and discussion is to be oriented toward the practical end of setting up groups to work in the shops in those locations that seem most promising. We would add, that outside the Labor Committee, SDSers who might consider working in such a situation should educate themselves in socialist politics. We, as socialists with an independent and revolutionary perspective, believe that those politics that are most relevant to the working class today are those that reject the old ideas and priorities of the Social Democrats (SP) and the Communists. We refuse to tie the working class to the policies of any nation, whether they pose as socialists or not, for to do so is to sap the revolutionary potential of the working class and to destroy the hope for a true working-class internationalism.

Notes

Introduction

1. US Bureau of Labor Statistics 2012, Table 1.
2. Cohen 2006.
3. McNally 2012.
4. Marx 1990, 125.
5. Ibid., 165.
6. Gruelle and Parker 1999.
7. See, for example, Draper 1992 and Draper 1978.
8. For a shortened version of this pamphlet and other works by Stan Weir, see Lipsitz 2004.
9. Marx and Engels 1965, 293.

Chapter 1: Marx's Theory of Class and the World Today

1. E. P. Thompson 1978, 46.
2. Ibid., 107–08.
3. Marx and Engels 1963, 48–49.
4. Marx 1995, 188.
5. Miliband 1977, 23.
6. Marx 1995, 189.
7. You will find this mistake in my essay "The Rank-and-File Strategy," chapter 4 of this book.
8. Graham 1992, 62.
9. E. P. Thompson 1978, 106.
10. Draper 1978, 40–41, 670n14.
11. Marx and Engels 1991, 42–45.

12. Marx 1963, 23.
13. Fernbach 1973, 341.
14. Marx 1990, 724.
15. Ibid., 874.
16. Ibid., 271–75.
17. Ibid., 899.
18. Ibid., 301.
19. Ibid., 450.
20. Ibid., 464; 1039–40.
21. Ibid., 518.
22. Ibid., 782.
23. Shaikh and Tonak 1996, 87.
24. Marx 1990, 1012–13.
25. Ibid., 1035–36.
26. Braverman 1998, 188–96.
27. US Census Bureau 2011, 409.
28. Ibid., 408.
29. Marx 1973, 769.
30. E. P. Thompson 1966, 194.
31. Marx and Aveling 2000, 70–72.
32. Marx 1991, 1025.
33. Moody 2014.
34. Marx and Engels 1953, 236.
35. US Census Bureau 2011, 378, 384.
36. Ibid., 390, 415, 421; Mishel et al. 2012, 43.
37. US Bureau of Labor Statistics 2013.
38. Engels 1980, 220–31.
39. Marx and Engels 1953, 293.
40. Marx 1995, 188–89.
41. Cited in Draper 1978, 84.
42. Marx and Engels 1953, 270–71.
43. International Labour Office 2008, 9–10; the ILO's definition of "employed" includes farmers, family workers, the self-employed, and those in the underground economy. If farmers and nonwaged family workers are excluded, the working class is certainly a real majority of those who work for a living.
44. Marx 1990, 659.
45. ILO 2008, introduction.
46. Glyn 2006, 191.
47. Mishel et al. 2012, 102.
48. McNally 2011, 54–58, 180–81.

Chapter 2: Unions, Strikes, and Class Consciousness Today

1. Marx and Engels 1974, 91.
2. Ibid., 95.
3. Ibid., 96.
4. Draper 1978, 81.
5. Ibid., 82.
6. Charlton 1997.
7. Hyman 1971, 4, 8.
8. Kelly 1988, 9–11; emphasis added.
9. Engels and Lafargue, cited in Lapides 1990, 149.
10. Marx and Engels 1953, 490.
11. Hyman 1971, 14–17; Moody 1988, 52–53.
12. Marx and Engels 1974, 80.
13. Engels 1885, 173.
14. Marx and Engels 1974, 79.
15. Marx 1973b, 150; emphasis added.
16. Ibid., 149; emphasis added.
17. For example, Newby 1977; Bulmer 1975.
18. Mann 1970.
19. Lash 1984.
20. Edwards and Scullion 1982, 198.
21. Croteau 1995, 139.
22. Moody 1996.
23. Mouffe 1983.
24. Radice and Pollard 1992, 555; Radice and Pollard 1993, 560; Radice and Pollard 1994, 568.
25. For example, Hall 1987 and Leadbeater 1988.
26. See London Hazards Centre 1994.
27. McDroy 1991.
28. "Before I got into this I thought socialists had horns on their heads"; "Capitalism doesn't work"; "I'm a socialist now": sample comments by Staley workers, quoted in Cooper 1996.
29. Moody 1997, 85–113, 180–95.
30. Deer 1996, 12–13.
31. For background on this period of the Teamsters and TDU, see La Botz 1990.
32. Carey had been president since 1968 of Local 804, a giant, mainly UPS-based local in New York City.
33. Parker 1997.
34. Ibid.
35. Cohen 1998.
36. Parker and Slaughter 1994.
37. Ward 1998.

38. Danford 1997.
39. Lucio and Stewart 1997.
40. Quoted in *Guardian* 1997.
41. Woodhouse and Pearce 1975, 87; Martin 1974, 174.
42. Martin 1974, 179.
43. Moody 1997, 249–67.
44. La Botz 1990.

Chapter 3: Contextualizing Organized Labor in Expansion and Crisis

1. Marx 1990, 763–70.
2. Shaikh 1987, 118–23; Shaikh and Tonak 1996, 147–49.
3. Mishel, Bernstein, and Shierholz 2009, 86; Shaikh 2010, 118–23.
4. McNally 2009, 47–53.
5. US Census Bureau 1981, 396; US Census Bureau 1985, 412; US Census Bureau 1986, 521; Bureau of Economic Analysis 2010a; Council of Economic Advisors 2010, 393.
6. Shaikh and Tonak 1996, 149.
7. McNally 2009, 45–51; Bureau of Economic Analysis 2010a; US Census Bureau 1986, 521.
8. Shaikh 2010, 48–50.
9. Mishel, Bernstein, and Shierholz 2009, 86.
10. Mohun 2006, 348; McNally 2009, 49–50; Shaikh 2010, 50–52; R. Brenner 2002, 72.
11. Shaikh and Tonak 1996, 129, 149; Mohun 2009, 1028; Mohun 2006, 357–58; US Census Bureau 1986, 423; Council of Economic Advisors 2010, 402.
12. Mike Davis 1986, 121–24; Metzgar 2000, 85–117.
13. Moody 2007, 99; Cohen 2006, 9–29.
14. For a detailed overview and analysis of this period see Brenner, Brenner, and Winslow 2010.
15. Moody 2007, 102.
16. Jeffreys 1986, 40; H. Thompson 2001, 214–16, 62; Nyden 1984, 109–18; La Botz 2010, 221–23; Moody 2010, 141–46.
17. Slaughter 1983, 10–41; Moody 1988, 151–54.
18. US Census Bureau 1982–83, 410; US Census Bureau 1986, 423; US Census Bureau 1989, 415; Moody 1988, 140–41.
19. Council of Economic Advisors 2010, 402; National Labor Relations Board 1990, 17; Moody 2007, 99; Chaison 2006, 118–22.
20. Craypo 1986, 62–63.
21. Shaikh and Tonak 1996, 127, 147–49; Council of Economic Advisors 2010, 386.
22. Moody 2007, 44.
23. Mishel, Bernstein, and Allegretto 2005, 253–54, 365–67; US Bureau of

Labor Statistics 2001.
24. Mike Davis 1986, 116; Chaison 2006, 107.
25. Hülsemann 1998, 1–9.
26. Benchich 2010, 8–9.
27. Horowitz 1997, 247–68, 276; Council of Economic Advisors 2010, 402.
28. Perry 1984, 235–68.
29. N. Johnson 1995, 101–12.
30. Perry 1986, 1, 104, 110; Council of Economic Advisors 2010, 402; Moody 2007, 47.
31. Keefe 1997, 31–66.
32. US Census Bureau 2001, 393–95.
33. Metzgar 2000, 121; Mangum and McNabb 1997, 89–92.
34. Moody 1988, 127–30.
35. Edsall 1984, 128.
36. Bureau of Economic Analysis, 2010b; US Census Bureau 1991, 411–12.
37. Beardwell and Clayton 2007, 6–8.
38. Torrington, Hall, and Taylor 2008, 115.
39. Keenoy 1995, 161.
40. Parker and Slaughter 1994, 24–38.
41. Babson 1995, 12–13.
42. Leary and Menaker 1995, 26–39.
43. Parker and Slaughter 1994, 177–220.
44. Smith 2000, 19–20.
45. Parker and Slaughter 1994, 107–10, 204–207.
46. Greenbaum 2004, 81–94.
47. Kumar 2010, 95. Six Sigma is a statistically based version of Total Quality Management developed by Motorola in the 1980s.
48. Smith 2000, 21–27.
49. Council of Economic Advisors 2010, 390, 393; US Census Bureau 1991, 411–12.
50. Smith 2000, 27.
51. Rachleff 1993; Early 1990; Brecher 1997, 330–35.
52. Tillman 1999, 137–63.
53. Council of Economic Advisors 2010, 403.
54. Shaikh 2010, 50–54.
55. Moody 2007, 106–20.
56. Buhle 1999, 244–52; Ashby and Hawking 2009.
57. McNally 2009, 59–65; Bureau of Economic Analysis 2010c.
58. Council of Economic Advisors 2010, 388; Shaikh 2010, 49.
59. US Bureau of Labor Statistics, 2000, 2006, 2007.
60. Bureau of National Affairs 2002, 2003, 2006, 2008.
61. FMCS 2000, 31; FMCS 2010, 8.
62. Hirsch and MacPherson 2000–2011.

63. Schmitt and Warner 2010, 266; US Bureau of Labor Statistics 2009, Tables 1, 3; US Census Bureau 1980, 430; US Census Bureau 1982–83, 408.
64. Milkman 2006, 117.
65. Getman 2010, 121–23.
66. Moody 2009b, 144–46.
67. Chaison 2010.
68. National Labor Relations Board 2000, 10; National Labor Relations Board 2009, 10; National Labor Relations Board 2008, 10.
69. FMCS 2000, 2004; see also chapter 8.
70. US Department of Labor 1995, 2010.
71. Eaton et al. 2009, 25, 32–33, 45–49; Early 2011a.
72. Eaton et al. 2009, 25, 32–33, 46–47; Schiavone 2008, 45–48; Early 2011a, 81–94; Milkman 2006.
73. Stern 2006, 105–106.
74. Early 2011a, 109–36.
75. Schiavone 2008, 50–53; Fletcher and Gapasin 2008, 125–30.
76. US Bureau of Labor Statistics 2008a, 2009; Hirsch and MacPherson 2000–2011.
77. US Department of Labor 2010a.
78. UNITE-HERE 2009a; Kaplan 2008.
79. Benson 2010, 297.
80. Winslow 2010 and 2011.
81. For a detailed account of the "civil war" and its impact, see Early 2011a and Winslow 2011.
82. Bureau of Economic Analysis, 2010c; Shaikh 2010, 48.
83. US Bureau of Labor Statistics 2010a, 1; US Bureau of Labor Statistics 2008b, 1; US Bureau of Labor Statistics 2007a, 1.
84. US Bureau of Labor Statistics 2010b; 2008.
85. US Bureau of Labor Statistics 2010c.
86. Bureau of National Affairs, 2010a, 117–18; Bureau of National Affairs 2010c, 3–4; Bureau of National Affairs 2008, 167–68.
87. FMCS 2009, 7.
88. Mead-Lucero 2010, 10, 16; Slaughter 2010, 1, 13; Gaus 2010, 6–7.
89. US Bureau of Labor Statistics 2010g, 1.
90. US Bureau of Labor Statistics 2010d, 2010e, 2010f.
91. Coy 2009.
92. McNally 2011, 4; Heintz 2009, 7–12.
93. Early 2011a.
94. Sewell 2011; AFL-CIO 2011; Ryan 2011b, 1, 14.
95. McNally 2011, 1–9.
96. Marx 1990, 574.
97. Rampell 2010; Bureau of Economic Analysis 2010d.

98. Mishel, Bernstein, and Shierholz 2009, 125–26.

99. Glyn 2006, 190–91.

100. International Labour Office 2008, xiii, 1–16.

101. For more on this see chapter 8.

102. For more on this see McNally 2011, 146–82.

103. Kelly 1998, 84–107; Clawson 2003, 13–25.

104. For a global look at the possible precursors of upsurge, see McNally 2011, 146–82.

Chapter 4: The Rank-and-File Strategy

1. United Automobile Workers 1996.

2. Quoted in Draper 1978, 91–92.

3. Quoted in Cliff 1975, 79–80.

4. Gramsci 1971, 419.

5. The particularly rapacious nature of US capitalism stems in part from its origins in English capitalism. As Ellen Meiksins Wood (1999) argues, in the seventeenth and eighteenth centuries England was still the only country with a truly integrated national market based on competition and accumulation. Its trade and colonial systems, unlike those of France and Spain, ran on capitalist principles of expansion, economic compulsion, and agrarian "improvement," i.e., productivity. It was John Locke who, in the seventeenth century, provided the capitalist rationale for expropriating Native American lands in the name of "improvement," basically the same as that for the land enclosures within England. The distinctly un-English rough-and-tumble culture of the United States flows in part from the decidedly "English" nature of its continental expansion from the seventeenth century through the nineteenth, unmitigated by the direct rule of England's highly centralized state even in colonial times.

6. For this point I am indebted to Deborah Simmons, whose "After Chiapas: Aboriginal Land and Resistance in the New North America" (1999) brought this point home to me.

7. Jones 1999.

8. Engels 1887, quoted in Lapides 1990, 141.

9. Brecher 1997.

10. Lens 1947, 33.

11. Labor's first major political effort in the 1870s and 1880s was the disgraceful campaign for state and national legislation excluding Asian workers from the United States. This occurred prior to the formulation of the AFL, but was supported by most of the unions that would join it and by the otherwise egalitarian Knights of Labor.

12. Brooks 1965, 97.

13. Ibid., 133.

14. Hinton and Hyman 1975, 10, 23.
15. Foner 1991, 323.
16. Barrett 1998, 315–16.
17. Their success in the amalgamation campaign and the Labor Party movement contrasted, according to the historian Philip Foner, with their general failure in the fight for racial inclusion and equality (Foner 1991, 338).
18. Barrett 1998, 312.
19. Lens 1947, 180.
20. Trotsky 1964, 9.
21. Dobbs 1972, 41–43.
22. Dobbs 1973, 24.
23. Lichtenstein 1982, 51.
24. Quoted in Horowitz 1997, 143.
25. An account of this period can be found in Moody 1988. For a somewhat different view of this period see Perusek and Worcester 1995.
26. An exception was the Independent Socialist Clubs, which became the International Socialists (IS) in 1970, whose members chronicled the events of that period and played a role in some rank-and-file movements. The IS was one of the groups, along with Workers Power and Socialist Unity, that founded Solidarity in 1986. The Sojourner Truth Organization and some Maoist groups also had a small presence in the working class toward the end of this period.
27. *Multinational Monitor* 1997.
28. *Wall Street Journal* 1996.
29. Moody 1998, 64–65.

Chapter 5: Updating the Rank-and-File Strategy

1. One mistake worth mentioning is the use of the term class "in itself" in reference to the development of a class consciousness "for itself." Class "in itself" is frequently used by Marxists, but as it turns out it wasn't Marx's phrase. Rather, in *The Poverty of Philosophy,* he wrote of a "class, as opposed to capital," a far more dynamic formulation. See Marx 1973b.
2. For a detailed analysis of this see Early 2011a.
3. See Moody 2009a for arguments and data on this failure.
4. Early 2012.
5. See chapter 9.
6. US Bureau of Labor Statistics 2001.
7. Many of management's barriers to success in NLRB elections are perfectly legal. See chapter 7.
8. Ibid.
9. See chapter 9.
10. See chapter 7.

11. See chapter 3.
12. Mishel et al., 2012.
13. Bureau of Economic Analysis 2013.
14. Bureau of National Affairs 2008, 2010b, 2012a, 2012b.
15. For a discussion of this see Draper 1978.
16. Bronfenbrenner 2003.
17. Moody 2007, 181-82.
18. See chapter 8.
19. Discussed in Dubofsky 2000, 181–83.
20. See chapter 9.
21. Slaughter 2012b, 1, 8–10.
22. For more detail on the breakup of national or industry-wide bargaining, see chapter 3.
23. While the example of Ron Carey as president of the Teamsters might seem to bring this view into question, and while not all leaders are the same or succumb to these pressures instantly, Carey's desire to retain office, which led him to reject a grassroots election campaign in 1996 and opt instead for a team of Democratic Party election pros, nonetheless ended in tragedy. See Cohen 2006 for more on these pressures.

Chapter 6: General Strikes, Mass Strikes
1. Mary Davis 2009, 61–62; Du Bois 1998, 53–83.
2. Renshaw 1967, 67–68; Dubofsky and McCartin 2000, 94.
3. Roller 1905.
4. Ibid., 6, 8–10.
5. Boyer and Morais 1979, 287.
6. Greeman 2011.
7. Singer 2002, 156–57.
8. The 1926 British general strike was a sort of hybrid. It was called by the Trade Union Congress (TUC) in solidarity with locked-out miners, lasted nine days, brought industry to a halt, and was then called off by the TUC precisely because it was taking on a revolutionary character with improvised Action Councils and increasingly challenging the government.
9. Luxemburg 1964, 11–16. This was somewhat of a caricature of some syndicalist positions that saw the general strike growing out of more limited struggles.
10. Ibid., 17.
11. Ibid., 19–25.
12. Quoted in Cohen 2006, 196.
13. Singer 2002, 156.
14. Luxemburg 1964, 25–26.
15. Brecher 1997, 13–37.
16. Quoted in Brecher 1997, 36.

17. Montgomery 1980, 92.
18. Brecher 1997, 47.
19. Friedman 1999, 78; Brecher 1997, 39–63.
20. Nelson 1988, 178–84.
21. O'Connor 2009, 121.
22. Lipsitz 1994, 120–54.
23. Weir n.d.
24. There have been both types of mass strikes north of the border in Canada, where something like a mass strike wave occurred in the mid-1970s and a more orderly series of one-day local general strikes was called in the mid-1990s during the Ontario Days of Action.
25. Preis 1964, 62–63.
26. For more on this see McNally 2011, Shaikh 2010, and chapter 3 of this book.
27. Even more useless is the notion that resolutions for a general strike will "expose" the union bureaucracy, as this assumes the consciousness for such action is already there among the ranks. Education is best pursued through discussion, not formal resolutions in poorly attended union meetings.

Chapter 7: Beating the Union

1. Mike Davis 1986; Goldfield 1987; Metzgar 2000; Lichtenstein 2002.
2. Cited in Barbash 1994, 46.
3. Georgine 1979, 20–21.
4. Cochran 1957, 199.
5. Jacoby 1991, 174–77.
6. Wheeler 1985, 113.
7. Atleson 1993, 162–70.
8. Jacoby 1991, 176–77; Lichtenstein 2002, 105–10.
9. Vogel 1978, 45–78.
10. Ibid., 45–46.
11. Cited in Logan 2006, 669.
12. Pope 2004.
13. Estlund 2007.
14. Pope 2004, 535.
15. Schwartz 1999, 6.
16. Gall 2010.
17. Freeman and Kleiner 1990, 352.
18. Bok 1964, 41–42.
19. Getman, Goldberg, and Herman 1976.
20. Eames 1976, 1181–93.
21. Dickens 1983, 560–75.
22. Bronfenbrenner and Juravich 1998; Bronfenbrenner 2000; Bronfenbrenner and Hickey 2004; Bronfenbrenner 2009.

23. Ferguson 2008, 16.
24. Preis 1964, 257–83.
25. Lipsitz 1994, 99–154.
26. Shaikh and Tonak 1994, 125.
27. Lipsitz 1994, 157–81.
28. National Labor Relations Board (NLRB) 1948–1955; Troy 1986, 81.
29. Sugrue 1996, 128–29.
30. Schatz 1983, 233–34.
31. Moody 2007, 44.
32. Goldfield 1987, 10.
33. US Census Bureau 1975, Part 1, 162–63.
34. Shaikh and Tonak 1994, 125; R. Brenner 2002, 72.
35. Mike Davis 1986, 121–24.
36. Mike Davis 1986, 121–22; Metzgar 2000, 94–117.
37. Pope 2004, 534.
38. NLRB 1955–1960.
39. NLRB 1950–1959.
40. Georgine 1979, 1; Logan 2002, 198.
41. US Census Bureau 1975, 179.
42. Brenner, Brenner, and Winslow 2010.
43. NLRB 1950–1970.
44. Georgine 1979, 32.
45. US Census Bureau 1975, 179; US Census Bureau 1982–83, 410.
46. Lichtenstein 2002, 240–41; Council of Economic Advisors 2011, 259.
47. R. Brenner 2002, 24–47.
48. Shaikh and Tonak, 126–27.
49. Edsall 1984, 128.
50. Lichenstein 2002, 236, Moody 1988, 27 135.
51. NLRB 1969–1979.
52. Georgine 1979, 1–8.
53. Imberman 1980, 275–83.
54. Ibid., 276.
55. Logan 2006, 658–65.
56. Troy 1986, 81–82.
57. NLRB 1950–1979.
58. Troy 1986, 80–87.
59. US Census Bureau 1982–83, 410; US Census Bureau 1986, 423.
60. Council of Economic Advisors 2011, 308.
61. Moody 2014; McNally 2009, 35–83; Fiorito, Lowman, and Nelson 1987, 113–23.
62. Babson 1995, 12–13.
63. Grabelsky 2007, 4–5.
64. La Botz 1990, 241–42.

65. Perry 1986, 110.
66. Lawler and West 1985, 411–12.
67. Bronfenbrenner and Hickey 2004, 39.
68. NLRB 1980–1999.
69. US Census Bureau 1982–83, 410; FMCS2000.
70. Bronfenbrenner 2000, 15.
71. NLRB 1950–1989.
72. NLRB *Annual Reports,* 1950–2009.
73. Lawler and West 1985, 412.
74. Bronfenbrenner 2000, 18, 66; Bronfenbrenner 2009, 2.
75. Fletcher and Hurd 1998, 37–53.
76. Milkman 2006, 155–62.
77. Moody 2007, 129–42, 169–72.
78. Brudney 2007, 26, n28, n29; Bronfenbrenner and Hickey 2004, 41.
79. FMCS 2000, 2004; Eaton and Kriesky 2001, 51; see also chapter 8.
80. See chapter 8.
81. Fine 2007, 38.
82. Bronfenbrenner and Juravich 1998, 25.
83. Ibid., 21.
84. Ibid., 25–29.
85. NLRB 2000–2009.
86. US Bureau of Labor Statistics 2008a, 2009.
87. US Bureau of Labor Statistics 2009, 2010c, 2012a.
88. NLRB 2012.
89. See chapter 8.
90. Bronfenbrenner 2009, 4.

Chapter 8: Union Organizing in the United States

1. Peter D. Hart Research Associates 2005, 6.
2. Harcourt and Lam 2007, 334.
3. Robinson 2008, 238.
4. Goldfield 1987, 10–11; Troy 1986, 81; US Department of Commerce 1972, 1991, 2001, 2004–05; US Bureau of Labor Statistics 2000, 2002, 2004, 2006a, 2008a.
5. Troy 1986, 81; Lewin 1986, 244; US Department of Commerce 1991, 1992, 2001, 2004–05; US Bureau of Labor Statistics 2000, 2002, 2004, 2006a, 2008a.
6. Moody 2007, 102; US Department of Commerce 1993, 2001.
7. US Department of Commerce 1972; US Bureau of Labor Statistics 2008c.
8. Moody 2007, 99–106.
9. Meyer and Cooke 1993, 533.
10. Bronfenbrenner 2003, 39.

11. Goldfield, 90–91.
12. Meyer and Cooke, 533; Moody 2007, 139.
13. Hurd 2004, 8.
14. Fiorito and Jarely 2008; Hurd 2007.
15. Hurd 2004, 13, 17.
16. NLRB 1999–2006.
17. Brudney 2007, 11–12.
18. Becker et al. 2006, 118; Jordan and Bruno 2006, 182–83.
19. Hurd 2008.
20. Benz 2002, 96.
21. Hurd 2008, 37–39.
22. UAW 2006, 103.
23. Jordan and Bruno 2006, 187.
24. Eaton and Kriesky 2001, 48.
25. Jordan and Bruno 2006, 188.
26. Hurd 2008, 41–42.
27. Brudney 2007, 12.
28. Greenhouse 2006.
29. NLRB 2005, Table 13.
30. Martin 2008, 1081.
31. Eaton and Kriesky 2001, 51.
32. Martin 2008, 1081.
33. NLRB 1998–2004; FMCS, 2000, 2004; National Mediation Board, 2001, 2006.
34. Hurd 2008, 39.
35. Woodruff 2008, 2.
36. Fiorito and Jarley 2008, Table 1; NLRB 2006–2007.
37. Brudney 2005, 26, n28, n29.
38. Bronfenbrenner and Hickey 2004, 41.
39. Eaton and Kriesky 2001, 51; Martin 2008, 1082.
40. Martin 2008, 1086.
41. Mishel and Walters 2003, 1.
42. Woodruff 2008, 2.
43. SEIU 2006a, 2006b, 2005.
44. Benz 2002, 104–105.
45. Bronfenbrenner and Hickey 2004, 45.
46. Fine 2007, 38.
47. NLRB 2007.
48. Gaus 2008a.
49. American Rights at Work 2008.
50. UAW 2006, 104.
51. Hurd 2004.
52. Gabriel 2006, 343–44; Ness 2005; Fink 2003.

53. Hirsch and MacPherson 2013.
54. Ibid.
55. NEA 2006.
56. US Department of Labor, 2000, 2007; California Nurses' Association 2008.
57. Hurd 2004, 7–8.
58. Fletcher and Gapasin 2008, 200.
59. De Turberville 2004, 782.
60. Brenner 2008, 3, 10.
61. Lustig 2002.
62. Bernstein 1969, 635–81.
63. Jordan and Bruno 2006, 194.
64. Bronfenbrenner 2003, 41; emphasis added.
65. Jordan and Bruno 2006, 182–85.
66. Bronfenbrenner 2003, 41; Bronfenbrenner 1998, 19–36.
67. Bronfenbrenner 2007, 144.
68. Fletcher and Hurd 1998, 48–51.
69. Rosenstein 2004, 10.
70. Fine 2007, 38.
71. Moberg 2006.
72. Gaus 2008b, 5.
73. AFL-CIO 2005, 55–57; Hurd 2007, 317.
74. Acuff 2006.
75. Freeman and Rogers 2002, 8–40.
76. Cobble 2001, 87.
77. Freeman and Rogers 2002, 25–28.
78. Bronfenbrenner 2003, 41.

Chapter 9: Striking Out in America

1. Becker 1994, 351.
2. Logan 2008, 171.
3. Private-sector workers on the railroads and airlines are covered by the Railway Labor Act of 1926, which will not be discussed in detail in this chapter.
4. Kelly 1998; Silver 2003; Clawson 2003.
5. Silver 2003.
6. Kelly 1998, 83–107.
7. Kelly 1998, 9; Silver 2003, 127.
8. Perry and Wilson 2004, 37.
9. Vandaele 2011, 8.
10. Ibid. 26–29.
11. Ibid., 30.
12. European Trade Union Confederation 2011.

13. Perry and Wilson 2004, 10–14.
14. Troy 1986, 81; Lewin 1986, 244; US Census Bureau 1982–83; US Bureau of Labor Statistics 2000–2009; FMCS 2000–2010.
15. Schwartz 1999, 10, 20.
16. Pope 2004, 518–19.
17. Compa 2000, 17.
18. Logan 2008, 172–73.
19. Pope 2004, 520–26.
20. Preis 1964, 62–63.
21. Pope 2004, 526; Becker 1994, 351–71.
22. A distinction needs to be made between actions that are illegal and those that are not "protected" under the NLRA. Unprotected activities may be legal, but the employer has the right to "retaliation," which usually means dismissal. So workers engaged in slowdowns or other unprotected "partial strikes," as the courts have defined these, can be dismissed without recourse to the law (see Schwartz 2006).
23. Pope 2004, 533–34.
24. US Census Bureau 1982–83, 410.
25. Logan 2008, 177.
26. Mike Davis 1986, 117–27.
27. Pope 2004, 533–34.
28. Moody 2010, 105–46.
29. Moody 1988, 127–46.
30. Pope 2004, 534.
31. Shaikh 2010, 44–63; Mohun 2006, 347–48; McNally 2011, 46–49.
32. See chapter 3 of this book.
33. Logan 2008, 175–76, 178.
34. See chapter 3.
35. Kochan et al. 2004a, 2004b.
36. FMCS 2000, 2006, 2010.
37. Bureau of National Affairs 2000–2010b; 2008.
38. Mishel et al. 2009, 123.
39. Freeman and Medoff 1984, 151–54.
40. Council of Economic Advisors 2011, 246.
41. Mishel et al. 2009, 86.
42. Fleck et al. 2011, 60.
43. McCammon 2001, 143–52.
44. Ibid., 156–60.
45. Moody 1988, 134; Logan 2008, 183–88.
46. Cited in Perry 1987, 1.
47. Ibid., 1.
48. Rachleff 1993, 53; Perry 1987, 61.
49. Rachleff 1993, 76.

50. Juravich and Bronfenbrenner 1999, 70–71.
51. Ashby and Hawking 2009, 224.
52. Perry 1987, 44, 75; Rachleff 1993, 78; La Botz 1991, 129–30.
53. See Brecher and Costello 1990.
54. La Botz 1991, 132–34.
55. Juravich and Bronfenbrenner 1999.
56. Ibid., 110–19.
57. Burns 2011, 76.
58. Juravich and Bronfenbrenner 1999, 81.
59. Juravich 2007, 25–39.
60. FMCS 2010, 7.
61. La Botz 1993, 117–25; Moody 1988, 238.
62. Boal 2005, 137.
63. Ashby and Hawking 2009, 45–93.
64. Ibid., 290–301.
65. Early 1990, 4–10.
66. Galpern 2005, 131–34.
67. See Schwartz 2006, 35–39, 112–24.
68. Slaughter 2011b, 1–2.
69. Becker 1994, 351–21.
70. Association of Flight Attendants–CWA 2002.
71. Gaus 2011, 6.
72. Burns 2011, 55–57.
73. Lydersen 2009.
74. Brecher 1997, 331–35.
75. Winslow 2010b, 2–3.
76. Kelly 199, 89.
77. McNally 2011, 21–24. While 2011 was characterized by social upheaval across the world, notably the Arab Spring, Occupy Wall Street, etc., with some trade union involvement, these were not primarily worker-led strike movements.
78. FMCS 2011.
79. ETUC 2011, 9.
80. Silver 2003, 123.
81. McNally 2011, 181–82; *Los Angeles Times* 2011; BBC News 2010.
82. Silver 2003, 13–16, 172–73.
83. Burns 2011, 182–83.
84. Moody 2007, 211–12.

Chapter 10: Competition and Conflict

1. US Bureau of Labor Statistics 2001, 2011.
2. Hirsch and MacPherson, 2011.
3. This union density estimate of 14 percent based on Current Population

Survey data almost certainly underestimates the real extent of hospital unionism by understating the numerator and overstating the denominator. By one trade union estimate, the number of workers covered by unions in US hospitals is closer to one million, while those eligible for union representation total 4.8 million, making density closer to 20 percent. Even this may understate true density, as the number of nonsupervisory workers in US hospitals is about four million, which would make density 25 percent.

4.   Getman, Goldberg, and Sage 1976; Heneman and Sandver 1983.
5.   Bronfenbrenner 2000; Bronfenbrenner et al., eds., 1998.
6.   Wheeler 1985,
7.   Weikle et al. 1998, 197–212.
8.   P. Clark 2009, 33,
9.   Clark et al. 1999, 61–67; Clark et al. 2001, 133–48.
10. Clark et al. 1999, 63.
11. Jarley and Fiorito 1991, 223–29.
12. Bronfenbrenner 2005, 2.
13. Schur and Kruse 1992; US Bureau of Labor Statistics 2011.
14. Bronfenbrenner 2005, 13–14; US Census Bureau 2010, 387.
15. Bronfenbrenner and Juravich 1998.
16. Clark et al. 1999.
17. Berkowitz 2008, 84; Gottschalk 2000, 43.
18. US Census Bureau 2009, 95.
19. Stevens 1989, 284–300.
20. Cited in Gordon 2005, 236–37.
21. MCOL 2011, 1; US Census Bureau 2009, 104.
22. Robinson and Dratler 2006, 139.
23. Kumar 2010, 100.
24. Brooks and Jones 1997, 701–702.
25. American Hospital Association 2011, 12.
26. Internal Revenue Service 2010.
27. Das 2009, 13–21.
28. Love et al. 2008, 22.
29. Internal Revenue Service 2010, 124, 143; National Union of Healthcare Workers 2011.
30. Kochan et al. 2009, 27–28.
31. Bureau of Economic Analysis 2010e, 2010f, 2010g.
32. Pearson 2009, 14.
33. American Hospital Association 2010, 161.
34. American Hospital Association 2009, 16–19; Bureau of Economic Analysis 2010e, 2010f, 2010g.
35. Weed 2010.
36. Kumar 2010, 95.

37. Allen 2009.
38. Kocakülâh et al. 2009, 80–82.
39. Gaus 2009, 1.
40. Lipsky et al. 2009, 74.
41. Eastaugh 2010, 27–30.
42. Institute for Health and Socio-Economic Policy 2009, 4–7.
43. Centers for Medicare and Medicaid Services 2010, 1–10.
44. NLRB 2000–2010.
45. Clark et al. 2001, 144–45.
46. Peter D. Hart Research Associates 2001.
47. Ibid., 11, 17, 18, 19.
48. Aiken et al. 2010, 9.
49. Clark 2009; Clark et al. 1999, 2001.
50. Clark et al. 1999, 65.
51. National Nurses United 2010a.
52. Benson 2010, 303.
53. Bronfenbrenner 2009, 1–14.
54. Bronfenbrenner 2000, 8–19.
55. Gruber and Kleiner 2010.
56. National Nurses United 2010b.
57. *Minneapolis Star-Tribune* 2010.
58. American Hospital Association 2011, 12–29; Delaney 1981.
59. Clark 2002, 110; Delaney 1981, 152–153; Farber 1999, 1–6.
60. Robinson 1988.
61. US Census Bureau 2010, 419.
62. Bronfenbrenner 2005, 14.
63. Benson 2010, 302.
64. Clark and Clark 2009, 22–23.
65. International Council of Nurses 2009.
66. Waldman et al. 2004, 4–6.
67. Kochan et al. 2009, 13.
68. Lafer 2005, 30–39.
69. Moody 2009a, 685–89.
70. Early 2011b, 68–71; Kaplan 2008.
71. NLRB 2000–2003, 2007–2009.
72. Clark 2002, 110.
73. Benson 2010, 297; National Nurses United 2010a; UNITE-HERE 2009b.
74. American Federation of Teachers 2010.
75. Benson 2010, 298–99.
76. United Food and Commercial Workers 2010; United Steelworkers 2007, 3.
77. American Nurses Association 2011.

78. Krehbiel 2009.
79. M. Brenner 2010, 3; Early 2011, 294–302, 329–31; Winslow 2011.
80. Bureau of National Affairs 2010a, 2010d, 2010e.
81. Hirsch and MacPherson 2011.
82. NLRB 2000–2009; NLRB 2010b.
83. Kochan et al. 2009, 1, 31–32, 41–42, 53–54; Early 2011, 65.
84. NLRB 2010b.
85. FMCS 2009, 6–7; FMCS 2010, 7–8.
86. US Bureau of Labor Statistics 2011, 144; US Census Bureau 2009, 402.
87. Bureau of National Affairs 2010a, 2010d, 2010e.
88. US Department of Labor 2010.
89. Evans 2010.
90. Olson 2010.
91. Labor Notes 2011, 4.
92. Brenner and Gaus 2011.
93. Kochan et al. 2009, 13.
94. Clark 2009; Clark et al. 1999, 2001.
95. Clark and Clark 2006, 60; Clark and Clark 2009, 24–25; US Department of Labor 2010.
96. LexisNexis search, newspapers, "Hospital Strikes," 2010, 2011.
97. Clark and Clark 2009, 25; US Department of Labor 2010.
98. US Department of Labor 2010.
99. Clark and Clark 2009, 25.
100. Gordon 2005, 278–79.
101. US Department of Labor 2010b.
102. Benson 2010, 302–303.
103. Kaplan 2008.
104. Harrison 2010b.
105. Clark and Clark 2009, 27.
106. Stern 2006, 105.
107. Kochan et al. 2009, 13.
108. Clark and Clark 2009, 27; Kochan et al. 2009, 43–44.
109. Preuss and Frost 2003, 86, 91–96.
110. Early 2011, 109–17.
111. Ibid., 289–94.
112. Ibid., 63.
113. Winslow 2010a, 25.
114. Ibid.
115. Brenner 2011.
116. US Department of Labor 1995, 2009.
117. NLRB 2010b.
118. US Department of Labor 2006, 2011.
119. Winslow 2011.

120. Eaton 1999, 75–81; Hirsch and MacPherson 2011.
121. Cobble and Merrill 1994, 447–89; Waddoups and Eade 2002, 137–77.
122. Getman 2010.

Chapter 11: Immigrant Workers and Labor in the United States
1. Archibold 2006.
2. Colias 2006; Grow 2006.
3. Watanabe and Matthews 2006.
4. *Labor Notes* 2000, 1, 14; *Labor Notes* 2001, 15, 16.
5. Ness 2005, 43.
6. *Labor Notes* 2006c, 13.
7. US Bureau of Labor Statistics 2005, Table 1; US Census Bureau 2006, 44–46; US Census Bureau 2001, 44–45.
8. US Census Bureau 2006, 45; US Bureau of Labor Statistics 2006b, Table 4.
9. US Department of Homeland Security, Office of Immigration Statistics 2006, 5.
10. Marshall 2007, 1.
11. Lens 1971, 269–71; Gonzales 2000, 58–60.
12. Sims 1992, 6; Gonzales 2000, 77.
13. Moody and McGinn 1992, 1–11; Gonzales 2000, 228–29.
14. Moody 1995, 102; Gonzales 2000, 239.
15. INS 1999, 26; US Department of Homeland Security 2006, Table 3.
16. Marshall 2007, 1.
17. US Bureau of Labor Statistics 2006b, Tables 4 and 5.
18. US Census Bureau 2001, 386; Council of Economic Advisors 2005, 266; US Bureau of Labor Statistics 2007b, 1; Mishel, Bivens, Gould, and Shierholz 2012, 179.
19. Waldinger 1996, 94–136.
20. Fine 2006, 69.
21. Ibid., 67.
22. Migration Policy Institute 2004, 4.
23. Milkman 2000, 13.
24. Milkman and Wong 2000, 170–77.
25. Milkman and Wong 2001, 111.
26. Ibid., 122–26.
27. *Labor Notes* 2006a, 1, 6.
28. Mathew 2005, 1–7, 68–69, 196–97.
29. Ness 2005, 150–61.
30. Ibid., 58–129.
31. Fink 2003, 2–6, 54–78, 96–97.
32. Fine 2006, 2–3, 11–14.
33. Ibid., 7–21.

34. Tait 2005, 165–69, 173–74; Fine 2006, 9.
35. Tait 2005, 188–92; Fine 2006, 9.
36. Fine 2006, 137–38, 174.
37. Ibid., 10–11.
38. Tait 2006, 178–81.
39. Make the Road by Walking 2005, 1–20.
40. Jenkins 2002, 65–68.
41. Slaughter 2005, 262–63.
42. Make the Road by Walking 2005, 12.
43. Fine 2006, 11.
44. Jayaraman 2003; Fine 2006, 17.
45. Fine 2006, 174–75.
46. *Labor Notes* 2003, 5; *Labor Notes* 2005, 1, 14; Slaughter 2005, 148–52; Fine 2006; 104–107.
47. Piven and Cloward 1979.
48. Jayaraman 2003.
49. Jenkins 2002, 72.
50. Fine 2006, 120–25; Slaughter 2005, 251–54.
51. *Labor Notes* 2006b, 1, 10–11.
52. *Labor Notes* 2007, 1, 14.
53. Lopez 2007, 4–9.
54. Ibid., 9.
55. Immigrant Solidarity Network 2007.

Epilogue

1. Most of the data from this and the three following paragraphs are taken from LM-2 forms (US Department of Labor 2008), annual US Bureau of Labor Statistics "Union Members" press releases, or from Gifford 2010, 206–208.

2. The SEIU's LM-2 forms show a net gain in active members of 110,703 from 2007 to 2008. The SEIU, however, had 204,000 agency fee payers in 2007. This fell to 159,000 in 2008. Thus almost half of the growth is explained by what appears to be a switch of nearly fifty thousand represented workers from agency fee payers to active members: a good thing, but not real growth. Alternatively, the SEIU lost these agency fee payers. Most of the other half of growth is explained by the affiliation in 2008 of the fifty-five-thousand-member North Carolina State Employees Association. The SEIU did win recognition for new members in fiscal 2008, notably twenty-two thousand Massachusetts home health care workers, but the big growth figures come from elsewhere.

3. For details on this see chapter 8.

4. For a thorough account and analysis, see Early 2011, from which much of this account is taken.

5. These include: Security Police Fire Professionals of America; Domestic Workers United; California Nurses' Association; Engineers and Architects Association; New York State Nurses Association; the Federación Maestros de Puerto Rico; and UNITE-HERE.

6. The six were SEIU, IBT, UFCW, UNITE-HERE, LIUNA, and the UFW. The Carpenters union, which had already left the AFL-CIO, also joined CTW.

7. There is also the matter of the Amalgamated Bank, of which Raynor was chair and which he claimed should go with him. Presumably this fact was of some interest to Stern. Eventually it went to SEIU.

8. Bureau of National Affairs 2008, 2010b, 2012a; FMCS 2011, 11.

9. First half 2012.

10. Bureau of National Affairs 2010b, 2012a.

11. US Bureau of Labor Statistics 2012b, 12, 36; US Bureau of Labor Statistics 2012c, 11; Bureau of Economic Analysis, 2012.

12. First half 2012.

13. Slaughter 2013, 1–3.

14. Lydersen 2009.

15. Harrison 2010a, 1, 14; Harrison 2010b.

16. Abowd 2010, 1, 13; Gutekanst 2012, 12–14.

17. Ryan 2011a, 1, 6; Slaughter 2011a, 1, 7, 14; Schirmer 2012, 15–16.

18. Slaughter 2012a, 8–10.

19. One could see this process of learning from one another's struggles in action at the 2012 *Labor Notes* conference.

20. For an account of workers' councils, see Cohen 2011.

21. Marx 1974, 79.

22. In fact, almost 90 percent of US employees work in traditional employment arrangements. Actual temp-agency workers compose less than 2 percent of the workforce. A related idea is that most US workers now work for small firms. In fact, nearly two-thirds of all workers work for firms with a hundred or more employees, while almost 40 percent work at companies with more than a thousand employees. US Census Bureau 2012, 389, 408–10; Mishel et al. 2012, 329–30.

23. Foner 1975, 200–204.

24. Montgomery 1989, 100–109; Ulman 1955, 468.

25. Slaughter, (2012); 8-10.

26. IWW 1962, 10–11.

27. Early 2013, 1, 3–5.

28. Draper 1970. The Workers' Party was a nonorthodox Trotskyist party, formed in the 1940 split from what was then a more orthodox Socialist Workers Party over the "nature of the Soviet Union," among other things.

Bibliography

Abowd, Paul. 2010. "Reformers to Lead Chicago Teachers." *Labor Notes* 376 (July).

Acuff, Stewart. 2006. "The AFL-CIO Union Movement: Strategy and Vision to Build Worker Power." *AFL-CIO Now.* http://blog.aflcio.org/2006/09/01.

AFL-CIO. 2005. *Executive Council Report 2005.* Twenty-Fifth Constitutional Convention. Washington, D.C.: AFL-CIO.

————. 2011. "Poll: Public Opposes Taking Away Freedom to Bargain." News release. February 22.

Aiken, Linda H., Douglas M. Sloane, Jeannie P. Cimiotti, Sean P. Clarke, Linda Flynn, Jean Ann Seago, Joanne Spetz, and Herbert L. Smith. 2010. "Implications of the California Nurse Staffing Mandate for Other States." *Health Services Research, Health Research and Educational Trust.* www.nationalnursesunited.org.

Allen, Scott. 2009. "No Waiting: A Simple Prescription that Could Dramatically Improve Hospitals—and American Health Care." *Boston Globe,* August 30. http://www.boston.com/bostonglobe/ideas/articles/2009/08/30/a_simple_change_could_dramatically_improve_hospitals_ndash_and_american_health_care/.

American Federation of Teachers. 2010. "About AFT Healthcare." www.aft.org.

American Hospital Association. 2009. "The Economic Crisis: Ongoing Monitoring of Impact on Hospitals." November. PowerPoint presentation. Chicago: American Hospital Association.

————. 2011. *AHA Hospital Statistics 2011.* Chicago: Health Forum.

American Nurses Association. 2011. "ANA Affiliates." http://nursingworld.org/AffiliatedOrganizations.

American Rights at Work. 2008. "Why Can't 60 Million Americans Get What They Want?" *AmericanRightsatWork.org,* April 10.

Archibold, Randal. 2006."Strategy Sessions Fueled Immigrant Marches." *New York Times,* April 12. www.nytimes.com/2006/04/12/us/12immig .html?pagewanted=print.

Ashby, Steven, and C. J. Hawking 2009. *Staley: The Fight for a New American Labor Movement.* Urbana: University of Illinois Press.

Association of Flight Attendants–CWA. 2002. "Midwest Express Flight Attendants Get Strategic Advice from Alaska Airlines CHAOSTM Strikers." www.afanet.org.

Atleson, James. 1993. "Wartime Labor Regulation, the Industrial Pluralists, and the Law of Collective Bargaining." In *Industrial Democracy in America: The Ambiguous Promise,* 142–75, edited by Nelson Lichtenstein and John Harris Howell. Cambridge: Cambridge University Press, 1993.

Babson, Steve. 1995. *Lean Work: Empowerment and Exploitation in the Global Auto Industry.* Detroit: Wayne State University Press.

Barbash, Jack. 1994. "Americanizing the Labor Problem: The Wisconsin School." In *Labor Economics and Industrial Relations: Markets and Institutions,* edited by Clark Kerr and Paul D. Staudohar, 41–65. Cambridge, MA: Harvard University Press.

Barrett, James R. 1998. "Boring from Within and Without." In *Labor Histories: Class, Politics, and the Working Class Experience,* edited by Eric Arnesen, Julie Greene, and Bruce Laurie. Chicago: University of Illinois Press.

BBC News. 2010. "Chinese Factories Hit by Wave of Strikes." June 28. http://www.bbc.co.uk/news/10434079.

Beardwell, Julie, and Tim Clayton. 2007. *Human Resource Management: A Contemporary Approach.* 5th edition. Harlow, UK: Pearson Education Limited.

Becker, Craig. 1994. "'Better Than a Strike': Protecting New Forms of Collective Work Stoppage under the National Labor Relations Act." *University of Chicago Law Review* 61(2): 351–421.

Becker, Craig, James Brudney, Charles Cohen, and Joan Flynn. 2006. "Neutrality Agreements Take Center Stage at the National Labor Relations Board." *Labor Law Journal* 57(2) (Summer): 117–28.

Beer, Michael, Bert Spector, Paul Lawrence, D. Quinn Mills, and Richard E. Walton. 1984. *Managing Human Assets.* New York: Free Press.

Benchich, Al. 2010. "Auto Worker Delegates: 'What, Us Worry?'" *Labor Notes* 376 (July).

Benson, Herman. 2010. "Unionization of the Nurses in the U.S.: Worker Power, Autonomy, and Labor Democracy." *Working USA* 13: 297–307.

Benz, Dorothy. 2002. "Organizing to Survive, Bargaining to Organize."

WorkingUSA 5(1), Summer: 95–107.

Berkowitz, Edward. 2008. "Medicare and Medicaid: The Past as Prologue." *Health Care Financing Review* 29(3): 81–92.

Bernstein, Irving. 1969. *Turbulent Years: A History of the American Worker, 1933–1941.* Boston: Houghton Mifflin.

Boal, E. 2005. "The Legal Limits of Working to Rule." In Slaughter 2005.

Bok, Derek. 1964. "The Regulation of Campaign Tactics in Union Representation Elections under the National Labor Relations Act." *Harvard Law Review* 78(1): 38–141.

Boyer, Richard O., and Herbert M. Morais. 1979. *Labor's Untold Story.* 3rd ed. Pittsburgh: United Electrical, Radio, and Machine Workers of America.

Braverman, Harry. 1998. *Labor and Monopoly Capital: The Degradation of Work in the Twentieth Century.* New York: Monthly Review Press.

Brecher, Jeremy. 1997. *Strike!* Rev. ed. Boston: South End Press.

Brecher, Jeremy, and Tim Costello. 1990. *Building Bridges: The Emerging Grassroots Coalition of Labor and Community.* New York: Monthly Review Press.

Brenner, Aaron, Robert Brenner, and Cal Winslow. 2010. *Rebel Rank and File: Labor Militancy and Revolt from Below During the Long 1970s.* London: Verso.

Brenner, Mark. 2008. "SEIU Reformers Challenge Union's Direction at Puerto Rico Convention." *Labor Notes* 352, July.

———. 2010. "Fear Wins as Service Employees Fend Off NUHW." *Labor Notes* 380: 3.

———. 2011. "NUHW Nurses Strike in Los Angeles over Staffing Levels." *Labor Notes,* March 3. www.labornotes.org/2011/03/nuhw-nurses-strike-los-angeles-over-staffing-levels.

Brenner, Mark, and Mischa Gaus. 2011. "21,000 Strike Giant California Hospital Chains." *Labor Notes.* www.labornotes.org/2011/09/21000-strike-giant-california-hospital-chains.

Brenner, Robert. 2002. *The Boom and the Bubble: The US in the World Economy.* London: Verso.

Bronfenbrenner, Kate. 2000. *Uneasy Terrain: The Impact of Capital Mobility on Workers, Wages, and Union Organizing.* Ithaca, NY: Cornell University ILR School, Digital Commons@ILR.

———. 2003. "The American Labour Movement and the Resurgence in Union Organizing." In *Trade Unions in Renewal: A Comparative Study,* edited by P. Fairbrother and C. Yates. London: Routledge.

———. 2005. "Unions Organizing among Professional Women Workers." AFL-CIO Department for Professional Employees. Washington, D.C.: AFL-CIO.

———. 2007. "Race, Gender, and the Rebirth of Trade Unionism." *New*

Labor Forum 16 (3–4), Fall.

———. 2009. *No Holds Barred: The Intensification of Employer Opposition to Organizing.* EPI Briefing Paper #235. Washington, D.C.: Economic Policy Institute.

Bronfenbrenner, Kate, ed. 2007. *Global Unions: Challenging Transnational Capital through Cross-Border Campaigns.* Ithaca, NY: Cornell University Press.

Bronfenbrenner, Kate, and Tom Juravich. 1998. "It Takes More than House Calls: Organizing to Win with a Comprehensive Union-Building Strategy." In Bronfenbrenner et al., eds., 1998.

Bronfenbrenner, Kate, and Robert Hickey. 2004. "Changing to Organize: A National Assessment of Union Strategies. In *Rebuilding Labor: Organizing and Organizers in the New Union Movement,* edited by Ruth Milkman and Kim Voss. Ithaca, NY: Cornell University Press.

Bronfenbrenner, Kate, Sheldon Friedman, Richard W. Hurd, Rudolph A. Oswald, and Ronald L. Seeber, eds. 1998. *Organizing To Win: New Research on Union Strategies.* Ithaca, NY: Cornell University Press.

Brooks, G. R., and V. G. Jones, 1997. "Hospital Mergers and Market Overlap." *Health Service Research* 31(6): 701–22.

Brooks, Thomas R. 1965. *Toil and Trouble: A History of American Labor.* New York: Delta Books.

Brudney, James. 2005. "Neutrality Agreements and Card Check Recognition: Prospects for Changing Labor Relations Paradigms." *Iowa Law Review* 90: 819–86.

———. 2007. "Neutrality Agreements and Card Check Recognition: Prospects for Changing Labor Relations Paradigms." *Advance* 1: 11–31.

Buhle, Paul. 1999. *Taking Care of Business: Samuel Gompers, George Meany, Lane Kirkland and the Tragedy of American Labor.* New York: Monthly Review Press.

Bulmer, Martin, ed. 1975. *Working-Class Images of Society.* London: Gregg Revivals.

Bureau of Economic Analysis. 2010a. "Net Stock of Private Nonresidential Fixed Assets." Table 4.1. www.bea.gov/national/nipaweb.

———. 2010b. "Chain-Type Quantity Index for Net Stock of Private Nonresidential Fixed Assets by Industry Group and Legal Form of Organization." Table 4.2. www.bea.gov/national/FA2004.

———. 2010c. "Corporate Profits by Industry." NIPA Table 6.6D. www.bea.gov/national/nipaweb.

———. 2010d. "Corporate Profits: Third Quarter 2010 (Preliminary)." Table 12. News release. BEA 10–54, November 23.

———. 2010e. "Chain-Type Quantity Indexes for Net Stock of Private

Fixed Assets by Industry," Table 3.2ES. www.bea.gov/national/nipaweb.

———. 2010f. "Chain Type Indexes for Net Stock of Private Equipment and Software by Industry," Table 3.2E. www.bea.gov/national/nipaweb.

———. 2010g. "Historical Cost Net Stock Private Assets by Industry," Table 3.3E. www.bea.gov/national/nipaweb.

———. 2012. "Corporate Profits: Second Quarter 2012." BEA-12-44, September 27.

———. 2013. "Price, Costs, and Profits Per Unit of Gross Value Added of Nonfinancial Corporate Business." Table 1.15.

Bureau of National Affairs, 2000–2010. *Collective Bargaining Bulletin.* Arlington, VA: Bureau of National Affairs.

———. 2002. *Collective Bargaining Bulletin(2).* Arlington, VA: Bureau of National Affairs.

———. 2003. *Collective Bargaining Bulletin (2),* January 23. Arlington, VA: Bureau of National Affairs.

———. 2006. *Collective Bargaining Bulletin (2)* 10, January 19. Arlington, VA: Bureau of National Affairs.

———. 2008. *Source Book on Collective Bargaining.* Arlington, VA: Bureau of National Affairs.

———. 2010a. *Collective Bargaining Bulletin (20),* October 7. Arlington, VA: Bureau of National Affairs.

———. 2010b. *Source Book on Collective Bargaining.* Arlington, VA: Bureau of National Affairs.

———. 2010c. *Collective Bargaining Bulletin (16),* August 12. Arlington, VA: Bureau of National Affairs.

———. 2010d. *Collective Bargaining Bulletin (1),* January 14. Arlington, VA: Bureau of National Affairs.

———. 2010e. "BNA Plus Contract Summaries Report." September. Arlington, VA: Bureau of National Affairs.

———. 2012a. *Source Book on Collective Bargaining.* Arlington, VA: Bureau of National Affairs.

———. 2012b. *Collective Bargaining Bulletin (20),* October 14. Arlington, VA: Bureau of National Affairs.

Burns, Joe. 2011. *Reviving the Strike: How Working People Can Regain Power and Transform America.* Brooklyn: Ig Publishing.

California Nurses' Association. 2008. "About Us." *California Nurses' Association.* www.calnurses.org.

Centers for Medicare and Medicaid Services. 2010. *Estimated Financial Effects of the 'Patient Protection and Affordable Care Act' as Amended.* Baltimore: Centers for Medicare and Medicaid Services.

Chaison, Gary. 2006. *Unions in America.* Thousand Oaks, CA: Sage.

————. 2010. "Union Membership Attrition." *Monthly Labor Review* 133(1), January 2010: 74–76.

Charlton, John. 1997. *The Chartists: The First National Workers' Movement.* London: Pluto Press.

Clark, Paul F. 2002. "Health Care: A Growing Role for Collective Bargaining." In Clark, Delaney, and Frost 2002, 91–136.

————. 2009. *Building More Effective Unions,* 2nd ed. Ithaca, NY: Cornell ILR Press.

Clark, Paul F., and Darlene A. Clark. 2006. "Union Strategies for Improving Patient Care: The Key to Nurse Unionism." *Labor Studies Journal* 31(1) (Spring): 51–70.

————. 2009. "Nurses' Unions' Efforts to Give RNs a Greater Voice in Patient Care." *Proceedings of the 61st Annual Meeting of the Labor and Employment Relations Association* (October), 19–30.

Clark, Paul F., Darlene A. Clark, David Day, and Dennis Shea. 1999. "Health Care Reform's Impact on Hospitals:Implications for Union Organizing." *Proceedings of the 51st Annual Meeting of the Industrial Relations Research Association* (January): 61–67.

————. 2001. "The Impact of Health Care Reform on Nurses' Attitudes toward Unions: The Role of Climate for Patient Care." *Industrial and Labor Relations Review* 55(1)(October).

Clark, Paul F., John Delaney, and Ann Frost, eds. 2002. *Collective Bargaining in the Private Sector: Current Developments and Future Challenges.* Champaign, IL: Industrial Relations Research Association.

Clawson, Dan. 2003. *The Next Upsurge: Labor and New Social Movements.* Ithaca, NY: Cornell University Press.

Cliff, Tony. 1975. *Lenin, Volume I: Building the Party.* London: Pluto Press.

Cobble, Dorothy Sue. 2001. "Lost Ways of Unionism: Historical Perspectives on Reinventing the Labor Movement." In Turner, Katz, and Hurd 2001, 82–96.

Cobble, Dorothy Sue, and Michael Merrill. 1994. "Collective Bargaining in the Hospitality Industry in the 1980s." In *Contemporary Collective Bargaining in the Private Sector,* edited by Paula B. Voos. Madison, WI: IRRA.

Cochran, Thomas C. 1957. *The American Business System: A Historical Perspective, 1900–1955.* New York: Harper Torchbooks.

Cohen, Sheila. 2006. *Ramparts of Resistance: Why Workers Lost Their Power and How to Get It Back.* London: Pluto Press.

————. 2011. "The Red Mole: Workers' Councils as a Means of Revolutionary Transformation." In *Ours to Master and to Own,* edited by Immanuel Ness and Dario Azzellini. Chicago: Haymarket Books.

Cohen, Sheila, ed. 1998. *What's Happening? The Truth about Work and the Myth of "Partnership."* London: Trade Union Forum.

Colias, Mike. 2006. "Immigrant Rally Chiefs Ponder What's Next." Associated Press, May 2.

Compa, Lance. 2000. *Unfair Advantage: Workers' Freedom of Association in the United States under International Human Rights Standards.* New York: Human Rights Watch.

Cooper, Marc. 1996. "Harley-Riding, Picket-Walking Socialism Haunts Decatur." *Nation,* April 8.

Council of Economic Advisors. 2005. *Economic Report of the President.* Washington, D.C.: US Government Printing Office.

———. 2010. *Economic Report of the President.* Washington, D.C.: US Government Printing Office.

———. 2011. *Economic Report of the President.* Washington, D.C.: US Government Printing Office.

Coy, Peter. 2009. "The Dark Side of the Productivity Surge." *Businessweek,* November 5.

Craypo, Charles. 1986. *The Economics of Collective Bargaining.* Washington, D.C.: Bureau of National Affairs.

Croteau, David. 1995. *Politics and the Class Divide: Working People and the Middle-Class Left.* Philadelphia: Temple University Press.

Danford, Andy. 1997. "The 'New Industrial Relations' and Class Struggle in the 1990s." *Capital and Class* 61 (Spring).

Das, D. 2009. "Factor Analysis of Financial and Operational Performance Measures of Non-Profit Hospitals." *Journal of Health Care Finance* 36(2): 13–23.

Davis, Mary. 2009. *Comrade or Brother? A History of the British Labour Movement.* London: Pluto Press.

Davis, Mike. 1986. *Prisoners of the American Dream.* London: Verso.

De Turberville, Simon. 2004. "Does the 'Organizing Model' Represent a Credible Union Renewal Strategy?" *Work, Employment and Society* 18(4).

Deer, Brian. 1996. "Still Struggling after All These Years." *New Statesman,* August 23.

Delaney, John Thomas. 1981. "Union Success in Hospital Representation Elections." *Industrial Relations* 20(2): 149–61.

Dickens, William. 1983. "The Effect of Company Campaigns on Certification Elections: *Law and Reality* Once Again." *Industrial and Labor Relations Review* 36(4): 560–75.

Dobbs, Farrell. 1972. *Teamster Rebellion.* New York: Monad Press.

———. 1973. *Teamster Power.* New York: Monad Press.

Draper, Hal. 1970. *Marxism and the Trade Unions,* III. www.marxists.org

/archive/draper/1970/tus/3.

———. 1978. *Karl Marx's Theory of Revolution, Volume II: The Politics of Social Classes*. New York: Monthly Review Press.

———. 1992. "The Two Souls of Socialism." In Haberkern 1992.

Du Bois, W. E. B. 1998. *Black Reconstruction in America, 1860–1880*. New York: Free Press.

Dubofsky, Melvyn. 2000. *Hard Work: The Making of Labor History*. Urbana: University of Illinois Press.

Dubofsky, Melvyn, and Joseph A. McCartin. 2000. *We Shall Be All: A History of the Industrial Workers of the World*. Abridged ed. Urbana: University of Illinois Press.

Eames, Patricia. 1976. "An Analysis of Union Voting Study from a Trade-Unionist Point of View." *Sanford Law Review* 28(2).

Early, Steve. 1990. *Holding the Line in '89: Lessons of the NYNEX Strike*. Somerville, MA: Labor Resource Center.

———. 2011a. "In Open Shop America: Dial 1-800-Unionism Is Not the Answer." *CounterPunch*, June 2.

———. 2011b. *The Civil Wars in US Labor: Birth of a New Workers' Movement or Death Throes of the Old?* Chicago: Haymarket Books.

———. 2012. "Bargaining to Organize: From Boon to Embarrassment." *Working In These Times*, August 21.

———. 2013. "House of Labor Needs Repairs, Not Just New Roommates." *Labor Notes* 415 (October).

Eastaugh, Steven. 2010. "Hospital Productivity and Information Technology." *Journal of Health Care Finance* 36(4): 27–37.

Eaton, Adrienne, and Jill Kriesky. 2001. "Union Organizing under Neutrality and Card Check Agreements." *Industrial and Labor Relations Review* 55(1): 43–59.

Eaton, Adrienne, Janice Fine, Allison Porter, and Saul Rubenstein. 2009. "Organizational Change at SEIU 1996–2009." http://scribd.com/doc/27928589/Organizational-Change-at-SEIU-1996–2009.

Eaton, S. 1999. "Changing Labor–Management Relations in Nursing Homes." In *Proceedings of the Fifty-First Annual Meeting of the Industrial Relations Research Association*. New York: IRRA.

Edsall, Thomas Byrne. 1984. *The New Politics of Inequality*. New York: W.W. Norton & Co.

Edwards, P. K., and Hugh Scullion. 1982. *Shop Stewards in Action*. Oxford: Blackwell.

Engels, Friedrich. 1885. "The History of the Communist League." In Karl Marx and Friedrich Engels, *Selected Works*, Vol. 3. Moscow: Progress Publishers, 1970.

———. 1887. "Preface to the American Edition of *The Conditions of the*

Working-Class in England." In Lapides 1990.

———. 1980. *The Conditions of the Working-Class in England: From Personal Observations and Authentic Sources.* Moscow: Progress Publishers.

Engels, Friedrich, and Laura Lafargue. 1889. *Correspondent,* Vol. 2. October 17.

Estlund, Cynthia. 2007. "The Ossification of American Labor Law and the Decline of Self-Governance in the Workplace." *Journal of Labor Research* 28: 591–608.

European Trade Union Confederation (ETUC). 2011. *ETUC Strategy and Action Plan.* Brussels: European Trade Union Confederation.

Evans, Melanie. 2010. "Pensions Picked Apart: Some Hospitals, Systems Freeze Defined-Benefit Plans." *Modern Healthcare,* April 19.

Farber, Henry S. 1999. "Union Success in Representation Elections: Why Does Size Matter?" Working Paper #420. Princeton, NJ: Industrial Relations Section, Princeton University.

Federal Mediation and Conciliation Service (FMCS). 2000. *Annual Report.* Washington, D.C.: FMCS.

———. 2001. *Annual Report.* Washington, D.C.: FMCS.

———. 2002. *Annual Report.* Washington, D.C.: FMCS.

———. 2003. *Annual Report.* Washington, D.C.: FMCS.

———. 2004. *Annual Report.* Washington, D.C.: FMCS.

———. 2005. *Annual Report.* Washington, D.C.: FMCS.

———. 2006. *Annual Report.* Washington, D.C.: FMCS.

———. 2007. *Annual Report.* Washington, D.C.: FMCS.

———. 2008. *Annual Report.* Washington, D.C.: FMCS.

———. 2009. *Annual Report.* Washington, D.C.: FMCS.

———. 2010. *Annual Report.* Washington, D.C. · FMCS.

Ferguson, John-Paul. 2008. "The Eyes of the Needles: A Sequential Model of Union Organizing Drives, 1999–2004." *Industrial and Labor Relations Review* 62(1): 3–21.

Fernbach, David, ed. 1973. *Karl Marx: The Revolutions of 1848, Political Writings,* Vol. I. New York: Vintage Books.

Fine, Janice. 2006. *Worker Centers: Organizing Communities at the Edge of the Dream.* Ithaca, NY: Cornell University Press.

———. 2007. "Why Labor Needs a Plan B: Alternatives to Conventional Trade Unionism." *New Labor Forum* 16(2): 35–44.

Fink, Leon. 2003. *The Maya of Morganton: Work and Community in the Nuevo New South.* Chapel Hill: University of North Carolina Press.

Fiorito, Jack, and Paul Jarley. 2008. "Why Don't They Organize?" Working paper, presented at the Labor and Employment Relations Association, New Orleans.

Fiorito, Jack, Christopher Lowman, and Forrest Nelson. 1987. "The Impact of Human Resource Policies on Union Organizing." *Industrial Relations* 26(2): 113–23.

Fleck, Susan, John Glaser, and Shawn Sprague. 2011. "The Compensation-Productivity Gap: A Visual Essay." *Monthly Labor Review* 134(1): 57–69.

Fletcher, Bill, and Richard W. Hurd. 1998. "Beyond the Organizing Model: The Transformation Process in Local Unions." In Bronfenbrenner et al., eds., 1998.

Fletcher, Bill, and Fernando Gapasin. 2008. *Solidarity Divided: The Crisis in Organized Labor and a New Path toward Social Justice.* Berkeley: University of California Press.

Foner, Philip S. 1975. *The History of the Labor Movement in the United States,* Vol. 2. New York: International Publishers.

———. 1991. *The History of the Labor Movement in the United States,* Vol. 9. New York: International Publishers.

Formbrun, Charles J., Noel M. Tichy, and Mary Anne Devanna. 1984. *Strategic Human Resource Management.* Chichester, UK: John Wiley and Sons.

Freeman, Richard B., and James Medoff. 1984. *What Do Unions Do?* New York: Basic Books.

Freeman, Richard B., and Joel Rogers. 2002. "Open Source Unionism: Beyond Exclusive Collective Bargaining." *Working USA* 5(4) (Spring).

Freeman, Richard B., and Morris Kleiner. 1990. "Employer Behavior in the Face of Union Organising Drives." *Industrial and Labor Relations Review* 43(4): 351–65.

Friedman, Gerald. 1999. "U.S. Historical Statistics: New Estimates of Union Membership in the United States, 1880–1914." *Historical Methods* 32(2).

Gabriel, Jackie. 2006. "Organizing the Jungle: Industrial Restructuring and Immigrant Unionization in the American Meatpacking Industry." *Working USA* 9 (September).

Gall, Gregor. 2010. "Statutory Union Recognition Provisions as Stimulants to Employer Anti-Unionism in Three Anglo-Saxon Countries." *Economic and Industrial Democracy* 31(7): 7–33.

Galpern, P. 2005. "Telephone Workers Pressure Verizon from Within." In Slaughter 2005.

Gaus, Mischa. 2008a. "Workers Win Test of 'Card Check' Ruling." *Labor Notes*, February 4.

———. 2008b. "Hotel Workers Rising Campaign Pays Off in L.A." *Labor Notes* 352, July.

———. 2009. "Technology Push in Hospitals Puts Stress on Workers." *Labor Notes* 364: 1, 13.

———. 2010. "Seven Unions Coordinate Six-State Strike, Red Cross Responds with Lockout." *Labor Notes* 376 (July).

———. 2011. "Grievance Strike Shutters Silicone Plant." *Labor Notes* 383 (February), 6.

Georgine, Robert. 1979. *From Brass Knuckles to Briefcases: The Changing Art of Union-Busting in America.* Washington, D.C.: Center to Protect Workers' Rights.

Getman, Julius. 2010. *Restoring the Power of Unions: It Takes a Movement.* New Haven, CT: Yale University Press.

Getman, Julius, Stephen Goldberg, and Jeanne Herman. 1976. *Union Representation Elections: Law and Reality.* New York: Russell Sage Foundation.

Gifford, Courtney. 2010. *Directory of U.S. Labor Organizations,* Arlington, VA: BNA Books.

Glyn, Andrew. 2006. *Capitalism Unleashed: Finance, Globalization, and Welfare.* Oxford: Oxford University Press.

Goldfield, Michael. 1987. *The Decline of Organized Labor in the United States.* Chicago: University of Chicago Press.

Gonzales, Juan. 2000. *Harvest of Empire: A History of Latinos in America.* New York: Penguin.

Gordon, Suzanne. 2005. *Nursing Against the Odds: How Health Care Cost Cutting, Media Stereotypes, and Medical Hubris Undermine Nurse and Patient Care.* Ithaca, NY: Cornell University Press.

Gottschalk, Marie. 2000. *The Shadow Welfare State: Labor, Business, and the Politics of Health Care in the United States.* Ithaca, NY: Cornell University Press.

Grabelsky, Jeffrey. 2007. "Serving the Public Interest: Preventing Double-Breasting in the Construction Industry." Testimony to the Standing Committee on Law Amendments, New Brunswick, Canada, October 17, 2007. Ithaca, NY: Cornell ILR Press.

Graham, Keith. 1992. *Karl Marx Our Contemporary: Social Theory for a Post-Leninist World.* Toronto: University of Toronto Press.

Gramsci, Antonio. 1971. *Selections from the Prison Notebooks.* New York: International Publishers.

Greeman, Richard. 2011. "General Strikes and Massive Demonstrations Challenge Neoliberal Reforms in France." *New Politics* 13(3): 9.

Greenbaum, Joan. 2004. *Window on the Workplace: Technology, Jobs, and the Organization of Office Work.* New York: Monthly Review Press.

Greenhouse, Steven. 2006. "Employers Sharply Criticize Shift in Union Organizing Method to Cards from Elections." *New York Times,* March 11.

Grow, Brian. 2006. "May Day: The Fight behind the Protest." *Businessweek.* April 28.

Gruber, Jonathan, and Samuel A. Kleiner. 2010. *Do Strikes Kill? Evidence from New York State.* Working Paper 15855. Cambridge, MA: National Bureau of Economic Research.

Gruelle, Martha, and Mike Parker. 1999. *Democracy Is Power: Rebuilding Unions from the Bottom Up.* Detroit: Labor Notes.

Guardian. 1997. "Cut and Thrust as Airline Brings In Its Grand Scheme." July 2.

Gutekanst, Norine. 2012. "How Chicago Teachers Got Organized to Strike." *Labor Notes* 404 (November).

Haberkern, E., ed. 1992. *Socialism from Below.* New Jersey: Humanities Press, 2–33.

Hall, Stuart. 1987. "Gramsci and Us." *Marxism Today* (June).

Harcourt, Mark, and Helen Lam. 2007. "Union Certification: A Critical Analysis and Proposed Alternatives." *Working USA* 10 (September).

Harrison, Marty. 2010a. "Hospital Workers Walk Out in Philadelphia." *Labor Notes* 374 (May).

———. 2010b. "Philadelphia Hospital Workers Victorious in Strike." *Labor Notes,* May 21. www.labornotes.org/2010/05/philadelphia-hospital-workers-victorious-strike.

Heintz, James. 2009. "The Grim State of the States." *New Labor Forum* 18(2) (Spring 2009): 7–15.

Heneman, Herbert G., and Marcus H. Sandver. 1983. "Predicting the Outcome of Union Certification Elections." *Industrial and Labor Relations Review* 36(4): 537–59.

Hinton, James, and Richard Hyman. 1975. *Trade Unions and Revolution: The Industrial Politics of the Early British Communist Party.* London: Pluto Press.

Hirsch, Barry, and David MacPherson. 2000–2011. "Union Membership, Coverage, Density and Employment by Industry." www.unionstats.com.

Hirsch, Barry, and David MacPherson. 2013. *Union Membership and Coverage Database.* www.unionstats.com.

Horowitz, Roger. 1997. *Black and White, Unite and Fight: A Social History of Industrial Unionism in Meatpacking, 1930–90.* Urbana: University of Illinois Press.

Hülsemann, Karsten. 2001. "Greenfields in the Heart of Dixie: How the American Automobile Industry Discovered the South." In *The Second Wave: Southern Industrialization from the 1940s to the 1970s,* edited by Philip Scranton. Athens: University of Georgia Press.

Hurd, Richard W. 2004. "The Failure of Organizing, the New Unity Partnership, and the Future of the Labor Movement." *Working USA* 8 (September 2004).

———. 2007. "US Labor 2006: Strategic Developments Across the Divide." *Journal of Labor Research* 28(2), Spring.

———. 2008. "Neutrality Agreements: Innovative, Controversial, and

Labor's Hope for the Future." *New Labor Forum* 17(1), Spring.

Hyman, Richard. 1971. *Marxism and the Sociology of Trade Unionism.* London: Pluto Press.

Imberman, Woodruff. 1980. "The Hocus Pocus in Union Avoidance." *Journal of Labor Research* 1(2): 275–83.

Immigrant Solidarity Network. 2007. "Coverage of May Day 2007." *Immigrant News Briefs* 10(12), May 6.

Immigration and Naturalization Service (INS). 1999. *1997 Statistical Yearbook.* Washington, D.C.: US Government Printing Office.

Institute for Health and Socio-Economic Policy. 2009. *Health Information Basics.* Oakland, CA: Institute for Health and Socio-Economic Policy.

Internal Revenue Service. 2010. "IRS Nonprofit Hospital Project: Final Report." www. irs.gov.

International Council of Nurses. 2009. "Nurses in the Workplace: Expectations and Needs, a Global Survey of Nurses." PowerPoint presentation. Geneva: International Council of Nurses. www.icn.ch/images/stories/documents/news/advocacy/nurses_in_the_workplace/survey.swf.

International Labour Office. 2008. *Global Wage Report, 2008/09.* Geneva: International Labour Office.

International Workers of the World (IWW). 1962. "Solidarity Forever." *Songs of the Workers to Fan the Flames of Discontent.* Chicago: IWW.

Jacoby, Sanford. 1991. "American Exceptionalism Revisited: The Importance of Management." In *Master to Managers: Historical and Comparative Perspectives on American Employers,* edited by Sanford Jacoby, 173–241. New York: Columbia University Press.

Jarley, Paul, and Jack Fiorito. 1991. "Unionism and Changing Employee Views toward Work." *Journal of Labor Research* 12(3): 223–29.

Jayaraman, Saru. 2003. "In the Wake of 9/11: New York Restaurant Workers Explore New Strategies." *Labor Notes,* August.

Jeffreys, Steve. 1986. *Management and Managed: Fifty Years of Crisis at Chrysler.* Cambridge: Cambridge University Press.

Jenkins, Steve. 2002. "Organizing, Advocacy, and Member Power." *Working USA* 6(2), Fall.

Johnson, Nancy. 1995. "Pay Levels in the Airlines since Deregulation." In *Airline Labor Relations in the Global Era: The New Frontier,* edited by Peter Capelli. Ithaca, NY: Cornell ILR Press.

Jones, Jacqueline. 1999. *American Work.* New York: W. W. Norton & Co.

Jordan, Lisa, and Robert Bruno. 2006. "Do the Organizing Means Determine the Bargaining Ends?" In *Union Recognition: Organizing and Bargaining Outcomes,* edited by Gregor Gall. London: Routledge.

Juravich, Tom. 2007. "Beating Global Capital: A Framework and Method for Union Strategic Corporate Research and Campaigns." In Bronfenbrenner, ed., 2007.

Juravich, Tom, and Kate Bronfenbrenner. 1999. *Ravenswood: The Steelworkers' Victory and the Renewal of American Labor.* Ithaca, NY: Cornell University Press.

Kaplan, Esther. 2008. "Labor's Growing Pains." *Nation,* May 29. www.thenation.com/print/article/labors-growing-pains.

Keefe, Jeffrey. 1997. "United States." In *Telecommunications: Restructuring Work and Employment Relations Worldwide,* edited by Harry Katz. Ithaca, NY: Cornell ILR Press.

Keenoy, Tom. 1995. "European Industrial Relations in Global Perspective." *European Journal of Industrial Relations* 1(1): 145–64.

Kelly, John. 1988. *Trade Unions and Socialist Politics.* London: Verso.

———. 1998. *Rethinking Industrial Relations: Mobilization, Collectivism and Long Waves.* London: Routledge.

Kocakülâh, Mehmet C., Laura M. Wiggins, and Marvin Albin. 2009. "Managing Manpower and Cutting Costs in the Health Care Industry." *Journal of Health Care Finance* 35(3): 80–92.

Kochan, Thomas A., Adrienne E. Eaton, Robert B. McKersie, and Paul S. Adler. 2009. *Healing Together: The Labor–Management Partnership at Kaiser Permanente.* Ithaca, NY: Cornell University Press.

Kochan, Thomas, Joel Cutcher-Gershenfeld, and John-Paul Ferguson. 2004a. *Report on the Federal Mediation and Conciliation Service Third National Survey.* Washington, D.C.: Federal Mediation and Conciliation Service.

———. 2004b. *Collective Bargaining in the 21ˢᵗ Century: Charting the Road Ahead.* PowerPoint presentation. Washington, D.C.: Federal Mediation and Conciliation Service.

Krehbiel, Paul. 2009. "Leaving SEIU and Joining NUHW." *Labor Notes,* December 1.

Kumar, Sameer. 2010. "Specialty Hospitals Emulating Focused Factories: A Case Study." *International Journal of Health Care Quality Assurance* 23(1): 94–109.

La Botz, Dan. 1990. *Rank and File Rebellion: Teamsters for a Democratic Union.* London: Verso.

———. 1991. *A Troublemaker's Handbook: How to Fight Back Where You Work—and Win.* Detroit: Labor Notes.

———. 2010. "The Tumultuous Teamsters of the 1970s." In Brenner, Brenner, and Winslow 2010.

Labor Notes. 2000. "In Dramatic Turnaround, AFL-CIO Endorses Amnesty for Undocumented Immigrants." *Labor Notes* 253 (April).

———. 2001. "Immigrant Rights Activists Try to Put Their Movement

Back on the National Agenda." *Labor Notes* 273 (December).

———. 2003. "Florida Farmworkers Stage Ten-Day Hunger Strike at Taco Bell Headquarters." *Labor Notes* 289 (April).

———. 2005. "Victory for Florida Farmworkers: Taco Bell Settles Boycott." *Labor Notes* 313 (April).

———. 2006a. "As Immigrants Strike, Truckers Shut Down Nation's Largest Port." *Labor Notes* 327 (June).

———. 2006b. "Organizing Meatpacking Hell." *Labor Notes* 329 (August).

———. 2006c. "Immigrant Workers Organize Mass Strikes." *Labor Notes* 332 (November).

_____. 2007. "Workers' Centers Increasingly Are Forging Alliances with Unions." *Labor Notes* 322 (January).

_____. 2011. "News Watch." *Labor Notes* 387 (June).

Lafer, Gordon. 2005. "Hospital Speedups and the Fiction of a Nursing Shortage." *Labor Studies Journal* 30(1): 27–46.

Lapides, Kenneth, ed. 1990. *Marx and Engels on the Trade Unions.* New York: International Publishers.

Lash, Scott. 1984. *The Militant Worker.* London: Heinemann.

Lawler, John, and Robin West. 1985. "Impact of Union-Avoidance Strategy in Representation Elections." *Industrial Relations* 24(3): 406–20.

Leadbeater, Charles. 1988. "Power to the Person." *Marxism Today.* October.

Leary, Elly, and Marybeth Menaker. 1995. *Jointness at GM: Company Unionism in the 21ˢᵗ Century.* Woonsocket, RI: New Directions Region 9A.

Lens, Sidney. 1947. *Left, Right, and Center: Conflicting Forces in American Labor.* Hinsdale, IL: Henry Regnery.

———. 1971. *The Forging of the American Empire.* New York: Thomas Y. Crowell.

Lewin, David. 1986. "Public Employee Unionism and Labor Relations in the 1980s: An Analysis of Transformation." In Lipset 1986.

Lichtenstein, Nelson. 1982. *Labor's War at Home.* New York: Cambridge University Press.

———. 2002. *The State of the Union: A Century of American Labor.* Princeton, NJ: Princeton University Press.

Lipset, Seymour Martin, ed. 1986. *Unions in Transition: Entering the Second Century.* San Francisco: ICS Press.

Lipsitz, George. 1994. *Rainbow at Midnight: Labor and Culture in the 1940s.* Urbana: University of Illinois Press.

Lipsitz, George, ed. 2004. *Single Jack Solidarity.* Minneapolis: University of Minnesota Press.

Lipsky, David B., Ariel C. Agvar, and James Ryan Lamare. 2009. "Organizational Strategies for the Adoption of Electronic Medical Records: Toward an Understanding of Outcome Variations in Nursing Homes." In *Proceedings of the 61st Annual Meeting*, 73–84. San Francisco: Labor and Employment Relations Association.

Logan, John. 2006. "The Union Avoidance Industry in the United States." *British Journal of Industrial Relations* 44(4): 651–75.

———. 2008. "Permanent Replacements and the End of Labor's 'Only True Weapon.'" *International Labor and Working-Class History* 74 (Fall 2008): 171–92.

London Hazards Centre. 1994. *Hard Labour: Stress, Ill-Health and Hazardous Employment Practices*. London: London Hazards Centre.

Lopez, Nativo V. 2007. "Strategy and Tactics for Immigrants' Rights in 2007. *Against the Current* 127 (March/April).

Los Angeles Times. "Chinese Factories Hit by Strikes amid Manufacturing Slowdown." November 28, 2011. http://latimesblogs.latimes.com /money_co/2011/11/chinese-factories-hit-by-strikes-amid-manufacturing -slowdown.html.

Love, Dianne, Lee Revere, and Ken Black. 2008. "A Current Look at the Key Performance Measures Considered Critical by Health Care Leaders." *Journal of Health Care Finance* 34(3): 19–33.

Lucio, Miguel Martinez, and Paul Stewart. 1997. "The Paradox of Contemporary Labour Process Theory: The Rediscovery of Labour and the Disappearance of Collectivism." *Capital and Class* 62 (Summer).

Lustig, Jeff. 2002. "New Leadership and Its Discontents." *Social Policy* 33.

Luxemburg, Rosa. 1964. *The Mass Strike, the Political Party and the Trade Unions*. Colombo, Sri Lanka: Sydney Wanasinghe.

Lydersen, Kari. 2009. *Revolt on Goose Island: The Chicago Factory Takeover, and What It Says about the Economic Crisis*. Brooklyn: Melville House.

Make the Road by Walking. 2005. "Building Power in Brooklyn and Beyond." In *Annual Report*. Brooklyn: Make the Road by Walking.

Mangum, Garth, and Scott McNabb. 1997. *The Rise, Fall, and Replacement of Industry-Wide Bargaining in the Basic Steel Industry*. Armonk, NY: M. E. Sharpe.

Mann, Michael. 1970. "The Social Cohesion of Liberal Democracy." *American Sociological Review* 35: 423–39.

Marshall, Ray. 2007. "Getting Immigration Reform Right." EPI Briefing Paper. March 15. Washington, D.C.: Economic Policy Institute.

Martin, Andrew W. 2008. "The Institutional Logic of Union Organizing and the Effectiveness of Social Movement Repertoires." *American Journal of Sociology* 113(4), January: 1067–1103.

Martin, Roderick. 1974. *The National Minority Movement*. Oxford: Blackwell.

Marx, Eleanor, and Edward Aveling. 2000. *The Working Class Movement in America*. Amherst, NY: Humanity Books.

Marx, Karl. 1963. *The Eighteenth Brumaire of Louis Bonaparte*. New York: International Publishers.

———. 1973a. *Grundrisse: Foundations of the Critique of Political Economy (Rough Draft)*. Harmondsworth, UK: Penguin.

———. 1973b. *The Poverty of Philosophy*. Moscow: Progress Publishers.

———. 1974. "Inaugural Address of the International Working Men's Association." In *Karl Marx: The First International and After, Political Writings*, Vol. III, edited by David Fernbach. New York: Vintage Books.

———. 1990. *Capital*. Vol. I. London: Penguin.

———. 1991. *Capital*. Vol. III. London: Penguin.

———. 1995. *The Poverty of Philosophy*. Amherst, NY: Prometheus Books.

Marx, Karl, and Friedrich Engels. 1965. *Selected Correspondence*. Moscow: Progress Publishers.

———. 1963. *The German Ideology*. New York: International Publishers.

———. 1974. *Manifesto of the Communist Party*. In *Karl Marx: The Revolutions of 1848*, edited by David Fernbach. New York: Vintage Books.

———. 1991. *Selected Works in One Volume*. London: Lawrence & Wishart.

Mathew, Biju. 2005. *Taxi! Cabs and Capitalism in New York City*. New York: New Press.

McCammon, Holly. 2001. "Labor's Legal Mobilization: Why and When Do Workers File Unfair Labor Practices?" *Work and Occupations* 28(2): 143–75.

McDroy, John. 1991. *The "Permanent" Revolution? Conservative Law and the Trade Unions*. London: Spokesman.

McNally, David. 2009. "From Financial Crisis to World-Slump: Accumulation, Financialisation, and the Global Slowdown." *Historical Materialism* 17(2): 35–83.

———. 2011. *Global Slump: The Economics and Politics of Crisis and Resistance*. Oakland, CA: PM Press.

———. 2012. *Monsters of the Market*. Chicago: Haymarket Books.

MCOL. 2011. Managed Care Fact Sheets. Modesto, CA: MCOL. www.mcareol.com/factsheets/factnati.htm.

Mead-Lucero, Jerry. 2010. "'Locked Out at Illinois Uranium Processing Plant, Steelworkers and Community Wait, Nervously." *Labor Notes* 379 (October).

Metzgar, Jack. 2000. *Striking Steel: Solidarity Remembered*. Philadelphia: Temple University Press.

Meyer, David G., and William M. Cooke. 1993. "US Labour Relations in Transition: Emerging Strategies and Company Performance." *British Journal of Industrial Relations* 31(4) (December), 531–52.

Migration Policy Institute. 2004. "Immigrant Union Members: Numbers and Trends." *Immigration Facts* 7 (May).

Miliband, Ralph. 1977. *Marxism and Politics*. Oxford: Oxford University Press.

Milkman, Ruth. 2006. *L.A. Story: Immigrant Workers and the Future of the U.S. Labor Movement*. New York: Russell Sage Foundation.

Milkman, Ruth, ed. 2000. *Organizing Immigrants: The Challenge for Unions in Contemporary California*. Ithaca, NY: Cornell University Press.

Milkman, Ruth, and Kent Wong. 2000. "Organizing the Wicked City: The 1992 Southern California Drywall Strike." In Milkman 2000, 169–88.

———. 2001. "Organizing Immigrant Workers: Case Studies from Southern California." In Turner, Katz, and Hurd 2001, 99–128.

Minneapolis Star-Tribune. 2010. "The Human Impact of Hospital Strikes." June 25. www.startribune.com/opinion/editorials/97113994.html.

Mishel, Lawrence, and Matthew Walters. 2003. "How Unions Help All Workers." Briefing paper. Washington, D.C.: Economic Policy Institute.

Mishel, Lawrence, Jared Bernstein, and Heidi Shierholz. 2009. *The State of Working America: 2008–2009*. Ithaca, NY: Cornell University Press.

Mishel, Lawrence, Jared Bernstein, and Sylvia Allegretto. 2005. *The State of Working America: 2004–2005*. Ithaca, NY: Cornell University Press.

Mishel, Lawrence, Josh Bivens, Elise Gould, and Heidi Shierholz. 2012. *The State of Working America*, 12th ed. Ithaca, NY: Cornell University Press.

Moberg, David. 2006. "Hotel Workers' Rising Tide." *In These Times*, April 19.

Mohun, Simon. 2006. "Distribution Shares in the US Economy, 1964–2001." *Cambridge Journal of Economics* 30 (2006): 347–70.

———. 2009. "Aggregate Capital Productivity in the US Economy, 1964–2001." *Cambridge Journal of Economics* 33 (2009): 1023–46.

Montgomery, David. 1980. "Strikes in Nineteenth-Century America." *Social Science History* 4(1).

———. 1989. *The Fall of the House of Labor*. Cambridge: Cambridge University Press.

Moody, Kim. 1988. *An Injury to All: The Decline of American Unionism*. New York: Verso.

———. 1995. "NAFTA and the Corporate Restructuring of North America." *Latin American Perspectives* 22(1), Winter: 95–116.

———. 1996. "A New American Politics: Who Will Answer the Invitation?" *New Left Review* I/216.

———. 1997. *Workers in a Lean World: Unions in the International Economy*. London: Verso.

———. 1998. "American Labor: A Movement Again." In *Rising from the Ashes? Labor in the Age of "Global" Capitalism*, edited by Ellen Meiksins Wood, Peter

Meiksins, and Michael Yates. New York: Monthly Review Press.

————. 2007. *US Labor in Trouble and Transition: The Failure of Reform from Above, the Promise of Revival from Below.* London: Verso.

————. 2009a. "The Direction of Union Mergers in the United States: The Rise of Conglomerate Unionism." *British Journal of Industrial Relations* 47(4) (December 2009): 676–700.

————. 2009b. "Immigrant Workers and Labour/Community Organisations in the United States." In *Community Unionism: A Comparative Analysis of Concepts and Contexts,* edited by Joe McBride and Ian Greenwood. Houndsmill, UK: Palgrave Macmillan, 2009.

————. 2010. "Understanding the Rank-and-File Rebellion in the Long 1970s." In Brenner, Brenner, and Winslow 2010.

————. 2014. "Competition and Conflict: Union Growth in the US Hospital Industry." *Economic and Industrial Democracy* 35(1), February: 5–25.

Moody, Kim, and Mary McGinn. 1992. *Unions and Free Trade: Solidarity vs. Competition,* Detroit: Labor Notes.

Mouffe, Chantal. 1983. "Working Class Hegemony and the Struggle for Socialism." *Studies in Political Economy* 12.

Multinational Monitor. 1997. "Editorial: Class War in America." *Multinational Monitor* 18(3), March. www.multinationalmonitor.org/mm/1997/03.

National Education Association (NEA). 2006. "Teachers Unions Merge in NY: NEA Grows to Largest Union in U.S. History." May 6.

National Labor Relations Board. 1948–2009. *Annual Report of the National Labor Relations Board.* Washington, D.C.: National Labor Relations Board.

————. 1990. *Fifty-Fifth Annual Report of the National Labor Board.* Washington, D.C.: US Government Printing Office.

————. 1998. *Sixty-Third Annual Report of the National Labor Relations Board.* Washington, DC: US Government Printing Office.

————. 2000. *Sixty-Fifth Annual Report of the National Labor Relations Board.* Washington, D.C.: US Government Printing Office.

————. 2001. *Sixty-Sixth Annual Report of the National Labor Relations Board.* Washington, D.C.: US Government Printing Office.

————. 2002. *Sixty-Seventh Annual Report of the National Labor Relations Board.* Washington, D.C.: US Government Printing Office.

————. 2003. *Sixty-Eighth Annual Report of the National Labor Relations Board.* Washington, D.C.: US Government Printing Office.

————. 2004. *Sixty-Ninth Annual Report of the National Labor Relations Board.* Washington, D.C.: US Government Printing Office.

————. 2006. *Seventy-First Annual Report of the National Labor Relations Board.* Washington, D.C.: US Government Printing Office.

————. 2007 *Seventy-Second Annual Report of the National Labor Relations*

Board. Washington, D.C.: US Government Printing Office.

———. 2007. *Dana/Metaldyne.* 351 NLRB No. 28. September 29.

———. 2008. *NLRB Election Report: Six-Month Summary—April 2008 through September 2008.* Washington, D.C.: National Labor Relations Board, October 10.

———. 2009. *NLRB Election Report: Six-Month Summary—April 2009 through September 2009.* Washington, D.C.: National Labor Relations Board.

———. 2010a. *NLRB Election Report: Six Months Summary—April 2010 through September 2010,* Washington, D.C.: National Labor Relations Board, October 19.

———. 2010b. *Election Report.* "Cases Closed October 2009–March 2011." Washington, DC: National Labor Relations Board.

———. 2012. "Explanation of Election Process Changes." Washington, D.C.: National Labor Relations Board.

National Mediation Board (NMB). 2001. *Annual Performance Report.* Washington, D.C.: NMB.

———. 2006. *Annual Performance Report.* Washington, D.C.: NMB.

National Nurses United. 2010a. "About National Nurses United. Who We Are: Nurse-Patient Ratios."

———. 2010b. "The Evidence Is In: California RN-to-Patient Ratios Save Lives."

National Union of Healthcare Workers 2011. "Floor Alert: AB 52 (Feuer)—SUPPORT." Oakland, CA: National Union of Healthcare Workers.

Nelson, Bruce C. 1988. *Beyond the Martyrs: A Social History of Chicago's Anarchists, 1870–1900.* New Brunswick, NJ: Rutgers University Press.

Ness, Immanuel. 2005. *Immigration, Unions, and the New US Labor Market.* Philadelphia: Temple University Press.

Newby, Howard. 1977. *The Differential Worker.* London: Penguin.

Nyden, Paul. 1984. *Steelworkers Rank-And-File: The Political Economy of a Union Reform Movement.* New York: Praeger.

O'Connor, Harvey. 2009. *Revolution in Seattle: A Memoir.* Chicago: Haymarket Books.

Office of Immigration Statistics. 2006. *Population Estimates.* August. Washington, D.C.: US Government Printing Office.

Olson, Jeremy. 2010. "Twin Cities Nurses Say 'No' on Hospital Contract Offers." *St. Paul Pioneer Press,* May 19. www.twincities.com/ci_15273390?nclick_check=1.

Parker, Mike. 1997. "Fighting UPS 'Teamwork' Prepared Union to Win the Big Strike." *Labor Notes* 224.

Parker, Mike, and Jane Slaughter. 1994. *Working Smart: A Union Guide to Participation Programs and Reengineering.* Detroit: Labor Notes.

Pearson, Mark. 2009. *Disparities in Health Expenditure across OECD Countries: Why Does the United States Spend So Much More than Other Developed Countries?* Paris: OECD Health Division.

Perry, Charles. 1984. *Collective Bargaining and the Decline of the United Mine Workers.* Philadelphia: Industrial Research Unit, University of Pennsylvania.

———. 1986. *Deregulation and the Decline of the Unionized Trucking Industry.* Philadelphia: Industrial Research Unit, University of Pennsylvania.

———. 1987. *Union Corporate Campaigns.* Philadelphia: Industrial Research Unit, University of Pennsylvania.

Perry, Len, and Patrick Wilson. 2004. "Trends in Work Stoppages: A Global Perspective." Working Paper 47. Geneva: International Labour Office.

Perusek, Glenn, and Kent Worcester. 1995. *Trade Union Politics: American Unions and Economic Change, 1960s–1990s.* New Jersey: Humanities Press.

Peter D. Hart Research Associates. 2001. *The Nurse Shortage: Perspectives from Current Direct Care Nurses and Former Direct Care Nurses.* Washington, D.C.: Peter D. Hart Research Associates.

Peter D. Hart Research Associates. 2005. "Labor Day 2005: The State of Working America." AFL-CIO.www.aflcio.org/aboutus/laborday/upload/ld2005_report.pdf.

Piven, Frances Fox, and Richard Cloward. 1979. *Poor People's Movements: Why They Succeed, How They Fail.* New York: Vintage.

Pope, James Gray. 2004. "How American Workers Lost the Right to Strike and Other Tales." *Michigan Law Review* 103(3): 518–53.

Preis, Art. 1964. *Labor's Giant Step: The First Twenty Years of the CIO: 1936–55.* New York: Pathfinder.

Preuss, Gil, and Ann C. Frost. 2003. "The Rise and Decline of Labor–Management Cooperation: Lessons from Health Care in the Twin Cities." *California Management Review* 45(2): 85–106.

Rachleff, Peter. 1993. *Hard-Pressed in the Heartland: The Hormel Strike and the Future of the Labor Movement.* Boston: South End Press.

Radice, Giles, and Stephen Pollard. 1992. *Southern Comfort.* London: Fabian Pamphlets.

———. 1993. *More Southern Comfort.* London: Fabian Pamphlets.

———. 1994. *Any Southern Comfort?* London: Fabian Pamphlets.

Rampell, Catherine. 2010. "Corporate Profits Were the Highest on Record Last Quarter." *New York Times,* November 23.

Renshaw, Patrick. 1967. *The Wobblies.* New York: Ivan R. Dee.

Robinson, Ian. 2008. "What Explains Unorganized Workers' Growing Demand for Unions?" *Labor Studies Journal* 33(3): 235–42.

Robinson, James C. 1988. "Workplace Hazards and Workers' Desire for Union Representation." *Journal of Labor Research* 9(3): 237–49.

Robinson, James C., and Dratler, Sandra. 2006. "Corporate Structure and Capital Strategy at Catholic Healthcare West." *Health Affairs* 25(1): 134–37.

Roller, Arnold. 1905. *The Social General Strike.* Corvus. http://libertarian-labyrinth.org/booklets/socialgeneralstrike.pdf.

Rosenstein, Hetty. 2004. "What Labor Needs: Thousands of New Shop Stewards." *Labor Notes* 309 (December).

Ryan, Howard. 2011a. "Wisconsin Labor Jams Capitol to Resist Governor's Attacks." *Labor Notes* 384 (March).

———. 2011b. "Democrats Join the Raid on Union Bargaining Rights." *Labor Notes* 387 (June).

Schatz, Ronald. 1983. *The Electrical Workers: A History of Labor at General Electric and Westinghouse, 1923–60.* Urbana: University of Illinois Press.

Schiavone, Michael. 2008. *Unions in Crisis? The Future of Organized Labor in America.* Westport, CT: Praeger.

Schirmer, Eleni. 2012. "Wisconsin Needs More than a Recall." *Labor Notes* 398 (May).

Schmitt, John, and Kris Warner. 2010. "The Changing Face of U.S. Labor, 1983–2008." *Working USA* 13: 263–79.

Schur, Lisa A., and Kruse, Douglas L. 1992. "Gender Differences in Attitudes toward Unions." *Industrial and Labor Relations Review* 46(1): 89–102.

Schwartz, Robert. 2006. *Striking, Picketing, and Inside Campaigns: A Legal Guide for Unions.* Cambridge, MA: Work Rights Press.

Schwartz, Robert, ed. 1999. *The Labor Law Source Book: Texts of Twenty Federal Labor Laws.* Cambridge, MA: Work Rights Press.

Service Employees International Union (SEIU). 2005. "Nearly 5,000 Janitors Form Union with SEIU." Washington, D.C.: SEIU, November 30.

———. 2006a. "Janitors' Victory in Houston Sparks Hope for New Era of Economic Gains for Families in America." Washington, D.C.: SEIU, November 20.

———. 2006b. "Janitors File More than a Dozen New Charges against Cleaning Contractors for Illegal Firings, Threats, and Harassment." Washington, D.C.: SEIU, November 6.

Sewell, Abby. 2011. "Protesters Out in Force Nationwide to Oppose Wisconsin's Anti-Union Bill." *Los Angeles Times,* February 26.

Shaikh, Anwar. 1987, "The Falling Rate of Profit and the Economic Crisis in the U.S." In *The Imperiled Economy,* Book I, edited by Robert Cherry et al. New York: Union for Radical Political Economics.

Shaikh, Anwar. 2010. "The First Great Depression of the 21st Century." In *The Crisis This Time: Socialist Register 2011,* edited by Leo Panitch, Greg Albo, and Vivek Chibber. New York: Monthly Review Press, 2010.

Shaikh, Anwar, and Ahmet Tonak. 1996. *Measuring the Wealth of Nations: The Political Economy of National Accounts.* Cambridge: Cambridge University Press.

Silver, Beverly. 2003. *Forces of Labor: Workers' Movements and Globalization since 1870.* Cambridge: Cambridge University Press.

Simmons, Deborah. 1999. "After Chiapas: Aboriginal Land and Resistance in the New North America." *Canadian Journal of Native Studies* 19(1): 119–48.

Sims, Beth. 1992. *Workers of the World Undermined: American Labor's Role in US Foreign Policy.* Boston: South End Press.

Singer, Daniel. 2002. *Prelude to Revolution: France in May 1968.* Boston: South End Press.

Slaughter, Jane. 1983. *Concessions—and How to Beat Them.* Detroit: Labor Education & Research Project.

———. 2005. *A Troublemaker's Handbook 2.* Detroit: Labor Notes.

———. 2010. "Victory in Miners' Lockout." *Labor Notes* 375 (June).

———. 2011a. "Wisconsin Changes Everything," *Labor Notes* 385 (April).

———. 2011b. "Rolling Sympathy Strikes Harass Food-Service Giant." *Labor Notes* 393 (December).

———. 2012a. "Supply Chain Workers Test Strength of Links." *Labor Notes* 397 (April).

———. 2012b. "The Vision Thing: Keeping Union Reform on Track." *Labor Notes* 398 (May).

———. 2013. "Right-to-Work Smacks Michigan: Sneak Attack, Long Buildup." *Labor Notes* 406 (January).

Smith, Tony. 2000. *Technology and Capital in the Age of Lean Production: A Marxian Critique of the "New Economy."* Albany: State University of New York Press.

Stern, Andy. 2006. *A Country That Works: Getting America Back on Track.* New York: Free Press.

Stevens, Rosemary. 1989. *In Sickness and in Wealth: American Hospitals in the Twentieth Century.* New York: Basic Books.

Sugrue, Thomas. 1996. *The Origins of the Urban Crisis: Race and Inequality in Postwar Detroit.* Princeton, NJ: Princeton University Press.

Tait, Vanessa. 2005. *Poor Workers' Unions: Rebuilding Labor From Below.* Boston: South End Press.

Thompson, E. P. 1966. *The Making of the English Working Class.* New York: Vintage.

———. 1978. *The Poverty of Theory and Other Essays.* New York: Monthly Review Press.

Thompson, Heather. 2001. *Whose Detroit? Politics, Labor, and Race in a Modern American City.* Ithaca, NY: Cornell University Press.

Tillman, Ray. 1999. "Reform Movements in the Teamsters and United Auto Workers." In Tillman and Cummings 1999.

Tillman, Ray, and Michael Cummings, eds. 1999. *The Transformation of U.S. Unions: Voices, Visions, and Strategies from the Grassroots.* Boulder, CO: Lynne Rienner.

Torrington, Derek, Laura Hall, and Stephen Taylor. 2008. *Human Resource Management.* 7th ed. Harlow, UK: Pearson Education Limited.

Trotsky, Leon. 1964. *The Death Agony of Capitalism and the Tasks of the Fourth International.* New York: Pioneer Publishers.

Troy, Leo. 1986. "The Rise and Fall of American Trade Unions: The Labor Movement from FDR to RR." In Lipset 1986.

Turner, Lowell, Harry C. Katz, and Richard Hurd, eds. 2001. *Rekindling the Movement: Labor's Quest for Relevance in the Twenty-First Century.* Ithaca, NY: Cornell University Press.

Ulman, Lloyd. 1955. *The Rise of the National Trade Union.* Cambridge, MA: Harvard University Press.

United Automobile Workers (UAW). 1996a. *Solidarity* (December): 5.

———. 2006. Department Reports. Submitted to the 34th UAW Constitutional Convention, National Organizing Department, June 12–15.

United Food and Commercial Workers. 2010. "Other Industries." United Food and Commercial Workers. www.ufcw.org/your_industry/other_industries.

United Steelworkers. 2007. *Stat Facts* (Summer): 3. Pittsburgh: United Steelworkers.

UNITE-HERE. 2009a. *Growing Pains: SEIU Campaigns against Other Unions.* Unpublished report.

———. 2009b. "SEIU Healthcare Organizing: A Report on Issues Related to Growth and Density." Washington, D.C.: UNITE-HERE.

US Bureau of Labor Statistics. 2000. "Union Members in 1999." News release. USDL 00-16, January 19, 2000.

———. 2001. "Union Members in 2000." News release. USDL 01–21, January 18.

———. 2004. "Union Members in 2003." News release. USDL 04-53, January 21, 2004.

———. 2005. "Labor Force Characteristics of Foreign-Born Workers in 2004." News release. USDL 05–834, May 12.

———. 2006a. "Union Members in 2005." News release. USDL 06-99, January 20, 2006.

———. 2006b. "Foreign-Born Workers: Labor Force Characteristics in 2005." News release. USDL 06–640, April 14.

———. 2007a. "Union Members in 2006." News release. USDL 07–0113, January 25.

———. 2007b. "Real Earnings in February 2007." News release. USDL 07–0377, March 16.

———. 2008a. "Union Members in 2007." News release. USDL 08–0092, January 25.

———. 2008b. "The Employment Situation: March 2008." News release. USDL-08–0448, April 4.

———. 2008c. "Employees on Nonfarm Payrolls by Detailed Industry." Table B-12. ftp.bls.gov/pub/suppl/empsit.ceseeb12.txt.

———. 2008d. *Establishment Data: Employment*, Table B-12. www.bls.gov/pub/sppl/empsit.ceseeb12.txt.

———. 2009. "Union Members in 2008." News release. USDL-09–0095, January 28.

———. 2010a. "The Employment Situation: October 2010." News release. USDL-10–1519, November 5.

———. 2010b. "Employees on Nonfarm Payroll by Detailed Industry." Table B-12. ftp.bls.gov/suppl/empsit.ceseeb12.txt.

———. 2010c. "Union Members in 2009." News release. USDL-10–0069.

———. 2010d. "Output per Hour Nonfarm Business." *Databases, Tables & Calculators by Subject.* http://data.bls.gov/PDQ.

———. 2010e. "Output per Hour Manufacturing." *Databases, Tables & Calculators by Subject.* http://data.bls.gov/PDQ.

———. 2010f. "Unit Labor Costs Manufacturing." *Databases, Tables & Calculators by Subject.* http://data.bls.gov/PDQ.

———. 2010g. "Major Work Stoppages in 2009." News release. USDL-10–0170, February 10.

———. 2011. "Union Members in 2010." News release. USDL-11-0063, January 21, 2011.

———. 2012a. "Union Members in 2011." News release. USDL-12-0094, January 27.

———. 2012b. "Employment Cost Index: Historical Listing, Volume IV, Constant-Dollar, March 2001–September 2012." July 2013.

———. 2012c. "Productivity and Costs." News release. USDL-12-2163, November 1.

———. 2013. "Union Members in 2012." News release. USDL-13-0105, January 23, table 3.

US Census Bureau. 1972. *Statistical Abstract of the United States.* Washington, D.C.: US Government Printing Office.

———. 1975. *Historical Statistics of the United States from Colonial Times to 1970.* Part 1. Washington, D.C.: US Government Printing Office.

———. 1980. *Statistical Abstract of the United States (101st Edition).* Washington, D.C.: US Government Printing Office.

———. 1981. *Statistical Abstract of the United States (102nd Edition)*. Washington, D.C.: US Government Printing Office.

———. 1982–83. *Statistical Abstract of the United States (103rd Edition)*. Washington, D.C.: US Government Printing Office.

———. 1984, *Statistical Abstract of the United States (104th Edition)*. Washington, D.C.: US Government Printing Office.

———. 1985. *Statistical Abstract of the United States (105th Edition)*. Washington, D.C.: US Government Printing Office.

———. 1986. *Statistical Abstract of the United States (106th Edition)*. Washington, D.C.: US Government Printing Office.

———. 1989. *Statistical Abstract of the United States.(109th Edition)*.Washington, D.C.: US Government Printing Office.

———. 1991. *Statistical Abstract of the United States (111th Edition)*. Washington, D.C.: US Government Printing Office.

———. 1992. *Statistical Abstract of the United States (112th Edition)*. Washington, D.C.: US Government Printing Office.

———. 1993. *Statistical Abstract of the United States (113th Edition)*. Washington, D.C.: US Government Printing Office.

———. 2001. *Statistical Abstract of the United States*. Washington, D.C.: US Government Printing Office.

———. 2004–05. *Statistical Abstract of the United States*. Washington, D.C.: US Government Printing Office.

———. 2006. *Statistical Abstract of the United States*. Washington, D.C.: US Government Printing Office.

———. 2008. *Statistical Abstract of the United States*. Washington, D.C.: US Government Printing Office.

———. 2011. *Statistical Abstract of the United States*. Washington, D.C.: US Government Printing Office.

———. 2012. *Statistical Abstract of the United States*. Washington, D.C.: US Government Printing Office.

US Department of Homeland Security. 2006. "Estimates of the Unauthorized Immigrant Population Residing in the United States: January 2005." *Population Statistics*, August. Washington, D.C.: Office of Immigration Statistics.

US Department of Labor. 1995. "LM2 Standard Reports." Washington, D.C.: US Government Printing Office.

———. 2000. "LM2 Standard Reports." Washington, D.C.: US Government Printing Office.

———. 2001. "LM2 Standard Reports." Washington, D.C.: US Government Printing Office.

———. 2006. "LM2 Standard Reports." Washington, D.C.: US Government Printing Office.

———. 2007. "LM2 Standard Reports." Washington, D.C.: US Government Printing Office.

———. 2008. "LM2 Standard Reports." Washington, D.C.: US Government Printing Office.

———. 2010a. "LM2 Standard Reports." Washington, D.C.: US Government Printing Office.

———. 2010b. "Listing of Public and Private Sector Agreements." Washington, D. C.: Department of Labor, Office of Labor-Management Standards.

Vandaele, Kurt. 2011. *Sustaining or Abandoning 'Social Peace'? Strike Developments and Trends in Europe since the 1990s.* Brussels: European Trade Union Institute.

Vogel, David. 1978. "Why Businessmen Distrust Their State: The Political Consciousness of American Corporate Executives." *British Journal of Political Science* 8(1): 45–78.

Waddoups, C. Jeffrey, and Vincent H. Eade. 2002. "Hotels and Casinos: Collective Bargaining During a Decade of Expansion." In Clark, Delaney, and Frost 2002.

Waldinger, Roger. 1996. *Still the Promised City? African-Americans and New Immigrants in Postindustrial New York.* Cambridge, MA: Harvard University Press.

Waldman, J. Dean, Frank Kelly, Sanjeev Aurora, and Howard L. Smith. 2004. "The Shocking Cost of Turnover in Health Care." *Health Care Management Review* 29(1): 2–7.

Wall Street Journal, June 17, 1996.

Ward, Dave. 1998. "Postal Workers Unite against Teamworking." In Cohen 1998.

Watanabe, Teresa, and Joe Matthews. 2006. "Unions Help to Organize 'Day Without Immigrants.'" *Los Angeles Times,* May 3. www.latimes.com/news/local/la-me-organizers3may,1,3363434,print.story.

Weed, Julie. 2010. "Factory Lessons Put to Use at Seattle Children's Hospital." *Seattle Times,* August 1. http://seattletimes.com/html/businesstechnology/2012485209_hospital01.html.

Weikle, Roger, Hoyt Wheeler, and John McClendon. 1998. "A Comparative Case Study of Union Organizing Success and Failure: Implications for Practical Strategy." In Bronfenbrenner et al., eds., 1998.

Weir, Stan. n.d. "1946: The Oakland General Strike." *LibCom.org.* libcom.org/book/export/html/1667.

Wheeler, Hoyt. 1985. *Industrial Conflict: An Integrative Theory.* Columbia: University of South Carolina Press.

Winslow, Cal. 2010a. *Labor's Civil War in California: The NUHW Healthcare*

Workers' Rebellion. Oakland, CA: PM Press.

———. 2010b. "Overview: The Rebellion From Below, 1965–81." In Brenner, Brenner, and Winslow 2010, 1–35.

———. 2011. "NUHW Wins in San Francisco; Strikes in L.A." *Znet,* June 5. www.nuhw.org/press-coverage/2011/6/5/nuhw-wins-in-san-francisco -strikes.

Wood, Ellen Meiksins. 1999. *The Origin of Capitalism.* New York: Monthly Review.

Woodhouse, M., and B. Pearce. 1975. *Communism in Britain.* London: New Park.

Woodruff, Tom. 2008. *Union Organizing in Difficult Times: How SEIU Became the Fastest-Growing Union in the United States.* Washington, D.C.: Service Employees International Union.

Index

About the Author

Kim Moody is a Senior Research Fellow at the Work and Employment Research Unit at the University of Hertfordshire in the UK. He is also a graduate student in US labor history at the University of Nottingham's Department of American and Canadian Studies. He was a cofounder and for many years director of *Labor Notes* and is author of *U.S. Labor in Trouble and Transition* (Verso, 2007); *From Welfare State to Real Estate: Regime Change in New York City from 1974 to the Present* (New Press, 2007); *Workers in a Lean World* (Verso, 1997); and *An Injury to All: The Decline of American Unionism* (Verso, 1988), as well as many articles on labor issues. He is a member of the University and College Union (UCU) and the National Union of Journalists (NUJ) in the UK.